Gender, Alterity and Human Rights

ELGAR STUDIES IN LEGAL THEORY

Series Editor: Wojciech Sadurski, *Sydney Law School, University of Sydney, Australia*

Elgar Studies in Legal Theory is a new series designed to cultivate and promote high quality works of scholarship on all aspects of legal theory. The focus of the series is on the development of original thinking in legal theory, with topics ranging from law and language, logic and legal reasoning, morality and the law, critical legal studies, and transnational law. Innovative work is encouraged from both established authors and the new generation of scholars.

Titles in this series include:

Understanding the Nature of Law
A Case for Constructive Conceptual Explanation
Michael Giudice

Comparative Law as Critique
Günter Frankenberg

Law's Political Foundations
Rivers, Rifles, Rice, and Religion
John O. Haley

Authority in Transnational Legal Theory
Theorising Across Disciplines
Edited by Roger Cotterrell and Maksymilian Del Mar

Legal Conversation as Signifier
Jan M. Broekman and Frank Fleerackers

Technology and the Trajectory of Myth
David Grant and Lyria Bennett Moses

Legal Theory and the Media of Law
Thomas Vesting

Gender, Alterity and Human Rights
Freedom in a Fishbowl
Ratna Kapur

Gender, Alterity and Human Rights

Freedom in a Fishbowl

Ratna Kapur

Queen Mary University of London, UK

ELGAR STUDIES IN LEGAL THEORY

Edward Elgar
PUBLISHING

Cheltenham, UK • Northampton, MA, USA

Published by
Edward Elgar Publishing Limited
The Lypiatts
15 Lansdown Road
Cheltenham
Glos GL50 2JA
UK

Edward Elgar Publishing, Inc.
William Pratt House
9 Dewey Court
Northampton
Massachusetts 01060
USA

A catalogue record for this book
is available from the British Library

Library of Congress Control Number: 2018932705

This book is available electronically in the **Elgar**online
Law subject collection
DOI 10.4337/9781788112536

Printed on elemental chlorine free (ECF)
recycled paper containing 30% Post-Consumer Waste

ISBN 978 1 78811 252 9 (cased)
ISBN 978 1 78811 253 6 (eBook)

Typeset by Columns Design XML Ltd, Reading
Printed and bound in the USA

Praise for *Gender, Alterity and Human Rights*:

'Ratna Kapur is one of the most stimulating, creative and challenging writers on law and human rights today. For those scholars and activists who have been thinking about how to respond to the limitations of the global human rights project this is a book whose publication we have been eagerly awaiting. Every single page offers insights into the problems and conundrums of the liberal human rights project and how alternative figurations of freedom are possible beyond, as Kapur puts it, the Western liberal "fishbowl". Utterly indispensable reading for anyone interested in the possibilities of freedom in our world.'
Ben Golder, University of New South Wales, Australia

'This enduring work invites us to rethink the human rights paradigm in the dazzling light of some non-European ideas of freedom, as we recede from the faith in "inherent capacity of rights to produce lasting freedom". Ratna Kapur boldly asks to "re-imagine" freedom in "tough, granular, committed practices of introspection" amidst the debris of human rights.'
Upendra Baxi, University of Warwick, UK and University of Delhi, India

'*Gender, Alterity and Human Rights: Freedom in a Fishbowl* is located within the best of critical theory traditions – thinking and rethinking orthodoxies around sexuality, rights and freedoms. Kapur not only deploys a late Foucauldian rethinking of freedom, but inherits the very spirit of intellectual engagement – of "shak(ing) up habitual ways of working and thinking, dissipate(ing) conventional familiarities, to reevaluate rules and institutions" (Foucault). It is a compelling, provocative read that will make its readers rethink what they think they already know.'
Brenda Cossman, University of Toronto, Canada

'This book offers a thought-provoking new critique of the liberal paradigm of human rights through skillfully weaving theoretical alternatives into contemporary rights discourse. Drawing upon Michel Foucault's theorization of "political spirituality" and Eve Sedgwick's engagement with Mahayana Buddhism, as well as the doctrine of non-dualism in traditional Indian philosophy, the author suggests that we radically rethink our definition of the free and unfree legal subject, and also reformulate our understanding of subjectivity itself.'
Kanchana Natarajan, University of Delhi, India

'Kapur's book not only offers a devastating critique of human rights as a global disseminator of liberal and neoliberal logics, but also probes us to reimagine freedom in ways that transcend the neoliberal imaginary. Traversing diverse philosophical and geo-political terrains, and considering questions ranging from LGBT rights to religious expression to sexual violence, Kapur shows us how a decoupling of rights from freedom can produce emancipatory possibilities that challenge the very notion of freedom on which the pursuit of rights is based. A pathbreaking contribution to critical scholarship on human rights and on transnational circulations of gender and sexuality.'
Elizabeth Bernstein, Columbia University, USA

'This scholarly impeccable, beautifully written book is broadening our political imagination. It is an important theoretical event for anyone interested in the future of emancipatory projects in a globalized world.'
Mikhail Xifaras, Sciences Po Law School, France

For

R.B.

&

My favourite heckler

Contents

Acknowledgements

Any book is the outcome of a journey, one that is undertaken not only in the intellectual realm but also within the space of the deeply personal and intimate. It involves a conversation with the many, and one that has no real beginning and also never ends. It is an inquiry and process of reflection and engagement, the value of which rests in its ability to change us and teach us to think differently. The writing process is at some level a solitary one, but it cannot be sustained without the threads of people, personal relations and institutions that form the weave of one's life. This book is stitched together by the many different threads that make up my life world.

I owe a special debt to a number of people for being so very encouraging and tireless interlocutors during the process of writing this book. My thanks to colleagues at Queen Mary University of London (QMUL), in particular, Elizabeth Barnes, Jessie Hohman, Penny Green, and Isobel Roele, for supporting, as well as engaging with, my work. I owe a special debt to Dianne Otto, whose input into the text has helped me reframe some of the central arguments in this book, and also to Smriti Vohra, for providing such incisive comments and bringing the gift of her scrutinizing eye to the manuscript as a whole. I am fortunate to be a part of the Institute for Global Law and Policy, Harvard Law School, which has provided me not only with a platform for sharing deeply provocative ideas, but also with colleagues who have been extremely generous with their time in discussing various aspects of my project and providing the most invaluable suggestions and insights during conversations had in this space: Karen Engle, Gunter Frankenburg, Vanja Hamzić, Adil Khan, Vasukhi Nesiah, Ben Golder and David Kennedy.

I am especially grateful for the wonderful friendship and the many significant personal exchanges with Saba Mahmood, who passed away before the completion of this manuscript. Her scholarship initiated an intellectual revolution in the humanities and social sciences to think beyond the liberal imaginary and her ideas have been a major inspiration for this endeavour.

There are a host of institutions that have provided me with an intellectual home during the years that this book has been in gestation:

the International State Crime Initiative, School of Law, QMUL; Melbourne Law School, where my appointment as a Senior Fellow has provided me the opportunity to develop this project and receive unparalleled research support; the Symbiosis School of Law, Pune; and the Anthropology Department at the Graduate Institute for International and Development Studies, Geneva, with special thanks to Shalini Randeira and Isabelle Milbert for their support.

I am fortunate to have been afforded the opportunity to share my research with various audiences around the world. I am especially indebted to the Berlin Institute for Cultural Inquiry; the University of Berlin; the Centre for Human Rights, University of Copenhagen; the Centre for Law and Society in a Global Context, QMUL; the Faculty of Law and Social Sciences, School of Oriental and African Studies; the Department of Gender Studies, London School of Economics; the Department of Legal Philosophy and the Gender Research Centre, University of Vienna; the Department of Philosophy, North-Eastern Hill University, Shillong; the École de Droit, SciencePo, Paris; the Faculty of Law and the Gender Research Centre, Geneva University; the Gender Research Centre, Hong Kong University; the Indian Council of Philosophical Research, New Delhi; the Institute of Advanced Studies, Simla; Faculty of Law, Jamia Millia Ismalia University, New Delhi; the Institute of Global Law and Policy, Harvard Law School; Jindal Global Law School, Sonepat; the University of Potsdam; and the School of Law and the Centre for Postcolonial Studies, Goethe University, Frankfurt. Thanks to Sealing Cheng, Hilda Romer Christensen, Nikita Dhawan, Gunter Frankenburg, Gina Heathcote, Clare Hemmings, Lys Kulamadayil, Elisabeth Holzleithner, Sumi Madhok, Sushila Mesquita, Bérénice Schramm, and Angela Wong, for hosting various events at which I presented my work, as well as to all those interlocutors who provided insights, comments and suggestions on my presentations. Thanks to Beverly Brown, Brenna Bhandar and Nadje Al-Ali for significant conversations and suggestions in the early phases of this research.

I am extremely indebted for the invaluable research assistance provided during different phases of this book and on different chapters by Darshan Datar, Emily Jones, Upasana Garnik, Radhika Gupta, Adil Khan, Gauri Pillai, Surabhi Shukla, Apurva Tripathi and Latika Vashisht. I am immensely fortunate to have had the excellent support of Robin Gardner, Fiona MacDowall and the Melbourne Law School Academic Research Service. I am especially grateful to Cate Read for her rigour in polishing the text through her highly skilful, meticulous edits and inputs, and for the research assistance of Abbey Lay and Chris Kaias. I would not have been able to acquire clarity and direction for the ideas that I have presented in this book had it not been for the time and effort of several colleagues and friends in being such patient readers of different chapters from this book. Each and every one has improved this book through offering helpful insights and constructive suggestions: Lakshmi Arya, Upendra Baxi, Brenda Cossman, Karen Engle, Gunter Frankenberg, Ben Golder, Kanchana Natarajan, Vasuki Nesiah, Dianne Otto and Isobel Roele. I would also like to thank Edward Elgar Publishing, in particular Stephen Gutierrez and Erin McVicar, for being consultative, thoughtful and unconditionally supportive throughout the publication process.

I am fortunate to have loved ones who, over many decades as well as during significant moments, have been the source of nourishment, encouragement and love in my life – Jyoti Sanghera, who saw the glint in my eye and encouraged me to write this book; and Kumar Shankardass, who revelled in describing himself as my number one heckler! Sadly, the heckler fell silent shortly after this manuscript was completed. Not only have they been my most important critics, but they did the caring and giving that kept me grounded and made it possible for me to attend to the nearly all consuming undertaking of writing this book. I am also grateful to my feline companions, Kaju and Misha, who have padded across innumerable drafts of each chapter, and weighed in heavily when it came to taking breaks and ensuring that I attended to the central tasks of their everyday lives – feeding, caring for and loving them.

I am so fortunate to have been constantly encouraged to write this book by those mentors and teachers who have sincerely believed in this project, and who have taught me to question the way in which we live now and encouraged me to think differently and to be otherwise. I could only dare to seek to move beyond the fishbowl and explore other constellations because of this inspiration.

Earlier versions of some portions of this book have appeared in print before. A much earlier version of sections in a different form from Chapter 2 appeared as ‘Precarious Desires and Ungrievable Lives: Human Rights and Postcolonial Critiques of Legal Justice’, *London Review of International Law* 3, no. 2 (2016) 267–294; from Chapters 5 and 7 appeared as ‘In the Aftermath of Critique, We are not in Epistemic Free Fall: Human Rights, the Subaltern Subject, and the Non-Liberal Search for Freedom and Happiness’, *Law and Critique* 25, no. 1 (2014) 25–45; and from Chapter 3 appeared as ‘Gender, Sovereignty, and the Rise of a Sexual Security Regime in International Law and Postcolonial India’, *Melbourne Journal of International Law* 14, no. 2 (2013) 1–26.

Prologue

I am sitting in the study of my family home in the picturesque foothills of the Himalayas, thinking through the desire for freedom and happiness that is a driving force behind many of the decisions that we take in life. As my thoughts gradually wander across the view of the Doon valley, in which the old city of Dehradun is nestled and which, from my perspective, appears as a peaceful oasis of calm and quiet, I become immediately aware of the contingency of my location. Like many smaller cities in India's new market economy, Dehradun is an overgrown bustling town where the cacophony of horns merges with whirls of smoke and dust, street vendors and overcrowded pavements. Masses of people stream in and out of brand-name stores offering the latest fashion accessories, electronic gadgets and luxury cars. This determined march into the neoliberal market sits against the nostalgic backdrop of this old colonial town, where an embattled past fends off the encroachments of a rapidly mutating present. Numerous idols of gods and goddesses adorn the streets and pavements, often squatting under the dusty majesty of large banyan trees that are scattered across the city, as if to take shelter from the sweltering heat. Loudspeakers deployed by those doing the bidding of local politicians blare interminably, making a brazen appeal to the electorate to return them to power despite a trail of broken promises. Other than the avid spectacle of consumerism, the city has little to show in terms of local 'development'.

But from the aperture of my location, as a light gathering of clouds descends from the mountaintops and covers the valley under a wistful haze, the clamour and clatter of the city resolves into silence. It is a noiseless peace – a freedom from the commotion of the world. How removed this perspective appears to be from the normative order of happiness and understandings of freedom that are continually restless, profit-driven, instrumental, transactional and directed towards an ever elusive goal whose true contours remain obscured.

At this moment, there is some commotion in the living room, which is at the end of a long corridor that separates it from the study. Walking towards the room, I glimpse a sudden undulation, like a wave flattening itself. Even as the snake retreats, I am fully aware that she is searching for a way out of the house. She finds shelter beneath the skirting of an old, battered chair. All the windows of the room are closed. I stay quiet and remain an observer on the threshold. Her head emerges hesitatingly from beneath her temporary haven, and then she swiftly glides towards the fireplace. She is on full display. Nearly five feet long and two inches thick. I see a flash of her yellow underbelly and a maquillage of thin green and black lines that adorn the entire length of her back. I marvel at how she *is*, inseparably, her very movement – an absolute fusion like fire and heat or water and wetness. She slides completely into the back of the fireplace, and it seems as if she has found her node of withdrawal from any impending threat of harm or danger.

So we wait – the two of us. I am certain now that all she wants is to find her freedom, a way out of the human structures surrounding and incarcerating her.

As the minutes slowly pass, she emerges again, looking sideways and upwards. She moves out of her impermanent refuge and then undertakes the most astonishing act – she gradually raises her entire pulchritudinous and supple form upwards, defying gravity and, also, the construction of her own anatomy. And within a moment she is quite literally standing. She rests on the tip of her tail, and she swivels her long and elegant neck, searching and seeking – a way out. She wants her freedom and to escape from a world that wants little to do with her; and, quite clearly, she wants little to do with it. As she remains fully upright on what seem to be invisible hind legs, I am struck by the surreal quality of this scene. No, there really *is* a snake standing in my living room!

While I am a mesmerized spectator to her performance, I also immediately have the urge to assist her in resolving her dilemma. I weigh up the different possible interventions. One strategy is a rescue-and-rehabilitation approach that entails grabbing her, putting her in a sack and delivering her to the nearest zoo or vet. There is something entirely imperialistic about this approach, given that I know nothing about snakes and their needs. I acknowledge the need to let go of the salvation mentality and shake off the conceit that I think I know what is best for her. Another option entails her physical destruction. After all, she could harm me. She might be poisonous. She is an intruder, an unwelcome and agitated presence, who has infiltrated my space of familiarity and has the capacity to cause fear and panic; annihilating her would ensure the peace I so cherish.

But then I ask: *who is the interloper*? Perhaps it is my world that has suddenly, inexplicably manifested in her world, rather than the other way around. Resolution lies not in my taking violent control of her fate, but in my recognizing that the space that we both inhabit should not be demarcated through the destruction of what we perceive to be 'Other' to ourselves. A final option is to adopt her as a pet. It is highly unlikely that she could be assimilated into the normative order of my world, where pets are usually furry, cute and eminently pettable. And she has already displayed her autonomy and subversive potential by defying the gravitational pull of the 'normal' order of things through her vertical feat.

It gradually becomes evident to me that none of these options give her what she desires – freedom. She desperately wants to escape her predicament.

As her perpendicular, staff-like posture gradually descends into a spiral that is almost a gesture of surrender, I take advantage of the opportunity to quickly open two windows at a distance from where she is, and then retreat back to my own spot on the threshold of the room. She senses a change, an opportunity, and an alternative possibility of freedom from any of the ones I had considered. With caution as well as excitement, she gradually undulates towards the windows. She raises herself to the ledge, stops and turns in a gesture of acknowledgement towards the human world she is leaving behind, and then slides out of the window and onwards in her journey.

Introduction

This book explores the imaginary possibilities of freedom in the aftermath of the critique of human rights. Addressing this issue in relation to gender and alterity, I specifically focus on how, in light of such critique, freedom is to be envisaged once the emancipatory claims of human rights have proven disingenuous, false or simply unrealizable. In the global context, freedom remains defined as a liberal, external pursuit, involving the accumulation of further rights by a rational, finite and individual subject. The critical legal project, including postcolonial and feminist interventions, has successfully dismantled the façade of this claim, exposing the regulatory and governance structures of human rights. The central endeavour of this book is to consciously explore the imaginary possibilities that have emerged in the aftermath of critique by centring and examining articulations of freedom available in non-liberal, alternative epistemologies. I address alternative registers that present radical insights on freedom as based on discrete understandings of the subject which are distinct from/remain beyond the reach of liberal individualism, and posit notions of self-scrutiny, reflection, discernment and the turn inwards as central features.

The focus on non-liberal (as opposed to illiberal) articulations of freedom pushes against the liberal positioning of human rights as indispensable central instruments in struggles for freedom, and further questions their capacity to realize this goal. The discussion not only exposes the parochial, provincialized identity of human rights as liberal, overwhelmingly Western and Eurocentric, but also displays the destructive capacities nestled in the liberal claim to ideological supremacy – one that ultimately seeks to retain its dominance over all others through its coercive formulations of how to be, and be free, in the world. The notion that divergent understandings of freedom have always existed outside of the liberal and neoliberal imaginaries and related market terms is either barely considered by those who shape, support and implement the rights regime, or considered inherently alien and therefore irrelevant to the recursive ideological currents within the fishbowl. This book sets the stage for the argument that freedom should be actively delinked from the human rights project as formulated and imposed by the liberal imaginary, and should instead be explored within a range of dynamic and existing alternative philosophical spaces. By exploring whether, and how, non-liberal vocabularies of freedom can address and alleviate the current disillusionment with human rights' capacity to deliver on their emancipatory promise, the book marks a conscious and productive shift in the direction of visualizing the concept of freedom from outside the liberal fishbowl, and exploring considerations of freedom that have always existed *beyond* the fishbowl.

My analysis is not framed within an either/or binary – that is, between support for the human rights project and a specific intervention (which can have disastrous and unintended consequences), and a refusal to intervene that closes its eyes to the repression and violence experienced by sexual and religious minorities and women (for the most part, it is generally alleged, in rogue, non-Western states). Instead, my starting premise accepts the idea of human rights as a project that is already affected by – and overtly and covertly implicated in – structures of power, laying bare the fallacy of human rights as linked to an external, optimistic pursuit of freedom. Thus, this book does not offer a comprehensive account of critical approaches to human rights, nor is it an encyclopaedic presentation of women's human rights and LGBT advocacy. Instead, in the initial chapters, I consider significant moments in gender and sexual rights advocacy and illustrate the work of human rights within these interventions. I set out the concerns around freedom that emerge from this line of inquiry, including the discursive and normative effects produced through these struggles for legibility and entitlement. Tracing the work of human rights within these specific advocacy pursuits, I demonstrate how even the minimalist claims of human rights advocates – that rights can alleviate human suffering and do not have wider effects – are invariably advancing maximalist projects, such as the need for thriving markets or the embedding of a particular notion of the female subject as unveiled, sexualized and autonomous. I offer insights into the core motives of rights strategies in relation to gender and alterity that are either seldom discussed or made visible, or not seen as politically relevant. The trail of disorder, chaos and, at times, unanticipated but irrefutably harmful outcomes produced in and through human rights advocacy, as delineated in the different chapters of this book, underscores the urgent need to identify new ways of pursuing freedom. I pose a direct challenge to the idea that rights accumulation by the individual can lead to freedom, thus shifting away both from the liberal conception of freedom as an exclusively external, progressive pursuit and from the assumption within human rights discourse that liberal understandings of freedom are the only available and valid ones.

My effort is partly to centre the idea that rights are techniques of governance which discipline and regulate the subject of human rights, and where practices of self-discipline and self-governance become normalized and experienced as freedom. Simultaneously, I question why the burgeoning critical scholarship on human rights more generally has not necessarily been productive or creative enough in scrutinizing this self-referential schema of entitlement. On the one hand, political interventions are regarded with paranoia, and all those features of human rights that hold out the possibility of hope and transformation are treated with suspicion. On the other, the scholarship has tended to offer reformulations and, somewhat awkwardly (and unsuccessfully), has sought to reinstall the project of human rights through proposals of pragmatic renewal and reinvestment. Rather than theorizing strategies of empowerment that take us further in the direction of freedom, these proposals speak more to anxiety and fear about 'letting go' of a project that has been so cherished over the past half-century. The theoretical turn back to human rights is in fact reflective of the anxiety that accretes around the notion of the epistemic void that, from the liberal perspective, would presumably result from any subversion or deconstruction of the existent rights framework. In this sense, as Golder asserts, despite delivering a devastating critique of human rights as 'a particular form of Western political liberalism that gets exported globally with great violence … critical commentators on human rights nevertheless make a curious return to human rights'.[1]

While I acknowledge the intrinsic, though qualified, benevolence associated with proposals that offer a reformulation and reinvestment in human rights, such reformulations *cannot* lead to freedom. The commitment to reimagining and reformulating human rights and its futurity is largely informed not only by a fear that the critique will send us into epistemic free fall, but also by the erroneous assumptions that there *are* no workable or sustainable alternatives outside of a liberal formulation or reformulation, and that any ventures beyond the liberal fishbowl are nihilistic and defeatist. Yet the persistent faith in human rights and allegiance to paradigms of freedom formulated and upheld within the liberal fishbowl not only remains embedded in a 'cruel optimism', but also represents a nihilistic move that can take us no further in the direction of freedom. The end result is a continuing subscription to the paradigms of freedom and happiness formulated and upheld within the liberal fishbowl, despite repeated evidence of the limitations of the human rights project and its ideological and material deployments, which have undeniably often produced ferocious outcomes and immense suffering.

Thus, contemporary critique finds itself at an impasse, and the core questions remain unaddressed: What happens when the faith in human rights as a liberal freedom project is so substantively eroded? Where does that leave us? If human rights cannot give us what we want – namely, freedom – then what *can*? In the final three chapters of this book, I identify new ways of pursuing freedom that involve a turn inwards and necessarily require the self-transformation of the subject. My argument draws partly on the radical thinking of critical Western scholars such as Michel Foucault and Eve Sedgwick. Foucault's theoretical engagement with political spirituality presented in relation to the early phases of the Iranian revolution, and his articulation of the self as distinct from the liberal subject, marks a profound intervention on the idea of freedom. Similarly, Sedgwick's inquiry into Mahayana Buddhist epistemology offers an alternative model of meaningful freedom, which partly emerges from her prescient insight that critique of the dominant normative order and deconstruction inevitably leads to non-dualism. I also draw on non-liberal philosophical and agnostic spiritual traditions, such as the ecstatic registers of Persian Sufism, where freedom is expressed in intensely affective and passionate release. Towards the end of this book, I present a close reading of the non-liberal, subcontinental episteme of non-dualism – *Advaita*, 'not two' – to demonstrate how an alternative register is not adversarial or irrelevant to human rights, even though its inscription of selfhood and of the processes of being and becoming may seem incommensurable with the parameters of subjectivity as enunciated and affirmed within the liberal project. In each instance, what becomes evident is that meaningful freedom is possible primarily through self-transformation and self-reflection.

The questioning of human rights as a freedom project and the turn towards non-liberal pursuits does not imply support for the rhetoric of cultural relativists, or ideologues of various persuasions, who foment collective practices that are inhuman and antihuman and who might embrace the critique as a justification for refuting the human rights project and embracing cultural orthodoxies. In fact, my argument seeks to occupy the semantic and political 'non-liberal' space that has all too often and easily been ceded to reactionary influences and orthodoxies by progressive, feminist, and leftist forces out of fear that it may mark them as 'religious' or unsecular. Nor does the proposed shift require abandoning human rights. Rather, it requires comprehending the work that human rights do primarily as regulatory and governance mechanisms. This process involves taking a step back and directing one's gaze behind the liberal paradigm of freedom and the notions of happiness and the 'good life' that arise from the fishbowl, and which comprise part of the ostensibly progressive and benevolent arsenal of human rights. Such critical objectivity is vital to any understanding of the full array, as well as the specific architecture, of the practices, assumptions and dogmas that shape the contemporary rights project.

Thus, the argument put forth in this book is not about negating the human rights project, even if that were desirable or possible in these exceedingly violent times. Rather, my analysis is underpinned by a call for a more mindful and diligent approach. It is a proposal to consciously take a step back and objectively evaluate what has been gained through the ethics and mechanics of the current model of human rights advocacy, and what has been – perhaps irretrievably – lost. Today, instead of promoting an arrogant triumphalism or succumbing to frustrated hopelessness, human rights advocacy requires substantive investment in practices of thoughtful self-scrutiny; scrutiny of one's 'Other/s', whomever or whatever they might be; and an inclusive dialogue not just within the rights establishment but also with those on whose behalf rights interventions are undertaken. The politics of my critical project resides in the process of *seeking*; that is, the foregrounding of a modality wherein our engagement with the human rights project and its proven limits provokes our *reflective* rather than our reflexive responses. Only such tough, granular, committed practices of introspection will enable us to pause and take heed of what needs our urgent attention.

HUMAN RIGHTS AND FREEDOM

Human rights advocacy is based on a fundamental belief that freedom rests in the accumulation of rights, and that these in turn are always both progressive and transformative. This belief draws on the dominant liberal idea that human beings are self-directing individuals capable of pursuing the goals that they have set for themselves, and of ensuring the existence of the conditions necessary to enable them to pursue their chosen end goals free from other people's will or the constraint of another's will. This understanding also involves adhering to the fundamental principle of liberalism – namely, that any exercise of freedom is to be respected only to the extent that it does not violate the equal freedom of the other. In classical liberal terms, this idea of freedom encompasses economic features that include ownership in the form of one's labour and material possessions, as well as private property. It involves a pursuit of the 'good life' – a particular existential modality arising from a particular self-concept that, in terms of the liberal paradigm, is essential to the wellbeing and happiness of the individual.

Human rights have become the essential mechanism for communicating this liberal understanding of freedom, specifically 'equal' freedom, at the international level. Faith in the inherent capacity of rights to produce lasting freedom for the individual partly rests on an assumption that we have, as a civilized world, moved forward, and that the coming together of nation states in the recognition of universal human rights is a critical part of the liberal project that is committed to individual and collective human freedom. This liberal narrative is driven by a view that history has a purpose and direction, coupled with an assumption that the world has emerged from a prolonged phase of superstitious and barbarian backwardness, and is evolving towards a universalist telos of justice and equality, based on reason, science and democratic values. The conviction that civilization has metamorphosed from the anarchic and primitive to a modern superior form has emanated from the heart of Europe;[2] the liberal assertion is that modernity has mostly been achieved, except in what are still regarded as 'the outposts of the empire'. The cartography of human rights has received a major impetus in the post-Cold War era in the form of liberal internationalism, which, it is claimed, no longer faces any ideological resistance except in those parts of the globe regressing into feudal despotism and/or xenophobic violence. A veneration of the ideals of modernity and a hubris born of persistent faith in the benevolence of this justice-seeking liberal project have come to characterize human rights advocacy as practised on the ground. There is a genuine earnestness on the part of well-intentioned activists, scholars, practitioners, jurists and legislators convinced that they are incontrovertibly pursuing a progressive, even righteous, universally desired goal of freedom for the individual.

This view generates and reinforces the consensus that the liberal framework within which freedom is located is the most progressive as well as civilizationally mature project for pursuing the goal of freedom. However, in recent times this assumption has been challenged as empirically and theoretically flawed: in purely factual terms, more human rights violations have been committed in the twentieth century – ostensibly the century most focused on human rights – than at any other point in human history.[3] There is a less benevolent side to human rights work that has been exposed by critical legal scholars, including feminist and postcolonial intellectuals.[4] These scholars have examined – and revealed – the costs of such work, including the often unanticipated damage inflicted in the name of procuring and securing freedom. This scholarship contests the idea of human rights as a liberatory project and one that will incontrovertibly secure our freedom, instead exposing it as a governance project – one that systematically regulates, disciplines and manages different lives and bodies. This critique produces a counter-narrative of human rights, subverting their unequivocally generous primary intent and the dominant assumption that they are a progressive, democratic and liberating force, integral to any experience of freedom. The rights rationale has also been efficiently co-opted to advance the agendas of large corporations and the military machines of powerful states.[5]

Contemporary critiques have increasingly identified what David Kennedy would describe as the 'dark side' of an ostensibly virtuous project, providing some insight into the interventionist conceits that human rights advocates consistently display with a disturbing lack of self-reflection.[6] This book builds upon that body of critical scholarship, which has challenged the accuracy of the claim that the human rights project – regarded as a manifestation of the liberal political episteme wherein the subject as a bearer of rights occupies a central position – can actually produce meaningful freedom and happiness through the continued acquisition of further rights. Locating the discussion within the context of gender and sexual rights advocacy, the first part of the book critically examines liberal conceptions of freedom *and* the assumption within human rights discourse that liberal understandings of freedom are the only available and valid ones. In the second part of the book, I identify new ways of pursuing lasting freedom without surrendering the terrain of human rights, although the relationship between the two projects may ultimately be incommensurable.

I draw considerably on critical legal theory to develop my critique of liberal freedom and the way that human rights attaches to the liberal enunciation. I demonstrate how the latter is in fact a technique of global governance and one in which the embrace of neoliberal markets serves as the most potent instrument through which such freedom is to be attained. In this vision, power operates to ensure that the governed themselves come to see behaving in a certain way as ethical and desirable, and as arising from their own freedom, procured and secured for them by those who govern. Furthermore, a postcolonial analysis that reconfigures dominant narratives by including the 'small voice of history'[7] destabilizes the primary assumptions about freedom on which the liberal human rights endeavour is based. It addresses how contemporary inequalities have been informed by their historical past, where the colonized 'Other' was deemed 'backward' by liberal political thinkers, both in terms of culture and in their ability to consent, and hence these features justified the legal difference in treatment. Under the conditions of liberalism and empire, juridical entitlements were integrally linked to recognition of the 'Other' as variously either fully human, a lesser human or a non-human.

Scholars differ on the 'origins' of human rights and when and how they became relevant,[8] or whether they remain relevant at all, given their inability to reduce harm and violence in an increasingly violent world.[9] My critical focus in this book concerns how the liberal worldview, which includes human rights – whether in the older guise of a civilizing mission or in its contemporary manifestation, where it is aligned with the market and global capital – is today intent on permeating *all* modalities of human relationships.[10] As a modality of liberalism, rights have without exception demonstrated an imperialistic trajectory and an understanding of freedom as a technique of governance as opposed to liberation. They have continued to be mapped and deployed along the axis of inclusion and exclusion – a discriminatory heuristic that is integral to the human rights endeavour, rather than a detour from or failure of the project. My analysis of this project brings into crisis the central pillars of liberalism – present regardless of its various disputatious guises and forms – on which the human rights enterprise is based: the universal, rational subject and the idea of freedom as an external pursuit; the march forward towards a common progressive end through the systematic accumulation of rights; and the valorizing of 'public' and 'private' as two distinct, separate spheres of human activity that must never infiltrate or influence each other.

Critical approaches to human rights have been enormously significant in unmasking the normative and regulatory arrangements that constitute human rights. The early chapters in the book work with this critical tradition to examine how gender and sexual rights advocacy has invariably reinforced these arrangements, rather than brought about transformation and meaningful freedom for the concerned disenfranchised constituencies. While such engagements produce moments of disruption in normative assumptions about gender, sexuality and culture, they are illustrative of the resistive capacities of the subaltern subject, rather than productive of meaningful freedom. Critical human rights scholarship has exposed the discursive operations of human rights as irrefutably hegemonic: a governance project primarily concerned with ordering the lives of non-European peoples and creating the conditions for the exponential flourishing of the neoliberal market with the bulk of profits channelled to further enrich a privileged few. And this governance project has intervened at the most intimate, epistemic level; that is, through infiltrating and moulding cognitive processes, the very modes of thinking, as well as the intricate spectrum of social and cultural practices.[11] In rereading/deconstructing the colonial legacies as well as the gender and sexual hierarchies that constitute human rights, the scholarship has exposed how this project is incapable of meeting its promise of delivering freedom to the disenfranchised. This scholarship has provincialized the universal claims of international human rights law and problematized the extractive and appropriative aspects of its proclaimed progressive sensibilities, where colonial-era conditioning and policies continue to resonate in the postcolonial present, and to reproduce the injustices of multiple marginalization and exclusion. While there is a compendious literature available on the strengths and limitations of human rights advocacy, I address the normative and regulatory effects of this advocacy specifically in relation to gender and alterity, including sexual and cultural difference, and examine the limits of human rights in its self-appointed role as a salvific force that can bring about freedom in these domains. I pursue this inquiry through a series of chapters that demonstrate the ways in which the freedom of a particular disenfranchised subject – the sexual subaltern, the exploited/abused woman, the veiled woman – is envisioned and pursued within the human rights paradigm. Specifically, I examine the human rights strategies of progressive groups, in particular feminists, and women's rights and sexual rights advocates, in the international legal arena as well as within specific domestic contexts, including various liberal democratic countries, recognizing the interconnections between the international and domestic legal regimes. I provide an alternative reading of this advocacy to illuminate how these engagements constitute and inscribe the subject into specific ways of being free – ways that are aligned with a neoliberal, wealth-producing, heteronormative, reproductive framework, as well as with sexual, cultural, racial and religious prescriptions. The analysis places into question whether the bestowal of more rights has resulted in less violence against women, more justice for sexual subalterns or more equality for the cultural 'Other', all of which would presumably be part of the end goal of freedom pursued through human rights. My discussion is illustrative and intended to highlight how concepts of freedom and subject formation are contingent upon dominant gender, sexual, cultural and religious norms becoming normalized, naturalized and universalized within the liberal/neoliberal framings of the rights project. In this guise, human rights appear incapable of delivering on their promise of freedom.

While the discussion does not provide a comprehensive account of freedom – an amorphous concept that means different things to different people – the illustrative examples counsel in favour of pausing for deeper reflection on the pursuit of freedom in and through human rights advocacy, given its contradictory and at times exclusive and disempowering effects. The central problematic that I confront in this book, then, is that human rights are universal and necessary tools that we cannot *not* want, to paraphrase Gayatri Spivak writing in a different context, even though they cannot give us what we *do* want – that is, freedom. And if this is indeed the case, then what *can* give us what we want? Part of the answer to this question rests in being open to the trajectories of freedom delineated within alternative, non-liberal philosophical registers.

METAPHORS OF FREEDOM

I make my arguments by working with two metaphors. The first is the fishbowl, which represents the liberal constellation that shapes and disseminates mainstream human rights advocacy and scholarship, as well as particular understandings of freedom. There is no hegemonic definition of freedom within the rights schema but, when the latter malfunctions, reparative and restorative solutions are inevitably sought within the fishbowl and the liberal episteme that underpins its operations. Solutions for rights-related problems and crises are rarely envisioned beyond it. Freedom continues to be articulated through the fishbowl knowledge and certitudes that are structured, reinforced and repaired within a limited liberal framework. Enclosed within the fishbowl, human rights and the pursuit of freedom within the liberal paradigm are partly defined, and their terrain of operations calibrated, against a powerful mistrust and fear of non-liberal epistemological traditions with sources outside this confining ideological sphere. These traditions, and their different understandings of freedom, are invariably viewed from within the fishbowl as an aggressive-cum-regressive threat to its hegemonies.

However, as systematically delineated in the chapters of this book, contemporary human rights advocacy is being engulfed by a sense of despair and stasis as it becomes increasingly evident that the accumulation of further rights, as well as efforts at repair, restoration or rehabilitation of the project, have clearly not resulted in more freedom for the disenfranchised. The accumulating fears and anxieties that inform human rights advocacy today ultimately expose the illusoriness of the modalities of freedom envisioned – for liberals themselves, as well as for their non-liberal 'Others'. I explain this illusion through the use of a second metaphor: the rope/snake metaphor wherein the perceiver mistakes the object of perception, a rope, to be a snake and reacts/acts accordingly. This metaphor, drawn from the non-liberal episteme of *Advaita* (lit. 'not two') mentioned above – a philosophical tradition of non-duality from the subcontinent – suggests that freedom can only be experienced through the perceiver understanding the root error of her (mis-)perception; that is, *the seeing of what is not, in what is.*[12] Such discernment, when consciously and repeatedly practised, corrects the perception and leads to correct external action and outcome. Quite specifically, in this episteme, the persistent, proliferating misjudgements that arise from the distorted logic of dualistic thinking resolve in the perceiver or observer.

In a Christian tradition, the snake is symbolic of evil, danger or a malevolent influence. Transposed into human rights terms, she represents the threat posed by the fear of an illiberal, unintelligible, regressive 'Other' to the very idea of human rights – and therefore, as undeserving of such rights, is to be coerced, incarcerated, subjugated or eliminated. However, the snake is read very differently within the non-liberal epistemology of non-dualism, where she is an illusion or appearance, produced by the perceiver. Fixating on the presence of this apparent snake, its particular features or its potential to harm brings the deluded observer no closer to discerning the truth – that the object perceived is actually the rope. The threat, the supposed 'snake', is not really there; the entity that actually does exist, the rope, becomes evident only through the perceiving subject. Through a constant practice of introspection/correction that alters and expands awareness, the perceiver's responses to both 'snake' and 'rope' are fundamentally transformed. And freedom rests in this understanding.

The metaphorical framing of my argument in terms of the rope-snake finds resonance in the latter part of this book – Chapters 6 and 7 – when I address the importance of self-scrutiny and the turn inwards as a central feature of freedom, as enunciated within non-liberal alternative epistemologies that focus on the concept of non-dualism. In terms of my argument in this book, the (mis)perceived entity of the 'rope-snake' – with its equivocations, contradictions and ambivalences – is, at one level, symbolic of the illusory rationale so cherished by its liberal adherents, proponents and actors: that human rights can actually, ethically and equitably procure and secure lasting freedom for all constituencies of the disenfranchised. Thus, while the rights apparatus may be viewed as a successful mode of emancipation for liberal advocacy, in real terms it may serve to further bind the disenfranchised through the overtly and covertly normative and regulatory functions of the project. The core illusion in the liberal rights paradigm rests specifically in two sets of exclusions that inform its universalist claims. First, the paradigm excludes those subjects who are constituted as either unassimilable or incommensurate, and thus fail to conform to the dominant normative arrangements that constitute part of the liberal scaffolding of freedom. Second, in monopolizing the space of freedom, this paradigm negates, suppresses or marginalizes alternative, non-liberal and, quite specifically, non-Western understandings of freedom.

At another level, and more importantly, the snake-rope metaphor is a subjective process – it is applicable only in reference to interiority and self-reflection. The metaphor is a technique for the observer or thinker or perceiver to correct the error in her perception. In this respect, the metaphor is an epistemological crux, where freedom lies in the discernment of the error – that the rope is not a snake. This understanding is arrived at through neither external pursuit nor external search, but through an internal process of reflection, correction and understanding that frees the observer from her misunderstanding and misperception, and precludes her from undertaking an action on the basis of this misunderstanding and misperception.

Using these two metaphors, I argue that after the disillusionment with human rights we are not in the epistemic free fall that seems to so unsettle the rights establishment, activists and scholars. The urge to alleviate the current critical despair by giving human rights a makeover and to retrieve it as a hopeful project within a liberal universe is not necessarily the only option, nor even a viable one. I suggest that the turn back to human rights in search of this goal – not only by liberal scholars, but also at times by critical scholars – is not a productive one.[13] This turn is actually reflective of the fear and anxiety underlying the refusal to explore alternative non-liberal registers and lifeworlds, not only because they are assumed to be illiberal and hence threatening, but also because of the entrenched hubris of the liberal conviction that the liberal project is *the* central means for securing freedom. Rather than succumb to paralysis and denial, we need to confront our despair – but, as I discuss in Chapter 5, the approach should not be through a renewed faith or reinvestment in the human rights project (as proposed by several scholars), nor through a bottom-up paradigm which seeks to recapture the originary dissonant and revolutionary spirit assumed to be integral to human rights. Instead, we need an approach that enables a delinking of the rights schema itself from dominant liberal understandings of freedom, and to explore whether and how non-liberal understandings of freedom can productively address and alleviate the current disillusionment with human rights.

Contemporary critiques erode the claims of liberal freedom to either secure the happiness of the individual through advocacy of 'the good life' or to focus primarily on the alleviation of suffering through a minimalist trajectory, and they also raise some crucial questions. Does freedom, understood as either the promotion of happiness or the reduction of suffering, inevitably marginalize other possible specific methods of personal and political emancipation? What kinds of subjects and political cultures are produced and manipulated, affirmed or negated through these types of interventions? I posit that the real project of human rights today is not its assumed salvific, benevolent, altruistic, universalist substrate but its constitutive, regulatory, exclusionary agenda that continues to produce and privilege certain 'free' subjects/subjectivities over a multitude of unfree/less free others. My argument in favour of a conscious shift towards exploring articulations of freedom beyond the fishbowl requires relinquishing the fear and anxiety that characterizes both critical and mainstream approaches to human rights, where non-liberal epistemological spaces are often equated with illiberalism, primitiveness, irrationality and threat. Such recognition involves taking seriously the reorientation and deconstruction of dominant thinking about human rights by critical scholars and acknowledging it as a governance project rather than a freedom project. It also involves taking this critique in a productive direction, which includes a willingness to turn towards and engage affirmatively with non-liberal epistemological spaces in the search for a genuinely meaningful articulation of freedom.

TEXTUAL CONTENT AND STRUCTURE

Several chapters in this book draw on lectures and keynotes that have been written and delivered at different points of time and for different occasions. These include invitations to speak about the complex relationship between human rights, justice and 'precarious desires'; to discuss the political possibilities of human rights in the context of the despair that has overtaken feminist and progressive politics; to analyse how women's rights advocacy on sexual violence at the domestic and international level may have reinforced the rise of a sexual security regime; to address the relationship between culture and freedom, and the coercive dimensions of human rights in relation to the Islamic practice of veiling; and to examine the understanding of freedom that is emerging in contemporary discourses on queer rights in both the postcolonial and international legal arenas. The adhesives that bind these interventions are all situated within a critical, quite specifically postcolonial feminist tradition, which does not assume that liberalism is the default position. Rather, this tradition has the ability to resist the northern gravitational pull of understanding and critiquing the world primarily through a liberal imaginary, as well as to accommodate in a productive way the inscriptions of freedom enunciated in various non-liberal philosophical traditions. At the same time, it does not subscribe to a nativist presentation of seemingly uncontaminated, indigenous epistemologies where, in fact, historically embedded caste and sexist and racist relations of power are also at work. Rather, the capacity to accommodate non-liberal philosophical possibilities may be the key to transforming the ways in which we imagine the world as well as catalyse more creative and meaningful imaginings of how to be free within it.

Liberal Freedom and the Fishbowl

As stated previously, the understanding of freedom that has informed human rights is fully framed within a liberal paradigm – what I designate as the fishbowl. And this paradigm includes a range of ways in which freedom is to be achieved, including through negative freedom, positive freedom, republican freedom and freedom in terms of the capabilities approach. In all these articulations, the individual is regarded as the central unit of the social sphere. Within the ambit of human rights, the key concern is how to maximize individual freedom through rights accumulation as well as how to hold states accountable for the withholding, suppression or violation of basic human rights. Battles are waged to secure rights set out in the main UN human rights documents in the conviction that more rights will lead to more freedom and happiness. In Chapter 1, 'Liberal Freedom in a Fishbowl', I argue that the central features of liberal freedom – as a progressive, external end goal, and as linked to liberal individualism – have been exposed by critical legal thinkers as obscuring the normative assumptions and political agendas that are reinforced or advanced in and through the discourse of rights. Such critiques have revealed how freedom is linked in the contemporary moment not only to an increasingly narrow understanding based on an economic formulation realized through a neoliberal market enterprise, but also to a distinct understanding of the subject as an unveiled, sexualized consumer. The critiques reveal how liberal freedom, valorized as the pinnacle of progressive thought and civilizational virtues, is explicitly and implicitly informed by political projects emanating from the fishbowl.

I analyse three key claims of liberal freedom in relation to human rights. The first is the claim that human rights are not linked to freedom, and that their only role is to reduce cruelty and suffering – they should, in this view, do nothing more in relation to the disenfranchised subject. The second is the belief that culture, antiquity and tradition have been obstacles to human flourishing, and that those oppressed and hindered through these modalities can be rescued through the universalist premise of human rights and liberal individualism. The third is the notion that human rights are based on the existence of a common universal subject. The analysis establishes my assertion that the current framework of human rights – which has its source in the liberal enunciation of freedom – is materially and ideologically grafted onto a governance project; this assertion informs the subsequent discussion in this book regarding the implications of such vascular fusion for human rights advocacy in relation to gender and alterity. The argument is not that the human rights terrain should be abandoned, but rather that it should be engaged precisely *because* it is an arena of power, even while there is a simultaneous need for rights to be actively dissociated from the assumption that they can deliver the disenfranchised into lasting freedom. Given the failure of the liberal-based rights schema, the rationales for such freedom must be sought through alternative non-liberal philosophical registers.

Evaluating LGBT and Feminist Human Rights Advocacy

In Chapter 2, 'Precarious Desires and the Pursuit of Rights', I discuss the anatomy of freedom and how certain subjects come to be recognized in human rights discourse as experiencing injuries and harms that are deemed as unjust, reparable or remediable, in a context where freedom is directly equated with securing rights that will render these marginalized groups more assimilated, that is, more mainstream. This chapter analyses how rights interventions occur within and against already established normative and material frameworks, namely, conventional racial, cultural, sexual and civilizational arrangements that inform both the ideology and the apparatus of human rights. The chapter specifically examines how pursuits of human rights have an impact on 'precarious desires', with a focus on LGBT advocacy. Further, it considers how such pursuits, while conferring recognition and legibility, not only reproduce the normative framework in which precarity and precarious identities are addressed, but also clearly incorporate the entitled subject, the rights-seeking subject and the illegible non-subject within a space where freedom is strongly defined in terms of the market and consumer agency.[14] I elaborate on how rights interventions simultaneously transform the disempowered 'unhappy queer' into a 'happy queer subject',[15] one whose experience of freedom is directly affiliated with the neoliberal rationality articulated by Foucault – specifically, the political/economic schema that finds its central manifestation in the logic of the market.

In Chapter 3, 'Freedom, Women's Rights and the Rise of the Sexual Security Regime', I illustrate how women's rights advocacy is moving further and further away from its promised goal of freedom in the context of human rights. As my starting point, I take the responses to the sexual assaults committed on women in Cologne on New Year's Eve in 2015, as well as those to the gang rape, and subsequent death in hospital from related injuries, of a young woman in Delhi on 16 December 2012 – an atrocity that catalyzed nationwide protests and received global attention. The chapter traces how these appalling episodes of violence against women invited activist and state responses that strengthened the security and sexual surveillance apparatus governing gender more generally and Third World women quite specifically, and witnessed an increased alignment with the state of progressive forces, including feminists. The consequent increase in overt and subtle control asserted over women's choices raises questions as to how and why decades of women's human rights advocacy have produced outcomes that have actually moved in the direction of *unfreedom* rather than freedom.

While rights discourse has indeed provided a platform for women to narrate and challenge abuses and harms that have been hidden from activist scrutiny, this evidentiary mode should not be equated with freedom. I illustrate how gender rights advocacy has been thoroughly implicated in maintaining gender binaries and promoting a carceral vision by discussing interventions in the context of anti-trafficking, as well as the Security Council Resolutions 1325 and 1820 on gender, peace and security in conflict situations. These interventions have invariably translated into a general tightening of the sexual security regime in accordance with national and cultural imperatives. Further, they have been displaced into a First/Third World divide, thus enabling a broader justification for the establishment of security regimes and the unleashing of military and 'civilizing' missions in developing countries in the name of women's rights. The work of protecting local women and procuring their freedom from various cadres of native oppressors, in what are regarded as illiberal contexts – dominated by hostile, unintelligible, irrational, misogynistic 'Others' – is, in fact, achieved through liberal forces imposing their own righteous counter-rhetoric and aggressive protocols of unfreedom in those regions.

The conflation of diverse issues within women's human rights advocacy with an almost exclusive focus on violence against women and related criminal justice measures, and directed partly by what Janet Halley has described as 'governance feminism', has moved decidedly away from the idea of human rights as a freedom project.[16] Women's human rights advocacy has instead come to operate as a tool for disciplining and intensifying the surveillance of women's sexual conduct and strengthening the security apparatus of the state. It remains no coincidence that this approach converges with the robust contemporary script of neoliberal governmentality and the increasing 'economization' of political life that I discuss in Chapter 2.

Chapter 4, 'Alterity, Gender Equality and the Veil', addresses the issue of gender in relation to equality and alterity, specifically in the context of the human rights controversies surrounding Muslim women's rights and the scripturally sanctioned, popular practice of veiling. Drawing upon the analytical insights of postcolonial feminism, this chapter demonstrates how the anatomy of the right to gender equality is shaped by dominant sexual, gender and cultural norms that set out fundamentally non-negotiable *unfree* terms for social inclusion and full citizenship. Focusing largely on the controversial French laws banning various manifestations of the veil, as well as on decisions of the European Court of Human Rights upholding the validity of such bans, I demonstrate how universality, which is claimed within the liberal constellation as the basis for freedom in human rights, is in fact a modality that is highly particular, exclusionary, differential and deeply conditioned by cultural and gender norms.

The argument illustrates how states deploy the logic of gender equality as a racist technique to profile and target French Muslims, render their religious *and* national identity suspect and deny them their rights. The veil bans are trumpeted in the name of advancing women's right to gender equality, but this process also ensures that a very specific understanding and desirable image of the gendered subject (essentialized, unveiled and sexualized) is presented as worthy of reinforcement and protection within the human rights regime. This understanding discounts the fact that liberal conceptions of freedom informing such interventions are based on the patronizing and paternalistic conceit that the West knows what is best for the inferior/oppressed 'Other'. And as Saba Mahmood has so eloquently and persuasively argued, opponents of veiling also completely ignore the intimate and affective dimensions of this practice; in particular, how articulations of the experience of freedom *through* the veil, rather than through freedom *from* the veil, can emancipate women for whom the veil functions simultaneously as a significant spiritual/cultural/ethical choice and as a way of life.[17]

Human rights as an advocacy tool, while prompted by radical movements and visions, are ultimately drawn into compliance with a specific normative order that is both de-radicalizing as well as regulatory and discriminatory. I do not take the position of scholars who consider the human rights project as a failed one that needs to be replaced,[18] or as a project that has repudiated its initial 'moral clarity' – a repudiation based on Eurocentric roots that have coerced rights advocacy into becoming an ally for the humanitarian and military interventions of powerful liberal states against various configurations of backward and violent 'Others'. I recognize not only that human rights are implicated in power and have powerful effects, but also that they constitute a terrain acquired arduously and at great cost – a terrain that cannot and should not be surrendered. As emphasized earlier in this Introduction, human rights are something 'we cannot not want', despite the injustice of preferential bestowal and the relentless reification of the liberal paradigm, wherein rights are embedded as the universal and desirable norm.

History continues to prove that the normative content of human rights can be altered and disrupted by those who have never been recognized as human by the entitled majority, or whose humanity has been positioned at the lower end of the civilizational hierarchy within the liberal (imperial) project. While these disruptive possibilities have concretely opened up some spaces of increased legibility and protection for racial and religious minorities, colonial subjects, queers and women, all of whom have sought to be recognized within the human rights apparatus, these 'victories' do not equate with the idea that rights have actually ensured more permanent freedom for these constituencies. The early chapters of this book illustrate that engagement with human rights, while at times urgent and compelling, has demonstrated little capacity to actualize the desire for lasting freedom, and that human rights are not simply pragmatic instruments for the pursuit of a minimalist agenda to alleviate suffering and ensure bare survival that puts the disenfranchised subject in a position to make more choices. The outcomes of the human rights interventions discussed in these early chapters provide little scope for understanding freedom outside of liberal conceptions generally, or the current phase of economic global expansion more specifically, where human life is subordinated to the neoliberal market and includes the commodification of suffering.[19] More significantly for the purposes of my book, the notion that divergent understandings of freedom have always existed outside of the liberal and neoliberal imaginaries and related market terms is either barely considered by those who shape, support and implement the rights regime, or considered inherently alien and therefore irrelevant to the recursive ideological currents within the fishbowl.

Chapter 4 sets the stage for the argument put forward in the final three chapters of the book, where it is proposed that the concept of freedom should be actively delinked from the human rights project as formulated and imposed by the liberal imaginary, and should instead be explored within affective as well as alternative philosophical registers. The stark realization that human rights do not equally deliver to all constituencies prompts us to ask: what do we do when the emancipatory hope incorporated into the liberal imaginary fades? Where do we turn when our critiques abandon us on the final precipice of the liberal vision – our backs to roiling violence, our thoughts overwhelmed by a sense of approaching apocalypse, even as we stare down into what seems like an epistemic abyss? Do we refashion the tools that have constituted the arsenal of liberal reform, and stage a hopeful reinvestment in the human rights project in anticipation that such reinvestment might draw aside the curtain of pessimism and allow in some streams of light? Do we continue to cling to our critical relationship with the human rights movement and the liberal concepts that have, with naive idealism and revolutionary fervour, held out hope for a different and better future? Or do we resign ourselves to embracing the *myth* of human rights as a minimalist endeavour or available firefighting technique that may alleviate some forms of human suffering, and do 'nothing more', despite knowing that they are always actively pushing, protecting and reinforcing other agendas? These and similar concerns are informed by an underlying fear on the part of human rights advocates and critical scholars that there are no other options, or only illiberal alternatives, available as solutions to the current crisis. In the later chapters of this book, I argue that these fears constitute obstacles to the work of shaping and implementing modalities of emancipation, and are based on an uninterrogated commitment to viewing liberalism as the default position or source of all emancipatory knowledge or as undisputedly the superior political philosophy.

Freedom beyond the Liberal Imaginary

What remains intriguing in the state of epistemic crisis is how the despair generated by the devastating critiques of human rights as instruments for the differential distribution of justice, or as facilitating a carceral politics, or as contradictory, or as a governance project that disciplines, regulates or constitutes subjects rather than emancipating them does not appear to have shaken the commitment to human rights as a moral and social good, or the continuing, unrelenting faith in its universal application. The terrain of rights is continually enhanced, reiterated and reinforced through its function as a site of continuous engagement by disenfranchised and marginalized groups, as well as by scholars who have recognized the limitations of human rights but found ways to reinvest in this project through re-theorizing its trajectories and thus nourishing the template of its futurity. The powerful critique of human rights has not undermined the foundations of the project or its power as a human ideal in the least. So we are compelled to ask: what is the allure of human rights, even when its promise of freedom that includes a specific vision of happiness or a better life remains unrealized, or elusive, or illusory for a large proportion of humanity? Does the terror and despair generated by the prospect of rejecting human rights, or by the conclusion that they have no redemptive or reparative value, galvanize the urge to pull it back from the brink and produce hopeful counter-narratives to these dystopian scenarios? Is there a limit to the capacity to envision human rights as the best route to political and personal freedom that can be hoped for in these dark times?

I argue that we need to take our sense of despair in a different direction. The human rights project has reached an impasse, and finds itself inhabiting a moment of stasis that also affords an opportunity for a more diligent and thoughtful consideration of the meaning of freedom in another set of registers – in particular, *outside* of the liberal imaginary and the structures of liberal legality that also construct the deserving, desirable, entitled, sovereign subject. I argue in favour of the politics of reflectivity and discernment, which can be utilized as a vital resource, method and modality in the current phase of global violence, chaos and upheaval. The tense equation of a liberal rights critique with pessimism, and a liberal rights deployment with optimism, has deferred a pending ideological implosion within the fishbowl, but has not defused it. This obdurate interlocking of scholarly and activist energies takes us not into clarity, but into further stagnation and confusion.

Chapter 4 marks the moment when my argument sloughs its skin through a controlled, purposive and complete peeling back. In the final three chapters of the book, I consciously stage a turn away from our conditioned view of human rights as a mechanism for freedom, towards possibilities for lasting freedom nestled in a turn to the intimate as well as alternative non-liberal registers where freedom rests in self-inquiry and the transformation of the self. In ideational terms, any fresh insight into the concept of freedom – one that would equally apply to and help *all* constituencies – mandates a calibrated loosening and inversion of the liberal sheath; a systematic, concentrated, diligent act of new cognition/re-cognition. This critical distancing from the familiar episteme and its hegemonies turns inside out the core framings of the human rights project – the rational subject, linear time and liberal freedom.

Chapter 5, 'Despair, Redemption and the Turn Away from Human Rights', elaborates on the enormous reluctance to let go of human rights as a redemptive moral pursuit, despite the knowledge that rights in their contemporary incarnation cannot deliver on their promise of freedom for women and cultural and sexual subalterns. I examine some of the efforts to reclaim the human rights project through renewal, recuperation and reinvestment, which all persistently adhere to the liberal vision of human rights as a proved mechanism for freedom. Though some of these efforts pursue the Foucauldian position on rights as regulatory and disciplinary techniques of governance, they resubmit to the coercive logic of the liberal universe as the sole location within which all solutions for human suffering and diagnostics of freedom must be found. This turn back to a schema of restoration via rights fails to explore the dynamic potential and generative capacities of experiential conditions of despair, hopelessness and failure. The second part of Chapter 5 draws on feminist and queer affect theory to explore the turn to the intimate. I discuss how this turn is inherently a valid source of self-affirmation and freedom. A continued yearning for or attachment to human rights may not be in the subject's best interest, and indeed may be a form of 'cruel optimism' that becomes an obstacle to human flourishing.[20] The existent human rights project requires compliance with the normative architecture of freedom and happiness instituted by liberal/neoliberal paradigms; those who do not comply become failed subjects.[21] Yet not only does this very site of negativity and failure draw attention to the granular aspects of daily suffering and the existential strategies that enable hope and survival within even the most hopeless, unliveable situations, but the foregrounding of affect and the intimate also opens up possibilities for examining freedom in alternative registers. It mandates a turn away from the doctrinaire liberal position that human rights are fundamentally a freedom project. It also inscribes the refusal of failed subjects to submit to a regulatory regime that compels conformity with the scaffolding of dominant sexual, gender and cultural norms which, in the liberal imaginary, constitute the enfranchised, empowered subject and the ideal of freedom.

Chapter 6, 'Seeking Freedom through Alternative Registers', explores the possibility of relocating the discursively constituted subject of human rights advocacy within a non-liberal philosophical tradition that may open up space for alternative understandings of, and realizing, the desire for lasting freedom through a crucial focus on the self and self-inquiry, and the adoption of a reflective rather than reflexive politics. The argument pushes back against the embedded notion that all political hope and possibility rests within a liberal philosophical tradition which can be actualized partly through the pursuit of human rights. To illustrate what I mean by the 'turn towards' understanding freedom in alternative registers, I examine the intellectual shift that manifested in the work of two critical theorists: Eve Sedgwick and Michel Foucault. I discuss Sedgwick's attraction to Buddhism and her engagement with Mahayana epistemology, which enabled her to theorize positive 'affect' and describe how the capacious and liberating idea of cyclic time, together with the interdependent, impermanent, experiential 'non-self' within this tradition, contrasts sharply with the limitations of liberal individualism and linear chronologies on which human rights are based. I also discuss Foucault's concept of 'political spirituality' in the context of his interest in the Iranian revolution, and the influence of canonical Shi'ism upon his thought. I describe how his theorizing of the notion of revolution beyond a liberal paradigm quite specifically involved a reconfiguration/ reinscription of the discursively constituted self and its finite potentialities.

I end the chapter with a discussion on how any such intellectual and emotional turn away from the liberal paradigm can be perceived as threatening and invite hostility and even, at times, violence. I conclude with a close reading of Iranian-born artist Shirin Neshat's video installation *Overruled* (2012), an allegorical work referencing Persian Sufism and based on a historic criminal trial that is ostensibly about a challenge to state-sanctioned freedom of expression, but is in fact about the expression of freedom in an alternative register. The work offers a complex appraisal of the embedded suspicions and phobias underlying the majoritarian resistance to individual and collective unfamiliarity or difference, including the turn, by those designated as failed subjects, away from a liberal episteme to embrace an alternative articulation of freedom. It also scrutinizes the reluctance to turn away from the assured taxonomies of sanctioned systems of thought and reorient towards alternative spaces of engagement and the narratives produced therein.

Chapter 7, 'Freedom from the Fishbowl', elaborates on the implications of a radical turn away from human rights and its normative prescriptions. I examine how re-conceptualizations of the subject, time and freedom within the epistemology of the specific subcontinental philosophical tradition of non-dualism (*Advaita*) offer possibilities for realizing the desire for meaningful freedom and happiness. I consider how engagement with this tradition is relevant for human rights advocacy, and how it opens up space for women and sexual subalterns to intervene on their own behalf and pursue strategies of freedom outside of a valorized liberal imaginary. Such a shift in perspective requires a willingness to detach from theoretical projects that have held out so much political hope and possibility, without fearing that nihilism will be the inevitable outcome. This turn away from the fishbowl is not a culturally exotic move. Rather, it reflects a serious concern with the question of *how* we can continue to pursue the idea of freedom and its connections to happiness and the 'good life', in the aftermath of the dismayed and immobilized contemporary critique of human rights.

In the epilogue, I bring together the analysis presented in the book and reread some historical and contemporary struggles, cases and texts involving alternative expressions of subjectivity against which our conventional concepts of freedom can be measured. These articulations illustrate the counter-hegemonic potential that resides in non-liberal epistemologies that are available, although not exclusively, in postcolonial spaces. They present alternative registers of being and becoming in the world, thus refuting the universalist assumption that freedom must already, and always, be schematized and instituted by a liberal imaginary. Without falling into the trap of convenient cultural relativism, the epilogue's narratives invoke the potential for human rights to be aligned with, though not necessarily commensurable with, a non-liberal paradigm of freedom.

This book avers that freedom is unlikely to be found in the insistent protocols of rights accumulation that serve to further embed the seeking subject within the terms of a liberal imaginary and, in the contemporary moment, impale the subject within a mode of uncompromising economic imperialism based on neoliberal rationality. The arguments presented in this book seek to displace liberal framings and international human rights understandings of freedom, even while rights remain important tools for conducting a conversation with the official state apparatus. The displacement operates at two levels: I thematically disorient and question the liberal human rights project through the 'fishbowl' and 'rope-snake' metaphors; and I provincialize and vernacularize the rights project by including non-Western, non-liberal epistemologies as valid and valuable strands of inquiry. My project is an audacious and radical one – in essence, it seeks to theoretically disrupt the axiomatic and hegemonic liberal positioning of human rights as the irrefutable core ideology for delivering the many constituencies of the disenfranchised into lasting freedom. Thus, the main contribution of this book is to identify new, revolutionary ways of pursuing freedom, highlighting the central features of non-liberal philosophical epistemologies and traditions that involve a turn inwards and necessarily require the self-transformation of the subject.

I end here by re-invoking the snake metaphor. What the passer-by erroneously observes as a snake forces her to instinctively move away or take another route to escape its menacing potential. However, if instead of deviating she engages in a closer investigation of both the external phenomenon and her internal responses to it, she may come to realize that the 'snake' is something else entirely: a rope, an object that in appearance resembles what she fears, but in actuality holds no threat. The real danger, in fact, is a profound error in perception that compels the observer to mentally superimpose what is not upon what is – an action that embeds her in confusion and may trigger an unsettling cascade of internal and/or external reactions. Transposing this logic of observation/self-observation onto the human rights schema, we might say, in the simplest terms, that rights advocacy intervention thus requires careful discernment and thoughtfulness. At a deep philosophical level, the rope/snake metaphor is about the subject and her discernment, which involves a simultaneous and meticulous scrutiny of the perceiving subject as well as of the perceived object, and through which fundamental errors in one's perception – of oneself and of one's 'other/s' – can be corrected. Discernment collapses the conventional categories of 'being' and 'doing', the distinction between the subject who 'is' and the subject who 'does'. And only through such discernment can the potential for further inscribing the wheel-ruts of error be appropriately curtailed, and the futile, recursive and endless ideological circumambulations within the fishbowl be effectively terminated.

NOTES

1. Ben Golder, 'Beyond Redemption? Problematising the Critique of Human Rights in Contemporary International Legal Thought', *London Review of International Law* 2, no. 1 (2014): 79. See also Ben Golder, *Foucault and the Politics of Rights* (Stanford, CA: Stanford University Press, 2015).
2. Wendy Brown, *Politics Out of History* (Princeton, NJ: Princeton University Press, 2001), pp. 5–6.
3. Costas Douzinas, *The End of Human Rights: Critical Legal Thought at the Turn of the Century* (Oxford: Hart Publishing, 2000), p. 2.
4. See, among others, Antony Anghie, 'International Human Rights Law and a Developing World Perspective', in *Routledge Handbook of International Human Rights Law*, eds. Scott Sheeran and Nigel Rodley (London: Routledge, 2013), pp. 109–25; Antony Anghie, *Imperialism, Sovereignty, and the Making of International Law* (Cambridge: Cambridge University Press, 2007); José-Manuel Barreto, *Human Rights from a Third World Perspective: Critique, History and International Law* (Newcastle upon Tyne: Cambridge Scholars Publishing, 2013); Dianne Otto, ed., *Gender Issues and Human Rights*, 3 vols (Cheltenham: Edward Elgar Publishing, 2013); Upendra Baxi, *The Future of Human Rights*, 3rd ed. (New Delhi: Oxford University Press, 2008); Doris Buss and Ambreena Manji, 'Introduction', in *International Law: Modern Feminist Approaches*, eds. Doris Buss and Ambreena Manji (Oxford: Hart, 2005), pp. 1–16; Subrata Sankar Bagchi and Arnab Das, eds., *Human Rights and the Third World: Issues and Discourses* (Lanham, MD: Lexington Books, 2012); David Kennedy, *The Dark Sides of Virtue: Reassessing International Humanitarianism* (Princeton, NJ: Princeton University Press, 2004); Makau Mutua, 'What is TWAIL?' *ASIL Proceedings* [2000]; Makau Mutua, *Human Rights Standards: Hegemony, Law, and Politics* (Albany, NY: State University of New York Press, 2016).
5. See, for example, Douzinas, *End of Human Rights*, p. 1.
6. For a further discussion on the 'dark side' or destructive consequences of the human rights project see Emma Larking, 'Human Rights Rituals: Masking Neoliberalism and Inequality, and Marginalizing Alternative World Views', *Canadian Journal of Law and Society/Revue Canadienne Droit et Société* 32, no. 1 (2017): 1–18; Kathryn McNeilly, 'After the Critique of Rights: For a Radical Democratic Theory and Practice of Human Rights', *Law and Critique* 27, no. 3 (2016): 269–88; Diana Tietjens Meyers, 'Recovering the Human in Human Rights', *Law, Culture and the Humanities* 12, no. 3 (2016): 474–84.

7. Ranajit Guha and Partha Chatterjee, *The Small Voice of History: Collected Essays* (Ranikhet: Permanent Black, 2010). See also Ranajit Guha, 'On Some Aspects of the Historiography of Colonial India', in *Subaltern Studies: Writings on South Asian History and Society*, ed. Ranajit Guha (Delhi: Oxford University Press, 1982), pp. 1–8. For recent postcolonial critiques of dominant narratives and hegemonic discourse see Fabian Klose, 'Human Rights For and Against Empire: Legal and Public Discourses in the Age of Decolonisation', *Journal of the History of International Law* 18, nos. 2–3 (2016): 317–38; Sebastian Bonnet, 'Overcoming Eurocentrism in Human Rights: Postcolonial Critiques – Islamic Answers?' *Muslim World Journal of Human Rights* 12, no. 1 (2015): 1–24.
8. See, for example, Samuel Moyn, *The Last Utopia: Human Rights in History* (Cambridge, MA: Harvard University Press, 2010). Moyn argues that human rights are contemporary in origin and emerged as globally relevant in the 1970s after the failure of revolutionary Communism and nationalism. A contrasting view is presented by Martinez, who traces the emergence of human rights law against the struggle to end the slave trade. See also Samuel Moyn, *Human Rights and the Uses of History* (London: Verso, 2014); Jenny S. Martinez, *The Slave Trade and the Origins of International Human Rights Law* (Oxford: Oxford University Press, 2012); Lynn Hunt, *Inventing Human Rights: A History* (New York: W.W. Norton, 2007); Christopher McCrudden, 'Human Rights Histories', *Oxford Journal of Legal Studies* 35, no. 1 (2015): 179–212.
9. See, for example, Stephen Hopegood, *The Endtimes of Human Rights* (Ithaca, NY: Cornell University Press, 2013); Eric A. Posner, *The Twilight of Human Rights Law* (New York: Oxford University Press, 2014).
10. Pheng Cheah, *Inhuman Conditions: On Cosmopolitanism and Human Rights* (Cambridge, MA: Harvard University Press, 2006). See also Anna Selmeczi, 'Who Is the Subject of Neoliberal Rights? Governmentality, Subjectification and the Letter of the Law', *Third World Quarterly* 36, no. 6 (2015): 1076–91. See further Nick Stevenson, *Human Rights and the Reinvention of Freedom* (Abingdon: Routledge, 2017).
11. Franz Fanon, *Black Skin, White Masks*, trans. Charles Lam Markmann (New York: Grove Press, 1967); Ashis Nandy, *The Intimate Enemy: Loss and Recovery of Self under Colonialism* (Delhi: Oxford University Press, 1983), p. 3; Albert Memmi, *The Colonizer and the Colonized* (New York: Orion Press, 1963); Walter D. Mignolo, *The Darker Side of the Renaissance: Literacy, Territoriality, and Colonization*, 2nd ed. (Ann Arbor, MI: University of Michigan Press, 2003); Edward Said, *Orientalism* (London: Penguin Books, 1978); Gayatri Chakravorty Spivak, 'Can the Subaltern Speak?' in *The Post-Colonial Studies Reader*, eds. Bill Ashcroft, Gareth Griffiths and Helen Tiffin (London: Routledge, 1995), pp. 24–8. For recent critical engagement with these texts, see Sarah Bracke, 'Is the Subaltern Resilient? Notes on Agency and Neoliberal Subjects', *Cultural Studies* 30, no. 5 (2016): 839–55; Bibhash Choudhury, *Reading Postcolonial Theory: Key Texts in Context* (Florence: Taylor and Francis, 2016).
12. The snake/rope metaphor is drawn from the expositions of the eighth-century philosopher Adi Śaṅkara, whose work is discussed in Chapter 7. See more generally Śaṅkarācārya, *Śaṅkara on the Absolute*, trans. A.J. Alston (London: Shanti Sadan, 2004).
13. See Golder, 'Beyond Redemption?' Golder discusses the redemptive aspects of the work of three critical legal scholars in international and human rights law: David Kennedy, Anne Orford and Makau Matua. See also my critique of the positions of three critical/postcolonial/feminist scholars – Costas Douzinas, Boaventura De Sousa Santos and Wendy Brown – and their recursive turn back towards human rights/liberal freedom in Chapter 5. For one response to Golder's arguments on the redemptive turn by critical scholars, see Geoff Dancy and Christopher J. Fariss, 'Rescuing Human Rights Law from International Legalism and Its Critics', *Human Rights Quarterly* 39, no. 1 (2017): 1–36.
14. See Wendy Brown, *Undoing the Demos: Neoliberalism's Stealth Revolution* (New York: Zone Books, 2015); Wendy Brown, 'Sacrificial Citizenship: Neoliberalism, Human Capital, and Austerity Politics', *Constellations* 23, no. 1 (2016): 3–14. See Foucault's lectures on neoliberalism as the new regime of governmentality in which 'homo economicus' is a particular mode of subjection and freedom is understood primarily in terms of freedom of

the market: Michel Foucault, *The Birth of Biopolitics: Lectures at the Collège de France, 1978–79*, ed. Michel Senellart, trans. Graham Burchell (Basingstoke: Palgrave Macmillan, 2008).

15. Sara Ahmed, *The Promise of Happiness* (Durham, NC: Duke University Press, 2010), pp. 88–120.
16. Janet Halley, 'Introduction to Governance Feminism,' in *Governance Feminism: An Introduction*, eds. Janet Halley, Prabha Kotiswaran, Rachel Rebouché, and Hila Shamir (Minneapolis: University of Minneapolis Press, 2018), pp. ix-xxii; Janet Halley, *Split Decisions: How and Why to Take a Break from Feminism* (Princeton, NJ: Princeton University Press, 2006), pp. 4–5; see also pp. 20–2.
17. Saba Mahmood, *The Politics of Piety: The Islamic Revival and the Feminist Subject* (Princeton: Princeton University Press, 2005)
18. Hopegood, *Endtimes of Human Rights*. Hopegood excoriates what he describes as the 'human rights industry' as a tool of conservative nationalists, religious forces and American power, arguing that the deployment of human rights serves the interests of international elites and assuages the guilt of the middle classes. See also Posner, *Twilight of Human Rights*. Posner argues that human rights are a failed project, incapable of functioning effectively to realize freedom due to their inherent ambiguities, sponginess and lack of consensus. He proposes that they be replaced by an economic framework based on a foreign aid model that has concrete and measurable indicators for poverty reduction.
19. Upendra Baxi, 'Voices of Suffering and the Future of Human Rights', *Transnational Law and Contemporary Problems* 8, no. 2 (1998): 159–60; Naomi Klein, *The Shock Doctrine: The Rise of Disaster Capitalism* (London: Allen Lane, 2007); Susan Marks, 'Four Human Rights Myths', London School of Economics and Political Science, LSE Law, Society and Economy Working Papers 10/2012 (2012), http://www.lse.ac.uk/collections/law/wps/WPS2012-10_Marks.pdf; Elaine M. Lazaro, 'Thinking with Irigaray: On Asian Women as Objects of Conquest and Exchange', *Kritike* 11, no. 1 (2017): 94–107.
20. Lauren Berlant, *Cruel Optimism* (Durham, NC: Duke University Press, 2011).
21. Ahmed, *Promise of Happiness*, 150; Judith Halberstam, *The Queer Art of Failure* (Durham, NC: Duke University Press, 2011). For a critical engagement with Ahmed and Halberstam, see Mari Ruti, *The Ethics of Opting Out: Queer Theory's Defiant Subjects* (New York: Columbia University Press, 2017).

1. Liberal freedom in a fishbowl

[F]ear destroys freedom.
—Judith Shklar, *Ordinary Vices*[1]

In truth that which you call freedom is the strongest of these chains, though its links glitter in the sun and dazzle your eyes.
—Kahlil Gibran, 'On Freedom'[2]

This chapter delineates how the concept of liberal freedom, which is central to the pursuit of human rights, is structured and articulated within what I metaphorically describe as the fishbowl. I do not attempt to provide a comprehensive account of liberal freedom, an elusive and paradoxical concept that has also already been the subject of extensive dispute and debate.[3] Rather, my intention is to pursue a philosophical inquiry into the common assumptions on which liberal freedom in the context of human rights is based, and how these become the basis of unfreedom.

LIBERAL FREEDOM AND THE FISHBOWL

Liberal freedom is based on two common assumptions: first, that freedom is a progressive, external pursuit, which is owned or possessed; second, related to the first, that freedom originates or is accessed through the consciously exerted will of a finite, thinking, individual subject. I interrogate these claims not only by building on existing and extensive critiques that have problematized the emancipatory claims of democratic political projects, but also by examining understandings of freedom that are left out or excluded – quite specifically, non-liberal understandings. In this chapter, I unpack how these two core features that are constitutive of liberal freedom, and on which human rights are based, in fact become the source of *unfreedom*. Centrally, these features obscure how release into the space of human rights, which is the international expression of liberal freedom, actually entails release into a governance regime that not only regulates and disciplines the subject, but also implicates her in specific ways of behaving, conducting herself and being that amount to being unfree. While resistance to the normative scaffolding of liberal freedom remains possible, my argument is that resistance and disruptions do not in and of themselves bring the resistive subject closer to lasting freedom.

Liberalism has long situated various conceptions of freedom at its core. It includes a range of ways in which freedom is to be achieved, including through negative freedom, positive freedom, republican freedom and the capability approach.[4] While liberal freedom has typically been defined in negative terms, with an emphasis upon maximizing individual freedom and preventing excessive state interference,[5] it has also been associated with happiness,[6] as well as with the maximizing of pleasure[7] – a tradition that established a strong cause-and-effect rationale between freedom and happiness, and which cohered over time into an ideology that John Rawls referred to as the 'liberalism of happiness'.[8] Some scholars have argued that human rights must be based on a far more robust understanding of liberal freedom, namely, one based on positive duties.[9] While the different approaches to freedom are complex, contradictory and at times confused, the various guises of liberal freedom adhere to the two key features that I have mentioned.

Human rights are the transnational expression of liberal freedom, where the protection of people from the state, together with ensuring their free involvement in/from the state, shifts from being the responsibility of local/state forces to being an international concern. This move towards a transnational mode seems a logical one, given the horrific violations of the Second World War, the scale of suffering and the traumatic dispossession of millions of people over large swathes of territory. There is thus a symbiotic relationship between liberalism, freedom and international human rights.[10] Liberalism – being centrally about freedom from the state – inherently *creates* rights that protect the individual from arbitrary intervention by the state. Thus human rights represent a modern attempt to formalize the relationship with liberal values – freedom being conceived as integral to both – although the question of whether human rights should solely focus on negative rights or also include positive rights remains an ongoing debate.[11] There is, however, a predominant assumption, set forth in the main UN human rights documents, that the accumulation of more rights brings about more freedom.[12]

The overarching configuration of the rights framework as creating a new, internationalized, universalizing discourse that purportedly offers equal freedom to all demographics has been exposed by, among others, critical legal scholars as having substantial political effects. They have revealed how liberal framings obscure the normative assumptions and the political and economic agendas that are being reinforced or advanced in and through the discourse of rights.[13] Human rights operate as a constituting discourse and thus a political tool, which can be wielded like any other and can produce outcomes that are not necessarily either progressive or liberating.[14] In other words, human rights have been used for political goals which seem to fundamentally clash with the very idea of human rights, and the freedom it purports to offer all constituencies.[15]

I revisit the symbiotic relationship between the liberal tradition and human rights, arguing that their connection is based not so much on a common pursuit of freedom, but rather on a shared, complex inheritance. This inheritance includes the cruelties and violence of the colonial encounter, aggressive conquests, claims to cultural, racial and civilizational supremacy, as well as the reproduction and reinforcement of gender stereotypes and hierarchies that are either obscured or justified in the name of good intentions and the alleviation of human suffering.[16] This inheritance is partly constitutive of liberal political thought and human rights.[17] These histories continue to inform the present, and frequently manifest as a form of muscular liberalism exerted over various demographics of often adversarial, non-liberal/illiberal 'Others'. They are also rechannelled into overt suspicion, distrust and/or rejection of anything that politically and philosophically pivots beyond the fulcrum of what I have described in this book's Introduction as the 'fishbowl', and beyond the field of the linked discourses that constitute fishbowl knowledge. And this schema of liberal hegemony continues to confine our understanding of freedom, and actively precludes or truncates other ways of being and of being free in the world.

The bulk of this chapter frames freedom within this complex inheritance and sets out the highly strategic and political nature of the work that freedom does in the context of human rights, even when rights are presented as being agnostic to the pursuit of freedom and concerned only with reducing the worst forms of human suffering and cruelty. Human rights emerge as part of the mode of governance wherein rights-enabled 'freedom' is the outcome of a regulatory endeavour that is increasingly articulated in terms of the neoliberal market, and which discursively constitutes the subject of rights. This endeavour establishes a discriminative hierarchy of who counts and who does not among the subjects so constituted. In the process, the central features of liberal freedom – as an aspiration and as an external pursuit by the autonomous subject with rational capacities – are revealed as being thoroughly embedded within relations of power: constrained, confined and managed from within the liberal fishbowl, and producing unfreedom.

CONTEMPORARY CRITIQUE OF LIBERAL FREEDOM IN HUMAN RIGHTS

Substantive critiques of the central features of liberal freedom on which human rights claim to be based already exist – specifically, that it is an external, linear, progressive pursuit by a universal, finite, thinking subject. While these critiques are diverse and diffuse, they can be diffracted into at least three main trajectories. First, human rights interventions have an expansive set of political effects that are invariably linked to a specific way of being, and of being free. This aspect is evident even in positions that claim to dissociate from freedom, and which are purportedly focused exclusively on alleviating human suffering and 'putting cruelty first', in Judith Shklar's term (discussed in the next section). Second, the work that human rights do in their encounters with culture and cultural difference reveals the contingency of their claims to universality, laid bare especially in the post-9/11 era. Third, the falsity of liberalism's foundational premise of freedom being integrally linked to a common 'universal', rational and thinking subject is exposed through the sharply hierarchical and differentiated understandings of the subject which permeate rights discourse and advocacy.

I briefly set out the critiques in relation to each of these aspects in the remainder of this chapter. I elaborate further on these trajectories in subsequent chapters, using the context of gender and alterity in human rights to reveal how the pursuit of freedom by disenfranchized and marginalized persons is structured explicitly, and fundamentally, by the parameters of the liberal fishbowl and its constitutive arrangement of dominant gender, sexual and cultural norms.

Rights Discourse and the Reduction of Suffering

In the contemporary moment, several key voices in liberal rights theory have focused primarily on the ethics and mechanics of freedom from human suffering caused by acts of cruelty. This position draws upon an influential strand of liberal thought – the 'liberalism of fear' (LoF) – developed initially in the work of American political theorist Judith Shklar. Claiming to be apolitical and agnostic to power, LoF emphasizes a rigorously defined concept of freedom – freedom from fear. LoF adopts an anti-foundational pragmatism, which proposes intervention in very specific instances only – namely, to alleviate acute human suffering and cruelty.[18] In its claim that it does not support the articulation of a political vision, either of happiness, the good life, or how to be and live in the world, LoF seeks to avoid some of the political implications or effects evident in the position that rights produce freedom. It vigorously adheres to its central position, which opposes state intervention, and in which the role of rights is primarily regarded as providing a bulwark for the private individual against the force of the 'public' state.[19] Although LoF promotes an avowedly apolitical stance, I probe the political project that informs it in the context of human rights. LoF is based upon an overly simplistic account of cruelty and fear that obscures how both are integral to the constitution of the subject of human rights and the modern state. I conclude that freedom in this limited guise obscures that human rights are not bulwarks of defence against state power, but are themselves deeply implicated in power, producing exclusions and justifying interventions against the perpetration of cruelty that are themselves cruel and violent.

In her foundational work, Shklar sets out the minimalist brief for LoF, stating that this strand of liberalism is fundamentally opposed to cruelty. The role of liberalism is to restrict itself to bringing about conditions that are essential for a citizen to be able to exercise freedom, including making decisions without fear or favour about most aspects of her life, as is compatible with the like freedom of every other adult subject.[20] Cruelty is understood as 'the willful inflicting of physical pain on a weaker being in order to cause anguish and fear',[21] and such 'fear destroys freedom'.[22] Shklar's work articulates a constrained and pragmatic understanding of freedom that concentrates primarily on 'putting cruelty first',[23] and on alleviating human suffering through the modality of rights to ensure 'bare survival'.[24] She is interested in enfranchising the disenfranchised, but only to the extent of enabling them to make existential choices that they were unable to make earlier, and helping them to intervene on their own behalf. Shklar depends on law as a central instrument to be applied in order to prevent cruelty, relying on law's claim to neutrality, even though she recognizes the political nature of law in terms of its links with liberalism.[25] In a similar vein, as American philosopher Richard Rorty states, cruelty is the 'worst thing we do';[26] beyond liberalism's imposition of the rights paradigm to counter cruelty, it has no business to either define happiness or to actively instruct citizens in how happiness, and hence even freedom, might be pursued. Michael Ignatieff, another important voice, makes the same minimalist claim, and specifically connects the project of liberalism with the justification for international human rights. He explicitly states: 'Human rights are an account of what is right, not an account of what is good. People may enjoy full human rights protection and still believe that they lack essential features of a good life.'[27]

The above scholars focus mainly on highlighting the idea that liberalism has the capacity to generate suitable conditions for the subject of rights to freely exercise 'choice' over the kind of life that she wants to have. In the context of human rights, this objective implies a logical connection between an increase in human rights protection and the expansion of such a subject's freedom to choose, even in this minimalist brief. The freedom in question is construed 'negatively' – in terms of 'negative liberty'.[28] This is an essentially negative politics of prioritizing action against manifestations of cruelty, with an interventionist emphasis on protecting the individual from physical injury, including torture, social and psychological degradation, dispossession, exile and the defeat of everyday expectation and hope.[29] The position of these influential voices is based on a pragmatic anti-foundationalism that refuses to claim a transcendental universal status for some essence of the human subject, such as human dignity or rationality, based on an older natural law tradition and a Kantian secular transcendentalism. This scholarship asserts that what we all share is not an *a priori* dignity or other aspect of our subjectivity, but an empirical vulnerability. This commonality is what connects us and establishes 'empathy' – that is, openness to the suffering of others – as the foundational ethic of human rights, thus distinguishing LoF from classical liberalism's universalist claims.

While formulating a particular script for 'bare survival', human rights are construed in essentially instrumentalist terms – as bulwarks or shields for vulnerable and powerless subjects – and schematize (political or social) power in negative and repressive terms: as that which denies, erodes, and erases the agency of subjects. The construction of both power and rights in negative terms, and as a zero-sum game in which more rights to individuals means less power to the 'repressive' institutions, is logically predicated upon considering *more* rights as necessarily entailing *more* freedom for the rights recipients. In this paradigm, rights are understood and deployed as a form of individual empowerment, providing the human subject with agency and the tools to fight injustice, and also enabling individuals to determine for themselves how they want to live and to use these rights in the way they see fit. As Ignatieff asserts, human rights are a 'systematic agenda of "negative liberty"'.[30] In this scholarship, the universalism of human rights ensures that the rights template remains open to plurality: to 'good lives' rather than a singular vision of the 'good life' to which everyone should aspire and seek to actualize. Provided that a subject has some freedom in the choice of how to live, the substance and content of her life should be left for her to determine in a way that accords with her desires, history and traditions.[31] Thus, the claim here is that such a position ostensibly accommodates a wide variety of civilizations, cultures and religions, including the non-liberal and illiberal.

There are varied perspectives on how the principle of putting cruelty first and the related reduction of suffering through rights modalities are to be actualized. For Rorty, this means expanding a set of welfare-oriented social rights, which includes getting enough to eat, finding shelter, having access to medicines for one's children – all of which enable the disenfranchised to avoid a kind of suffering that consists in the humiliation of humans at the hands of other humans; such interventions preserve human dignity.[32] In this respect, the reduction of suffering is equated with an increase in happiness, and the solutions are found within the fishbowl from knowledge infused with the liberal assumption that liberalism embodies a progressive, evolutionary trajectory, and that its inscribed values represent the zenith of civilized thought. Rorty does not support the engagement of any form of radicalism in uncovering the hidden, systematic causes of injustice and exploitation, or in bringing about social and economic transformation. His attention remains primarily on developing the ability to become sensitive to the suffering of others, and identifying with them rather than seeking radical change.

In contrast, Ignatieff opposes social rights, or what he describes as collective rights, which he views as leading to 'rights inflation' – 'the tendency to define anything desirable as a right' – and which 'ends up eroding the legitimacy of a defensible core of rights', namely, the entitlements that fall into the category of civil and political rights.[33] Wendy Brown, in her critique of Ignatieff, has argued that the institution being generated and exponentially strengthened by these 'defensible' rights is the free market.[34] In this sense, faith is invested in the possibility of greater happiness being achieved through greater rights, the latter of which entails free participation as an economic entity in thriving markets, which will purportedly assist in actualizing one's vision of the 'good life'. Freedom is thus directly linked to happiness or the good life – a modality that envisages a central role for the market,[35] and the continuous production of the consumer-subject. As long as an expansive plethora of rights ensuring 'civil and political freedoms' is in place, happiness can definitely be achieved by these free agents themselves (only) by recourse to the market, posited as the ideal node for exercising personal choice. Thus, for Ignatieff, rights interventions preclude achievement of the 'good life' through formations other than the market, in which these autonomous entitled subjects of rights are free to obtain any 'good' they happen to desire. The discussion makes evident that even while advancing a position which seemingly 'puts cruelty first', this position ultimately endorses a normative script for freedom that includes a happy and 'good' life made possible through self-assertion, and one that can *only* be negotiated and overcome by invoking the discourse of human rights.[36] This rationale implies that any other mode of self-empowerment and agency adopted by the subject will necessarily be at odds with the prescriptions of human rights, and therefore may be justifiably targeted as illiberal and repressive, or alienating, or irrelevant.

Theorists who use LoF or similar arguments in human rights vary greatly, as exemplified by the different positions adopted by Ignatieff and Rorty. The branch of scholars who advocate *for* humanitarian intervention agree that human rights should primarily be about reducing human suffering and fear. While the link between these scholars and LoF is not necessarily explicitly made, similar reasons and justifications are often used in both positions, especially when discussing the nature and meaning of human rights dispensation and the manner in which it is theorized. Peters, for example, argues this point, stating that sovereignty should be based on 'humanity'; that is, if the state crosses a threshold in failing to protect its citizens against extremely grave human rights abuses such as physical suffering and cruelty, either at the hands of the state or another actor, then other states have a duty to intervene to protect the afflicted citizens of that state.[37] This argument suggests that human suffering precedes all other modalities, including sovereignty, the state and possibly democracy. The LoF, in this sense, comes to mean that global society should primarily aim to protect individuals from cruelty and fear.[38]

Another strand of human rights theorists who work within the trend of LoF are those who promote human dignity as the value that should be given precedence before anything else. In the International Covenants on both Civil and Political Rights (ICCR) and Economic, Social and Cultural Rights (ICESCR), human dignity is proclaimed in the preamble: 'these rights derive from the inherent dignity of the human person.'[39] Human dignity is similarly affirmed in the Universal Declaration of Human Rights (UDHR).[40] Hasson states that human dignity is the '"ultimate value" that gives coherence to human rights'.[41] Yet exactly what dignity means remains unclear and disputed, with Donnelly concluding that in fact it is best not to define human dignity, but rather to leave it open so as not to sell it short.[42]

Baxi is one such scholar who is deeply concerned about preventing cruelty and suffering, in particular 'the barbarism of power', and uses notions of humanness and human dignity to justify human rights interventions. He states that '[h]uman rights languages are all that we have to interrogate the barbarism of power, even when these remain inadequate to humanize fully the barbaric practices of politics'.[43] However, Baxi is also very critical of human rights, noting that they are elitist and work to exclude as much as to include. He further notes that human rights have an 'ambivalent relationship' to suffering,[44] highlighting how they can sometimes work to create hierarchies of human suffering and arguing, for example, that 'the paradigm of the Universal Declaration of Human Rights is being steadily supplanted by a trade-related, market-friendly, human rights paradigm'.[45]

At the same time, Baxi does not give up on human rights, but instead suggests that they need to be re-appropriated. He argues that 'the historic mission of "contemporary" human rights is *to give voice to human suffering*, to make it visible, and to ameliorate it'.[46] He notes that the notion of human rights being used in 'the pursuit of happiness' is an elitist notion, stating that '[f]or the hundreds of millions of the "wretched of the earth", human rights enunciations matter, if at all, as and when they provide, even if contingently, shields against torture and tyranny, deprivation and destitution, pauperization and powerlessness, de-sexualization and degradation'.[47] Baxi also notes the importance of non-state actors (such as global corporations) and their role in causing human suffering, and in turn not only argues for human rights that prevent human suffering at the hands of the state but also uses the human suffering paradigm to call for a broader use of and intervention through human rights law, with a re-appropriation of the term to suit people's needs according to context.

A key limitation of the argument that projects human rights primarily as a method of reducing suffering and cruelty is that such logic is based on an outmoded notion of power as a monolithic apparatus to be wrested away from the state or institution by the disenfranchised individual.[48] This articulation of the 'repressive hypothesis' refuses to take into account the discursive operations of human rights so effectively theorized by Foucault – the fact that human rights are always profoundly implicated in power and operate as technologies of governance that produce and inscribe the very subject to be governed as well as the choices made available to her.[49] Rather than merely defending or protecting her, these controlling forces limit the choices the rights holder has and stipulate how that choice may be exercised and what kind of freedom is to be realized. Rights are not bulwarks of defence against state power, but are a crucial aspect of power's aperture and governmentality – in other words, rights can *themselves* be tactics and vehicles of governance and domination, as well as resistance.[50] Golder provides a reading of Foucault's work on human rights which illustrates how they are simultaneously political tools used by political subjects to capture and subvert power as well as regulatory technologies that constitute these very subjects and manipulate their conduct.[51] Thus, human rights are thoroughly implicated in power, with their directed understandings of freedom and happiness, primarily towards the market. In the following two sections, I elaborate on how human rights are further implicated in power with their claims to universality and the construction of the subject, as well as their idea of what constitutes fear.

Rights Discourse and the Politics of Universality

In relation to the logic of 'Othering', there is a need to further interrogate the understanding of freedom that informs human rights by examining how they construct 'traditional' cultures (read as 'not the West') as 'cultural collectives', which are assumed to inherently constrain the capacity to choose or the agency of their members. This interpretation is principally energized by the idea of the universality of human rights, coupled with the concept of liberal individualism, wherein every individual is recognized as having the capacity to realize rational intentions and the right to a good life, however conceived, without restrictions or obstructions.[52] Universality is tethered to this form of individualism, which is assumed to be effective in fighting tyranny and has been regarded as attractive to oppressed people suffering exploitation and abuse across a broad range of cultures. The ascription to human rights of a universal essence, as enabling and all-inclusive, becomes a coveted object possessing the capacity to release this constituency into a space of lasting freedom.

At least two problems can be identified in relation to this argument. First, the practices of 'traditional' collectives are ultimately judged against the universal values of human rights which are always calibrated in consonance with the liberal paradigm, thus reiterating, without question, that human rights are the *only* 'universal' language which can effectively challenge tyrannies and hegemonies, and secure freedom for the disenfranchised. Although the purported 'universality' of the international human rights discourse is grounded upon an openness towards cultural difference, this very 'universality' functions to deny or preclude other possible visions of freedom and the 'good life'. The liberal claim is that human rights are the primary and central – if not the only – universally available moral language that upholds and validates the rights claims of vulnerable subjects/non-subjects requiring protection from the oppression which they continuously experience in illiberal, patriarchal and 'primitive' cultures and societies. The rights discourse is presented as effectively enabling such dependent groups to see themselves as moral agents. Through rights, they can empower themselves to resist or challenge cultural practices such as the veil, or female genital mutilation, or arranged marriages. When these constituencies resort to human rights protection, it legitimizes their protest against cultural oppression.[53] This argument reflects the classic ruse of liberalism: purposively engaging in politics while donning anti-political garb, that is, positing itself as being prior to or transcending politics, and thus universal.

This duplicitous logic occludes the fact that specific, targeted decisions underpin the liberal conceptions of freedom which inform human rights when they are deployed as a technology of emancipation in the domain of 'cultural collectives'. Instead of being critically problematized and examined as a political construction, human rights thus deployed are assumed to be universal, essentially and naturally benevolent, with the good intentions of their advocates viewed as unassailable. Even when the rhetoric claims to be hospitable to plurality, this projected expansiveness is ultimately an exclusionary gesture as it operates to install only *one* possible and desirable script of freedom, namely, happiness or the good life – lives made manifest through full enfranchisement, and ensured by the international human rights that are a given and are enjoyed in liberal societies. Therefore, if struggles are waged to change oppressive traditions and the social order in 'cultural collectives', and thus to deliver conditions for a different, 'good' life, then this line of argument dictates that this can only be done by invoking the hegemonic discourse of human rights. The claim to the universality of human rights functions to deny or preclude all other possible visions of freedom outside of the liberal fishbowl.

Second, the reactive core of the political project that informs human rights has become acutely evident in the post-9/11 period, where the conceptual emphasis on universality and plurality is displaced by a very clear assertion of the distinction between 'us' and 'them'. Certain unruly and transgressive actors are located outside the order of liberal societies, and the threat they pose to the fishbowl generates acute fear followed by a xenophobic political call for a return to true liberal values.[54] The us/them dialectic is reflective of the constant perceived threat to the fishbowl posed from outside which has legitimated, and continues to legitimate, 'illiberal' responses from within – thus exposing the hollowness of the concept of universality. This critical redrawing of the 'self'/'other' boundary as an intellectual parallel to unfolding political–militaristic events on the ground is also a reinscription of the closed circuit of the fishbowl. As noted earlier, this 'dark side' of liberal freedom draws upon its colonial legacy and a complex inheritance characterized by the violent domination of 'Others'. This dark side is evident both historically, in the context of slavery and the colonial encounter, and in its contemporary imposition of a form of muscular liberalism – deploying strategies of liberal governance infused with attributes reminiscent of 'responsible' empire, in a context where the very survival of liberalism is purported to be under threat from barbaric, illiberal 'Others'.[55] Proposals such as Walzer's quest to establish mandates or trusteeships to govern societies when self-determination fails, or when famine or civil war destroys a polity, are illustrative of this move.[56]

A similar, more explicit proposal is evident in Ignatieff's open embrace of small doses of 'empire' post-9/11, wherein he argues that the suspension of rights through mechanisms of liberal governance may be the best hope for democracy and stability in certain anarchic parts of the world. He claims that a new imperialism in the form of military occupation and the torture of intractable, adversarial 'Others' may be prescribed in order to save liberalism and its global project of human rights from the chaotic violence of feudal, illiberal societies that exponentially breed evildoers such as terrorists who do not cherish or respect human rights, and hence are not entitled to their protections.[57] This form of 'Empire lite' – consisting of democracy, human rights and the free market – is to be 'enforced by the most awesome military power the world has ever known'.[58] Such violence is justified not only to save the world from illiberalism, but also because these counter-measures are in the hands of the United States, which stands as liberalism's vanguard and whose good intentions are apparently beyond reproach. And for liberal ideologues, such aggression is justified as an act of compassion and benevolence, necessary to bring good governance to those oppressed 'Others' who are the helpless victims of the illiberalism that is the socio-political fulcrum of 'cultural collectives'.[59]

Inevitably, 'Empire lite' is a hegemonic modality, but it is one that claims to operate 'without consciousness of itself as such', and which is 'constantly shocked that its good intentions arouse resentment abroad'.[60] It depicts the choice between liberalism and empire as a tragic one for a liberal society, but one that is necessary in the context of rapidly escalating barbarism and a world of non-believers (in the liberal project). The agony and despair experienced by the liberal establishment in making this tragic choice serves as an affective reminder of the fundamental character of the liberal state – as liberal, and also conscious of the emotional cost of fidelity to liberal ideals in this chaotic world.[61] The image of the United States as a reluctant imperialist thrust by conscience onto the global stage to do good in the world may be more visible in the current moment, but it is of course not something new. This deceptive formulation does not attend to the ways in which illiberalism and normative and literal violence are characteristic of the liberal project's response to the expanding scenarios of manifest barbarity being witnessed. 'Lite' interventions resonate with the historical assertion of empire, warranted as part of a 'civilizing mission'[62] or, in the contemporary moment, to bring about gender liberation or happiness or to alleviate suffering and ensure bare survival. These interventions have amounted to nothing less than a call for the recolonization of 'failed states' and have strengthened what Mamdani describes as 'human rights fundamentalism'.[63] This renewed call in the post-9/11 period reinscribes the boundaries of the fishbowl and recalibrates the limits of liberal freedom against an 'Other' perceived as ever threatening and ever intent on subverting or rupturing the securities of the fishbowl, thus resulting in the incarceration of its inhabitants within their own fears. This call not only justifies the logic underlying the new imperialism, but also perversely justifies the liberal resort to the stunted, suffocating rationale of illiberalism as the appropriate chosen response – specifically, an unequivocal counter-hostility directed at the unintelligible violent 'Other'. And this choice falls *within* liberal ideology and constitutes part of its shared, complex inheritance with human rights. A constant measuring of the liberal self against constituencies of regressive 'Others', who were once outside the fishbowl but are now avidly infiltrating it via political opportunities, generates and nourishes a crippling sense of embattlement that views all 'Others' as a threat to the very survival of liberalism – the preferable and superior philosophy or way of life. Post-9/11, assertions of universality have become a thin veneer over a response that has catalyzed increased surveillance, military interventions and a strengthened security apparatus, building on a colonial legacy which assumes that there is nothing to be gained from non-violent forms of engagement with the 'Other', who must be corralled, policed, expelled or eliminated if liberalism's adherents, allies and structures are to be protected from the constant threat of imminent violent destruction.

As several postcolonial scholars have argued, this choice is a false one, as liberalism is *itself* constituted through and expressive of imperialistic motives.[64] The forceful rhetoric of protectionism and 'Othering' deflects attention from the symbiotic relationship between historical imperialism and its contemporary embodiment, both of which are equal exertions of liberal hegemony. It also cloaks the way that liberalism – which has always seen itself as having to actively save the world from illiberalism – may be fully complicit in creating the contemporary conditions that now require it to save the world.[65] In the process, the critical genealogies of the relationship between liberalism and empire, its colonial legacies and violent conquests, become more visible and the ploy of universality is fully unmasked. Adding this ongoing account of liberal empire to the historical narrative of human rights is an effort to produce a more disruptive testimonial of liberal hegemonies that inform the project. These unsettling truths diminish the claims to universality and account for the increasingly aggressive 'us and them' dialectic that has structured liberal freedom in human rights and that continues to do so.

Rights Discourse and Avatars of the Subject

This discussion enables the emergence of at least three distinct avatars of the subject within human rights discourse. One is that of the utterly vulnerable, suffering and powerless subject, identifiable and identified on account of abject dispossession, yet who has the power to move the entire project of human rights due to the scale of this very dispossession. A second is the successful, empowered subject, who is autonomous and has sufficiently developed sentiments to respond to the suffering of the vulnerable, abject subject. And the third is the belligerent or dangerous subject, who threatens liberal freedom either by a refusal to assimilate with dominant gender, sexual and cultural norms or/and by turning away to pursue an alternative conception of freedom.

The suffering or abject subject is evident in Shklar's discussion, where she grounds the liberal project in the methodology of determining what counts as 'cruelty' and the response of the abject powerless subject to modes of oppression as well as to modes of intervention. She argues that the test for determining which cruelties can be endured and what would constitute efficient LoF interventions is to ask those who are the likeliest victims: 'Until that is done there is no reason not to assume that the liberalism of fear has much to offer to the victims of political tyranny.'[66] Rorty is less ambivalent, declaring that at times 'these people' will be misguided and short-sighted and want the wrong things. This may be the result of 'superstition' or 'false consciousness', but it might nevertheless require liberal intervention or actions that strip such people of their dignity even while it reduces their suffering. Rorty justifies his position via the rationale of unqualified paternalism: 'We may decide to use their present selves as means to the novel ends that their future selves, or their descendants, will be better off for having adopted.'[67] This argument prefigures the justification for 'Empire lite', discussed earlier and advanced by Ignatieff, as well as a host of interventions that often discount the views of the subject who is being rescued or aided on the grounds that they do not know what is good for them. For Rorty, such non- or negligible subjects are to be made to progress towards a desirable completeness through liberal removal of the conditions that cause them unnecessary suffering. This removal shifts the sufferers into the position of empowered 'subjects' who – having been sufficiently endowed with adequately developed 'sentiments' – can now themselves respond to the 'suffering of others'. The removal of conditions that cause the unnecessary suffering of powerless victims is a process that invariably casts the suffering 'Others' as thoroughly alien to the liberal norm, and not in any way structurally connected to the operations of the liberal project.

Ignatieff, who sharply distinguishes the powerful agent from the powerless subject, presents a very similar understanding. He asserts that human actions can be judged by a simple test of whether, as he puts it, 'we would wish to be on the receiving end' of those actions.[68] He states '[t]hat we are capable of this thought experiment – that is, that we possess the faculty of imagining pain and degradation done to other human beings as if it were our own – [which] is simply a fact about us as a species'.[69] Further, he continues by noting that since we have the capacity to empathize, and we possess a conscience, 'we wish to be free to make up our own minds' about whether to intervene.[70] That some humans are indifferent to the pain of others does not mean that they do not have a conscience – it means that this conscience is free to not/to preferentially/to partially empathize with suffering. Thus, by this logic, opting to be indifferent to the pain of others does not necessarily signify cruelty or solipsism; it may instead signify liberal freedom of choice.

The abject or vulnerable subject has been analysed within feminist legal scholarship in relation to the broader critiques of the universal autonomous liberal subject.[71] Martha Fineman, for example, has advanced the notion of the 'vulnerable subject' in arguing in favour of the need for human rights specifically, and politics more generally, to prevent human suffering and to pay more attention to 'bodily fragility, material needs, and the possibility of messy dependence'.[72] Fineman understands the term 'vulnerability' as a heuristic device that represents a common universal experience, which is a part of the human condition and beyond human control. It cannot be hidden, is enduring and is ever present at the institutional and individual levels.[73] She broadens the conception of suffering through her focus on vulnerability and the vulnerable subject, and asks liberals to rethink human suffering through this expanded lens and to actively engage with institutions to respond to this vulnerability. While her discussion is largely directed at the United States, her position draws upon a human rights edifice which addresses these vulnerabilities through institutional and structural commitments to providing basic social goods to human beings. In seeking to dislodge the primacy of the sovereign, self-determining, entitled rational liberal subject by foregrounding the vulnerable subject/non-subject, she notes that, unlike liberal autonomy, the concept of vulnerability has the potential to describe 'a universal, inevitable, enduring aspect of the human condition'.[74]

Fineman's work is situated within a larger, now highly familiar, feminist critique of the liberal legal subject and how it is structured by gendered and sexual assumptions and norms.[75] This critique has in turn led to alternative articulations of the gendered subject in law that move beyond this limited construction. While the foregrounding of a vulnerable subject exposes the universal subject as fractured and not whole, a focus on vulnerability risks slipping into a politics of victimization, which negates the victim's subjectivity and views her as an object of rescue. More significantly, and as I illustrate in various chapters in this book, such interventions do not necessarily alter the ways in which dominant gender and sexual norms structure the formation of the subject. Thus efforts to re-engage with rights may result in the reinscription of the subject's subordination and exclusion. As Brown states, 'the first imaginings of freedom are always constrained by and potentially even require the very structure of oppression that freedom emerges to oppose'.[76] Rights may be alluring, and the risk of re-subordination worthwhile, if pitted against an option of no rights and, hence, no recognizable subjectivity. But, in continuing to centralize the role of the state in protecting the vulnerable subject, such interventions continue to run the inevitable risk of subordination and exclusion, and remain confined within a liberal fishbowl. The point here is that the vulnerable or abject subject continues to be articulated in terms of her subordination and against an already empowered autonomous subject.

This discussion brings me to a second related avatar of the subject, that is, the successful subject. This avatar takes the form of a dyadic relationship between the two distinct subjectivities engendered through human rights: the fully developed, able, empowered, autonomous agent; and the vulnerable or abject victim just discussed, who is also conceived of as a failed subject. The question that arises is whether there are particular scripts formulating how such failed selves – that is, inherently or circumstantially incapable subjects – can be shaped through rights accumulation into successful entities capable of properly exercising choice as legible, empowered, entitled and autonomous self-determining agents. In the well-established liberal tradition, especially that of the English Utilitarians, it is only through undergoing proper education that these failed subjects can become 'successful'. This is the tradition whose mandates involved excluding colonized subjects from the realms of consensual representative government unless they achieved civilizational maturity by internationalizing the colonial model, developing the capacity to reason outside existent native intellectual and cultural systems and assimilating without dissent into the practices of liberalism. However, for scholars such as Rorty, it is not rationality that is sought to be developed, but rather 'sentiments' or, as he puts it, 'sentimental education'.[77] In other words, human rights education, through which we develop the capacity to respond to the suffering of others, enables us to become fully successful rights-bearing subjects. Human rights, which operate through empathy to establish an emotional relationship between empowered and disempowered subjects, is thus utilized as a transformative methodology – one that not only transforms failure into success, but simultaneously transforms the illiberal into liberal, the regressive into progressive.

Paradoxically, the abject, failed subject of human rights is fated to 'be' always in the process of 'becoming' – that is, to experience a constant deferral of the self-actualization that, in the liberal view, can only be enabled through conditioning and formal education in the normative scripts of the 'good life', procured and secured by human rights. Such training in liberal aspiration and action is efficiently provided by international human rights implementers, defenders and experts – who are themselves always already the successful, legible, realized, free subjects/actors as visualized within the fishbowl. Thus, the failed non-subjects are assisted in their evolution not by their own states or societies or knowledge systems, but by international human rights agencies and defenders; that is, the successful subjects. A central contradiction, then, in the liberal construction of both the successful and the failed/abject subject of human rights is that the term 'subject' cannot be simultaneously applied to an already empowered agent whose choice must be respected in all circumstances, and to a powerless entity who can validly claim human rights protection. The dialectical relationship between the sovereign subject who has agency and the disenfranchised subject who does not has to be rigorously and continuously upheld if human rights are to retain their place as an effective mode of governance. This is achieved through the education, transformation and ideological compliance of the failed, abject, vulnerable, illegible and/or illiberal 'Others' who, prior to this education, are always frustratingly located beyond the ideological purview of fishbowl hegemonies. This differential underscores the fact that while human rights unceasingly disseminate a particular script of 'happiness' and the 'good life' – in other words, the liberal norm – as an ideal for both successful rights-bearing and failed subjects, it simultaneously operates to ensure that the latter will never be able to attain that norm, or be in the precarious position of imminent lapse from it. This precarity is illustrated by the withdrawal or conditioning of the rights of Muslim citizens in liberal democracies, either through screening or through the removal of a woman's veil, as in the United States and France respectively, or by the decriminalization of homosexuality only for it to be subsequently recriminalized, as in India. Thus, the unequal subject–abject power relationship inherently encodes failure, and the failed are forever consigned to the 'waiting-room of history'[78] or, rather, the 'waiting-room of liberal happiness'.

The third avatar of the subject arises from the liberal fear of the 'Other', presumed as belligerent, threatening and dangerous. Elaborating on my discussion in the previous section, in the age of the global 'war on terror' and in the context of human rights violations in an increasingly phobic and violent world, this fear is of the very real possibility of ideological contagion and physical infiltration by radicalized cadres of illiberal 'Others' whose threatening actions invoke a possible subversion and collapse of the liberal order. Liberal responses to this escalation lay bare the true orientation of human rights as a political project – which is not just about addressing and alleviating the pain of those who have suffered cruelty. Rather, the rights framework is fully co-opted into the annihilatory mechanisms of militarism, forming part of the justification for inflicting cruelty to ensure the survival of liberalism. The rights paradigm is now firmly part of the neo-imperialistic rationale that justifies the unconscionable inflicting of cruelty and violence on untold numbers of innocent civilians/'non-combatants', who are potentially threatening, to ensure the permanent local embedding of the liberal agenda.[79] The liberal fear that underpins this appropriation of the rights discourse involves much more than crippling anxiety, panic and paranoia – it is a totalizing, visceral horror of an 'Other' envisioned as dangerous, monstrous, perverse and incomprehensible, and the expurgation of this barbaric 'Other' through various political and military means is essential if liberalism is to retain its political supremacy.[80] In the process, the state is given extensive powers to prevent liberalism's imminent destruction – powers that find their manifestation in military intervention and torture, while also in the process diminishing the political freedoms of those on behalf of whom such interventions are made.

It is in precisely such situations of extremity, crisis and trauma that the sinister side of human rights comes into full display as an embedded component in a liberal schema of assault against a threatening/potentially threatening 'Other', in just the same way that human rights operate as a technology of governance. And it is truly ironic that illiberal measures such as cruelty – the perennial primary focus of rights advocacy – in the guise of delivering emancipation, and channelled into a narrative of liberal righteousness, are what centrally inform policy and tactics in this violent targeting of the 'Other'. The very cruelty from which the abject or suffering subject is to be rescued through rights is mirrored in the violence applied by militarized liberalism to counter those cruelties and prevent the world from further disintegrating into primitivism, bigotry and chaos. Shklar's original claim that 'fear destroys freedom' comes home to roost in the gut of liberalism itself, since it now has to continually offer a convincing rationale for the continued use of illiberal methods to ensure its own survival and the survival of human rights. To this end, liberal rhetoric constantly and forcefully alludes to a self-righteous reiteration of 'who we are'; namely, a superior, evolved, Western or westernized human.[81] Similarly, liberal advocacy arrives at the point where experiencing empathy for the 'Other', and witnessing the massive pain of the abject, vulnerable, failed, terrorized and violated non-subject, no longer forms the motivational substrate of human rights interventions; instead, human rights are unmasked as centrally concerned with, and firmly committed to, the retrenchment of liberalism and the entitled, successful and currently fearful subject, through 'Empire lite' and the targeting of the threatening 'Other'; thus the implicit political project of liberalism becomes aggressively explicit.

There are ample human rights mechanisms for soliciting the views of those on whose behalf human rights interventions are made. These include the special procedures in the form of special rapporteurs and treaty bodies that enable, in some instances, individual complaints to be made and testimonies to be documented. However, despite these consultative processes and mechanisms, the hierarchized framing of humans that underpins rights protocols remains largely in place. In the liberal rights schema, these 'Others' are masses of unintelligible, faceless beings who have no particularity, subjectivity or agency; they are either humanized/deemed as worthy of being saved through the bestowal and reinforcement of rights, or they are dehumanized/deemed as unworthy and excluded from protection. If classified as the latter, they are either neglected, manipulated through 'lite' strategies or, if considered a threat to liberal interests, annihilated. As a key instrument deployed to implement 'Empire lite' agendas, rights are thus procured and secured either for the greater good of saving liberalism itself from insidious or violent predation by illiberal, adversarial, radicalized 'Others', or for saving primarily those constituencies who demonstrate a willingness to embrace liberalism as the only desirable tool of emancipation. The hierarchy of the human subject within human rights is developed through the next three chapters of this book in relation to the precarious sexual subject, the gendered subject and the female 'Other'. Each chapter further illustrates how she is assembled and assigned, rendered perpetually unstable and insecure, and never fully free within the fishbowl.

LIBERAL FREEDOM AS UNFREEDOM

My discussion thus far has deconstructed two significant dimensions of the rights schema co-opted for the idealization and implementation of liberal 'freedom'. First, human rights do not lead to lasting freedom, but are mechanisms tied to a specific and normative script of freedom that is in turn tied to a very specific, and narrow, understanding of happiness and the 'good life'. In fact, the methodology for procuring and securing freedom through rights emerges as thoroughly complicit in an aggressive global political project where even the minimum intervention is productive of specific subjects and political outcomes. Moreover, it is strongly aligned with liberal individualism and human freedom which, in the current moment, are specifically defined in market terms. Human rights not only create, execute and refine a particular script of intervention – whether it is for 'bare survival' or eliminating the threat to liberalism posed by the 'Other' – but also impose a particular script of freedom to which the failed subject must aspire to become successful. While different chapters in this book explore, in depth, the core postulates of liberal freedom or the lack of it in the lives of both 'free' and 'unfree' subjects, here I make the generalized assertion that the various strands of liberal freedom are significantly more agenda-driven, in implicit and explicit terms, than they claim to be.

Second, my critical account also makes evident the manner in which human rights actively sequester liberalism from its role in the production and proliferation of the very horrors that human rights actively seek to confront and resolve today. The complex and violent inheritances of liberalism inform the contemporary moment, and within this broader framing human rights emerge not as a righteous, benevolent or minimalist enterprise, but as a governance project and a disciplinary mechanism for generating appropriate, homogenous political subjects and assimilating them into a script of ideological compliance and irreversible social transformation, or eliminating those who refuse to comply or turn away from such a mandate. Human rights advance a specific script of freedom even while they simultaneously suspect, denigrate and/or demolish any other vision of freedom. Alternatives are inevitably cast as skewed, grotesque, unworthy and invariably illiberal, deserving to be extinguished so as to stop the slide into political violence and chaos that threatens the supremacy of liberal thought and liberal governance – and this claim to supremacy becomes the central preoccupation of the human rights project. Thus, within the fishbowl, the choice is cast as being between what are perceived as two incommensurable objectives; of these, the idea of liberalism being resisted, refuted or supplanted in any way by any other modalities is simply intolerable. This proven inability to be 'open to', to 'engage with' and to 'learn from' the 'Other', whomever or whatever that 'Other' might be, has resulted in a renewed and just as ferocious project of empire that is somehow continually free to pursue ideological and material conquests, even as it ensures its futurity through the constant gestation of those 'Others' continuously assimilated into the liberal womb.

NOTES

1. Judith Shklar, *Ordinary Vices* (Cambridge, MA: Harvard University Press, 1984), p. 2.
2. Kahlil Gibran, 'On Freedom', in Kahlil Gibran, *The Prophet*, ed. Suheil Bushrui (London: Oneworld Publications, 2012), p. 47.
3. See, for example, Ronen Shnayderman, 'On "Being Forced to Be Free" between Republican and Liberal Freedom', *Ethical Perspectives: Journal of the European Ethics Network* 22, no. 2 (2015): 247–70; Lars Svendsen, *A Philosophy of Freedom* (London: Reaktion Books, 2014); Katrin Flikschuh, *Freedom: Contemporary Liberal Perspectives* (Cambridge: Polity, 2007).
4. For some examples, see Robert Nozick, *Anarchy, State, and Utopia* (New York: Basic Books, 1974); Martha Nussbaum, *Creating Capabilities: The Human Development Approach* (Cambridge, MA: Harvard University Press, 2011); Philip Pettit, *A Theory of Freedom: From the Psychology to the Politics of Agency* (New York: Oxford University Press, 2001); Amartya Sen, *Commodities and Capabilities* (Amsterdam: Elsevier Science Publishing Company, 1985); Jeremy Waldron, 'Theoretical Foundations of Liberalism', *The Philosophical Quarterly* 37, no. 147 (1987): 127–50.
5. For example, John Locke, who is considered one of the founders of modern-day liberalism and a defender of the negative concept of freedom, promoted the 'natural freedom of mankind': John Locke, *Two Treatises of Government*, prep. Rob Hay, vol. 5 (London: Thomas Tegg, 1823; McMaster University Archive of the History of Economic Thought, 2000), p. 15. For an important early critique of this position, see Uday Singh Mehta, *The Anxiety of Freedom: Imagination and Individuality in Locke's Political Thought* (Ithaca, NY: Cornell University Press, 1992), analysing the central tension in Locke's idea that human beings have a natural potential to live free lives as individuals, and the political and educational structures which mould the individual. His analysis puts into question the idea that individuality exists outside of these structures which compel external conformity and internal self-restraint.
6. The English Utilitarians made an explicit connection between freedom and happiness, and supported legislative interventions to ensure maximum happiness and minimum pain for the individual: see Jeremy Bentham, *An Introduction to the Principles of Morals and Legislation* (London: T. Payne, and Son, 1789); John Stuart Mill, *Utilitarianism* (London: Parker, Son and Bourn, 1863).
7. Bentham, *Principles of Morals and Legislation*, ch. I, para. I. In this schema, the operations of pleasure are linked with morality – thus, for Bentham, 'it is the greatest happiness of the greatest number that is the measure of right and wrong': Jeremy Bentham, *A Comment on the Commentaries and A Fragment on Government*, eds. J.H. Burns and H.L.A. Hart (London: Athlone Press, 1977), 393. His theory of utility was thus about pleasure and its maximization. He stated that it was inherent to human nature for the individual to think of his own self-interest before that of the 'social': Jeremy Bentham, *The Book of Fallacies: From Unfinished Papers of Jeremy Bentham* (London: J. and H.L. Hunt, 1824), pp. 392–4. Similarly, Mill, having been brought up a Benthamite, also believed in the principle of utility and its conception of freedom, stating that 'pleasure, and freedom

from pain, are the only things desirable as ends': John Stuart Mill, *Utilitarianism*, 2nd ed. (London: Longman, Green, 1864), p. 10. Mill's theorization emphasized that, in liberalism, '[t]he *à priori* assumption is in favour of freedom': John Stuart Mill, *Essays on Equality, Law, and Education*, vol. 21 of *Collected Works of John Stuart Mill*, ed. John M. Robson (Toronto: University of Toronto Press, 1984), p. 262.

8. John Rawls, *Lectures on the History of Moral Philosophy*, ed. Barbara Herman (Cambridge, MA: Harvard University Press, 2000), p. 366. An additional strand of this type of argument is also found in the liberals of the American revolutionary era, such as Thomas Jefferson, who introduced the term 'pursuit of happiness' in the same sentence as the right to 'life' and 'liberty' in the Declaration of Independence and the American Constitution: George M. Stephens, *Locke, Jefferson, and the Justices: Foundations and Failures of the US Government* (New York: Algora Publishing, 2002), pp. 5–6.
9. Sandra Fredman, *Human Rights Transformed: Positive Rights and Positive Duties* (Oxford: Oxford University Press, 2008); Amartya Sen, *Development as Freedom* (Oxford: Oxford University Press, 1999); Hugh Breakey, 'Positive Duties and Human Rights: Challenges, Opportunities and Conceptual Necessities', *Political Studies* 63, no. 5 (2015): 1198–1215.
10. See, for example, Tomuschat, who begins his history of human rights with John Locke: Christian Tomuschat, *Human Rights: Between Idealism and Realism* (Oxford: Oxford University Press, 2014), p. 17. Hunt, too, notes the influence on human rights theory of many liberal thinkers, such as Rousseau: Hunt, *Inventing Human Rights*, p. 25. Central human rights documents such as the American Declaration of Independence in 1776 and the French *Déclaration des Droits de l'Homme et du Citoyen* of 1789 both follow the tradition of liberalism with their focus on creating a new (democratic) state, free from the British/monarchy.
11. This ongoing conflict can even be seen in the de facto priority given to the ICCPR over the ICESCR, not only in terms of imagination and resource allocation, but also explicitly in the wording of the two, with civil and political rights (the 'negative freedom' rights) often being defined in absolute or more absolute terms. For example, 'Every human being has the inherent right to life. This right shall be protected by law. No one shall be arbitrarily deprived of his life' (International Covenant on Civil and Political Rights, 19 December 1966, 999 UNTS 171, Art. 6(1)), which contrasts with the coached language used in relation to economic, social and cultural rights (the 'positive freedom' rights), for example, 'Each State Party to the present Covenant undertakes to take steps, individually and through international assistance and co-operation, especially economic and technical, to the maximum of its available resources, with a view to achieving progressively the full realization of the rights recognized in the present Covenant by all appropriate means, including particularly the adoption of legislative measures' (International Covenant on Economic, Social and Cultural Rights, 16 December 1966, 993 UNTS 3, Art. 2(1)).
12. See Universal Declaration of Human Rights, 10 December 1948, GA Res. 217A (III); International Convention on the Elimination of All Forms of Racial Discrimination, 21 December 1965, 660 UNTS 195; International Covenant on Civil and Political Rights, 19 December 1966, 999 UNTS 171; Convention on the Elimination of All Forms of Discrimination Against Women, 18 December 1979, 1249 UNTS 13.
13. See, for example, Dianne Otto, 'Rethinking the "Universality" of Human Rights Law', *Columbia Human Rights Law Review* 29, no. 1 (1997): 1–46; Douzinas, *The End of Human Rights*; David Chandler, ed., *Rethinking Human Rights: Critical Approaches to International Politics* (Houndmills: Palgrave Macmillan, 2002). See also important critical Marxist arguments that refashion human rights as a social and economic project, and bring into analysis the very structure of the market that has come to bound notions of freedom and justice to economic explanations, including economic justice and economic inequalities: for example, Brad R. Roth, 'Marxian Insights for the Human Rights Project', in *International Law on the Left: Re-Examining Marxist Legacies*, ed. Susan Marks (Cambridge: Cambridge University Press, 2006), pp. 220–51; Susan Marks, 'Exploitation as an International Legal Concept', in *International Law on the Left: Re-Examining Marxist Legacies*, ed. Susan Marks (Cambridge: Cambridge University Press, 2008), pp. 281–307;

B.S. Chimni, *International Law and World Order: A Critique of Contemporary Approaches* (Cambridge: Cambridge University Press, 2017), pp. 534–43.

14. David Kennedy, 'The International Human Rights Movement: Part of the Problem?' *Harvard Human Rights Journal* 15 (Spring 2002): 103–4.
15. Ibid., p. 119. See, for example, the implications of the US invasion of Afghanistan after the 9/11 attacks: Oz Hassan and Andrew Hammond, 'The Rise and Fall of American's Freedom Agenda in Afghanistan: Counter-Terrorism, Nation-Building and Democracy', *International Journal of Human Rights* 15, no. 4 (2011): 432–51.
16. See, for example, Talal Asad, who argues that human rights have been used, among other things, by colonial empires against the native subject to advance their civilizing missions: Talal Asad, 'What Do Human Rights Do? An Anthropological Enquiry', *Theory & Event* 4, no. 4 (2000): muse.jhu.edu/article/32601.
17. Note, for example, that while Kant believed in the power of 'common human reason' (at p. 19), thus believing law should be 'derive[d] ... from the universal concept of a rational being in general' (at p. 28), there is extensive analysis and critique of Kant's racism – which included the endorsement of slavery and the defence of racial hierarchy – demonstrating how it was integral to his political thought, rather than aberrational or marginal: Immanuel Kant, *Groundwork for the Metaphysics of Morals*, trans. and ed. Allen W. Wood (New Haven, CT: Yale University Press, 2002). See further Robert Bernasconi, 'Who Invented the Concept of Race? Kant's Role in Enlightenment Construction of Race', in *Race*, ed. Robert Bernasconi (Malden, MA: Blackwell Publishers, 2001), pp. 11–36; Emmanuel Chukwudi Eze, 'The Color of Reason: The Idea of 'Race' in Kant's Anthropology', in *Postcolonial African Philosophy: A Critical Reader*, ed. Emmanuel Chukwudi Eze (Cambridge, MA: Blackwell Publishers, 1997), pp. 103–40. Also consider John Stuart Mill's defence of liberal imperialism and his justification for withholding rights from the native colonial subject, whom he claimed lacked the capacity to consent or for self-rule, as ostensibly evidenced by their primitive culture and lack of civilizational development: Mill, *Essays on Equality, Law, and Education*, pp. 118–19. See Uday Singh Mehta, *Liberalism and Empire: A Study in Nineteenth-Century British Liberal Thought* (Chicago: University of Chicago Press, 1999).
18. Michael Ignatieff, 'I. Human Rights as Politics; II. Human Rights as Idolatry' (lecture, Princeton University, 4–7 April 2000); Richard Rorty, 'Hope and the Future', *Peace Review* 14, no. 2 (2002): 149–55; Shklar, 'Liberalism of Fear', pp. 21–38; Michael Walzer, 'On Negative Politics', in *Liberalism without Illusions: Essays on Liberal Theory and the Political Vision of Judith N. Shklar*, ed. Bernard Yack (Chicago: University of Chicago Press, 1996), pp. 17–24; Bernard Williams, 'The Liberalism of Fear', in *In the Beginning was the Deed: Realism and Moralism in Political Argument*, ed. Geoffrey Hawthorn (Princeton, NJ: Princeton University Press, 2005), pp. 52–61.
19. LoF, like classical liberal thought, is opposed to state intervention, but maintains the centrality of a 'public–private dichotomy'. What is important is not where this crucial line is drawn, but that it *is* drawn and, once drawn, is not forgotten or ignored: Judith N. Shklar, 'The Liberalism of Fear', in *Liberalism and the Moral Life*, ed. Nancy L. Rosenblum (Cambridge, MA: Harvard University Press, 1989), p. 24. There has been much writing on LoF in recent years: see Bernard Yack, 'Political Liberalism: Political, not Philosophical', *Perspectives on Politics* 15, no. 1 (2017): 116; Elisabeth Anker, 'The Liberalism of Horror', *Social Research* 81, no. 4 (2014): 795; Thom Brooks, 'Bernard Williams, Republicanism, and the Liberalism of Fear: Problems and Prospects', in *The Moral Philosophy of Bernard Williams*, eds. Alexandra Perry and Chris Herrera (Newcastle upon Tyne: Cambridge Scholars Publishing, 2013), pp. 57–60; Andreas Hess, *The Political Theory of Judith N. Shklar* (Basingstoke: Palgrave Macmillan, 2014); Robert Talisse, 'On the Liberalism of Fear: A Reply to Brooks', in *The Moral Philosophy of Bernard Williams*, eds. Alexandra Perry and Chris Herrera (Newcastle upon Tyne: Cambridge Scholars Publishing, 2013), pp. 114–18; Michael Ignatieff, *Human Rights as Politics and Idolatry* (Princeton, NJ: Princeton University Press, 2011).
20. Shklar, 'Liberalism of Fear', p. 21.

21. Shklar, *Ordinary Vices*, p. 8.
22. Ibid., p. 2. Subsequent work on LoF both rejects and accepts certain aspects of Shklar's argument: see Corey Robin, *Fear: The History of a Political Idea* (Oxford: Oxford University Press, 2004); Williams, 'Liberalism of Fear'; and Brooks, 'Bernard Williams, Republicanism, and the Liberalism of Fear'.
23. Judith N. Shklar, 'Putting Cruelty First', *Daedalus* 111, no. 3 (1982): 17–27.
24. Judith N. Shklar, *The Faces of Injustice* (New Haven, CT: Yale University Press, 1990), p. 73.
25. Shklar understood law's political link to liberalism and that this link exposed the contradiction of law; it revealed law's lack of neutrality while at the same time recognizing that law's power relied upon its so-called neutrality: Judith N. Shklar, *Legalism* (Cambridge, MA: Harvard University Press, 1964).
26. Richard Rorty, *Contingency, Irony, and Solidarity* (Cambridge: Cambridge University Press, 1989), p.xv.
27. Ignatieff, 'Human Rights as Idolatry', p. 321.
28. Isaiah Berlin, 'Two Concepts of Liberty', in *Four Essays on Liberty* (Oxford: Oxford University Press, 1969), pp. 118–72.
29. Walzer, 'On Negative Politics', pp. 17, 20.
30. Ignatieff, *Human Rights as Politics and Idolatry*, p. 57.
31. Ibid., pp. 55–7. See Stevenson, *Human Rights and the Reinvention of Freedom*, pp. 17–18.
32. Rorty, *Contingency, Irony, and Solidarity*, p.xv, on the perspective taken by liberal ironists. See critique by Kapoor, who argues that all of these 'basic needs' advanced by development practitioners and gender and human rights advocates, and through international development programmes, are complicit in advancing neoliberal policies and contemporary forms of imperialism: Ilan Kapoor, *The Postcolonial Politics of Development* (London: Routledge, 2008). See also Stevenson, *Human Rights and the Reinvention of Freedom*, p. 16.
33. Ignatieff, *Human Rights as Politics and Idolatry*, p. 90. Gearty is more nuanced in his discussion of rights inflation. He argues that rights are more often than not viewed as markers of modernity in the contemporary period, and thus they are embraced and used without the meaning and theory behind rights necessarily being understood. For example, the fact that in many ways they restrict popular democracy, and thus can be seen and even used against some of the aims of groups who are calling for such rights, may not at all be appreciated: see Conor Gearty, *Can Human Rights Survive?* (Cambridge: Cambridge University Press, 2006).
34. Wendy Brown, '"The most we can hope for …": Human Rights and the Politics of Fatalism', *South Atlantic Quarterly* 103, nos. 2–3 (2004): 451–63. See Stevenson, *Human Rights and the Reinvention of Freedom*, p. 17. See also James D. Ingram, *Radical Cosmopolitics: The Ethics and Politics of Democratic Universalism* (New York: Columbia University Press, 2013), pp. 226–62.
35. Ignatieff, *Human Rights as Politics and Idolatry*, pp. 70–1.
36. For slightly different approaches to happiness and the good life, see, for example, Martha C. Nussbaum, 'Capabilities and Human Rights', *Fordham Law Review* 66, no. 2 (1997): 273–300. Nussbaum applies her 'capabilities' approach to development to the context of human rights, and suggests that human rights and the human rights discourse should focus on the question '[w]hat is A actually able to do and to be?' (at 285). Nussbaum's liberalism is an expansive and explicitly interventionist one, which rests on the belief that politics should have a larger role in human life and the promotion of 'their good life' than merely the prevention of human suffering. Nussbaum's position remains explicitly embedded in the fishbowl and promotes a liberal, universal idea of freedom as something to be obtained through a 'capabilities approach' version of equality, albeit more nuanced.
37. Anne Peters, 'Humanity as the A and Ω of Sovereignty', *European Journal of International Law* 20, no. 3 (2009): 513–44.
38. It is worth noting, however, that while Peters believes human rights should limit sovereignty in the name of cruelty, Moyn has critiqued the collapse of humanitarian

interventions to prevent all human suffering and human rights, stating that the two have become the same in many ways: Moyn, *The Last Utopia*, pp. 220–1. In his view, this result is why and how humanitarian intervention is often wrongly justified in the name of human rights: Samuel Moyn, 'Judith Shklar versus the International Criminal Court', *Humanity* 4, no. 3 (2013): 473–500.

39. International Covenant on Civil and Political Rights, 19 December 1966, 999 UNTS 171; International Covenant on Economic, Social and Cultural Rights, 16 December 1966, 993 UNTS 3.
40. Universal Declaration of Human Rights, 10 December 1948, GA Res. 217A (III).
41. Kevin J. Hasson, 'Religious Liberty and Human Dignity: A Tale of Two Declarations', *Harvard Journal of Law & Public Policy* 27, no. 1 (2003): 83.
42. Jack Donnelly, *Universal Human Rights in Theory and Practice*, 3rd ed. (Ithaca, NY: Cornell University Press, 2013), pp. 130–2.
43. Baxi, 'Voices of Suffering', pp. 126–7.
44. Ibid., p. 132.
45. Ibid., p. 163.
46. Ibid., p. 127.
47. Baxi, *The Future of Human Rights*, p. 7.
48. Michel Foucault, 'The Body of the Condemned', in Michel Foucault, *Discipline and Punish: The Birth of the Prison*, ed. Alan Sheridan (New York: Vintage, 1995), pp. 3–31.
49. See Michel Foucault, 'The Subject and Power', in Michel Foucault, *Power*, ed. James D. Faubion, trans. Robert Hurley et al., vol. 3 (London: Penguin Books, 1994), pp. 474–5. See also Ben Golder's excellent analysis of Foucault's politics on rights: Ben Golder, 'Foucault, Rights, and Freedom', *International Journal for the Semiotics of Law* 26, no. 1 (2013): 5–21; Golder, *Foucault and the Politics of Rights*. See Bal Sokhi-Bulley, *Governing (through) Rights* (Oxford: Hart Publishing, 2016).
50. Brown, '"The most we can hope for …"', 459; Golder, *Foucault and the Politics of Rights*, pp. 115–47. See also Bal Sokhi-Bulley, 'Government(ality) by Experts: Human Rights as Governance', *Law and Critique* 22, no. 3 (2011): 251–71.
51. Golder, *Foucault and the Politics of Rights*, pp. 115–47. Golder's reading challenges the view that Foucault capitulated to the terms of liberalism in his 'embrace' of human rights in his later work; I elaborate upon this argument in Chapter 6. See also Michel Foucault, *'Society Must be Defended': Lectures at the Collège de France, 1975–76*, eds. Mauro Bertani and Alessandro Fontana, trans. David Macey (London: Allen Lane, 2003), where he refutes the idea that the subject has a pre-existing ontological status or essence; rather, it is constituted through power which operates through 'bodies, gestures, discourses, and desires' that are named as 'individual' (at pp. 29–30). See also Golder, 'Beyond Redemption?'; Joe Hoover, *Reconstructing Human Rights: A Pragmatist and Pluralist Inquiry into Global Ethics* (Oxford: Oxford University Press, 2016).
52. Ignatieff, *Human Rights as Politics and Idolatry*, p. 57; Joseph Raz, *The Morality of Freedom* (Oxford: Clarendon Press, 1986); Will Kymlicka, *Liberalism, Community and Culture* (Oxford: Clarendon Press, 1989), pp. 10–20.
53. Ignatieff, 'Human Rights as Idolatry', 330. See also Martha C. Nussbaum, 'Human Capabilities, Female Human Beings', in *Women, Culture, and Development: A Study of Human Capabilities*, eds Martha C. Nussbaum and Jonathan Glover (Oxford: Clarendon Press, 1995), pp. 61–104.
54. Jeanne Morefield, *Empires Without Imperialism: Anglo-American Decline and the Politics of Deflection* (New York: Oxford University Press, 2014), especially her discussion of this recursive position in Michael Ignatieff's work (at pp. 201–31). See also Ann Laura Stoler, *Duress: Imperial Durabilities in Our Times* (Durham, NC: Duke University Press, 2016), on how colonial histories inform the conditions of the current world.
55. Nikita Dhawan, 'Introduction', in *Decolonizing Enlightenment: Transitional Justice, Human Rights and Democracy in a Postcolonial World*, ed. Nikita Dhawan (Opladen: Barbara Budrich Publishers, 2014), pp. 9–10.

56. Michael Walzer, 'The Politics of Rescue', *Social Research* 62, no. 1 (1995): 61–2. Walzer repeated his support for the establishment of a mandate or trusteeship system in the context of the refugee crisis that assailed Europe in the summer and autumn of 2015, when large numbers of migrants were fleeing the horrors of the war in Syria. In this respect, Walzer commented: 'There are countries in the world today that ought to be, for a time, not-independent and not-sovereign. What the world needs, and what the UN might provide if it were the organization it was meant to be: a new trusteeship system for countries that are temporarily unable to govern themselves ... Libya and Syria ought to be UN trusteeships, with some coalition of countries, different in each case, taking responsibility for maintaining law and order and providing basic services to the population – under strict UN supervision': Michael Walzer, 'The European Crisis', *Dissent* (blog), 11 September 2015, www.dissentmagazine.org/blog/michael-walzer-european-refugee-crisis. This move finds support in Ignatieff's scholarship (for example Michael Ignatieff, 'The Seductiveness of Moral Disgust', *Social Research* 62, no. 1 (1995): 95).
57. Michael Ignatieff, *Empire Lite: Nation Building in Bosnia, Kosovo and Afghanistan* (London: Vintage, 2003). See also Michael Ignatieff, 'Human Rights, Global Ethics, and the Ordinary Virtues', *Ethics & International Affairs* 31, no. 1 (2017): 3–16. In doctrinal terms, see Scheinin and Vermeulen's critique regarding the denial or reduction of the application of human rights norms in combating terror: Martin Scheinin and Mathias Vermeulen, 'Unilateral Exceptions to International Law: Systematic Legal Analysis and Critique of Doctrines that Seek to Deny or Reduce the Applicability of Human Rights Norms in the Fight against Terrorism', in *Terrorism and Human Rights*, ed. Martin Scheinin (Cheltenham: Edward Elgar Publishing, 2013), pp. 3–56. See also Ariane Bogain, 'Security in the Name of Human Rights: The Discursive Legitimation Strategies of the War on Terror in France', *Critical Studies on Terrorism* (7 April 2017), doi: 10.1080/17539153.2017.1311093; Ipek Demirsu, *Counter-Terrorism and the Prospects of Human Rights: Securitizing Difference and Dissent* (Cham: Palgrave Macmillan, 2017).
58. Michael Ignatieff, 'The American Empire: The Burden', *The New York Times Magazine*, 5 January 2003, www.nytimes.com/2003/01/05/magazine/the-american-empire-the-burden.html. Former UK prime minister David Cameron invoked the term 'muscular liberalism' in a speech critical of multiculturalism, in which he stated that '[w]e've ... tolerated these segregated communities behaving in ways that run completely counter to our values': 'PM's Speech at Munich Security Conference', *GOV.UK*, February 2011, www.gov.uk/government/speeches/pms-speech-at-munich-security-conference. In the context of preventing extremism through education, Tony Blair used the term 'muscular centrism' as an alternative to 'flabby liberalism', which he cautioned against, stating that '[t]he centre has become flabby and unwilling to take people on. We concede far too much': quoted in Sean Coughlan, 'Tony Blair Warns of "Flabby Liberalism"', *BBC News*, March 22, 2016, www.bbc.com/news/education-35862598. See also Nicola Perugini and Neve Gordon, *The Human Right to Dominate* (New York: Oxford University Press, 2015).
59. Asad, for example, argues that cruelty and violence are integral to compassion and good intentions: Talal Asad, 'Reflections on Violence, Law, and Humanitarianism', *Critical Inquiry* 41, no. 2 (2015): 390–427. See also Talal Asad, 'On Torture, or Cruel, Inhuman, and Degrading Treatment', *Social Research* 63, no. 4 (1996): 1081–1109, where he challenges the universalist discourses generated around the idea of cruelty which obscure the ways in which cruelty is integral to the modern state.
60. Ignatieff, *Empire Lite*.
61. Morefield, *Empires Without Imperialism*, pp. 213–15.
62. Anghie, 'International Human Rights Law', pp. 109–25.
63. Mahmood Mamdani, 'Beware Human Rights Fundamentalism!' *Mail & Guardian*, 20 March 2009, https://mg.co.za/article/2009-03-20-beware-human-rights-fundamentalism; Mahmood Mamdani, *Saviors and Survivors: Darfur, Politics, and the War on Terror* (London: Verso, 2009).
64. See, for example, Mehta, *Liberalism and Empire*; Said, *Orientalism*; Dhawan, 'Introduction'. There remains a consistent refusal to work through the legacies of colonialism

and the hostility that it has generated against the 'Other': Paul Gilroy, *Postcolonial Melancholia* (New York: Columbia University Press, 2005).

65. Morefield, *Empires Without Imperialism.*
66. Shklar, 'Liberalism of Fear', p. 35.
67. Rorty, 'Hope and the Future', p. 154.
68. Ignatieff, *Human Rights as Politics and Idolatry*, pp. 88–9.
69. Ibid., p. 89.
70. Ibid., p. 89.
71. See, for example, Martha Fineman, *The Autonomy Myth: A Theory of Dependency* (New York: New Press, 2004); Martha Albertson Fineman and Anna Grear, *Vulnerability: Reflections on a New Ethical Foundation for Law and Politics* (Surrey: Ashgate Publishing Company, 2013). See also Nedelsky, who develops the idea of a relational autonomy, arguing that relations with other humans is in fact constitutive of the human and that autonomy is something that can primarily be developed in the context of relationships with others: Jennifer Nedelsky, *Law's Relations: A Relational Theory of Self, Autonomy, and Law* (New York: Oxford University Press, 2011). See further Rosemary Hunter, 'Deconstructing the Subjects of Feminism: The Essentialism Debate in Feminist Theory and Practice', *The Australian Feminist Law Journal* 6 (1996): 135–62; Carol Smart, 'The Women of Legal Discourse', *Social & Legal Studies* 1, no. 1 (1992): 29–44; Margaret Davies, *Delimiting the Law: 'Postmodernism' and the Politics of Law* (London: Pluto Press, 1996). See also Kate Brown, 'Introduction: Vulnerability and Social Justice', *Social Policy and Society* 16, no. 3 (2017): 423–7.
72. Martha Albertson Fineman, 'The Vulnerable Subject and the Responsive State', *Emory Law Journal* 60, no. 2 (2010): 263.
73. Martha Albertson Fineman, 'The Vulnerable Subject: Anchoring Equality in the Human Condition', *Yale Journal of Law & Feminism* 20, no. 1 (2008): 11.
74. Ibid., p. 8.
75. For example, several feminist critiques have focused on how liberal legalism has contributed to the construction of gender as a binary system – as male and female, masculine and feminine: Dianne Otto, 'International Human Rights Law: Towards Rethinking Sex/Gender Dualism', in *The Ashgate Research Companion to Feminist Legal Theory*, eds. Margaret Davies and Vanessa E. Munro (Farnham: Ashgate, 2013), pp. 197–215; Davies, *Delimiting the Law*; Hunter, 'Deconstructing the Subjects of Feminism', p. 160. Smart, for example, argues that law functions as a technology of gender and produces fixed identities and gendered subjects. In her analysis, legal discourse not only brings into being the categories of woman and man, but also normalizes and naturalizes the specific attributes associated with each category: Smart, 'Women of Legal Discourse', pp. 34–9. Postcolonial feminism has further complicated this analysis through an examination of how these categories are displaced onto a developed/developing world, 'us' and 'Other' divide: Ratna Kapur, *Erotic Justice: Law and the New Politics of Postcolonialism* (London: Glass House Press, 2005); Sara Ahmed, 'Deconstruction and Law's Other: Towards a Feminist Theory of Embodied Legal Rights', *Social & Legal Studies* 4, no. 1 (1995): 58.
76. Wendy Brown, *States of Injury: Power and Freedom in Late Modernity* (Princeton, NJ: Princeton University Press, 1995), p. 7.
77. Richard Rorty, 'Human Rights, Rationality, and Sentimentality', in Richard Rorty, *Truth and Progress: Philosophical Papers*, vol. 3 (Cambridge: Cambridge University Press, 1998), pp. 181–2; José-Manuel Barreto, 'Ethics of Emotions as Ethics of Human Rights: A Jurisprudence of Sympathy in Adorno, Horkheimer and Rorty', *Law and Critique* 17, no. 1 (2006): 73–106. See also Nussbaum, who argues that emotions are an important capability to support as they are crucial to human development: Nussbaum, 'Capabilities and Human Rights', p. 287; Michalinos Zembylas, 'Emotions, Critical Pedagogy, and Human Rights Education', in *Human Rights Education: Theory, Research, Praxis*, ed. Monisha Bajaj (Philadelphia: University of Pennsylvania Press, 2017), p. 47; José-Manuel

Barreto, 'Rorty and Human Rights: Contingency, Emotions and How to Defend Human Rights Telling Stories', *Utrecht Law Review* 7, no. 2 (2011): 93–112.

78. Dipesh Chakrabarty, *Provincializing Europe: Postcolonial Thought and Historical Difference* (Oxford: Princeton University Press, 2000), p. 8.
79. Günter Frankenberg, *Political Technology and the Erosion of the Rule of Law: Normalizing the State of Exception* (Cheltenham: Edward Elgar Publishing, 2014), addressing how the resort to securitization as a response to perceived threats is becoming a normalized response by a number of liberal democratic states; Andreas Krieg, *Commercializing Cosmopolitan Security: Safeguarding the Responsibility to Protect* (New York: Palgrave Macmillan, 2016).
80. Anker describes this as a shift from fear to horror – a more intense feeling of terror and disgust – and uses Thomas Hobbes' *Leviathan* to analyse how the liberal state capitalizes on this idea of horror: Anker, 'Liberalism of Horror'.
81. Morefield, *Empires Without Imperialism*, pp. 2, 4.

2. Precarious desires and the pursuit of rights

> [T]here are 'subjects' who are not quite recognizable as subjects, and there are 'lives' that are not quite – or, indeed, are never – recognized as lives.
>
> —Judith Butler, *Frames of War*[1]

In December 2013, the Supreme Court of India unexpectedly reversed a lower court's 2009 decision that had decriminalized gay sex by reading down a colonial-era provision on homosexuality – Section 377 of the Indian Penal Code, 1860 (IPC).[2] Arguments presented on the part of those opposed to de-criminalization ranged from the assertion that homosexuality was an illness that could be cured, to expressions of anxiety over the cultural crisis in relation to morality that had been triggered in part by the 2009 decision. Most of the challenges overtly or covertly invoked a paradigmatic narrative of nationalism, asserting that homosexuality in India was a reprehensible 'Western' import, that its supposedly hedonistic predilections were not part of the genetic substrate of 'Indian culture' and that it constituted a repudiation of 'Indian cultural values'.[3] In reversing the lower court's decision, the Supreme Court withdrew the legal potential for gay people to become fully legible subjects entitled to the same rights, protections and privileges as all other Indian citizens. The re-criminalization of sexual conduct under the penal code, after a gap of nearly four years, brought to a halt efforts by LGBT and human rights groups working to consolidate the triumph of the 2009 decision, which had included advocacy in favour of same-sex marriage.

Following the Supreme Court ruling, public protests in the form of rallies and demonstrations by the LGBT community, activists and a spectrum of heterosexual citizenry received significant attention from the print media and television. The protests focused on the denial of agency, dissent and failed subjectivity, as well as the pain of the abject and precarious queer Indian subject. An immediate consequence of the media narrative produced by the legal narrative was that the LGBT community – stigmatized and demonized, but largely invisible and generally unmentionable in Indian public discourse – was suddenly made hypervisible through daily reportage of strident, violent and absurd expressions of cultural panic rooted in a homophobia that often validates itself through quoting scripture and classical sources. The few sympathetic editorials and interviews that appeared after the ruling were subsumed by self-aggrandizing opinions (including by legislators, jurists and religious leaders) that LGBT Indians could be indoctrinated into heterosexual 'normalcy' through marriage. Equally confident were the cacophonous claims that queer sexual impulses and practices could be permanently eradicated by therapies such as psychiatry and yoga. And while some Western governments and international LGBT human rights groups, among others, also condemned the Supreme Court ruling, their responses continued to operate against the problematic civilizational and cultural divides that have shadowed the emergence of the 'gay international' or 'gay imperialism' in such advocacy – a concept on which I elaborate later in this chapter.

The re-criminalization of the homosexual through the 2013 Indian Supreme Court decision emphasizes the crucial role of queer visibility and an aggressive strategy based on rights claims for ensuring queer legitimacy and equality. I would nevertheless question what is actually achieved when freedom as an end goal is envisaged primarily as the procurement of human rights, especially with regard to 'precarious' desires. In this chapter, I specifically examine how pursuits of human rights have an impact on precarious desires, and how these pursuits, while conferring recognition and legibility, not only reproduce the normative framework in which precarity and precarious identities are addressed, but also clearly incorporate the rights-seeking subject and illegible non-subject within a space where freedom is strongly defined in terms of the market and consumer agency.

Drawing on the discussion about the hierarchy of the subject presented in Chapter 1, I first examine how gendered and sexual subaltern subjects, among others, are considered as less legible; less human and, at times, even non-human. This hierarchy is partly structured by a reproductive heteronormative order and dominant cultural narrative about sex and gender, as well as the complex legacies of the colonial encounter. I then examine the normalizing role, function and outcome of LGBT human rights advocacy drawing upon examples from postcolonial India, as well as the broader international human rights responses to gender and sexual rights violations. I illustrate how these interventions – while initially disruptive, subversive and exposing the contingency of the rights project – ultimately serve to regulate, discipline, normalize and sustain governing norms, including dominant gender and sexual norms, as well as to negate the aspirations for lasting freedom of those subjects who fail or refuse to conform to these norms. In the last part of this chapter I continue to use the example of postcolonial India, to examine the specific ways in which the neoliberal space within which rights claims are being made and secured ensnares the desiring subject within an understanding of freedom linked to the market, and into inevitably becoming a consumer subject.

GRIEVABLE LIVES AND THE COVERT ANATOMY OF RIGHTS CLAIMS

In *Precarious Life*, Judith Butler argues that some lives cannot be apprehended as grievable or lost if they cannot be apprehended as living.[4] Writing in the aftermath of the 9/11 attacks on the United States and the response to these attacks, she questions whether the reaction to grief must inevitably be a cry of war combined with the incarceration of humans who do not count as adequately human and are thus denied the protection of international law. Discussing the idea of recognition and liveable lives, with specific reference to Muslim and Arab lives in the context of a post-9/11 global politics, Butler asks: 'Is Muslim life as valuable as legibly first-world lives? Are the Palestinians accorded the status of "human" in U.S. policy and press coverage? … Is our global capacity to mourn not foreclosed precisely through the failure to conceive of Muslim and Arab lives as lives?'[5]

Butler has analysed the collective response to grief in several historical contexts, most notably in the context of the 1980s AIDS epidemic and the consequences flowing from the refusal to publicly acknowledge and mourn the many dead young and mostly homosexual men, whose suffering received little or no social empathy, and who were simply denounced for their particular mode of being. Butler astutely summarizes how such erasure can have cruel and catastrophic effects on the marginalized – those not deemed worthy of being mourned: 'Insofar as the grief remains unspeakable, the rage over the loss can redouble by virtue of remaining unavowed. And if that rage is publically proscribed, the melancholic effects of such a proscription can achieve suicidal proportions.'[6] Her central inquiry is how some lives become grievable and are consecrated in public spaces and obituaries, while other losses become unthinkable and ungrievable.[7] Butler argues that 'the differential allocation of grievability that decides what kind of subject is and must be grieved, and which kind of subject must not, operates to produce and maintain certain exclusionary conceptions of who is normatively human: what counts as a liveable life and a grievable death?'[8] Further, in *Frames of War*, she elaborates upon this concern and asks under what conditions it becomes possible to apprehend a life as possible.[9] She concludes that such apprehension partly depends upon 'that life being produced according to norms that qualify it as a life or, indeed, as part of life'[10] and that, as stated in the epigraph to this chapter, some lives 'are never … recognized as lives'.[11]

I present Butler's discussion on precariousness in order to examine which harms or injuries are recognized in human rights as deserving of repair and remedy and which are not, specifically in relation to sexual subaltern lives. An obvious prerequisite to any kind of rights bestowal is that the subject who experiences the harm or injury is recognized in the first place. Recognition is contingent on the subject's 'recognizability' – an aspect of personhood arising from an existent set of general conditions that 'prepare or shape a subject for recognition – the general terms, conventions, and norms "act" in their own way, crafting a living being into a recognizable subject'.[12] As a result of these norms' operation, there are certain subjects that are recognized as persons and others that are not, or that receive less recognition. Human rights produce a hierarchy of who counts as human and who does not; who is more or less human; who is non-human or inconceivable as human. Moreover, it is important to note that those subjects who meet the terms of recognizability – and whose injuries or wounds are thus attended to – may not necessarily find the relief that they seek. The injury may continue to fester, as recognition of the injury or harm can in fact reinscribe the injury or harm rather than successfully mitigate it by addressing/resolving the broader social, historical and economic conditions that have produced the discrimination, harm or injury.[13]

By this same logic, those who are considered non-human, or whose subjectivity is effaced – in the sense that there was either no recognizable human there in the first place, or no life worthy of recognition – cannot experience injury, or harm, or erasure; there *are* no lives to be socially accounted for, lost, mourned or grieved.[14] If this is the case, then it also renders the idea of a universal subject in human rights as either not realizable, or only realizable on terms that are exclusive. As discussed in Chapter 1, theorizing such exclusion places into crisis the idea of the universal subject at the core of human rights, and the concept of 'human', the rights-bearing individual entity that grounds rights discourse, itself becomes a problem that requires critical investigation.

This chapter focuses on how precariousness plays out in specific ways within the material and discursive domains of gender and sexuality. In some jurisdictions, the rape or sexual assault of a lesbian woman or a sex worker receives no recognition, for the legal regime regards her and her kind as criminals/deviants to be profiled, targeted, incarcerated or even eliminated.[15] Even if she is not regarded as a criminal, the cultural and social space views her as a contaminant, as corrupting and toxic. Her injuries are unworthy of recognition, for she is unworthy of recognition as a human subject. The harm that she endures is not reparable; her life, if lost, is not grievable. Her body, her selfhood and her life can only be humanized by her voluntary or coerced submission to a corrective, social, reproductive, heteronormative order. Indeed, her very survival may be contingent on such submission. A human rights intervention may confer recognition on her as a victim of sexual marginalization/discrimination and/or sexual violence. However, as I discuss in Chapter 3, interventions responding to violence against women operate within an existing set of gender and sexual arrangements, and only the victim-subject who complies with such arrangements is accommodated. The pursuit of rights requires compliance with existing normative orders. Failure to comply results in penalization of the disruptive, disobedient individuals who are rendered de-constituted subjects in law.

Postcolonial critiques of human rights have deconstructed the ways in which the project of Empire has operated and continues to operate in and through international human rights law, and how the specific gender and sexual arrangements forged on the anvil of the colonial encounter inform this endeavour. Legal interventions in the lives of colonial subjects initially included rescuing the 'Other' woman from the native man.[16] Such interventions not only forcibly eliminated other legal traditions, by codifying and entrenching a specific understanding of the world, but also bonded the colonized subject to a specific understanding of the human. For the colonial power, such interventions would also serve as a justification for the continuation of colonial rule and its civilizing mission, partly pursued through legal reform. At the same time, for the native subject, resistance to reform took the shape of affirming the private sphere of the heteronormative family and crafting a very narrow cultural project of native selfhood distinct from, and to be aggressively defended against, the hegemonic West, Western masters, Western women and Western notions of sexuality. This resolve was a deeply conservative and narrow one that defined tradition and culture in, and through, women's bodies and established sexual norms that served as a fulcrum in the forging of cultural and national identity. It was a manoeuvre that further excluded, disenfranchised, and stigmatised sexual subalterns and desires that resided outside of this framing.

This complex legacy of Empire, civilizational maturity, cultural nationalism and alterity continues to inform human rights, and how precarious desires are addressed in the present moment. Those who claim knowledge of the 'right way' to be gendered and sexual in the world also presume to know how to categorize a human as recognizable, legible and grievable – or not. In turn, this process of regulative categorization produces an exclusionary understanding of freedom. Human rights are a relativistic intervention – that involve a struggle over messy, non-idealized conceptions of freedom. Encrusted by the weight of history and context, the fraught processes of human rights are always at an intractable distance from the immaculate and humane ideal of freedom that is claimed as the end goal.

NORMALIZING 'QUEERS' THROUGH RIGHTS CLAIMS

As discussed earlier, human rights perform a normalizing function in the context of precarious desires: they operate to preserve a hegemonic gender, sexual, cultural and racial order by vetting out elements considered threatening, dangerous and contaminating. Although human rights also open space for resistance, this space remains confined within the fishbowl, where liberal freedom – even after its critical makeover – remains the exclusive universe within which understandings of freedom can be articulated.

The term 'queer' reflects a location of resistance, and refers to a critical anti-normative project. It is intended as an analytical tool designed to disrupt and subvert the dominant normative order, and to introduce a polymorphous, diverse understanding of gender, sex and sexuality. It is this anti-normative critical capacity that distinguishes the 'queer' and queer theory from 'LGBT' advocacy and scholarship. However, the insights of queer theory have not found their way into the logic of LGBT human rights advocacy and, as I discuss later in this chapter, can in fact be used to entrench orthodoxies. LGBT advocacy, for the most part, has focused on the universalizing and homogenizing dynamic of rights claims, accreting around specific constituencies/identities and directed at legal inclusion and the bestowal of rights on those subjects who have been disenfranchised, subordinated, stigmatized, criminalized and regarded as less than human.[17] Based on faith in universal human rights, this advocacy culminates in the globalization of a 'global gay' identity: '[a] claim to "gay and lesbian rights" as human rights depends on an understanding that the identities "gay" and "lesbian" are universal in the sense that they are present in all cultures, not just in the west.'[18] The point to note is that the processes of globalization have enabled the proliferation of gay and lesbian identities alongside the proliferation of sexuality rights, also enabling the genesis of a certain kind of liberal queer – the exclusive, Western or westernized, progressive, out or selectively out queer consumer – the 'gay international' or 'global gay'.[19] This particular sexual subjectivity seems more affirmed, in contrast to the spectrum of less privileged, less visible or invisible 'local' queers not affiliated with cosmopolitanism, and about whom 'global gays' may wish to know very little or nothing at all.

The distinction between 'queer' and 'LGBT' has become increasingly blurred in the human rights arena, with 'Q' at times being added as part of the LGBT acronym and with LGBT advocacy on occasion designated as a modality of 'queer' work. And the purported redeployment of 'queer' by queer persons for radical political purposes has produced its own set of racial and cultural exclusions.[20] Thus, in the context of human rights, even though 'queer' is understood as providing a critical intellectual impulse that questions normativity and drives the political agenda, such efforts frequently end up reinforcing the dominant normative order of gender and sexuality rather than producing freedom from it.

The rights claims of stigmatized and marginalized sexual subjects remain a compelling and important aspect of the queer political project, especially given that LGBT persons in great swathes of the world are reduced through state and social collusion to truncated, demeaned, incapable, silenced subjects, ever vulnerable to exploitation and hate crimes, and rendered continually precarious through a lack of legal recognition.[21] While this goal of queer enfranchisement is laudable, I question the claim that the degradation of LGBT persons can be substantively alleviated by human rights interventions, especially as they have largely failed to challenge the normative framework within which sexuality is addressed. Moreover, these interventions have at times not only inscribed particular fishbowls of their own – namely, sets of sexual normativities – but also reproduced racial and cultural binaries between societies viewed as 'progressive' and 'civilized', and societies that, as per the liberal vision, remain in a state of transition until the human rights of their LGBT persons are secured.

At one level, there is clearly no reasonable argument that can be invoked against a human rights challenge to legal provisions that call for the imposition of life imprisonment or the death penalty for being gay. For all possible reasons, being an affirmed, legitimate citizen-subject is preferable to being a negated criminal deviant. In the choice between criminality and legitimacy, at one level, legitimacy is clearly preferable given that it affords access, protection, public standing and legibility. For example, in April 2014, the transgender community in India was ecstatic over the Supreme Court's decision that transgender persons – disenfranchised, considered unworthy and grotesque, yet paradoxically accepted for millennia as a visible and valid social presence in 'Indian culture' –

are entitled to their human and fundamental rights to health and education, to be included in the category of 'Other' on government documents and to marry.[22] The transgender community, as well as other queer communities, hailed the decision as a victory due to its official and formal recognition of the humanity of sexual minorities. The landmark case represents the realization of an excluded non-subject's struggle for recognition, with the state allowing those excluded 'Others' to enter into all the rights, privileges and protections conferred through recognition as a legible juridical subject. Regardless of his/her sexual orientation, preference or practice, which may or may not be same-sex, the Indian transgender person is now allocated full selfhood through legal categorization as an entitled 'third gender'.

Similarly, prior to the 2013 Indian Supreme Court ruling referred to at the beginning of this chapter, a lower court ruled in 2009 that Section 377 of the IPC, a colonial-era law criminalizing sodomy – defined as an act of 'carnal intercourse against the order of nature' – would no longer cover consensual adult sexual relations. While the decision did not confer full legibility on LGBT subjects in law or reduce the traumatic pressure of being homosexual in a homophobic environment, it at least removed a significant impediment to the full pursuit of LGBT rights. Following the decision, many Indian gays and lesbians participated in public discourse, stating that homosexuality was legitimate and extending the rights discourse into discussions about the possibility of same-sex marriage. Some queers even married in the presence of temple deities, with traditional priests conducting ceremonies, or through the formal exchange of garlands, a ritual central to Indian marriage ceremonies. The reviled sexual subaltern, an outsider to 'Indian culture', was transcending the disciplinary limits of the Court's decision, through a provocative and subversive appropriation of the ruling.

These cases reflect excluded bodies' struggle to realize their desire for recognition and humanity through human rights. It is doubtlessly important that illegible constituencies continually pursue their political and personal desires through rights mechanisms. In the context of homosexuality, it is indeed better to have legal recognition, including the option to get married as a gay person, rather than having an active discriminatory law that, as mentioned earlier, not only persecutes homosexual conduct but also criminalizes and thus endeavours to annihilate the very selfhood of homosexuals.

At the same time, procuring and protecting gay rights requires further scrutiny through a critical lens that illuminates how the pursuit of rights claims does not move smoothly in a linear, progressive direction towards a better space and a better time inhabited by freedom. This discussion prompts, and provokes, crucial questions regarding queer advocacy and its increasing alignment with the regulatory apparatus of the state and emergence as a governance project. The cases and advocacy suggest a series of questions: Is the primary objective of partially enfranchised queers to acquire respectability and align with the constructs of familial domesticity? By using law to modify illegitimate and 'unnatural' desire to produce a mimetic representation of more approved and 'natural' forms, do sexual subalterns intend a wholesale pursuit of aspirations sanctioned and valorized by the heterosexual regime, in order to prove their own humanity – to feel and hope to be treated as 'normal', thereby 'equal', and to achieve a stable sense of social belonging? Do such processes of desirable 'naturalization' somehow sanitize and make reasonable the 'abnormality' of queer sexual desires to the 'natural', 'normal' majority? While it is important to give greater acknowledgement to the moments of social disruption produced by same-sex marriage, the logic underlying the act and its outcomes do mandate deeper scrutiny. More specifically, these disruptions need to be addressed within an understanding of what Foucault identifies as the extremely complex configurations of power and how it functions in the small moments – in the minutiae of daily life – and how it operates within the larger frames of relationships such as marriage, adoption or consensual sex. It is to understand how power is not something to be possessed through rights claims; it is to know how it is capillary, and how it is most immediately exercised and felt.[23]

A further concern requires that attention is paid to the racial and cultural assumptions that inform LGBT human rights pursuits. The broader global struggle for LGBT rights manifests in polarized responses to the sexual subject and claims to legibility and legitimacy. These range from increased criminalization of same-sex conduct and/or simply identifying as homosexual,[24] to increased legal recognition in other countries, where the culmination of the struggle for legitimacy and equality is the judicial recognition of same-sex marriage,[25] generally seen as the ultimate validation of LGBT advocacy. Such trends are invariably presented as evidence of the primitiveness or backwardness of non-Western, developing countries, against the more civilized, evolved approach of Western/liberal democracies. However, if same-sex marriage is permissible in various Western nations, this mode of legitimizing queer subjectivity cannot be based on one-dimensional, paternalistic reasoning which posits that these societies are inherently better, more civilized and mature than, for example, Uganda, Kenya or Nigeria, or other 'underdeveloped' parts of the world, including India. Such reasoning deflects attention from the way in which Christian evangelicals from the United States have been partially implicated in the construction of an anti-gay agenda in these African nations.[26] It is not Islamic orthodoxy but rather this type of Christian evangelicalism that is driving a homophobic agenda easily received within a context where conservative gender and sexual norms, constituted partly by the legacies of the colonial past, continue to resonate in the postcolonial present. Economic sanctions – or the withdrawal of aid by the home countries of citizens centrally implicated in producing or reinforcing homophobia in countries being punitively targeted by such measures – require that both the injury and the restorative/rehabilitative interventions be rigorously problematized.[27]

International LGBT human rights advocacy has also tended axiomatically to associate freedom with the West and Western liberal values, while African, Islamic and non-Western societies and their leaders are cast as retrogressive and barbaric. Such a position neglects to implicate the ways in which homophobia continues to be a feature of Western liberal democracies. Abhorrence of homosexuality and the homosexual continues to exist as an ideological position *across* these hemispheric divides. For example, in May 2013, France witnessed some of the largest protests seen in Paris since the 1960s, with vast rallies attended by those opposed to the move to legalize same-sex marriage; this opposition has been sustained and continuous.[28] There was a simultaneous upsurge in violence against the gay community when the law was enacted, illustrating how – even in the liberal ethos – precarious desires remain precarious. The Paris protests suggest that despite legal recognition, homosexuals continue to be regarded as less valid, less worthy, less legitimate subjects within the French cultural and political space – a space in which dominant Catholic theological notions constitute the liberal subject and the frames of recognizability that determine who is entitled to recognition and who is not. Likewise, in the United States discriminatory initiatives against LGBT people persist, despite the Supreme Court's recognition of same-sex marriage. For example, in July 2017, Donald Trump reinstated the ban on transgender persons serving in the US military. In June 2016, the brutal massacre of 49 LGBT persons at a gay nightclub in Florida elicited comments of reprehensible bigotry from some Christian religious leaders and groups, including 'The tragedy is that more of them didn't die',[29] as well as public citations from the Bible such as 'You shall reap what you sow', thus reinforcing the conservative claim that homosexuality is both sinful and evil. While legal challenges to discriminatory measures continue to be brought and receive judicial favour, these responses are also indicative of the continuing prevalence and influence of homophobia in the 'free world'.

International LGBT human rights advocacy has not necessarily challenged the normative framework within which precarious desires are pursued and addressed. As discussed, LGBT activist interventions have at times not only inscribed a set of gender and sexual normativities of their own, but also reproduced the binary between those societies that are viewed as 'progressive' and 'civilized' and those societies that remain in a state of transition until the human rights of LGBT persons within them are secured. The subversive term 'queer' can be skilfully deployed in ways that are complicit with dominant formations of heterosexuality or homonormativity.[30] A necessary component of this assimilative process involves the indoctrination of sexual subjects with a belief in the liberal superiority and positioning of the West/First World liberal democracies as progressive and inclusive cultures, particularly in relation to the United States. 'Queer' serves not as a signifier of sexual identity or sexual subversion, but merely as a defused inscription of socio-political difference within a larger modality of hierarchical regulation and governance.[31] For example, in the context of the torture of Iraqi men by US soldiers at the Abu Ghraib prison, as depicted in the photographs subsequently released to the media, it is significant that this testimonial of atrocity was almost exclusively crafted and interpreted through a sexual lens by queer scholars, with the prisoners being intentionally humiliated not through excessive interrogation protocols but through sexualized practices that were assumed to be repulsive, emasculating and shameful to Muslims.[32] Occluded in such readings were the overwhelmingly racial, cultural and gendered dimensions of the torture. These erasures reinforced the liberal media's xenophobic practice of caricaturing Muslims, here through traumatic images of pure abjection that violently satirize Muslim sexuality/subjectivity as primitive and grotesque. The racist and sexist dimensions of this avidly consumed cache of brutality remained largely unquestioned by queer scholars and LGBT advocates, thereby leaving unchallenged the Western supposition that repressed sexuality is a defining characteristic of the Muslim, who is pinioned fetishistically into a default position as the West's most prominent, phobogenic and adversarial cultural 'Other'. The Muslim remains a fully objectified genus enwombing that malignant subgenus – the jihadi/Muslim terrorist. Queer critique has thus effectively reinforced this dominant supposition about the Muslim to shore up US 'sexual exceptionalism' – an ideology used to indoctrinate 'Other' sexual subjectivities into the reification of liberal superiority. In the case of Abu Ghraib, acts of pure sadism were converted into a 'positive register of the valorization of (American) life'[33] – a manifestation of Western hubris that confidently continues to applaud this particular fishbowl as unequivocally progressive and inclusive.

A further example of this exclusionary politics and the recurrent predication of rights recognition for LGBT subjects against the politics of Empire, racism and militarism is found in the UN Security Council. The Council called its first organized session on gay rights, which was open to all member states, in August 2015, a few months after footage emerged on social media of Islamic State (IS) militants throwing a blindfolded man off a seven-storey tower block in Tal Abyad, Syria, as punishment for having a homosexual relationship. The man survived the fall, but was then stoned to death by the crowd waiting at the foot of the tower. In a closed-door meeting sponsored by the United States and Chile, the Security Council focused on IS and its ongoing persecution of LGBT Syrians and Iraqis.[34] Of the 15 countries sitting on the Security Council, 13 participated in the meetings, with China, Russia, Nigeria and Malaysia present but silent, and Chad and Angola absent. The event was celebrated as a landmark, with the Security Council taking up the cause of LGBT rights for the first time in its 70-year history.[35] What remains troubling is that this new locus of LGBT rights is centrally fixed within a security discourse that reproduces binaries based on racial and cultural exclusions, and also finds its justification in the rescue of the sexual subaltern from what is viewed as the primitive, homophobic 'Other'. This event further illustrates how LGBT human rights advocacy can become linked to exclusionary and highly aggressive broader agendas and projects, where threats to freedom are refracted through the liberal fishbowl as imminent and justifying violent militarism. Interventions – where the righteous trajectory of human rights drives and justifies the impulse to action – go unquestioned, and have a cost: the erasure of subjectivity and choice for those marked by such interventions as simultaneously in need of rescue and threatening to the prevailing social norm. As argued in Chapter 1, the sexual and gendered 'Other' is thus brought into being – produced through a set of disciplinary and regulatory mechanisms that are coextensive with human rights and the liberal epistemology on which they are based. Liberal templates of freedom, while cast as a virtuous endeavour, serve to control and manage the 'Other', with such altruistic processes ultimately reinforcing a neo-imperial, racist and often militaristic project.

LGBT human rights advocacy has been critiqued precisely for pursuing agendas that are based on prevalent models in the United States and Europe – schemas that erase or marginalize articulations of non-Western perspectives on sex and sexuality, while also reinforcing the purported civilizational superiority of Western states. At one level, the critique suggests that the gay rights movement, which produces a particular kind of tolerable homosexual – the 'gay international' – is nothing more than a neo-colonial enterprise that annuls the possibility of a valid, authentically postcolonial, non-Western narrative of queer sexuality, rights claims and identity politics.[36] The discussion in this chapter highlights the importance of scrutinizing and complicating the ways in which postcolonial sexual subjectivities are constructed and deployed in human rights advocacy, as well as the liberal media. My argument moves away from a thesis based upon unproblematized binaries of 'us' and 'them', and from the counter-positions of sexual liberation and sexual repression, which are based upon a First/Third World divide.

Within contemporary human rights discourse, the radical features of 'queer' thought and subjectivity have failed to gain traction and instead 'queer' has frequently moved in the direction of gay governance, where sexuality becomes both normalized and naturalized. The critical capacities of 'queer' have thus been shorn away by the assimilative gravitational pull of human rights. As a political/social/sexual category, 'queer' appears unable to transform or destabilize the normative foundations of human rights that remain firmly embedded in dualistic gender categories, a gender hierarchy and a set of racial and cultural exclusions.[37] In fact, as I argue in the later sections of this chapter, 'queer' – far from going rogue – has *itself* gone normative.

Homosexuality within the liberal paradigm is inevitably presupposed and constituted against a cultural 'Other', which thus assumes something about freedom, and what queer freedom *should* look like – namely, adherence to the virtue of outness as opposed to the deception of the closet. The influential framework of 'coming out' narratives tends to repudiate the varied genealogies and modalities of queer subjectivity, instead locating the issue of sexuality within the narrow dialectic of visibility and invisibility. It captures neither the very real and particular ambivalences, dangers, dilemmas and crises of homoerotic experience, nor the local imperatives and complexities negotiated by queers in postcolonial contexts. Invisibility comes at a high emotional cost, but it may be a necessary form of self-protection – which may also mean the protection of others, both homosexual and heterosexual – in many parts of the world, especially where homosexuality is criminalized, and where being an out queer automatically means risking all modes of direct and indirect penalization. The assertion of queer selfhood through visibility may involve great losses, ranging from familial and social rejection and ostracism, to being deprived of home, livelihood and services, to discrimination and humiliation, to violent assault and, sometimes, even death at the hands of the bigoted and/or the ignorant.

It is certainly problematic to allege that the out 'gay international' produced by hegemonic 'Western' notions of sexuality/sexual subjectivity is clear evidence of an imposition by 'the West on the Rest', as suggested, for example, in Massad's work cited previously. It is just as problematic to assume a monolithic 'Rest' in this equation, for the West's 'Others' form a set constituted by heterogeneous, culturally specific, internally differentiated yet cohesive subsets committed to varied ideologies, groupings, practices and knowledge paradigms that are not present in the progressive narratives of reform and rights.[38] Moreover, given such diversity, it is obvious that queer subsets within the set of any particular queer culture would be wholly or partially invisible to one another, may function hierarchically and/or may not have a common language or common interactive ground: for instance, metropolitan queers may have no grasp of what it means to be queer in provincial/rural contexts, and vice versa; queer men and queer women might have different priorities and approaches to complex identity or rights issues, and so on. The equation nevertheless urges us to interrogate the idea of human rights as the universally preferred mechanism for procuring freedom. We also need to scrutinize the belief that the current model of human rights has the ability to actually remedy, repair or restore the lives of stigmatized sexual others.

International LGBT human rights advocacy has incorporated gay sexuality into a linear regulatory framework that may, in some instances, be a safer option than adopting a more radical approach. Given the prevalent climate of homophobia – in both the Global North and the Global South – it is arguable that an uncomplicated approach to sexual subjectivity based on identity and framed within the heterosexual/homosexual binary is always welcomed. And given the precarity of LGBT rights, such a strategy might be all that stands between advocates and the virulent homophobia of orthodox and conservative religious groups at the international and domestic levels. While such interventions may indeed breach the borders of heteronormativity and foster empowerment through successfully eliding the distance between mainstream and margins, the deeper meta-issue is that the legal inscription of some sexual minorities through human rights, and their protection from discrimination and persecution, is neither radical nor moving in the direction of lasting freedom. Instead, it is a regulatory heuristic. By transforming illegitimate desire into a mimesis of more approved forms, current LGBT human rights advocacy appears to involve nothing more than the wholesale pursuit of aspirations sanctioned and valorized by the heterosexual regime, in order to prove one's own humanity, feel 'normal' and attain a sense of stability and social belonging. Thus, queer advocacy emerges as a governance project. In the pursuit of entitled 'normality', the 'abnormality' of the queer subject is thoroughly sanitized, with those aspects of homoeroticism most objectionable to the 'normal' and 'natural' heterosexual majority – that is, the spectrum of queer sexual practices – rendered reasonable and endurable.

While it is important to acknowledge the moments of social disruption produced, for example, by the recognition of LGBT persons as human, or by the legalization of same-sex marriage – that is, to affirm the terrain of rights acquired through activist heroism and sacrifice – the logic underlying such acquisition and its outcomes mandates deeper scrutiny. In the next section, I discuss how the entrance of LGBT/queer communities to the stage of human rights signifies release not into a space of lasting freedom, but rather into the regulatory space of the neoliberal market. This trajectory compels the 'new' queer subject as market actor into being – as *'homo' economicus* in the contemporary neoliberal moment.[39]

THE 'HAPPY QUEER' AS *HOMO ECONOMICUS*

I elaborate here on how the acquisition of rights for those who have been recognized as human does not, in and of itself, release the precarious subject into a space of freedom. Rather, through such acquisition, the LGBT person is coercively channelled into a competing normative order that disciplines and dictates how she can be in the world. On the one hand, queer sexuality, sexual identity and sexual practices continue to be directly or indirectly constrained once they enter the terrain of rights; on the other, conferring legal recognition could prompt movement towards a totalized response and invite regulation of these once radical subjectivities. In the context of Foucault's conceptualization of power relations and subjectivity as discussed in Chapter 1, the LGBT person becomes eligible and possible, secure and liveable, *only* when reproduced through the legal regulation and governance of difference and the alignment of marginalized otherness with mainstream normativity. It is crucial to emphasize that this trajectory, while of course different from one that criminalizes and outlaws queer sexuality, is also regulative and constraining. It is not self-evident that sexual recognition/legitimacy through rights acquisition ensures greater freedom for the entitled sexual subject. Instead, this understanding fails to take the discursive operations of human rights into account – how human rights are implicated in power, operating as technologies of governance that produce and inscribe the very subject to be governed, and the choices available to her. They reproduce a specific normative order, which continues to regulate, discipline and monitor the sexual subject. This order is framed within a script of the 'good life' or happiness which is equated with thriving markets and the rise of consumer-citizens or 'human capital',[40] as discussed in Chapter 1. Thus, the end goal of human rights as freedom simultaneously transforms 'unhappy queers' into 'happy queer subjects'[41] in a scheme of neoliberal rationality, where economic imperatives and state-enabled forces of market governance are identified as the source of general well-being, social inclusion and personal affirmation.

Ahmed discusses the example of the unhappy queer subject who never belongs, or can only belong on the terms prescribed by the dominant narrative of happiness; these terms are prescribed by a heteronormative, reproductive framework and, in the contemporary moment, are most powerfully inscribed within the neoliberal market.[42] In the process, unhappy queers, or those who ideologically and/or materially resist such coerced conformity, are a significant and under-acknowledged part of queer genealogy. Ahmed offers a reconceptualization of happiness through queer politics, deconstructing the emotion of happiness to illustrate how it is not just a 'good feeling', but also attaches to a moral economy. Tracing the experience of unhappiness in queer literature, Ahmed stitches together a meta-textual archive of the experience of queer unhappiness/the unhappy queer as negative affect, and as part of a shared social inheritance.

Transposing Ahmed's analysis onto the human rights context, we see that the legal recognition of same-sex relationships and the queer family, where this has been achieved, does not necessarily release the queer into a space of unfettered freedom. While such recognition produces a celebratory moment – and, no doubt, one to which postcolonial queers or those denied subjectivity or recognition as legible subjects or as having 'real' relationships also aspire – it is partly secured through an alignment with normative social arrangements. As noted earlier, in the contemporary moment, the queer non-subject can only become a subject/belong on terms prescribed by the dominant normative order – that is, a heteronormative, reproductive framework, embedded in a lifestyle propagated by a neoliberal market. These normative alignments involve marriage, parenthood and material success – all of which are made possible through the acquisition of rights within the alluring cartography of the neoliberal market, and according to the terms of this market. Ultimately, such recognition ends up simulating the standard heterosexual model. In her discussion on queer happiness and queer reproduction, Ahmed questions whether queers can 'sustain the struggle for recognition, the struggle to make the world bearable for queers, without approximating the very forms of happy heterosexuality?' She reflects upon whether '[i]t might be that queers are rewarded with happiness in return for approximating signs of straightness', but goes on to consider the potential for happiness associated with unconventional routes – that being 'happily queer' might be preferable to being a 'happy queer'. For example, Ahmed suggests that being 'happily queer' might mean moving 'beyond the straight lines of happiness scripts'.[43] The proliferation of cosmopolitan queer lifestyles and the 'normalized' lives of entitled queer subjects attest to how far the claim for rights has aligned with the logic of the neoliberal market, where nearly every aspect of socially privileged queer life – the life of the Western or Westernized 'global gay' – is increasingly defined through modalities of consumption.

While neoliberalism is a 'loose and shifting signifier' that operates differently according to the historical and political context, the notion of governing for the market is a consistent feature, in which financialization and competition, rather than rights, become the central preoccupation.[44] I illustrate this argument in the remainder of the chapter by examining the specific ways in which rights claims are being subsumed by the increasing economization of every dimension of life, including the configuring of human beings as market actors, with reference to the context of contemporary India. The (apparently) greater recognition of sexual and queer subjectivities within the larger domain of (apparently) increased gender rights is being rigorously aligned with very specific economic arrangements.

In the 1990s, as India began pursuing and implementing a package of neoliberal reforms to become a 'global player', there was heightened anxiety over emergent proliferating discourses of sexual desire, expression and agency, which appeared to challenge the very identity of the Indian nation and its 'cultural values' – values which rest upon their innate distinction from the West as discussed earlier in this chapter. Hindu nationalists, who have publicly declared their intention to reconstitute secular India as a Hindu state, routinely attacked heterosexual couples celebrating Valentine's Day, or stores selling Valentine's Day cards, for being 'Western' contaminants. Police raided cyber cafes, popular nodes of sociality (for young people) within the new technological culture, allegedly to catch consumers surfing the Internet for pornography. There was increased surveillance of female sexual conduct in public, with police periodically launching 'clean-up' operations in city parks and harassing heterosexual couples as well as suspected gay people. Local vigilantes disrupted public displays of affection, and self-appointed right-wing guardians of Indian morality also protested celluloid representations of the 'kiss' as the iconic gesture of true love – in today's Bollywood, extended kiss sequences have replaced the marriage scene as the climactic signifier of plot complications being resolved to produce the desired, socially validated happy ending. The Hindu nationalists – key players in the movement to purge India and Indians of sexual agency and modes of sexual discourse – have remained intent on degrading sexual diversity and banishing overt expressions of sexuality that contrast with the model of the chaste and subservient Hindu wife, heteronormative arrangements and the images of sexual relationships valorized in classical 'Indian culture' and constitutive of Indian national identity. They have enabled and exaggerated the narrow, rigid and immutable interpretation of scripture and mythology, an interpretation partly informed by the colonial encounter and resistance to colonial rule, in order to oppose sexual rights and the legal recognition of non-normative sexualities, A conservative Hindu majoritarianism not only reifies culture and fixes gender and sex as physiological categories, but also erases the cultural pluralism and alternative practices that have always been important features of gender and sexuality in India and throughout the subcontinent. In the process, right-wing spokespersons and functionaries have, through various modes of public hate speech, promoted unceasing bigotry and hate crimes, while projecting this ideological vilification and distortion of otherness – including sexual alterity – onto marginalized groups and religious minorities, particularly Muslims and Christians, sex workers, migrants and homosexuals.

The rights claims of Indian sexual subalterns must be understood within a context characterized by the parallel rise of politico-religious right-wing politicians and groups, and the emergence of India as a neoliberal economy. On the one hand, rights advocacy invokes queer desire as a challenge to the dominant heterosexual, familial, cultural norms that have defined the borders of sexual legitimacy. On the other hand, such advocacy also invokes queer desire to counter some of the state and non-state efforts that seek to confine or censor alternative sexual expression and representations, especially those present in celluloid and popular culture.[45] However, the space from which these challenges are made, and in relation to which recognition is sought, remains understood, structured and reinforced almost entirely in terms of the seductive fishbowl of the neoliberal market.

To illustrate this argument, I discuss the representation of queer sexuality in the 2008 Bollywood Hindi blockbuster *Dostana* (used as a noun, the word translates as 'friendship'; used as an adjective, it translates as 'amicably', 'companionably', 'characteristic of/befitting a friend'). The film represents one of the first attempts to boldly pull queer sexuality from its elusive and erratic margins and serve up an ironic full-frontal enunciation of a very particular mode of gayness – a theatrical transplant far removed from the sinister edict of Section 377.[46] The spectator witnesses the makeover of two hot, straight superstars of

Bollywood cinema, Abhishek Bachchan and John Abraham, who are scripted into the most unlikely avatars: transnational 'queer folk'. Sameer and Kunal, two straight 'friends', present themselves as a gay couple to secure a lease on a penthouse apartment in downtown Miami, which they ultimately end up sharing with Neha, the ambitious, high-powered editor of a glossy high-end fashion magazine – played by the equally hot, straight Priyanka Chopra, who oozes the confident sexuality of the cosmopolitan '*desi* (Indian/indigenous) girl' or the 'new Indian woman' in the global market. The two men also learn that their gay façade makes them eligible to be fast-tracked through the US immigration process, to claim that ever coveted green card. Through a series of plot twists, this audacious faux queering of the Bollywood hunks and their real attraction to Neha receives the ultimate seal of approval from Sameer's mother, Ama, who – after much handwringing, expressed in the song *Mama's Boy Has Gotten Spoilt* – blesses the relationship during the standard Hindu wedding scene, which unfolds in classic Bollywood style with a signature song-and-dance sequence.

Throughout the film, the two 'queer' actors are on the frontlines of the defence of an aestheticized hyper-masculinity. Beefcake and sculpted brawn are on lavish display for the heroine, and no doubt also for the spectator, male or female. These privileged macho 'friends' are not transgressive, alien or threatening. Their onscreen sexuality is flaunted as familiar, lovable and even desirable. Ultimately, they are forced to confess their deception and reveal their 'true' sexuality to Neha. She forgives them only after they perform a very public 30-second lip-locking kiss. The film closes with both heroes' pleasurable recollection of the kiss, putting into question the certainty of their heterosexual status.

Queer desires are becoming more visible, and are increasingly claiming space in law, in culture and on the streets, with efforts to eliminate or incarcerate these desires being regularly challenged as human rights violations; however, the core issue is whether LGBT advocacy is actually bringing disenfranchised sexual subalterns closer to freedom? Legitimacy – a goal that seemed unrealizable only a decade ago – remains a valid pursuit; yet a teleological, progressive reading of how sexual subalterns are in the process of becoming full and equal members of the polity through rights claims masks the regulatory and normative apparatus into which certain sets of 'recognizable' queers are being incorporated, attaining respectability and affirmation and securing membership. One such scripting of aspiration is undertaken through neoliberal economics, as exemplified in *Dostana*. While social inclusion and assimilation appear to be the end goal for the two 'queer' protagonists, the model of freedom on display involves the pursuit of these goals through a complete, explicit affiliation of apparently subversive sexuality with the hegemonies and homogeneities of the global market. The apartment that Sameer and Kunal share with Neha is exquisitely modern, adorned with all the accoutrements of stylish living. Their clothes and mobile phones are branded, luxurious and 'fabulous'; they drive a flaming-pink vintage Chevrolet convertible and own Harley-Davidson motorbikes. Almost all the characters in the film are rich and consumption-oriented. These cosmopolitan gay men and women inhabit the elite universe of private enterprise glutted with shining signifiers of the 'happy' life, from glitzy bars, to fashion magazine offices, to the swimwear shoots at which Kunal clicks away as a fashion photographer. The desiring gay subject emerges as an energetic consumer of all these exclusive, queer-friendly spaces and services.

In many ways, the film invokes the emerging consumer-citizen in an emerging market economy, where the market is seducing the socio-economically privileged subject, whether homosexual or heterosexual, to indulge until satiated in a shopping spree of luxury brand names, new gadgets and haute couture styles. The cosmopolitan queer and his/her lifestyle is produced through his/her participation in this marketized space, where the desire to consume, rather than subversive sexual desire, is the core feature of queer personal identity. Those who critiqued *Dostana* for reinforcing gay stereotypes missed the broader discursive significance of the film and the new models of citizenship that it invokes – the queer subject apparently defused of subversive potential; gay desire efficiently normativized through the neoliberal market, with the production of a tamed, well-groomed, moneyed, reliable and responsible citizen. This form of representation is implicitly supported by an LGBT politics that focuses on assimilationist activism and which has not rigorously interrogated the neoliberal treatment of sexuality *itself*, which as a commodity, as with any material commodity, can be voraciously and profitably produced, manipulated and consumed.

The critical capacities of LGBT human rights advocacy are attenuated, depoliticized and stalled in this transformation of the socially disruptive sexual subject into a compliant consumer or market citizen, through which markets can function efficiently. The market is a means for increasing the citizen's power and control over her own life, and a mechanism for ostensibly ensuring greater equality and justice.[47] It reflects a homonormative pursuit in which individual and collective success is calibrated and judged not necessarily by how one negotiates one's sexual location and its imperatives, but more or also through the discriminatory indices of wealth accumulation and the wealth-enabled practices of responsible citizenship. The seduction and metamorphosis of the rogue – the radical sexual subject – into a malleable consumer-citizen through the neoliberal market order may be experienced as a form of freedom and entitlement for those who have lived precarious lives on the anxious terrain of unacceptability and non-recognition. At the same time, the desiring marginal subject is mapped with increasing finesse along a neoliberal graph of craving and fulfilment, demand and supply, through a process of continually modulated and mainstreamed sexual image, identity and aspiration; this momentum is designed to push economic and social responsibility away from the state and into the private arena. Here, groomed into straight-seeming model behaviour through his/her purchasing power, the intractable sexual subaltern is disciplined into becoming a satisfied, respectable, entitled and apparently equal subject – in other words, a 'happy queer'.

'BECOMING' QUEER SUBJECTS

Although precarious desires are being liberated through legal recognition, they are simultaneously being subjected to greater self-regulation, self-discipline and responsibility through the market, which is overtly and covertly appropriating the private sphere, including in terms of sexuality. It is through compliance with the normative call for greater self-governance and responsibility that queers – assembled through various modalities of state, market and advocacy-enabled normativization – manage to move from undesirability to desirability and from precarity to stability as legible, respectable citizen-subjects. The pursuit of recognition through rights can erode and/or efface the subversive and radical possibilities of queer politics. More significantly, such a pursuit can converge with the increasing regulation and governance of society, including the meticulous annexation of sexual subjectivity, within the coordinates of the omnivorous global market. This thesis is further developed in Chapter 3, where I discuss women's human rights advocacy and its relationship to statist and market configurations of freedom in the sphere of gender.

The analysis raises several urgent questions. In relation to LGBT rights, when do international human rights become a project of 'norming the queer', rather than a queering of the norm, and when do they become complicit in the new imperialism that presents in the guise of the 'gay international'? Can queer freedom in the realms of 'the Rest' ever be realized through human rights diffracted through the prism of racial/cultural othering, or the profit-oriented fishbowl of neoliberal rationality? Can rights ever perform an authentically counter-hegemonic role, even when sufficiently and effectively appropriated by radical or subversive identities or arguments? And can precarious desires be recognized and affirmed via the human rights project, without in the process consolidating the ability of both state and market to define the terms and contours of these desires and their freedom?

As discussed in earlier sections of this chapter, the reconstitution of queer subjectivities through the liberal paradigm of assimilative LGBT activism inscribes once excluded, disruptive, disobedient sexualities with the linked schemas of social entitlement, desirability, normativity and regimes of governance. Life in a state of exclusion does affirm the subversive potential of queer precarity, but the continuous strain of living on one's own terms as a precarious subject also extracts its costs, especially in locations where queers are formally categorized as criminal deviants and have no protection under law. Thus, the argument is not that pursuit of recognition through human rights is a false end goal. Rather, I argue that it does not give us what we want: unfettered freedom. Instead, it provides a 'fishbowl' modality, an illusory emancipation that in fact continues to operate in accordance with a set of binaries – 'us' and 'them', the legible subject and the cultural 'Other', First/Third World – which are sustained, reinforced and even perpetuated through rights advocacy and rights acquisition.

Cossman argues in favour of a more expansive and hospitable theoretical focus on the process of 'becoming' – one that introduces a politics which *cannot* be captured in the oppositional terms of assimilation or transgression, exclusion or inclusion, but rather orients itself to the spaces somewhere in between.[48] This argument does pull us away from thinking only in terms of normalizing or subverting, conforming or dissenting. It is never either/or. Focusing on how legitimate or illegitimate sexual subjects come into being, or on how some desires are deemed by state/society as worthy of expression while others are not, certainly makes visible the ingrained ambivalences that underscore human rights pursuits in relation to precarious desires. And there is no doubt that some process of deep and, perhaps, irreversible transformation of subjectivity takes place in the process of 'becoming', which itself may be important to illuminate. Precarious desires may be normalized in the process of becoming, yet may remain charged with subversive potential in the process of becoming legible.

For example, while at one level *Dostana* can be read as invoking how subject formation of the 'desirable' queer occurs through economic logic, it also suggests that even while such sexual subjectivity can be rendered compliant through assimilation, it is also inherently incapable of being wholly disciplined. *Dostana* ends with the two straight heroes daydreaming about their 'queer' kiss, and remembering the performance with some pleasure and delight. Their heterosexual credentials remain disrupted – not only by the fact of this sensual recollection, the denouement of their fictive queer action, but also by the fact that they are, after all, married to one another. The final 'ruling' and 'sentencing' for their 'gay' deception, based on a seemingly light-hearted 'let the punishment fit the crime' logic, can be decoded as pushing past satire, absurdity and taboo into the unsettled and unsettling space of pure paradox. The spectacle of the mock kiss – initially a meeting of two sets of lips each first extended in a reluctant *moue* – ultimately climaxes in a vigorous collision of mouths on stage in front of a visibly shocked Neha and a hall of cheering witnesses, accompanied by a celebratory soundtrack. The experience of 'becoming', in this moment, hovers as tantalizingly non-manifest, since the thoroughly equivocal same-sex kiss simultaneously affirms and annuls the 'being' of the two straight 'happy queers' – eliding intimacy and dissociation, it is a gesture in which legibility and illegibility, truth and illusion, flex uneasily against each other like tectonic plates poised to grind their massed forces into convulsion.

For the spectator, this untypical yet conventional Bollywood cocktail of riotous romance, suspense and dramatic irony offers a serious subtext: the issue of whether the fraught existential process of queer becoming, and becoming legible, contains within itself the possibility of meaningful freedom. What politics or understanding of freedom is produced after precarious desiring non-subjects become 'becoming' – that is, desirable – subjects through assimilative acts? Whether legal or not, same-sex marriage, consensual sodomy and other queer sexual practices, judged in India and elsewhere to be 'against the order of nature', are a profound challenge to the sexual and social norm. Two men or two women who perform the sanctioned cultural rituals of marriage, even while not legally recognized as valid, grievable human subjects, are at one level simulating heterosexuality and gesturing towards assimilation. At the same time, they are also unsettling the normative understandings of the 'natural' marital relationship. The subversive erotic of queer sexual choice becomes the basis of the marriage claim, and the performance of 'sodomy as consummation' unravels the tight seams of what constitutes marriage legally and culturally.[49] While dependent upon victories or defeats in legislatures and courtrooms, freedom for the 'unbecoming' queer subject may also perhaps be traced to such personal moments of sexualized self-affirmation.

Recognition does indeed bestow humanity, legibility and grievability. But such recognition, whatever its parameters, can be fragile, tentative and vulnerably grafted onto political exigencies. Thus, the criminalized sodomite may transition across the discursive threshold from 'unbecoming' outlaw into a legally recognizable subject, one who is tolerated in law, only to become a criminalized sodomite again – as occurred relatively recently in India. As noted at the outset of this chapter, the Indian Supreme Court reversed the 2009 decision decriminalizing homosexuality on appeal in 2013.[50] While the challenges to colonial and persecutory laws have been important, this pursuit of 'becoming' legal has also served to abrade/erase the radical substrate of what it means to 'be' queer. As the term 'queer' finds increasing traction within the arena of human rights, it also becomes more embedded within dominant racial, religious and cultural norms that continue to operate along an inclusionary and exclusionary divide. This pursuit may be indicative of how 'queer', once a descriptor of rogue alterity, has now perhaps irreversibly gone normative. Even though queerness, as a manifestation of social–sexual dissent, has invariably sought to distinguish itself from normative projects, and also from LGBT politics that have been cast as a distinctly more liberal enterprise, it is not apparent that this once essential distinction has been maintained in the field of either the discourse or the practice of human rights. As I have illustrated, the consistent feature of these seismic shifts from non-recognition to recognition to de-recognition of the queer – as happened in India – is that precarious desires continue to be managed and policed, governed and regulated, in one way or another. It is important to acknowledge activist passion, effort and sacrifice, and just as important to highlight rights-enabled moments of successful queer subversion – but, no matter how disruptive, these are after all contingent outcomes rather than lasting freedom.

'Becoming' respectable, responsible queer citizens through the assimilative process of marriage, reproduction or adoption, even while 'being' reliably queer in terms of sexual choice, ultimately contributes to the neoliberal politics of normalization and respectability.[51] LGBT human rights advocacy can be read as simply operating in accordance with the logic of producing a happy queer subject within the framework of queer reproduction, as Ahmed argues, or as operating within the logic of neoliberal governmentality, in relation to which the queer consumer-citizen must comply so as to become recognizable and thus socially included. At one level, then, queer *has* gone normative. And it may be that there *is* no place outside the norm from which it would be possible to 'possess an otherness which would actually make it other'; that '[t]he norm, or normative space, knows no outside'.[52] It may be that within the human rights arena, strategic sets and subsets of interdependent norms abound; yet this project is *itself* rigorously bounded, limited by a liberal scaffolding which provides little room for radical alternatives or for the 'failed subject' who cannot be regulated into normativity.[53] The assimilative pull of human rights has decanted an entitled, legible, respectable, desirable queer subject while simultaneously producing its opposite – the unsuccessful sexual subaltern/non-subject; the silent or vocal queer dissident navigating the existential pressures of stigmatized criminal deviance, unable/unwilling to comply with the prescriptions of freedom in a fishbowl, who aspires to equality, legibility and grievability but does not/cannot participate in the frameworks that bring about recognition through this set of arrangements.

The contemporary rights paradigm leaves us with some troubling questions. What are the consequences of the conditional bestowal of rights for the 'failed subject'/'unhappy queer' who, through choice or circumstance, cannot or does not acquiesce to the normative registers through which precarious desires become desirable and worthy of enunciation and celebration? What are the critical capacities that are available or that reside in this 'unsuccessful' queer, who does not surrender her search for freedom, but rather seeks it *outside* of the normative apparatus that is the fishbowl, and the governance and regulatory apparatus that it enfolds? And what avenues are available for the one who seeks her freedom outside of the confines of the fishbowl? How might these elusive, enigmatic possibilities unfold? I suggest that this disenfranchised subject subscribes to a wider and deeper logic of 'becoming' and 'being', one that manifests beyond the claustrophobic normative/anti-normative trap of the liberal fishbowl. Such spaces flourish with the norm as well as without it, and offer an epistemic alternative upon which I elaborate in the later chapters of this book.

NOTES

1. Judith Butler, *Frames of War: When is Life Grievable?* (London: Verso, 2009), p. 4.
2. *Suresh Kumar Koushal v. Naz Foundation* (2014) 1 SCC 1. *Naz Foundation v. Government of NCT of Delhi*, 160 Delhi Law Times 277 (2009). By way of background, see Ratna Kapur, 'Unruly Desires, Gay Governance and the Makeover of Sexuality in Postcolonial India', in *Global Justice and Desire: Queering Economy*, eds. Nikita Dhawan et al. (Abingdon: Routledge, 2015), pp. 115–31. For an elaborate discussion on the legal regulation of homosexuality in India, see Jyoti Puri, *Sexual States* (Durham, NC: Duke University Press, 2016); Yeshwant Naik, *Homosexuality in the Jurisprudence of the Supreme Court of India* (Cham: Springer International Publishing, 2017); Savina Balasubramanian, 'Contextualizing the Closet: *Naz*, Law and Sexuality in Postcolonial India', in *Perverse Politics? Feminism, Anti-Imperialism, Multiplicity*, eds. Ann Shola Orloff, Raka Ray and Evren Savci (Bingley: Emerald, 2016), pp. 135–58. On 24 August 2017, a nine-judge Supreme Court bench unanimously recognized the right to privacy as a fundamental right under the Indian Constitution: *Justice K.S. Puttaswamy (Retired) v.*

Union of India, No. 494 of 2012 (Supreme Court of India, 24 August 2017). Several judges were clearly of the view that sexual orientation is an essential attribute of privacy and that the Koushal decision was unsustainable: *Puttaswamy v. Union of India* at 124 [127]. As the *Koushal* case is pending reconsideration before a larger bench, the Court refrained from deciding the issue in the *Puttaswamy* case. See A.K. Aditya, 'What the Right to Privacy Bench has said about Emergency and Section 377', *Bar and Bench*, 24 August 2017, https://barandbench.com/right-privacy-bench-said-adm-jabalpur-suresh-koushal/; *The Wire* Staff, 'Right to Privacy Judgement Sets Stage to Decriminalise Gay Sex For All Time', *The Wire*, 24 August 2017, https://thewire.in/170565/section-377-right-to-privacy-supreme-court/.

3. India's judicial architecture is uniquely complicated and influenced by – and frequently in adversarial relationship with – the array of prescriptions and prohibitions enunciated by cohesive parallel traditional systems that manifest formally and informally, directly and indirectly, as a form of law: the rules and sanctions of canonical religious philosophy, the logic of caste, cultural practices, and social codes and conditioning. The timeless force of Indian 'tradition' can function as both violator and upholder of rights; that is, as both perpetrator and punisher. This schema of tradition-as-law may exert itself anywhere, but does so most frequently in the fraught domains of gender and sexuality, where it becomes constitutive of these domains, producing verdicts and penalties that at times are unjust, disempowering and sometimes even fatal, as well as offering tools of resistance, subversion and legitimacy for the subaltern subject.

   Under Indian law, the personal laws of each community govern familial or domestic matters. Faith-based rulings in cases involving family matters, differently enunciated in different religions, are symbiotically bound to 'tradition-as-law'. Thus, religious authorities or their authorized delegates adjudicate in petitions presented under 'Muslim personal law', 'Hindu personal law', and so on, although these rulings can be challenged in the secular courts.
4. Judith Butler, *Precarious Life: The Powers of Mourning and Violence* (London: Verso, 2004); See also Judith Butler, 'Explanation and Exoneration, Or What We Can Hear', *Grey Room* 7 (Spring 2002): 56–67; Judith Butler, 'Afterword: After Loss, What Then?' in *Loss: The Politics of Mourning*, eds. David L. Eng and David Kazanjian (Berkeley: University of California Press, 2003), pp. 467–73.
5. Butler, 'Explanation and Exoneration', p. 63.
6. Judith Butler, *The Psychic Life of Power: Theories in Subjection* (Stanford, CA: Stanford University Press, 1997), p. 148.
7. Butler, Precarious Life, p.xiv.
8. Ibid., pp.xiv–xv.
9. Butler, *Frames of War*, p. 2.
10. Ibid., p. 3.
11. Ibid., p. 4.
12. Ibid., p. 5.
13. Wendy Brown, *States of Injury*.
14. Butler, *Precarious Life*, p. 147.
15. United Nations High Commissioner for Human Rights, *Discrimination and Violence against Individuals Based on their Sexual Orientation and Gender Identity*, UN Doc. A/HRC/29/23, 4 May 2015. See, for example, paras 31 and 35.
16. See Gayatri Chakravorty Spivak, A Critique of Postcolonial Reason: Toward a History of the Vanishing Present (Cambridge, MA: Harvard University Press, 1999). See more generally, Karuna Mantena, Alibis of Empire: Henry Maine and the Ends of Liberal Imperialism (Princeton, NJ: Princeton University Press, 2010) discussing how law and culture were contested terrains, deployed in ways that advanced the mission of Empire; Anna Millan and Ali Can Yildirim, 'Decolonizing Theories of Global Justice', in *Decolonizing Enlightenment: Transnational Justice, Human Rights and Democracy in a Postcolonial World*, ed. Nikita Dhawan (Opladen: Barbara Budrich Publishers, 2014), pp. 195–208 examining how Eurocentric frameworks of liberal theories of global justice

produce violent exclusions and elisions, silencing and marginalizing subaltern groups, especially women. See also, for example, Shenila S. Khoja-Moolji, 'The Making of Humans and Their Others in and through Transnational Human Rights Advocacy: Exploring the Cases of Mukhtar Mai and Malala Yousafzai', *Signs* 42, no. 2 (2017): 377–402.

17. These efforts have culminated, for example, in the adoption of the Yogyakarta Principles, which identify areas of discrimination faced by LGBT persons and include measures to alleviate such discrimination: International Commission of Jurists, *The Yogyakarta Principles: Principles on the Application of International Human Rights Law in Relation to Sexual Orientation and Gender Identity* (March 2007), icj.wpengine.netdna-cdn.com/wp-content/uploads/2012/08/Yogyakarta-Principles-publication-2007-eng.pdf.
18. Kristen L. Walker, 'Capitalism, Gay Identity and International Human Rights Law', *Australasian Gay and Lesbian Law Journal* 9 (2000): 62.
19. Joseph Massad, 'Re-Orienting Desire: The Gay International and the Arab World', *Public Culture* 14, no. 2 (2002): 361–85; Niamh Ní Mhaoileoin, 'The Ironic Gay Spectator: The Impacts of Centring Western Subjects in International LGBT Rights Campaigns', *Sexualities*, 5 June 2017, doi: 10.1177/1363460717699778; Katarzyna Korycki, 'Desire Recast: The Production of Gay Identity in Iran', *Journal of Gender Studies* 25, no. 1 (2016): 50–65.
20. Judith Butler, *Bodies that Matter: On the Discursive Limits of 'Sex'* (New York: Routledge, 1993), pp. 223–42.
21. UNHCHR, *Discrimination and Violence against Individuals*. See also United Nations High Commissioner for Human Rights, *Discriminatory Laws and Practices and Acts of Violence against Individuals Based on Their Sexual Orientation and Gender Identity*, UN Doc. A/HRC/19/41, 17 November 2011. See also Paula Gerber and Joel Gory, 'The UN Human Rights Committee and LGBT Rights: What Is It Doing? What Could It Be Doing?' *Human Rights Law Review* 14, no. 3 (2014): 403–39; United Nations Office of the High Commissioner for Human Rights, *Living Free and Equal: What States are Doing to Tackle Violence and Discrimination against Lesbian, Gay, Bisexual, Transgender and Intersex People*, UN Doc. HR/PUB/16/3 (2016); United Nations Office of the High Commissioner for Human Rights, *Born Free and Equal: Sexual Orientation and Gender Identity in International Human Rights Law*, UN Doc. HR/PUB/12/06 (2012).
22. *National Legal Services Authority of India v. Union of India* (2014) 5 SCC 438. See Spence Jones, 'Towards a Universal Construction of Transgender Rights: Harmonizing Doctrinal and Dialogic Strategies in Indian Jurisprudence', *The Indonesian Journal of International & Comparative Law* 4, no. 1 (2017): 91–121.
23. Foucault, 'The Subject and Power', pp. 336–7.
24. For a list of countries where same-sex conduct and/or the identity of homosexuals have been legally criminalized, see '76 Countries Where Homosexuality Is Illegal', *Erasing 76 Crimes*, last updated 19 May 2017, https://76crimes.com/76-countries-where-homosexuality-is-illegal/.
25. For a list of countries that have legalized same-sex marriage, see 'Gay Marriage around the World', *Pew Research Center*, last updated 8 August 2017, www.pewforum.org/2017/06/30/gay-marriage-around-the-world-2013/. See also Robert Wintemute, 'From "Sex Rights" to "Love Rights": Partnership Rights as Human Rights', in *Sex Rights: The Oxford Amnesty Lectures 2002*, ed. Nicholas Bamforth (Oxford: Oxford University Press, 2005), pp. 186–224.
26. Sally Kohn, 'Hillary, "The Family" and Uganda's Anti-Gay Christian Mafia', *The Daily Beast*, 25 February 2014, www.thedailybeast.com/hillary-the-family-and-ugandas-anti-gay-christian-mafia. Scott Lively is a US evangelical who has participated in anti-gay campaigns in Uganda and elsewhere. In *The Pink Swastika*, a book that Lively co-authored with Kevin Abrams, the authors argue that homosexuals were the true inventors of Nazism, and that they were responsible for the Nazi atrocities: Scott Lively and Kevin Abrams, *The Pink Swastika: Homosexuality in the Nazi Party* (Sacramento, CA: Veritas Aeterna Press, 2002). See also Ciara Bottomley, 'Unintended Consequences of International Human

Rights Advocacy in Uganda', *SOAS Law Journal* 2, no. 1 (2015): 49–75; Kevin Ward, 'The Role of the Anglican and Catholic Churches in Uganda in Public Discourse on Homosexuality and Ethics', *Journal of Eastern African Studies* 9, no. 1 (2015): 127–44.

27. The fact that Sexual Minorities Uganda (SMUG), a non-profit umbrella group for LGBT persons in Uganda, filed a lawsuit in a US federal court against Scott Lively, charging him with spreading extremist homophobic propaganda in African countries, is extremely significant. Although the lawsuit was ultimately dismissed, the case represented an important example of 'pushback' from the Global South, and one that exposes homophobia as both a cultural feature of and an export from the West: see Henriette Gunkel, 'Some Reflections on Postcolonial Homophobia, Local Interventions, and LGBTI Solidarity Online: The Politics of Global Petitions', *African Studies Review* 56, no. 2 (2013): 67–81; Floribert Patrick and Calvain Endong, 'LGBT Rights Movement in Africa and the Myth of the Whiteman's Superiority', *Journal of Globalization Studies* 7, no. 1 (2016): 139–51.
28. Bruno Perreau, *Queer Theory: The French Response* (Stanford: Stanford University Press, 2016). See Loi n° 2013-404 du 17 mai 2013 ouvrant le mariage aux couples de personnes de mêmesexe, *Journal Officiel de la République Française [JO] [Official Gazette of France]*, 18 May 2013, 8253; 'France: Loi n° 2013-404 du 17 mai 2013 ouvrant le mariage aux couples de personnes de même sexe', *Fabregat Perulles Sales Abogados* (blog), 29 May 2013, www.fabregat-perulles-sales.com/blog/france-loi-n-2013-404-du-17-mai-2013-ouvrant-le-mariage-aux-couples-de-personnes-de-meme-sexe/.
29. Meg Wagner, "California pastor rejoices in massacre at Orlando gay club," *New York Daily News*, 14 June 2016, www.nydailynews.com/news/national/california-pastor-celebrates-massacre-orlando-gay-club-article-1.2673335.
30. Jasbir K. Puar, *Terrorist Assemblages: Homonationalism in Queer Times* (Durham, NC: Duke University Press, 2007). See generally Lisa Duggan, 'The New Homonormativity: The Sexual Politics of Neoliberalism', in *Materializing Democracy: Toward a Revitalized Cultural Politics*, eds. Russ Castronovo and Dana D. Nelson (Durham, NC: Duke University Press, 2002), pp. 175–94.
31. See, for example, David M. Halperin, *One Hundred Years of Homosexuality: And Other Essays on Greek Love* (New York: Routledge, 1990); John C. Hawley, ed., *Postcolonial, Queer: Theoretical Intersections* (Albany, NY: State University of New York Press, 2001); Puar, *Terrorist Assemblages*, 79–114. On whether it is possible to develop a queer politics/theory and avoid aligning with an anti-normative stance, see Robyn Wiegman and Elizabeth A. Wilson, 'Introduction: Antinormativity's Queer Conventions', *Differences: A Journal of Feminist Cultural Studies* 26, no. 1 (2015): 1–25.
32. Puar, Terrorist Assemblages, pp. 79–114.
33. Ibid., p. 3.
34. Michael K. Lavers, 'Islamic State Focus of U.N. Security Council's First LGBT Meeting', *Washington Blade*, 25 August 2015, www.washingtonblade.com/2015/08/24/islamic-state-focus-of-u-n-security-councils-first-lgbt-meeting/.
35. US Department of State, 'UN Security Council Holds Inaugural Meeting on LGBT Issues', news release, 24 August 2015, https://2009-2017.state.gov/r/pa/prs/ps/2015/08/246296.htm; Kerry Brodie, 'In a Historic First, U.N. Security Council Convenes to Discuss LGBT Rights', *Human Rights Campaign* (blog), 24 August 2015, www.hrc.org/blog/in-a-historic-first-u.n.-security-council-convenes-to-discuss-lgbt-rights.
36. Massad, 'Re-Orienting Desire'; Joseph A. Massad, *Desiring Arabs* (Chicago: University of Chicago Press, 2007); Stewart Chang, 'The Postcolonial Problem for Global Gay Rights', *Boston University International Law Journal* 32, no. 2 (2014): 309–54. For a more critical perspective, see Momin Rahman, *Homosexualities, Muslim Cultures and Modernity* (Basingstoke: Palgrave Macmillan, 2014); Rahul Rao, *Third World Protest: Between Home and the World* (Oxford: Oxford University Press, 2010). For an example of how to counter the franchise of the 'gay international' through the resurrection of a Third World, authentic lesbian subject, see Gayatri Gopinath, 'On *Fire*', *GLQ: A Journal of Lesbian and Gay Studies* 4, no. 4 (1998): 631–6.

37. Dianne Otto, 'Queering Gender [Identity] in International Law', *Nordic Journal of Human Rights* 33, no. 4 (2015): 299–318. See generally Dianne Otto, ed., *Queering International Law: Possibilities, Alliances, Complicities, Risks* (Abingdon: Routledge, 2018). For recent examples of the subversive elements of 'queer' emerging in the UN structure, see United Nations Human Rights Council, *Report of the Independent Expert on Protection against Violence and Discrimination Based on Sexual Orientation and Gender Identity*, UN Doc. A/HRC/35/36, 19 April 2017. For a more elaborate discussion, see Cynthia Weber, *Queer International Relations: Sovereignty, Sexuality and the Will to Knowledge* (New York: Oxford University Press, 2016).
38. See, for example, Arondekar, on the erasure of pluralist histories of sexuality under the weight of a colonial and racist past, and the hegemonic histories of nationalism and colonialism: Anjali R. Arondekar, *For the Record: On Sexuality and the Colonial Archive in India* (Durham, NC: Duke University Press, 2009). For a critique of Arondekar, see Jessica Hinchy, 'The Eunuch Archive: Colonial Records of Non-Normative Gender and Sexuality in India', *Culture, Theory and Critique* 58, no. 2 (2017): 127–46.
39. The relationship between *homo economicus* and neoliberalism, as described by Foucault, is instilled in the moment when '*Homo economicus* is an entrepreneur, an entrepreneur of himself': Foucault, *Birth of Biopolitics*, p. 226.
40. Brown, *Undoing the Demos*, p. 83.
41. Ahmed, *The Promise of Happiness*, pp. 105–6, 112–13. For a contrasting position, see Sri Craven, 'Challenging Queer as "Neoliberal": The Radical Politics of South Asian Diasporic Lesbian Representational Culture', *Journal of International Women's Studies* 18, no. 2 (2017): 45–58.
42. Ahmed, *The Promise of Happiness*, pp. 88–120.
43. Ibid., pp. 114–15. See also Aeyal M. Gross, 'Sex, Love, and Marriage: Questioning Gender and Sexuality Rights in International Law', *Leiden Journal of International Law* 21, no. 1 (2008): 235–53.
44. Brown, *Undoing the Demos*, pp. 20, 66–67.
45. Some earlier serious representations include *Phir Milenge* (2004), a Bollywood portrayal of a single woman who contracts HIV after unprotected sex during a one-night stand; *My Brother … Nikhil* (2005), a small-budget film sympathetically depicting the discrimination and homophobia experienced by an HIV patient in contemporary Indian society; and *Dedh Ishqiya* (2014), on the reworking of the relationship between Muslim identity and lesbian desire. More recently, *Aligarh* (2015) presented the true story of a gay Hindu professor at the famed Aligarh Muslim University in the north Indian city of Aligarh who, in 2010, was fired by the institution for his sexuality. He was subsequently reinstated after winning his legal case against the university; his challenge was based on discrimination and violation of his right to privacy, and relied upon the 2009 Delhi High Court decision. However, the professor was found dead in suspicious circumstances within days of securing his legal victory. These films have featured at a time when the rights of sexual minorities have been increasingly claimed in the courts, amid a climate of rising cultural intolerance. See also Pawan Singh, 'Staging Sexuality through the Familial, the Performative and the Activist: Bollywood's Queer Repertoire in the Twenty-First Century', *South Asian Popular Culture* 13, no. 2 (2015): 125–39, and Rohit K. Dasgupta, *Digital Queer Cultures in India: Politics, Intimacies and Belonging* (New Delhi: Routledge, 2017), on the opening up of the digital space and formation of queer identities in India.
46. Aaron Rohan George, 'Bollywood's Queer Dostana: Articulating a Transnational Queer Indian Identity and Family in 2008's *Dostana*', *Asia Colloqiua Papers: 2014 Critical Approaches to South Asian Studies Workshop* 5, no. 2 (2015): 1–14.
47. Amanda Root, *Market Citizenship: Experiments in Democracy and Globalization* (Los Angeles: SAGE, 2007), p. 57.
48. Brenda Cossman, *Sexual Citizens: The Legal and Cultural Regulation of Sex and Belonging* (Stanford: Stanford University Press, 2007), pp. 9, 18. See also Diane Richardson, 'Rethinking Sexual Citizenship', *Sociology* 51, no. 2 (2017): 281–96; Leti Volpp,

'Feminist, Sexual, and Queer Citizenship', in *The Oxford Handbook of Citizenship*, eds. Ayelet Shachar et al. (Oxford: Oxford University Press, 2017), pp. 153–77.

49. Cossman, *Sexual Citizens*, pp. 165–6.
50. In February 2016, the Indian Supreme Court allowed a curative petition against its 2013 ruling on Section 377, and directed that the case involved significant constitutional issues. It has placed the matter before a constitutional bench of five judges. This case will, once again, raise issues of recognizability and the processes of becoming a legible queer subject.
51. Yuvraj Joshi, 'Respectable Queerness', *Columbia Human Rights Law Review* 43, no. 2 (2012): 415–67; Yuvraj Joshi, 'The Trouble with Inclusion', *Virginia Journal of Social Policy & the Law* 21, no. 2 (2014): 207–65; Diane Richardson, 'Desiring Sameness? The Rise of a Neoliberal Politics of Normalisation', *Antipode* 37, no. 3 (2005): 515–35; Apoorva Ghosh, 'LGBTQ Activist Organizations as "Respectably Queer" in India: Contesting a Western View', *Gender, Work and Organization* 22, no. 1 (2015): 51–66.
52. François Ewald, 'A Power without an Exterior', in *Michel Foucault Philosopher*, ed. Timothy J. Armstrong (New York: Harvester Wheatsheaf, 1992), p. 173.
53. Ahmed, *Promise of Happiness*; Halberstam, *Queer Art of Failure*.

3. Freedom, women's rights and the rise of the sexual security regime

> I knew what I wanted to run to. But it didn't exist, so I didn't leave.
> —Chimamanda Ngozi Adichie, *Half of a Yellow Sun*[1]

At the end of December 2015, hundreds of women were sexually molested during New Year's Eve celebrations near the main cathedral and central train station in Cologne. Headline news around the world suggested that men of Middle Eastern or North African appearance had carried out most of the assaults. At the time, Europe was engulfed in a highly fraught debate on the refugee crisis,[2] in relation to which the allegations concerning the Cologne attacks proved a turning point. Specifically, the attacks seriously challenged German chancellor Angela Merkel's open-door policy, which was labelled 'irrational' and 'dangerous'. Under the policy, more than one million refugees fleeing from conflict zones, mainly Syria and Iraq, had been permitted to enter the country. While only 3 of the 58 men ultimately charged were actually refugees, the racial origins of the perpetrators, who were mostly non-white, non-German citizens, led to immediate conflation with Islam and generated hysterical xenophobic phrases such as 'Islamic Rape of Europe' and 'Europe's Muslim Rape Epidemic', or the term 'Rape refugee'.[3] The response of *Charlie Hebdo* – the French satirical magazine that emerged as a global icon of free expression following the lethal terrorist attacks on Paris in January 2015 – was to run the famous image of the Syrian refugee toddler who drowned along with his mother and brother while crossing the Mediterranean, his body later washing up on a Turkish beach. The *Hebdo* cartoon was captioned: 'What would little Aylan Kurdi have grown up to be? Ass-groper in Germany.'[4]

Given that sexual violence against women rarely triggers this level of alarm – or even interest – in Europe, including in Germany, the question that arises is whether the nationality and religion of the attackers, rather than the criminal treatment of women, was more at issue. For example, the 'rape refugee' slogan brandished by supporters of Pegida, an extreme right-wing German political party, at a rally after the assaults seems to confirm that the victims had become mere background features in the heated discussions and muscular assertions of nationalism surrounding the refugee debate. The dominant narrative, supported partly by the media, took the form of an iteration that sexual violence is a crime usually committed by 'Others' – 'non-white', 'non-European', 'Muslim' men, originating from elsewhere. This familiar orientalist discourse, which underpinned the colonial rhetoric, is coupled in the contemporary period with an Islamophobia that is rife in Europe, has flourished ever since 9/11 and has been strengthened by subsequent terror attacks in major Western European cities. Denial and disavowal of the 'Other' are exposed as being integral to human rights in the post-9/11, postcolonial era.[5] The failure to acknowledge that violence against Western women is not perpetuated solely by 'Others', or that Western liberal democratic states are themselves thoroughly implicated in having triggered the current mass migrations into Europe, is an instance of how the solutions to the problem – in this case, combating the perceived threat through bigotry, xenophobia and carcerality – can miss the point altogether and, in the process, do further harm. In the subsequent reforms enacted by the German national parliament, MPs backed stricter rape laws that included making the victim's lack of consent central to the definition of the crime.[6] At the same time, law reform has enabled the prosecution of entire groups for a sex crime, regardless of whether any individual in the group is involved in the crime. Under the new law, it is a crime just to be present in a group that carries out a sexual assault. The relevant provision is specifically intended to address the events that occurred in Cologne, and places a powerful tool in the hands of authorities by making it easier for them to deport migrants who commit sexual offences.[7]

In a contrasting case, thousands of Indian citizens of all ages and backgrounds marched in protest against the brutal gang rape and murder of 23-year-old medical student Jyoti Singh Pandey and the vicious assault of her male companion, which occurred in a moving bus on the Delhi streets during the night of 16 December 2012.[8] The sadistic attack triggered national and international outrage, with protestors demanding an end to the culture of pervasive sexism and violence against women. While at one level the protests were similar to those responding to the Cologne attacks, in which outrage was directed against migrants,[9] they were also distinct from them in a number of respects. They signalled both deep anger and exhaustion with a profoundly misogynistic culture that enables women to be ogled, groped, molested, stalked, threatened, bullied and harassed while traversing public space, using public transport, or otherwise spending time outside the home pursuing everyday activities. Thus, the protests represented a defiant demand for the recognition of women's rights not only concerning public safety, but also in relation to bodily integrity and sexual autonomy. They also vociferously confronted the entrenched understanding of women's rights as located exclusively within a familial framework and upon an outdated notion of 'Indian womanhood' – a cultural archetype and historical assumption that all Indian women should unswervingly align with the classical image of the female as perennially self-sacrificing, obedient, malleable, dutiful, honourable, heterosexual, marriage-oriented and, most importantly, chaste.[10] The protests provided a thorough challenge to and repudiation of calcified conventional understandings of 'Indian womanhood' and its accompanying stereotyped assumptions about female and male, femininity and masculinity. Holding aloft placards that declared 'I am not just your mother, daughter, sister or wife. I am a citizen. I demand equal rights', some demonstrators overtly distanced themselves from customary perceptions of what it means to be subject to the 'Indian cultural values' that have shackled women's freedom.

At the same time, the protests also represented a sharp shift in the direction of a neoliberal political rationality that is increasingly characterizing and shaping the terms of gender within India, as well as within the global context and the international legal arena. Jyoti Pandey's parents, who came from a lower income bracket, sold their land to support her desire to become an educated professional; she, in turn, had intended to support the education of her younger siblings once she began earning enough. The image of an aspiring Indian woman creating a valid, hard-earned place for herself within a sexist national order – which is now also linked to a global economic order – marked a significant moment in the inscription of a new generation within the neoliberal schema of gender, and the foregrounding of the *femme economicus*. Pandey was perceived as embodying the aspirations of millions of such women.[11]

The government responded to the protests by enacting a series of reforms focused exclusively on the criminal law. These included provision for the death penalty where rape resulted in the death or maiming of the victim, the strengthening of law enforcement machinery and increased surveillance on public transport.[12] However, the government refused recommendations to remove the marital rape exemption from the criminal law and to do away with colonial and Victorian provisions concerning the outraging of a woman's modesty and chastity, which reflected a dominant nationalist view that equated Indian women's virtue with the 'honour' of the nation itself.[13] The new legal edifice focused primarily on security. It left gender dualisms intact – that is, the fixed categorization of what constitutes a 'man' and what constitutes a 'woman' – and it reinforced intractable gender stereotypes, where women are seen as passive and vulnerable, as victims and as subservient repositories of 'Indian culture', whereas men dominate as either patriarchs, perpetrators, protectors or custodians. A spate of measures targeting women's mobility and freedom were also promoted at local and state levels, and included allegations that women were 'inviting' rape by 'flaunting' their sexuality through personal practices such as wearing Western clothing and adopting Western patterns of sociality.[14]

The gruesome Delhi attack also became the subject of a documentary entitled *India's Daughters* (2015), which was made by a little-known UK-based filmmaker called Leslie Udwin.[15] The film includes lengthy interviews with one of the convicted rapists/killers, who justifies the fatal violence of his group on the basis of the woman's dress and behaviour and the fact she was out late at night with a man – which, for the rapists, was apparently sufficient proof of her promiscuity and immorality. Igniting furious controversy, the filmmaker's 'whiteness' and gender were noted in conjunction with strong criticism that the film 'denigrated' Indian men and concerns that it would simply reinforce stereotypes of them as 'barbaric' and 'misogynists'.[16] In this sense, the film was seen as an affront to the Indian nation, laden with 'patriarchal undertones' and essentially depicting India as a 'place of ignorance and brutality toward women'.[17] The film was ultimately banned, partly for the reason that it posed a law and order problem. Somewhat problematically, the ban was supported by at least one segment of the Indian feminist movement, which objected to the 'white woman's saviour complex' and the civilizing mission purportedly embodied by the film.

The responses to the Delhi rape, much like those to the Cologne assaults, demonstrate how gender can be taken up by discourses that have little to do with women's rights – in this instance, sexual violence. Instead, gender was incorporated into three parallel modalities: first, a security discourse combined with neoliberal rationalities; second, a nationalist narrative that valorizes tradition and is opposed to external intervention; and third, the configurations of what is perceived as a new kind of gender imperialism.

The compelling question that arises from these two sets of narratives is: how did these appalling episodes of sexual violence come to be articulated within the discourses of security and sexual surveillance, nationalism and cultural identity, and also displaced onto a First/Third World, 'us and them' divide? More specifically, it compels us to ask why and how decades of women's human rights advocacy has produced outcomes moving in the direction of unfreedom rather than freedom?

This chapter discusses how the stability of gender concepts and gender categories – prioritized as integral to gender rights advocacy in international human rights law (IHRL) – are maintained partly through appeals to the state for redress, and partly through an overwhelming focus on violence against women (VAW) and the criminal justice framework. I use the term 'gender' interchangeably with 'woman'/ 'women' largely to reflect the practice in IHRL, where 'gender' has been used as a synonym. Women's rights advocacy is directed at the state to demand redress and protection, primarily in the form of carceral measures, which in turn translates into a general tightening of the sexual security regime in accordance with national and cultural imperatives. This carceral vision is also embedded within a neoliberal paradigm that views VAW as an obstruction to women's participation in the market, with the market epitomizing the desired coalescence of subjectivity, choice and economic agency – crucial variables in the calculus of liberal freedom.

In this deeper reading of rights, attention should be drawn to the historical co-optation of gender to serve the political ends of imperialism and colonialism, through the discursive construction of the powerless and victimized Third World woman. This history in part explains the dominance of the script of violence in women's rights advocacy within the realm of international human rights.[18] The foregrounding of this violence helps make the case for categorizing women as victims who are unfree and require saving and empowerment.[19] This focus reproduces the first two avatars of the subject that figure in the scholarship on liberalism and human rights discussed in Chapter 1 – that is, the abject powerless subject and the powerful subject. It is my contention that women's human rights advocacy on sexual violence has partly contributed to a reaffirmation of the dualistic and heteronormative categories of gender and sexuality, and has also strengthened the policing of these categories, which have been displaced onto a First/Third World divide. The reproduction and preservation of these categories within the liberal fishbowl becomes a justification for the establishment of security regimes and militaristic interventions which have increasingly come to frame women's human rights, and where apparent freedom from the threat of hostile, unintelligible, irrational 'Others' – the third avatar of the subject – is, in fact, achieved through the imposition of modalities of unfreedom.

The sexual and cultural dichotomies permeating the narratives of nation states deeply inform and influence the vocabulary of gender rights advocacy. I illustrate this argument by tracing the work that gender does in international human rights advocacy, specifically in the areas of sexuality rights and anti-trafficking, as well as gender, peace and security.

The analysis explains the outcomes of the Cologne and Delhi violence, clarifying how such interventions are moving inexorably in the direction of *less* socio-sexual freedom for women, *increased* regulation of gender and *more* vigilant surveillance of women's sexual conduct, as well as of the presence of the undisciplined 'Other'.

UNPACKING GENDER, SEX AND SEXUALITY IN HUMAN RIGHTS ADVOCACY

Since the 1990s, the scholarship on gender in international law has been prolific.[20] While prior to the 1990s feminists prioritized the goal of gender equality and directed their efforts towards greater inclusion of women in all domains, in the early 1990s their primary focus shifted to addressing VAW. The same period also witnessed the emergence of more critical and postcolonial feminist legal voices. These critical positions have drawn attention to the structural biases in international law (IL) more generally, noting how women's inequality has been positioned as either being outside the remit of IL or included on terms that reproduce both gender and cultural stereotypes, as well as the limited emancipatory effects of IHRL for women more specifically.[21] The critical, feminist and activist objective, then, was to advocate for an overall restructuring of IL parameters to further accommodate women's rights, rather than to struggle for greater inclusion within the skewed existing arrangements, and to shape interventions that could resist collusion with abusive power structures while supporting the development of new understandings of state responsibility.[22] However, it was no easy task to challenge the foundations of IL and its modes of operation, and such efforts continue to meet considerable resistance.[23] As Buss and Manji have argued, 'international lawyers may not change *what* they do or *how* they do it, but they now seem willing to tolerate feminists at their side *as* they do it'.[24]

Feminist legal scholarship has unpacked the normative/naturalized assumptions on which the categories of gender, sex and sexuality are based. These include interrogation of the following: gender dualism and the idea that there are only two biologically distinct genders – male and female; gender hierarchy, and the assumption that women are naturally weak and vulnerable, and entirely dependent on – and the property of – men who are cast as their protectors, breadwinners and saviours; sex as a natural, physiological and stable category; and sexuality as essentialized and presumptively based on reproductive heterosexuality. The scholarship has specifically struggled to dislodge these categories from the vicelike grip of the 'real', 'authentic' or 'natural' – conceptualizations that have reproduced gender stereotypes and invited protectionist responses which continue to treat women as vulnerable, weak, victimized and incapable.

Significant inroads have been made in articulating gender as a social construction and in exposing the gendered nature of law – in terms of procedure, substance and its differential impact on women. This understanding has enabled feminists to challenge a broad range of issues including discrimination and violence in the home, sexual violence and harassment, and inequality and sex discrimination in the workplace. However, there remains a constant risk of interventions falling into and reproducing the biological traps that cause gender to become fixed and frozen. And in the international legal arena, where the term 'gender' has been increasingly deployed within human rights advocacy and by UN institutions,[25] the normative inscriptions of the category of gender remain largely unchallenged.

Similarly, there have been persistent feminist challenges to understandings of sex and sexuality as natural and physiological. The dominant narrative of gender in IL more generally, and in IHRL more specifically, is based on the reiterated idea that biological sex is a stable, anatomical, natural category, and that gender is a social construction which can be altered and manipulated. The theoretical sex/gender binary has reinforced the conventional understanding of sex/sexuality as a purely biological category, and thus of selfhood as inextricably bound up with personal physiology. It has further privileged a specific form of sexuality – that is, reproductive heterosexuality – as superior, 'natural', and desirable, relegating all deviations from this norm to an inferior and/or 'unnatural', 'abnormal' status.

Challenges to the idea of sex and sexuality as natural, physiological categories initially emerged in the writings of radical/dominance/power feminists, such as Catharine MacKinnon.[26] Her central argument is that the differences between men and women are instituted by an exercise of power through which sexuality is entirely defined and dominated by men, and where women are subordinated, oppressed and disadvantaged through male dominance. Gender is thus a product of the way in which sexuality is constructed as a form of power, quite specifically through the patriarchal oppression of women and their sexuality. This argument contends not only that the very culture and substance of law is gendered, but also that notions of neutrality and objectivity are, in fact, based on male experiences and a male point of view. From this perspective, sex – that is, the body – is treated as the primary site for female subordination and viewed as an ever available, easily accessible terrain for all modes of ideological, social and cultural inscription. This position has had an overwhelming influence on women's rights advocacy strategies, which have been directed almost exclusively at combating sexual violence, including rape, pornography, sexual harassment and prostitution.

POSTSTRUCTURAL, QUEER AND POSTCOLONIAL CRITIQUES

Poststructural, queer and postcolonial feminist critiques have further troubled the categories of gender, sex and sexuality, as well as the continued prevalence of gender dualism and the idea of sexuality as the central site of women's oppression. A significant early critique initiated more than two decades ago by poststructuralist feminist scholar Judith Butler interrogated the overly deterministic position of radical/dominance/power feminists, which conflated sexuality and gender, and limited the possibility of theorizing sexuality outside of gender difference.[27] Butler's work theorizes sex not as the natural manifestation of the body's innate physiological drives, but as a discursive and cultural production made existent in and through the modality of gender.[28] Butler casts the givens of gender into a new mould: as performance, or a set of conditioned re-enactments that simultaneously involves a constant re-experiencing of meanings socially attached to it.[29] Gender is thus a scripted construct: a seemingly predictable yet equivocal apparatus through which sex is *produced* and rendered as fixed and incontrovertible – that is, as 'pre-discursive' and 'natural'/'normal'.[30]

Drawing upon Foucault's notions of disciplinary and regulatory power, Butler argues that sex operates as a norm whose regulatory power 'produces the bodies it governs'.[31] Through a 'stylized repetition of acts' that congeal over time, gender is an effect of discourse and performance.[32] And this performance has normative effects through repetition, reiteration and exclusion. This argument rejects the distinction between sex as natural and sexuality/gender as socially constructed, but rather views sex as a product of the discourses of gender and sexuality and, in this sense, as denoting the impossibility of exercising agency outside of these sets of discursive practices.[33]

Relating this argument to the specific context of law, Margaret Davies argues that neither sex nor gender are natural.[34] Rather than referring to the idea of law as gendered, she refers to law as sexing and heterosexing its subjects, thus exposing its heteronormative moorings and marking a move away from the sex/gender distinction, the naturalness and immutability of which are disavowed. These positions resonate with Foucault's critique of the understanding of political power primarily in terms of sovereignty exercised by the various components of a nation state.[35] As discussed in Chapter 2, Foucault argues that this account of the functioning of power disguises the minute and intimate ways in which it is deployed – the capillary operations that infiltrate the personal, and influence the constitution of the subject.[36]

Subsequent developments in queer theory have built on Butler's analysis and have sought to more comprehensively challenge concepts of gender, sex and sexuality, with a view to creating space for more polymorphous and pluralistic genders, sexes and sexualities.[37] They have argued that these concepts are fractured and contingent, and have sought to fully disengage sex/gender from its biological moorings. Efforts to envisage the sex/gender binary as a fully social category, and to dislodge the naturalized and universalized hegemonies in which this binary has been – and continues to be – embedded, seek to push back against protectionist representations and responses that are built on gender, sexual and cultural stereotypes.[38] The re-conceptualizing and reimaging of the entire category of sex/gender as fluid and fluctuating rather than based on an asymmetrical gender dualism remains crucial to confronting the tenacious grip of biological determinism as an explanation for women's subordination (and male dominance), as well as countering the constant re-emergence of protectionist and paternalistic responses to women and developing understandings of how gender, sex and sexuality operate as technologies of power.

Postcolonial feminist critiques have similarly outlined not only how male and female bodies have been overwhelmingly understood within the human rights discourse as naturally different, but also how they have been consistently displaced onto a First/Third World divide. Colonial understandings of the gendered 'Other' are constructed by equating tradition and antiquity with primitiveness and libidinal aggression – a perspective central to the colonizers' moral judgements about the native subject and his treatment of women. This equation served to reinforce civilizational differences and to inscribe the cultural superiority of the West, both of which remain highly potent ideas in the postcolonial era. Non-European societies were, and continue to be, treated as objects of knowledge to be reconstituted through various techniques, including law, and made comprehensible to the West. This knowledge was informed by liberal definitions of colonial masculinity, femininity, heteronormativity, culture and historical difference, in addition to liberal postulations of what and who constitutes the universal subject.[39] These arguments were deployed to facilitate the continuation of colonial rule through gender, as well as to manage and regulate the native population. Civilizational maturity or achievement became a prerequisite to legal entitlements and other state-bestowed benefits.[40]

Liberal imperialism mobilized the mission of empire as a disciplining and civilizing tool through which gender, sexuality and culture were sutured together as key sites for structuring the contest between the colonial power and the native subject. As observed elsewhere in this book, colonial attempts to outlaw harmful cultural practices – characterized by Spivak as white men 'saving brown women from brown men' – were as much about establishing the civilizational and cultural supremacy of the West as they were a justification for denying self-rule to the backward and/or barbaric native subject.[41] Postcolonial feminism emerged from the politics of the colonial encounter and its aftermath – namely, the global wave of decolonization that followed the Second World War. This position addresses the manner in which liberation is advanced through the discourse of liberal democracy, and plays out specifically within the context of women's human rights and a global feminism informed centrally by the '"moral superiority" of American geopolitical discourse'.[42] This process 'construct[s] "American" feminists as saviors and rescuers of "oppressed women" elsewhere within a "global" economy run by a few powerful states'.[43] It is an approach that reinstates liberal selfhood at the cost of obscuring heterogeneity and structural inequality, and which retains human rights as a virtuous technology of rescue and emancipation.

These critiques expose and illustrate the governance work being conducted by gender, historically, since the period of the colonial encounter – where economic global expansionism was not only coupled with a civilizing mission, but also a rescue mission. In contemporary women's rights advocacy, interventions regarding gender also involve an intervention on existing racial, religious and sexual norms and prevailing civilizational discourses. Interrogating the idea of pre-existing subjectivities awaiting emancipation and affirmation through the liberal paradigm of gender and sexuality rights exposes how rights discourses are implicated in the construction and inscription of these very identities, and highlights the cultural and civilizational hierarchy that continues to inform contemporary women's rights advocacy – which thus materializes as a governance project.

Although contemporary poststructural, queer and postcolonial scholarship has problematized the categories of gender, sex and sexuality, women's human rights advocacy continues to operate primarily along the fraught sex/gender binary, with an apparent acceptance of traditional gender dualisms. Re-imagination of gender, sex and sexuality entirely outside of biological and naturalized embeddedness has found little traction in the international legal arena. Biological explanations persist, which not only restore gender dualisms and reinforce gender stereotypes, but also ensure that several closeted forms of sexuality and categories of people who do not adhere to or fall into the rigidly defined categories of gender, sex and sexuality are excluded from protection.[44] Similarly, the unmasking of colonial strategies, which have been integral to the structural formations of gender vis-à-vis reformist interventions on behalf of 'native' women, has not shaken the commitment of human rights to the sex/gender binary and its accompanying racial and civilizational underpinnings. There remains considerable resistance to the ambivalences produced by these critiques in respect of those for whom the sex/gender binary (as well as racial and civilizational hierarchy) is axiomatic.

Women's human rights advocacy has embraced gender, sex and sexuality in ways that have not been unequivocally emancipating or liberating for women. A protectionist approach towards women – coupled with biological determinism and dualistic understandings of gender – has retained its tenacious grip on this advocacy. While this development is evident in the context of several issues pertaining to women's rights, including gender equality and the gendered 'Other', which I examine in Chapter 4,[45] the focus of my discussion in the remainder of this chapter is the campaigns pursued by women's human rights advocates, which target VAW.

GOVERNANCE FEMINISM, SECURITY DISCOURSE AND CAMPAIGNS TARGETING VIOLENCE AGAINST WOMEN

In the international human rights arena, freedom in contemporary gender advocacy has been largely framed within the logic of campaigns confronting VAW. The turning point came at the 1993 Vienna World Conference on Human Rights, when the human rights community recognized that violence against women in the home or private sphere should be subject to human rights scrutiny.[46] Accordingly, the Vienna Declaration stressed the significance of eliminating VAW, including 'all forms of sexual harassment, exploitation and trafficking in women',[47] and recognized that '[v]iolations of the human rights of women in situations of armed conflict are violations of the fundamental principles of international human rights and humanitarian law'.[48] While the 1994 Cairo Conference on Population and Development, the 1995 Beijing World Conference for Women and the adoption of the 1999 Optional Protocol to the Convention on the Elimination of All Forms of Discrimination against Women have been important milestones for women's human rights,[49] the proliferation of resolutions and declarations addressing sexual violence against women has received the most attention.[50]

Anti Sex-Trafficking Interventions

As discussed earlier, states have responded to the recognition of sexual violence in IHRL largely through an overall strengthening of the law and order agenda and a tighter focus on criminal justice provisions. A carceral vision has been acutely evident in the area of anti-trafficking interventions, where intensification of border controls, raid-and-rescue operations by law enforcement and a zero-tolerance campaign aimed at targeting individuals engaged in sex trafficking are among the dominant responses by the state.[51] In the context of anti-trafficking interventions undertaken in the 1990s and the first decade of the twenty-first century, gender continues to be primarily aligned with victimization, vulnerability and sexual oppression. The Protocol to Prevent, Suppress and Punish Trafficking in Persons, especially Women and Children (UN Trafficking Protocol) illustrates how the discourse of IHRL is complicit in the constitution of the trafficked subject, as well as how freedom visualized by activists in relation to the trafficked subject is aligned with a criminal justice and law and order agenda. The Protocol was specifically attached to the UN Convention on Transnational Organized Crime, which falls under the remit of the UN Office on Drugs and Crime (UNODC).[52] The definition of trafficking under the Protocol is arguably intended to cover a broad range of activities, including forced labour and services. While the definition is gender neutral and extends beyond the specific issue of prostitution, the document retains a core focus on prostitution and violence against women in the broader public arena, where freedom is largely seen as an outcome of law enforcement, enhanced border security, prosecution and the criminal justice system – processes inscribed as the primary methods by which to protect the human rights of persons who are trafficked.

Consistent with such anti-trafficking campaigns, which have become central to women's rights advocacy, a number of states have been moving towards what is described as the 'Nordic model', which criminalizes the clients of sex workers and various other aspects of the sex industry.[53] It is well known that, in this model, the sex worker is recognized only as a victim to be rescued. Critiques of this position highlight the 'victimization and rescue' mentality that informs anti-trafficking campaigns, which frequently focus on representing Third World women or women from the Global South exclusively as victims sold into the sex industry.

Thus, a carceral and criminal justice framework becomes central to addressing the problem of trafficking.

Several larger projects are served by the focus on anti-trafficking in relation to prostitution, which specifically targets sex workers and migrants. This approach has been supported and promoted, in part, by a specific strand of feminism that classifies and targets *all* sex work, voluntary *and* involuntary, as a form of violence against women perpetrated through the conduit of trafficking. For some women's rights advocates, freedom lies in dismantling the very structure of the sex industry and in erasing the sex worker as a legible or eligible category of person in law, or making the sex worker only eligible in the identity of a victim. This paradigm encourages criminal law to sweep up any remnants of the industry, the dismantling of which serves to reinforce both governing norms and the moral crusade against sex work. These interventions have become a magnet for other actors and stakeholders who view *all* voluntary and coerced sex work/workers as 'sinful' – a position that dovetails specifically with the moral topographies of well-funded evangelical Christian 'humanitarian' organizations and individuals involved in projects to rehabilitate victims trafficked for this purpose.[54]

The entrenchment of anti-trafficking interventions in the criminal law can be traced through earlier international legal instruments that focused on transnational trafficking and, quite specifically, on criminalizing the trafficking of women and young girls for the purposes of prostitution.[55] While the turn to criminal law to redress human rights violations has been more evident in other areas of law since the early 1990s,[56] in the specific area of trafficking, criminal prosecution and punishment have been central features for the past century.[57] These interventions claim to emancipate women through the elimination of trafficking, but have instead further entrenched the control and regulation of women's cross-border movements, while also establishing a precedent for characterizing female transnational migration as invariably forced and for the purpose of prostitution and/or sexual slavery. In the contemporary context, an important feature of anti-trafficking interventions is how feminists and conservatives alike share the state's construction of gender and its focus on a carceral vision that seeks to penalize men who behave badly. These seemingly politically opposed groups have a common commitment to supporting interventions that, in actuality, target, police and criminalize economically and racially marginalized populations, through an emphasis on tough border controls and the use of threats to withdraw donor funding and non-humanitarian aid in order to coerce countries into actively curtailing prostitution.

In some jurisdictions, the definition of 'trafficking' and the scope of related interventions has extended beyond sex trafficking to include a broader array of activities – such as forced labour – which do not necessarily involve any migratory movement, and which are then classified as various forms of exploitation under the generic term 'slavery'.[58] This expansion has emphasized, and been facilitated by, prosecution-oriented strategies that have focused on the accountability of individual perpetrators. These measures affect a wide range of people and provide the state with enormous power over them, as well as over their movement across borders – control, in this sense, being a central plank in liberal governance and its embrace of a security agenda. The overall trajectory is one that privileges a criminal law approach with accountability sought through prosecution – an approach that works via the reductive traditional dialectic of victim protection and offender incarceration, and which does not move in the direction of freedom. Traffickers are not the root problem – they are responding to demand from desperate people and 'helping' them, while also charging exorbitant prices and using unsafe means of transport. In the clamour to demonize traffickers, advocacy loses sight of how their prosecution is used to obscure the larger picture and to justify a host of other agendas, including carceral responses in relation to sex work and cross-border migrations. The imposition of discourses and technologies of control, such as the state security apparatus, which seem so removed from women's human rights has produced fierce rejoinders as to whether these carceral initiatives have contributed anything at all towards women's freedom, or even marginally eased the suffering of trafficked persons.[59]

Anti-trafficking interventions are also part of a larger move by states to address VAW as part of the 'second-generation' reforms that have shifted the focus from macroeconomic and financial considerations to those seeking to address the broader structural dimensions of development, including gender.[60] VAW is understood as being a barrier to women's participation in the market, including as a cheap exploitable labour resource. A specific set of prescriptions designed to promote women's participation in the market thus accompany this 'modern-day slavery' abolitionist project.[61] These strategies visualize women specifically as human capital whose potential is being impeded by gender-based violence; as a demographic, they are viewed as a significant repository and resource that needs to be unleashed as well as exploited. Importantly, this reflection upon the structural dimensions of development has not invited analysis of the reasons for cross-border migrations. The complex issue of safe migration remains at the periphery of analysis, where trafficking and migration are treated as separate spheres – despite their overlap in practice – and consciously dissociated for address under separate juridical regimes.[62] Nor have responses to the movement of women inquired into the possibility of developing local, regional and international mechanisms to address labour migration, migrant rights and ethical work practices, so that people would not be compelled to migrate for livelihood purposes. This argument is not to suggest that drawing attention to migrant rights would bring freedom; however, it *would* draw attention to the larger global issue of neoliberal markets, which are often sequestered from human rights scrutiny, even though these processes remain in plain sight.[63]

The central strategy of using criminal law is embedded in the neoliberal agenda, where state intervention is limited to the penal sphere to ensure security in the interests of market stability and efficiency.[64] These interventions divert attention from the deeper truth underlying the political accommodation of voluntary and/or involuntary migration – particularly the national and international need for a large, stable, malleable labour force, which includes the terrain of sexual labour. Therefore, these measures are ultimately less about women and more about means to other ends. Opposition to sex trafficking is thus presented as a modernizing, sanitizing project. Solutions to the problem of violence against women are articulated in terms of the restoration of the heterosexual familial order, law making and physical control, and individual perpetrator accountability – all viewed as means for creating a stable economic environment that enables women's freedom to participate in the market. At one level, women rescued from sex trafficking are reintegrated into their original familial spaces, or incarcerated for their own protection. At another, the solutions are imagined in corporate and consumer terms – in other words, an economic logic becomes a significant motive for securing sexual freedom, alleviating sexual trauma, resettling uprooted lives and bringing about gender justice. Under this logic, rescued women are encouraged to set up small-scale business enterprises to manufacture goods that are advertised as having been produced by 'traffick[ed] victims'.[65] The increasing obsession with national security, law and order modalities, surveillance and border policing serves not only as a deterrent to traffickers and a form of protection for the trafficked victim, but also to protect advocacy-linked special interests in the context of globalization and free-market ideology.

A carceral vision remains embedded in a neo-colonial as well as neoliberal paradigm. The analysis does not suggest that the antidote rests in simply shifting to a focus on rights that promote mobility, freedom of movement, and equality – which already exist in international and domestic laws. Such rights do not in and of themselves either disrupt the normative assumptions about female autonomy and agency, or unmask the broader agendas that are being advanced through anti-trafficking interventions. This does, however, partly illustrate how an entire regulatory regime of anti-trafficking interventions – that focus on clandestine profiteering networks of handlers, traffickers and smugglers – can be established *without* tackling the root causes behind exploitation of and violence against women, which include the failure to formulate effective migration strategies as well as to challenge conservative sexual morality. Such a focus removes or hides the responsibility of the state, the market and neoliberal ideology, as well as of sex work abolitionists, in the production of these clandestine networks. The interventions depend upon a law and order, criminal justice approach; on the objectification of women, viewed simultaneously as victims and as sinful contaminants; and on appeals to states for redress – all of which contribute to a legal edifice that may appear to support women's freedom, but which, in fact, could be bypassing the core problem altogether.

This misperception does not bring the trafficked woman any closer to *her* goal of freedom. She remains immobilized within the state-cum-advocacy panoptic: one that constructs her almost exclusively as a victim, controls her sexual autonomy and facilitates a host of exploitative agendas that have little to do with her freedom. Moreover, the focus on criminal law has not in the least discouraged irregular movement; on the contrary, it has strengthened the operations of an illegal, transnational, transcultural migrant mobility circuit, which continues to facilitate the movement of people determined and desperate to move, and pushes them into situations of increasing vulnerability, exploitation and abuse.[66] The central point here is that a human rights regime which protects the normative arrangements of gender and sexuality by disentitling the sex worker and the migrant – thus reinscribing their precarity – does so in the first instance by rendering their very livelihood as per se constituting violence against women, and in the latter instance by projecting and stigmatizing them as a threat to the social cohesion, security and law and order of the receiving state. This disentitlement thus sustains the dominant exclusionary rationales of the liberal paradigm, as well as the normative prescriptions that constitute 'fishbowl' freedom.

Gender, Peace and Security

Similarly, the continued focus on sexual violence – from a perspective based on fixed and static representations of gender – continues to inform women's human rights advocacy in relation to gender, peace and security. Dualistic understandings of gender have informed the United Nations

Security Council Resolutions 1325 ('Resolution 1325')[67] and 1820 ('Resolution 1820')[68] on women, peace and security.[69] The three principal features of Resolution 1325 call for greater participation of women in conflict prevention, resolution and peace processes;[70] for renewed attention to and focus on women as victims of violence, particularly sexual violence in the context of armed conflict;[71] and for 'gender mainstreaming' in all activities of the UN and member states pertaining to their conflict-related operations.[72] Resolution 1820 focuses on the issue of violence against women, particularly on sexual violence against women in the context of armed conflict, and enumerates the responsibilities and commitments of the UN, parties to a conflict and member states.[73] Resolution 1325 has been lauded as a landmark political moment. Not only have the resolutions offered a route for gender advocacy to be both heard and addressed,[74] but they have also served to shore up the Security Council's credentials on gender.[75]

Embedded in Resolution 1325, its accompanying resolutions and the scaffolding of UN documents and mechanisms that enable them is the notion that women are inherently peace loving, speak 'in a different voice' – a gentler, more modulated tone – than men and are innately more committed to the pursuit of peace and conflict resolution. These conventional and culturally sanctioned assumptions are strewn across the field of IL more generally, and the women's human rights industry more specifically.[76] Women are not only portrayed as more peaceful than men, but are also – in the statements surrounding these resolutions – described as being 'better equipped than men to prevent or resolve [conflict]', and as having for generations played a crucial role in preserving social order when communities have collapsed.[77]

In the process, women's human rights are increasingly absorbed into the hegemonic discourse of security, militarism and war that often has little to do with the realization of freedom. The securitization of gender continues to be grafted onto existing power structures and inscribed into a gender binary, where gender is equated with women, and women remain essentially differentiated from men. The persistent representation of women as victims in need of protection and men as either perpetrators or rescuers/custodians continues within the gender, peace and security initiatives. In the process, the military and security apparatus within which this issue is addressed increasingly becomes the overarching paradigm for taking up women's rights. Freedom comes to be articulated within an earlier discourse of protectionism in relation to gender and, within this rhetoric, women remain objects needing protection. Quite specifically, an earlier version of American feminism based on an 'ethic of care' has been retrieved, and is now centrally deployed to characterize women's moral perspectives and to frame the discourse of gender in women's rights advocacy.[78]

The paradoxical incorporation of women's capacity and role as empathetic peace makers into the coercion and militarism of security discourse has at one level enhanced the value attached to women's human rights within the larger UN discourse, especially as the move has the backing of the Security Council and its most powerful members.[79] At the same time, the resolution reproduces responses to women's human rights. The work that gender does in the context of peace and security provides a clearer understanding of how gender, as a category/sphere for intervention, serves to enhance security as well as to provide a justification for militarism and war, since women are presented as in need of rescue and protection. For example, the military invasion of Afghanistan in 2003 was glazed with a call, supported by feminists among others, to rescue the 'Other' woman from the barbaric 'Other' man (an issue further explored in Chapter 4). The rhetoric used to legitimize the call for militarism presents women as being genetically conditioned to be peaceful, inclined to promote peace and in need of protection from violent, culturally regressive 'Other' male predators. A broader and newer definition of security emerges in the context of the Security Council resolutions, extending beyond existent frameworks, and frenetically concerned with individual and group security. This definition continues to encase women within a static relationship of protector/protected, masculine/feminine, male/female, under an umbrella binary of (liberal) 'us' and (illiberal) 'them', which obscures the actual insecurities and vulnerabilities of women and others in conflict and post-conflict societies.

Moreover, the political and radical claims of women directly involved in conflict on equal terms with men – as, for example, armed combatants, members of rebel militia cadres or guerrilla groups – remain unacknowledged, unaddressed or dismissed in the very terms of peace promotion. There is no questioning or challenging of the very basis on which peace, security or the category of 'woman' is understood.[80] Examples of those with such agency include the female guerrilla fighters in the People's Liberation Army who actively participated in the civil conflict in Nepal from 1996 to 2006; or female Tamil Tiger soldiers in Sri Lanka's civil war; or those in the active battle zones of the 'war against terror', such as the Kurdish women who, in 2015, formally joined the Peshmerga as frontline soldiers to fight the Islamic State (IS); or the Yazidi women who, in 2015, audaciously refuted obscurity, domesticity and traumatic displacement to organize themselves into all-female squads, wearing battle fatigues and training to defend their communities from the ravening bloodlust of IS jihad.

More significantly, in the aftermath of war, peace *itself* comes to be structured alongside a wholesale restoration of normative gender and familial arrangements. In this scheme, women participants in conflict are 'rehabilitated' through training in domestic skills and reintegration into the normative structures of gender and family, whereas fighters – assumed in most instances to be men – are rewarded with positions of authority in new governing structures, including the military, police and security apparatus. Local security and society is rcordered in the image of liberal governance. The newly restored peace becomes an enabling condition for a reinstatement of the normative orders of gender based on privileged hegemonic masculinities; for the re-subordination of gender, equated entirely with women, through a protectionist lens; and for the restored state and gender apparatus to welcome, and embrace, liberal market forces. And the unprecedented expansion of the Security Council's power in this arrangement is further enhanced and strengthened in the name of gender, peace and security, in which women have a prescribed role. The justification for this framing is reminiscent of the logic of 'Empire lite', a new colonialism that celebrates global hegemony in the form of free markets, human rights and democracy – the principal architecture of 'fishbowl' freedom. It is a humanitarian vision of empire, where rule of law rationales become part of a technocratic enterprise that incorporates gender/gender activism and women's rights in thorough accordance with the diktat of neoliberal govermentality.

The portrayal of women largely as idealistic non-aggressors is an example of how gender is inscribed within the international legal regime in a way that reflexively reinforces the standard framework of gender advocacy, without any real scrutiny or critical reworking of the standard model of 'woman'. Nor do these interventions play any role in problematizing the way gender is deployed as a category that remains contingent on the traditional male/female binary, fixed and intact, a construction that enables or enhances the securitization of women's human rights.[81] The foregrounding of the vulnerable subject is, in this instance, taken up within the discourse of security, where gender is framed within the terms of a biologically determined perspective assumed to be common to all women, rather than utilized as an analytical category for interrogating the *a priori*, stereotypical assumptions of the international legal regime.[82] At the same time, the homogenizing vision of 'liberal peace', which remains the end goal of these interventions, does not accommodate any assertions of autonomy that disrupt the conventional gender order, even when evidence of such disruption is regularly produced in the theatre of war itself. As discussed, this vision takes no account of the agency of militarized women – female combatants, guerrilla fighters or suicide bombers – who fail or refuse to comply with the gender order of their own traditions and seek alternative expressions of identity and selfhood, but who are generally regarded as anomalous to this essentialist discourse.

The discussions on sex trafficking and on peace and security – both longstanding central concerns for the state and civil society in women's human rights within the wider ambit of IHRL – exemplify the particular ways in which gender, sex and sexuality have manifested in international and human rights circuits. The Security Council resolutions, like the anti-trafficking interventions, are a manifestation of what Janet Halley describes as governance feminism; they illustrate how the 'international legal order is increasingly receiving feminists into its power elites and that feminist law reform is emerging there as a formidable new source of legal ideas'.[83] Governance feminism maintains the idea that gender operates along the binary of man/woman, male/female, masculine/feminine; that it is committed to a theory of subordination, where woman/female/feminine are subordinated to men/male/masculine; and also that feminists carry a brief for women, femininity, the female/feminine gender.[84] In this description, then, the gender category 'woman' remains distinct, stable and closed. Within this arrangement, women's human rights manifest as a form of governance feminism, especially when the discourse coincides with the linked parameters of the neoliberal market, securitization and imperialistic ambition.[85]

Governance feminism finds literal manifestation in the international legal regime, where gender is regulated, disciplined and managed in ways that do *not* necessarily emancipate women. While 'doing gender' enhances the 'progressive' credentials of states and non-state actors, the work that gender does and that is being done through gender tells a somewhat different story. As discussed, gender is addressed primarily through carceral measures and the criminal law, which offer and validate 'fishbowl' freedom – finite, conditional, preferential, duplicitous and, in essence, illusory. The strong focus on sexual violence and victimization has invited the state's selective engagement with feminist ideas and the pursuit of a carceral vision and, in the process, deflected attention from the broader structural, political and economic arrangements that produce violence. At the same time, the state's appropriation of gender advocacy to strengthen the security apparatus clearly serves the state's priorities, which are directed towards establishing social and political stability – partly to ensure that the market performs efficiently and optimally. In the guise of protecting women and protecting the right to free choice, state and market forces collude to ensure the political and economic regulation of the citizen-subject. The emergent narrative is a description of how the deployment of stable, solidified understandings of gender serves other larger projects of empire, neoliberalism and the free market.

RESISTANCE OR COMPLIANCE? THE POLITICAL LOCUS OF 'VIOLENCE AGAINST WOMEN' CAMPAIGNS IN INTERNATIONAL HUMAN RIGHTS LAW

I return to the discussion regarding the Cologne attacks and the Delhi rape which introduced this chapter so as to reiterate that the procession of state and non-state responses to these events was deeply influenced by the global response to VAW in IHRL. The translation of rights into a security discourse informed the interventions by various state and non-state actors in the 'Delhi rape' case, and, with the sometimes violent barring of refugee entry by border guards, acted as part of the highly racialized and paranoid response to the Cologne assaults. The broader structural causes that serve as a trigger for VAW either remain unaddressed through these paternalistic and culturally claustrophobic interventions or are addressed in purely economic terms, where the remedies are seen to lie in market access and participation – a logic that further entrenches and exacerbates the conditions of social inequality, marginality and disempowerment.

The exponential increase in security, sexual surveillance and law and order has augmented the muscular power of the state to regulate and discipline the sexual behaviour of its citizens in the direction of *fewer* rights, *more* surveillance and *less* freedom. The state uses crisis, such as the Cologne and Delhi rape protests, to extend the tentacles of criminal law into women's personal lives and intensify its powers of regulation and surveillance; moreover, it does so by building upon the existing legal edifice, without any scrutiny or deconstruction of the normative assumptions about gender, women's vulnerability and the lack of autonomy embedded in the discriminatory sexist substrate of women's bodies as repositories of 'national honour' and integrity. Nor does it challenge the hubris underlying the assumption of superior civilizational values. It simultaneously uses these events to construct the 'Other' – whether refugee or Muslim, for example – as a threat to the liberal paradigm, and to develop interventions for expelling, incarcerating or severely restricting the unprecedented, unforeseen surge of the unruly, irrational, illegible 'Other' into the safe, sanctioned, sanitized, serene fishbowl of European space.

It is increasingly apparent that the state is utilizing carcerality as a central feature of neoliberal governance, to manage the civic insecurities, disruptions, equivocations and contradictions being produced in these neoliberal times. In the process, the language of rights is used to justify state or state-supported interventions that remain focused on security, imprisonment and identifying and executing 'solutions' to social 'problems' through criminal law. The burden of responsibility for the overall welfare of vulnerable citizen-subjects is shifted away from the state, which is complicit in producing the existing environment of insecurity and predation, and which absolves itself by providing and operating technologies of increased control over citizens' lives. Doubling back on itself like a Möbius strip, this approach does little to curtail the enactment of prevalent sexist norms and, in part, explains why so little has changed with regard to the lack of public safety for women in 'developed' Germany or 'underdeveloped' India, despite several decades of women's human rights advocacy.

It is also a fact that the security apparatus, which was strengthened by both the Cologne and the Delhi assaults, is partly propelled by market demands for an economic environment of continual stability and efficiency, and hence the need for greater policing. This apparatus becomes the means for suppressing counter-opinion, choking dissent and directly and indirectly reinforcing the rightist panopticon.[86] Such interventions serve to reinforce existent political, social and economic hegemonies, rather than to empower disenfranchised communities who are using the rights discourse to demand recognition, action and inclusion.

It must be remembered that while security, sexual surveillance, law and order and the rhetoric of rights are perceived as the primary tools to fight sexual inequality and sexual violence, this amalgam of enforcement mechanisms and activist interventions is a core feature of neoliberal governance more generally rather than a specific feature of German or Indian society, or a necessary means for responding to the criminal abrogation of purportedly superior civilizational or cultural values. The deliberate and prominent use of the security discourse deflects attention away from the dysfunctional social and economic structures that pervade many aspects of daily existence. Little attention is paid to concretely addressing the stark material deprivation that is the perennial substrate of so many women's daily lives and is opportunistically used to perpetrate violence against them. Nor does a security discourse interrogate the grossly and unapologetically sexist educational and social conditioning that nurtures specific archetypes and valorizes certain images of desirable/undesirable, 'good'/'bad' women.

Moreover, the trend in security discourse is to target men belonging to already marginalized communities – whether religious and racial minorities, migrants, those of lower caste or 'the poor' in broad terms – and displace responsibility for sexual violence onto them. These men are systematically represented and stigmatized as sociopathic deviants whose 'naturally' ignorant, misogynist, predatory treatment of women may be partly attributed to their religious, class or caste affiliations, illiteracy or poverty. The surveillance and incarceration of profiled offenders is lauded as the most effective means for having apparently ensured greater security and autonomy for women. However, state, non-state and social actors all collude to validate the sexist hegemonies, hierarchies and rhetoric that perpetuate socio-economic inequality and injustice via increasingly refined security discourses and instruments.

The categories of gender, sex and sexuality are also being managed and controlled by an aggressive neoliberal political rationality that is not confined to economic transactions, but extends and disseminates market values to *all* institutions and social actions.[87] It is an implementation strategy in which market demands for efficiency and stability are partly pursued in and through legal discourse – the latter being consciously applied as a normalizing mechanism through which citizens are rendered recognizable or non-recognizable, enfranchised or disenfranchised, variously able or less able or unable to function as economic units. As discussed in Chapter 2, differential participation in the voracious neoliberal market becomes the primary index for calibrating human worth and value, and for the bestowing of entitlements. Legal discourse, which includes the narrative of human rights, is utilized to discipline and regulate all spheres of life, including the economic life of both the powerful and the powerless. At the same time, the move towards a society of control reinforces itself through carceral means to suppress those unruly, undesirable, illegal subjects who can, sometimes – even through mere visibility – threaten the prosperity, stability and viability of the neoliberal enterprise.

One significant outcome of the way in which the market is harnessing gender to advance the neoliberal economic project, together with the framing of gender issues within a carceral vision, is that traditional gender categories continue to be reproduced as normalized, naturalized and stable. This process remains problematic, as 'gender' remains a noun – a static object of focus – rather than a performance that is normatively reproduced and reinforced. The swathe of diverse practices that constitute gender are contracted into and elided with the existing narrow understanding of 'woman' as a fixed biological category within an axiomatic sex/gender binary, as discussed earlier in this chapter. Such essentialism also operates on the formulaic assumption that the woman is always inherently vulnerable, a victim in need of rescue and protection from predatory men. This distorted logic is primarily offered as a solution within the context of sexual violence, soliciting and implementing interventions that conform to the normative gender script. Such approaches are not useful in procuring freedom for women in general, or even specific justice for the criminally violated, such as the 'Delhi rape victim', the victims of the Cologne sexual assaults or anyone else subject to gender inequality. Replicating these normative arrangements inevitably produces ahistorical, decontextualized and universalist accounts of gender. Moreover, such reiteration effectively forecloses any possibility of change in the existing patriarchal gender and sexual arrangements.

'TAKING A BREAK' FROM (ANGLO-AMERICAN) FEMINISM?

Women's groups and human rights groups have not adequately confronted the fact that advocacy, like other modalities, is being embedded in international and national legal orders, which are heavily consolidated by a top-down understanding of sovereign power. The interventions have proved restrictive and have *not* provided positive benefits for women; nor have they addressed the dispersed and disguised forms of power that have an impact on, or constitute, the reification of the term 'gender'. Halley argues that a specific thread of feminism is being co-opted within the larger agenda of IL, and is exercising considerable power in international institutions.[88]

In the specific context of IHRL, feminist activists have been forced to dilute their demands and homogenize their ideological differences in order to secure visibility, consensus and a strong critical voice in the international legal arena, where policy makers and strategists turn to feminists for 'expertise' on gender advocacy issues – thus feminism becomes a technocratic enterprise. It is no longer a means of interrogating and challenging current practices and structures – including the neoliberal political rationality that serves to perpetuate gender inequality, or indeed the very categories of 'man', 'woman', 'male', 'female', 'masculinity', 'femininity' – but rather has become a means of facilitating and legitimizing the (neo)liberal project of IHRL in the guise of addressing women's concerns. For this reason, feminism is trapped in its own recursive rhetoric and has become its own obstacle – which, as Halley proposes, may be overcome by 'taking a break' from feminism to review the role of feminism in mechanisms directed towards securing women's human rights.[89]

The call to 'take a break' is tempting in light of the perception that feminism appears to have become an obstacle in the pursuit of what are deemed as emancipatory projects. Yet several scholars have expressed concern over the implications of Halley's call to step back from the current model of gender justice and emancipation, and regarding her overestimation of feminist power within the international legal arena. Otto argues that despite substantial victories at the UN, the feminist project is losing ground.[90] She views the institutional reception of feminist ideas as part of the management of feminist ideas, which serves to divest them of their emancipatory content. She therefore prefers to represent the results of such management as 'co-option' rather than 'governance feminism', the latter of which implies that the result is desired by feminists.[91] Charlesworth further argues that governance feminism may be overstating the case, as feminist critiques of IL in the academy have been largely regarded as a frill, with such efforts remaining in a 'scholarly ghetto'.[92] At the institutional level, feminists have been engaged with normative projects largely to secure women's equality based on gender mainstreaming, but their gains have been partial and not without costs. Charlesworth argues in favour of a more sustained critical engagement, and reasserts her earlier call to pursue feminist messages through feminist methods, such as searching for the silences on gender in the international legal arena as well as highlighting how this arena excludes women's lived experiences.[93]

Other scholars object to the demoralizing and demobilizing impact of the formal call to 'take a break' from feminism, since this clearly risks ceding the hard-won terrain of gender justice to regressive forces, as well as producing other costs that are incurred not by those who make this call but those on behalf of whom the call is made. By rejecting the call, these scholars are not endorsing a narrow vision of gender, but are arguing in favour of paying more attention to the reconstructive potential of IL and human rights, which rests somewhere between resistance and compliance.[94] The debate illustrates how feminists are confronted with a dilemma posed by the possibilities of resistance and compliance, whereby they recognize that human rights excludes or marginalizes women from the human rights boardroom even as entry is sought in the hope that the project still has some potential for promoting women's rights. And, indeed, admission seems contingent on feminists speaking only with the master's voice and undertaking action only with the master's tools.

Scepticism about the potential clarities that might manifest through literalizing Halley's call to 'take a break' from feminism is important and useful, insofar as Halley's position emerges largely from an American Left tradition, and targets the American feminist Catharine MacKinnon's work as exemplifying the partiality and imperfections of feminism in law. Halley's narrative of feminism erases the specific cultural formations and colonial histories that constitute the ground upon which rights are deployed and through which rights must be procured. Instead, it valorizes the emergence of a hegemonic contemporary global (read American) feminism that, in the international legal arena, has consolidated around the issue of violence against women and the victimized, specifically 'Third World', woman's body. Since Halley's call is based largely on Anglo-American debates and context, it may be more appropriate to provincialize her call – namely, to treat it as a call to take a break from *Anglo-American* feminism.

The proliferation and reinforcement of American feminism is integral to the hegemonic imaging of 'the West', particularly the United States, as the ideal site of freedom, including women's freedom, where personal rights are a political reality; this position is systematically exported to 'the Rest' through the mechanism of IHRL. Contemporary feminism is actively complicit in the global embedding of the American imperium. In this analysis, the goal of freedom remains one of incorporating the 'Other' woman into a dominant model that is largely driven by Western feminists, and especially American feminists. The call to 'take a break' from the old certainties of feminism is helpful if read as a break from Anglo-American feminism and the colonial, racial and civilizational certainties that have and continue to shape this project. This shift should not invariably move back in the direction of human rights as holding out the possibility of freedom for women. My argument is that such a break can take us in another direction – it can help create space for feminism that emerges from elsewhere in the world and is influenced by the diverse and complex genealogies that have emanated from a colonial past. These other modalities of feminism do not assume to speak for *all* women, do not carry a brief *only* for women and do not view Anglo-American feminism as *the* solution to developing world gender injustices but, in fact, experience it as part of the problem. Postcolonial feminism is an example of how gender can be productively theorized along the intersections of gender, race, caste, ethnicity and religion. This discursive operation challenges the First/Third World divide that privileges feminist thinking from 'the West', and along which feminist advocacy, including that by and about 'the Rest', previously habitually aligned itself. At the same time, the call for such a break from Anglo-American feminism can create space for alternative understandings of gender as well as freedom, as delineated in the remainder of this book, that are not confined within the generic liberal fishbowl and its accompanying hegemonies.

Critical engagement with human rights must continue for the purpose of calibrating the work that is being done by gender in human rights advocacy, and tracking how this may have little to do with advancing women's rights and freedom and more with legitimating discriminatory governance – whether through the modality of a civilizing mission or colonial knowledge project, as in the past, or in service of neoliberal economic forces or right-wing political agendas from the contemporary moment. It is only through persistent, if not necessarily optimistic, engagement with the current discourses and instruments of gender advocacy that we might come to see what is continuously and constantly revealed, and what is just as continuously and constantly concealed, in the name of women's empowerment and freedom.

NOTES

1. Chimamanda Ngozi Adichie, *Half of a Yellow Sun* (New York: Anchor Books, 2006), p. 77.
2. On the scale of the crisis, see, for example, Elias Groll, 'A Record Year in Misery: The World Has Never Seen a Refugee Crisis This Bad', *Foreign Policy*, 18 June 2015, http://foreignpolicy.com/2015/06/18/a-record-year-in-misery-the-world-has-never-seen-a-refugee-crisis-this-bad/.
3. Harriet Sherwood, 'Polish Magazine's "Islamic Rape of Europe" Cover Sparks Outrage', *The Guardian*, 18 February 2016, www.theguardian.com/world/2016/feb/18/polish-magazines-islamic-of-europe-cover-sparks-outrage.
4. '"Charlie Hebdo": Riss imagine le petit Aylan en "tripoteur de fesses",' *Le Point*, 13 January 2016, www.lepoint.fr/societe/charlie-hebdo-riss-imagine-le-petit-aylan-en-tripoteur-de-fesses-13-01-2016-2009640_23.php.
5. Ali Behdad, 'Inhospitability, European Style: The Failures of Human Rights', in *The Postcolonial World*, eds. Jyotsna G. Singh and David D. Kim (Abingdon: Routledge, 2016), pp. 291–307.
6. Ed Adamczyk, 'New German Law Broadens Definition of Rape', *UPI*, 7 July 2016, www.upi.com/Top_News/World-News/2016/07/07/New-German-law-broadens-definition-of-rape/9361467899775/.
7. Stephanie Kirchner and Rick Noack, 'New Stricter Sexual-Assault Laws in Germany are Making Refugee Activists Uneasy', *The Washington Post*, 7 July 2016, www.washingtonpost.com/news/worldviews/wp/2016/07/07/why-stricter-sexual-assault-laws-in-germany-make-refugee-activists-uneasy/?utm_term=.62a764bc34c9.
8. Jyoti Singh Pandey and her male friend were returning home at night after watching a film at a well-known multiplex cinema in New Delhi. They waited at a bus stop on a main road for one of the city's unreliable and erratic public buses, and even tried to hail a three-wheeler auto-rickshaw, but to no avail. Eventually, a private bus with tinted windows slowed, and a youth posing as a conductor invited them aboard. Along with the driver, the bus held four other men pretending to be passengers. As the bus pulled away, a sadistic nightmare unfolded on the streets of the nation's capital. Two hours later the couple, stripped naked and bleeding, were dumped on a road near the glistening new international airport. The young woman had been brutally gang raped and had suffered traumatic

injuries as the result of penetration with an iron rod. She subsequently died of these injuries in hospital. Her friend had been gruesomely beaten by the rapists, but survived and later testified in court. The six assailants – all young, one a minor, and all from socio-economically deprived backgrounds – were swiftly arrested and jailed by the city police. One of the accused died while in prison, prior to sentencing. Four of the other accused were convicted and sentenced to death in 2013. In May 2017, the death sentences were affirmed by the Indian Supreme Court. The sixth accused was a minor at the time of the assault. He was convicted and sentenced to three years at a remand home for juveniles, in line with the legal provisions governing juveniles. He was released in December 2015 upon completion of his sentence.

9. Poulami Roychowdhury, '"The Delhi Gang Rape": The Making of International Causes', *Feminist Studies* 39, no. 1 (2013): 283–4.
10. See, for example, Pundita Ramabai Sarasvati, *The High Caste Hindu Woman* (Philadelphia, PA: Jas. B. Rodgers Printing Co., 1888). See also Manali Desai, 'Gendered Violence and India's Body Politic', *New Left Review* 99 (May/June 2016): 67–83.
11. Lakshmi Chaudhry, 'Rape in the "New India,"' *The Nation*, 16 January 2013, www.thenation.com/article/rape-new-india/. For a critical and nuanced analysis of this perception, see Roychowdhury, 'The Delhi Gang Rape'.
12. The definition of rape under the existing law was expanded to include acts that were not confined to vaginal penetration by the penis against a woman's will: Criminal Law (Amendment) Act, 2013 (India), s. 9, amending the Indian Penal Code, 1860 (IPC), ss. 375, 376, 376A, 376B, 376C, 376 D. The addition of the death penalty clause seems somewhat superfluous given that rape resulting in death is tantamount to murder, which is already a capital offence under sections 302 and 303 of the IPC.
13. The government largely ignored the findings of a committee constituted shortly after the Delhi rape, which recommended repeal of the marital rape exception in the IPC, and also sought to address gender outside the constraints of familiality through rights to bodily integrity and sexual autonomy: see J.S. Verma, Leila Seth, and Gopal Subramanium, *Report of the Committee on Amendments to Criminal Law* (New Delhi: Centre for Social Research, 2013).
14. Palash Ghosh, 'Delhi Gang-Rape: Right-Wing Leader Claims Sex Crimes Caused by Western Influences, Urban Living', *International Business Times*, 1 August 2013, www.ibtimes.com/delhi-gang-rape-right-wing-leader-claims-sex-crimes-caused-western-influences-urban-living-999992.
15. *India's Daughters*, film, dir. Leslee Udwin (United Kingdom: Berta Film, 2015).
16. Amrita Ibrahim, '*India's Daughter* and How Not to Talk about Rape', *Dissent*, 19 March 2015, www.dissentmagazine.org/blog/indias-daughter-and-how-not-to-talk-about-rape
17. Ellen Barry, 'Broadcast of India Gang Rape Documentary Is Banned by Court', *The New York Times*, 4 March 2015, www.nytimes.com/2015/03/05/world/asia/indian-court-bans-broadcast-of-documentary-on-delhi-gang-rape.html.
18. Ratna Kapur, 'The Tragedy of Victimization Rhetoric: Resurrecting the "Native" Subject in International/Post-Colonial Feminist Legal Politics', *Harvard Human Rights Journal* 15 (Spring 2002): 1–37; Kristin Bumiller, 'Victims in the Shadow of the Law: A Critique of the Model of Legal Protection', *Signs* 12, no. 3 (1987): 421–39.
19. See generally Makau Mutua, 'Savages, Victims, and Saviors: The Metaphor of Human Rights', *Harvard International Law Journal* 42, no. 1 (2001): 201–45.
20. The most important early work was Hilary Charlesworth, Christine Chinkin and Shelley Wright, 'Feminist Approaches to International Law', *The American Journal of International Law* 85, no. 4 (1991): 613–45. This was followed by a rapid proliferation of scholarship on feminism and international law. For an excellent compilation of these seminal works see Otto, ed., *Gender Issues and Human Rights*.
21. See, for example, Sari Kouvo and Zoe Pearson, eds., *Feminist Perspectives on Contemporary International Law* (Oxford: Hart, 2011); Karen Engle, 'International Human Rights and Feminisms: When Discourses Keep Meeting', in *International Law: Modern Feminist Approaches*, eds. Doris Buss and Ambreena Manji (Oxford: Hart, 2005), pp. 47–66. See

generally Geeta Chowdhry and Sheila Nair, eds., *Power, Postcolonialism and International Relations: Reading Race, Gender, and Class* (New York: Routledge, 2002).

22. Charlesworth, Chinkin and Wright, 'Feminist Approaches to International Law', p. 644.
23. Hilary Charlesworth, 'Cries and Whispers: Responses to Feminist Scholarship in International Law', *Nordic Journal of International Law* 65, nos 3–4 (1996): 557–68.
24. Doris Buss and Ambreena Manji, 'Introduction', in *International Law: Modern Feminist Approaches*, eds. Doris Buss and Ambreena Manji (Oxford: Hart, 2005), p. 3.
25. See, for example, United Nations High Commissioner for Refugees, *Sexual and Gender-Based Violence against Refugees, Returnees and Internally Displaced Persons: Guidelines for Prevention and Response* (May 2003), www.unhcr.org/en-au/protection/women/3f696bcc4/sexual-gender-based-violence-against-refugees-returnees-internally-displaced.html. However, resistance to a more fluid and interpretative understanding of gender in human rights has remained intractable, as reflected by the term's invariable bracketing in significant UN documents. See, for example, the extremely ambiguous definition of the term in the statement from the President of the Fourth World Conference on Women, which reflected the tension between feminists and conservatives: United Nations, *Report of the Fourth World Conference on Women (Beijing, 4–15 September 1995)*, UN Doc. A/CONF.177/20/Rev.1, 27 October 1995, Annex IV ('Statement by the President of the Conference on the Commonly Understood Meaning of the Term "Gender"').
26. Catharine A. MacKinnon, *Toward a Feminist Theory of the State* (Cambridge, MA: Harvard University Press, 1989); Andrea Dworkin, *Pornography: Men Possessing Women* (London: Women's Press, 1981).
27. Butler, *Bodies that Matter*, pp. 238–9.
28. Judith Butler, *Gender Trouble: Feminism and the Subversion of Identity* (1990; repr., New York: Routledge, 1999); Butler, *Bodies that Matter*.
29. Butler, *Gender Trouble*, pp. 179–80.
30. For a discussion on the implications of Butler's theoretical interventions regarding gender in international law, see Brenda Cossman, 'Gender Performance, Sexual Subjects and International Law', *Canadian Journal of Law and Jurisprudence* 15, no. 2 (2002): 281–96.
31. Butler, *Bodies that Matter*, p. 1.
32. Butler, *Gender Trouble*, p. 179.
33. Ibid., p. 189.
34. Margaret Davies, 'Taking the Inside Out: Sex and Gender in the Legal Subject', in *Sexing the Subject of Law*, eds. Ngaire Naffine and Rosemary J. Owens (North Ryde: LBC Information Services, 1997), pp. 25–46.
35. Michel Foucault, *Discipline and Punish: The Birth of the Prison*, ed. Alan Sheridan (New York: Vintage, 1995); Michel Foucault, *The History of Sexuality: Volume I – An Introduction*, trans. Robert Hurley (New York: Pantheon Books, 1978).
36. Foucault, 'The Subject and Power', pp. 336–7. See also Ben Golder and Peter Fitzpatrick, *Foucault's Law* (Hoboken, NJ: Taylor & Francis, 2009), pp. 11–52.
37. Eve Kosofsky Sedgwick, *Epistemology of the Closet* (Berkeley, CA: University of California Press, 1990); Halley, *Split Decisions*. See also Carl F. Stychin, *Law's Desire: Sexuality and the Limits of Justice* (London: Routledge, 1995).
38. Dianne Otto, 'International Human Rights Law: Towards Rethinking Sex/Gender Dualism', in *The Ashgate Research Companion to Feminist Legal Theory*, eds. Margaret Davies and Vanessa E. Munro (Farnham: Ashgate, 2013), pp. 197–215.
39. Bonny Ibhawoh, *Imperialism and Human Rights: Colonial Discourses of Rights and Liberties in African History* (New York: State University of New York, 2007), pp. 1–17. Regarding the production of colonial masculinity, see, for example, Mrinalini Sinha, *Colonial Masculinity: The 'Manly Englishman' and the 'Effeminate Bengali' in the Late Nineteenth Century* (Manchester: Manchester University Press, 1995). See also Leela Gandhi, 'A Case of Radical Kinship: Edward Carpenter and the Politics of Anti-Colonial Sexual Dissidence', in *The Phobic and the Erotic: The Politics of Sexualities in Contemporary India*, eds Brinda Bose and Subhabrata Bhattacharyya (London: Seagull

Books, 2007), pp. 91–116, arguing that Empire and the anti-colonial nation were both profoundly heteronormative projects.

40. See generally Anghie, *Imperialism, Sovereignty, and the Making of International Law*. For a contrasting position, see Andrew Fitzmaurice, 'Scepticism of the Civilizing Mission in International Law', in *International Law and Empire: Historical Explorations*, eds. Martti Koskenniemi, Walter Rech and Manuel Jiménez Fonseca (Oxford: Oxford University Press, 2017), pp. 359–84. See further Mehta, *Liberalism and Empire*. Mehta explores the ways in which liberalism was based on promises of universality, but justified exclusions in practice. See also Javed Majeed, *Ungoverned Imaginings: James Mill's The History of British India and Orientialism* (Oxford: Oxford University Press, 1992), which discusses how James Mill's six-volume series on *The History of British India* (1817) provided part of the theoretical basis for the liberal endeavour to 'liberate' India from its own culture. In contrast, see Sankar Muthu, *Enlightenment against Empire* (Princeton, NJ: Princeton University Press, 2003), who traces the understudied strand of eighteenth-century liberal thought on anti-imperialism in the work of Denis Diderot, Immanuel Kant and Johann Gottfried Herder. Similarly, in Jennifer Pitts, *A Turn to Empire: The Rise of Imperial Liberalism in Britain and France* (Princeton, NJ: Princeton University Press, 2005), the author tracks the way in which critiques of Empire by eighteenth-century liberal political theorists (who nevertheless remained staunch believers in European superiority) are eclipsed by nineteenth-century imperial liberalism. Dhawan challenges such claims to a more humane liberalism, arguing that eighteenth-century thinkers were in fact advocating for a more humane imperialism or enlightened colonialism, rather than being anti-imperialist and interested in overcoming normative violence: Nikita Dhawan, 'Affirmative Sabotage of the Master's Tools: The Paradox of Postcolonial Enlightenment', in *Decolonizing Enlightenment: Transitional Justice, Human Rights and Democracy in a Postcolonial World*, ed. Nikita Dhawan (Opladen: Barbara Budrich Publishers, 2014), pp. 45–6. See also Gerrit W. Gwong, *The Standard of 'Civilization' in International Society* (Oxford: Clarendon Press, 1984).
41. Gayatri Chakravorty Spivak, 'Can the Subaltern Speak?' in *The Post-Colonial Studies Reader*, eds Bill Ashcroft, Gareth Griffiths and Helen Tiffin, 2nd ed. (London: Routledge, 2006), p. 33.
42. Inderpal Grewal, *Transnational America: Feminisms, Diasporas, Neoliberalisms* (Durham, NC: Duke University Press, 2005), p. 152. See also Sara de Jong, *Complicit Sisters: Gender and Women's Issues across North–South Divides* (New York: Oxford University Press, 2017).
43. Grewal, *Transnational America*, p. 152.
44. Otto, 'Towards Rethinking Sex/Gender Dualism', 204; Cynthia Rothschild, *Written Out: How Sexuality is Used to Attack Women's Organizing*, eds Scott Long and Susana T. Fried (New York: International Gay and Lesbian Human Rights Commission; Center for Women's Global Leadership, 2005). Also see Puar, *Terrorist Assemblages*, pp. 79–113, on how queer interventions have also produced their own set of cultural and racial exclusions.
45. Darren Rosenblum, 'Unsex CEDAW, Or What's Wrong with Women's Rights', *Columbia Journal of Gender and Law* 20, no. 2 (2011): 98–194.
46. United Nations, World Conference on Human Rights, *Vienna Declaration and Programme of Action*, UN Doc. A/CONF.157/23, 12 July 1993, I, para. 18 ('Vienna Declaration').
47. Ibid., II, para. 38.
48. Ibid.
49. United Nations Population Fund (UNFPA), *Report of the International Conference on Population and Development*, UN Doc. A/CONF.171/13/Rev.1 (1995); see United Nations, *Report of the Fourth World Conference on Women (Beijing, 4–15 September 1995)*, UN Doc. A/CONF.177/20/Rev.1, 17 October 1995, Annex I ('Beijing Declaration') and Annex II ('Platform for Action') ('Beijing Declaration and Platform for Action'); Optional Protocol to the Convention on the Elimination of All Forms of Discrimination against Women, 10 December 1999, 2131 UNTS 83.

50. See, for example, United Nations General Assembly, *Declaration on the Elimination of Violence against Women*, UN Doc. A/RES/48/104, 20 December 1993. See also United Nations General Assembly, *Report of the Committee on the Elimination of Discrimination against Women*, UN Doc. A/47/38 (1993); United Nations Commission on Human Rights, *Question of Integrating the Rights of Women into the Human Rights Mechanisms of the United Nations and the Elimination of Violence against Women*, Res. 1994/45, UN Doc. E/CN.4/1994/132, 4 March 1994; United Nations Commission on the Status of Women, *Report on the Fifty-Seventh Session, 4–15 March 2013, Economic and Social Council*, UN Doc. E/2013/27–E/CN.6/2013/11, 2 April 2013; and the UN Secretary General's campaign to end violence against women: *United Nations Secretary-General's Campaign to End Violence against Women (UniTE)*, www.un.org/en/women/endviolence/; United Nations General Assembly, *Intensification of Efforts to Prevent and Eliminate All Forms of Violence against Women and Girls: Domestic Violence*, UN Doc. A/RES/71/170, 7 February 2017; United Nations General Assembly, *Addressing the Impact of Multiple and Intersecting Forms of Discrimination and Violence in the Context of Racism, Racial Discrimination, Xenophobia and Related Intolerance on the Full Enjoyment of All Human Rights by Women and Girls*, UN Doc. A/HRC/RES/32/17, 18 July 2016; United Nations General Assembly, *Accelerating Efforts to Eliminate Violence against Women: Preventing and Responding to Violence against Women and Girls, including Indigenous Women and Girls*, UN Doc. A/HRC/RES/32/19, 19 July 2016; United Nations General Assembly, *Violence against Women Migrant Workers*, UN Doc. A/RES/70/130, 8 February 2016. Note how this logic has extended beyond the traditional remit of IHRL into international law. For example, see Janet Halley's discussion on feminist engagement with the drafting process of the Rome Statute of the International Criminal Court, 17 July 1998, 2187 UNTS 90 ('Rome Statute'), in which she outlines how a consensus emerged on women's rights, specifically regarding wartime rape – a consensus that was based on a radical feminism committed to a structuralist understanding of female subordination and male domination: Janet Halley, 'Rape at Rome: Feminist Interventions in the Criminalization of Sex-Related Violence in Positive International Criminal Law', *Michigan Journal of International Law* 30, no. 1 (2008): 1–123. See also Janet Halley, 'Rape in Berlin: Reconsidering the Criminalisation of Rape in the International Law of Armed Conflict', *Melbourne Journal of International Law* 9, no. 1 (2008): 78–124.
51. Elizabeth Bernstein, 'Militarized Humanitarianism Meets Carceral Feminism: The Politics of Sex, Rights, and Freedom in Contemporary Anti-trafficking Campaigns', *Signs* 36, no. 1 (2010): 45–71. See also Janie Chuang, 'Redirecting the Debate over Trafficking in Women: Definitions, Paradigms, and Contexts', *Harvard Human Rights Journal* 11 (1998): 65–107; Prabha Kotiswaran, *Dangerous Sex, Invisible Labor: Sex Work and the Law in India* (Princeton: Princeton University Press, 2011); Svati Pragna Shah, *Street Corner Secrets: Sex, Work, and Migration in the City of Mumbai* (Durham, NC: Duke University Press, 2014).
52. See Protocol to Prevent, Suppress and Punish Trafficking in Persons, Especially Women and Children, 15 November 2000, 2237 UNTS. 319, supplementing the United Nations Convention against Transnational Organized Crime, 15 November 2000, 2225 UNTS 209. Subsequent UN initiatives include United Nations General Assembly, *Trafficking in Persons, especially Women and Children: Protecting Victims of Trafficking and Persons at Risk of Trafficking, especially Women and Children in Conflict and Post-Conflict Situations*, UN Doc. A/HRC/RES/32/3, 20 July 2016.
53. Several countries and influential international women's rights groups have endorsed the Swedish or Nordic model, which views the sex trade as incompatible with gender equality. In 2014, the Council of Europe adopted a resolution endorsing the Nordic or Swedish model, thus signalling member countries to do the same: Council of Europe, *Prostitution, Trafficking and Modern Slavery in Europe*, Resolution 1983, 8 April 2014, para. 12.1.1.
54. Noy Thrupkaew, 'The Crusade against Sex Trafficking', *The Nation*, 16 September 2009, www.thenation.com/article/crusade-against-sex-trafficking/; Samantha Power, 'The Enforcer: A Christian Lawyer's Global Crusade', *The New Yorker*, 19 January 2009,

www.newyorker.com/magazine/2009/01/19/the-enforcer. See also Yvonne C. Zimmerman, 'Christianity and Human Trafficking', *Religion Compass* 5, no. 10 (2011): 567–78; Letitia M. Campbell and Yvonne C. Zimmerman, 'Christian Ethics and Human Trafficking Activism: Progressive Christianity and Social Critique', *Journal of the Society of Christian Ethics* 34, no. 1 (2014): 145–72.

55. International Convention for the Suppression of White Slave Traffic, 4 May 1910, 211 CTS 45; International Convention for the Suppression of the Traffic in Women and Children, 30 September 1921, 9 LNTS 415; International Convention for the Suppression of the Traffic in Women of Full Age, 11 October 1933, 150 LNTS 431; Convention for the Suppression of the Traffic in Persons and of the Exploitation of the Prostitution of Others, 21 March, 1950, 96 UNTS 271. These conventions all focus, almost exclusively, on trafficking in relation to prostitution and sexual exploitation. For a review of the human rights framework addressing trafficking, see Alice Edwards, 'Traffic in Human Beings: At the Intersection of Criminal Justice, Human Rights, Asylum/Migration and Labor', *Denver Journal of International Law & Policy* 36, no. 1 (2007): 9–53. On gender and trafficking, see Sanja Milivojevic and Marie Segrave, 'Responses to Sex Trafficking: Gender, Borders and "Home"', in *Trafficking and Human Rights: European and Asia-Pacific Perspectives*, ed. Leslie Holmes (Cheltenham: Edward Elgar, 2010), pp. 37–55.

56. Karen Engle, 'Anti-Impunity and the Turn to Criminal Law in Human Rights', *Cornell Law Review* 100, no. 5 (2015): 1069–1127. See also Sarah M.H. Nouwen, 'Justifying Justice', in *The Cambridge Companion to International Law*, eds. James Crawford and Martti Koskenniemi (Cambridge: Cambridge University Press, 2012), pp. 327–51. Nouwen examines how an overwhelming focus on the international criminal justice process, and individuals, has reduced the visibility of structural wrongs that have produced poverty and extreme inequality, 'the causes of which are located in the structure of the same international community in whose name "international justice" is performed': Nouwen, 'Justifying Justice', pp. 343–4.

57. Edwards, 'Traffic in Human Beings', pp. 15–16.

58. Janie A. Chuang, 'Exploitation Creep and the Unmaking of Human Trafficking Law', *American Journal of International Law* 108, no. 4 (2014): 611.

59. Elizabeth Bernstein, 'Carceral Politics as Gender Justice? The "Traffic in Women" and Neoliberal Circuits of Crime, Sex, and Rights', *Theory & Society* 41, no. 3 (2012): 233–59; Global Alliance Against Traffic in Women (GAATW), *Collateral Damage: The Impact of Anti-Trafficking Measures on Human Rights around the World* (2007); Janie A. Chuang, 'Rescuing Trafficking from Ideological Capture: Prostitution Reform and Anti-Trafficking Law and Policy', *University of Pennsylvania Law Review* 158, no. 6 (2010): 1655–1728; Kotiswaran, *Dangerous Sex*; Sabrina Balgamwalla, 'Trafficking in Narratives: Conceptualizing and Recasting Victims, Offenders, and Rescuers in the War on Human Trafficking', *Denver Law Review* 94, no. 1 (2016): 1–41; Anne T. Gallagher and Joy Ngozi Ezeilo, 'The UN Special Rapporteur on Trafficking: A Turbulent Decade in Review', *Human Rights Quarterly* 37, no. 4 (2015): 913–40.

60. Kerry Rittich, 'The Future of Law and Development: Second-Generation Reforms and the Incorporation of the Social', in *The New Law and Economic Development*, eds. David M. Trubek and Alvaro Santos (Cambridge: Cambridge University Press, 2006), pp. 203–52; Ellis Ward and Gillian Wylie, eds., *Feminism, Prostitution and the State: The Politics of Neo-Abolitionism* (London: Routledge, 2017).

61. Aziza Ahmed, '"Exploitation Creep" and Development: A Response to Janie Chuang', *AJIL Unbound* (blog), 11 June 2015, www.asil.org/blogs/%E2%80%9Cexploitation-creep%E2%80%9D-and-development-response-janie-chuang; Kiril Sharapov, 'Traffickers and *Their* Victims' Anti-Trafficking Policy in the United Kingdom', *Critical Sociology* 43, no. 1 (2017): 91–111; Barbara G. Brent, 'Neoliberalism's Market Morality and Heteroflexibility: Protectionist and Free Market Discourses in Debates for Legal Prostitution', *Sexuality Research and Social Policy* 13, no. 4 (2016): 402–16.

62. Jayne Huckerby, 'Same, but Different: Assessing the Interaction of the Migrant Workers' Rights and Anti-Trafficking Regimes Under International Law', *New York University*

Journal of International Law and Politics 47, no. 3 (2015): 593–645. See the International Convention on the Protection of the Rights of All Migrant Workers and Members of their Families, 18 December 1990, 2220 UNTS 3.

63. On 'looking at the world without actually seeing it', see Marks, *Four Human Rights Myths*, pp. 13–14, 16–17.
64. Bernard E. Harcourt, *The Illusion of Free Markets: Punishment and the Myth of Natural Order* (Cambridge, MA: Harvard University Press, 2011).
65. Bernstein, 'Militarized Humanitarianism', p. 64; Seo-Young Cho, 'Liberal Coercion? Prostitution, Human Trafficking and Policy', *European Journal of Law and Economics* 41, no. 2 (2016): 321–48.
66. GAATW, *Collateral Damage*.
67. United Nations Security Council, *Resolution 1325 (2000)*, UN Doc. S/RES/1325, 31 October 2000 (*Resolution 1325*).
68. United Nations Security Council, *Resolution 1820 (2008)*, UN Doc. S/RES/1820, 19 June 2008 (*Resolution 1820*).
69. UNSC, Resolution 1325; UNSC, Resolution 1820.
70. The resolution '*[e]ncourages* the Secretary-General to … increase … the participation of women at decision-making levels in conflict resolution and peace processes': UNSC, Resolution 1325, para. 2.
71. Ibid., para. 10.
72. Ibid., preamble; para. 17.
73. Subsequent resolutions include Security Council Resolutions 1888 and 1889 (*Resolution 1888* and *Resolution 1889*). Resolution 1888 sets out the specific ways in which to implement Resolution 1820. It further emphasizes the problem of sexual violence in armed conflict and reiterates the demands of Resolution 1820, in addition to asking the Secretary-General to undertake certain reporting requirements in this regard: United Nations Security Council, Resolution 1888 (2009), UN Doc. S/RES/1888, 30 September 2009. The purpose behind women's participation in Resolution 1325 is explained in Resolution 1889, where the Security Council '[*reiterated*] the need for the full, equal and effective participation of women at all stages of peace processes given their vital role in the prevention and resolution of conflict and peace-building', and also '[*reaffirmed*] the key role women can play in re-establishing the fabric of recovering society': United Nations Security Council, Resolution 1889 (2009), UN Doc. S/RES/1889, 5 October 2009, preamble. Resolution 1889 puts in place institutional measures to ensure greater implementation of Resolution 1325. See further United Nations Security Council, Resolution 2242 (2015), UN Doc. S/RES/2242, 13 October 2015; United Nations Security Council, Resolution 2282 (2016), UN Doc. S/RES/2282, 27 April 2016, paras 6, 21, 22, 27. For an excellent analysis regarding the broader relationship between gender equality, peacekeeping and security in international law, see Dianne Otto and Gina Heathcote, 'Rethinking Peacekeeping, Gender Equality and Collective Security: An Introduction', in *Rethinking Peacekeeping, Gender Equality and Collective Security*, eds. Gina Heathcote and Dianne Otto (Basingstoke: Palgrave Macmillan, 2014), pp. 1–20. See also Louise Olsson, *Gender, Peace and Security: Implementing UN Security Council Resolution 1325* (Hoboken, NJ: Taylor and Francis, 2015).
74. Vasuki Nesiah, 'Feminism as Counter-Terrorism: The Seduction of Power', in *Gender, National Security and Counter-Terrorism: Human Rights Perspectives*, eds. Margaret L. Satterthwaite and Jayne C. Huckerby (Abingdon: Routledge, 2013), pp. 127–51.
75. Dianne Otto, 'The Security Council's Alliance of Gender Legitimacy: The Symbolic Capital of Resolution 1325', in *Fault Lines of International Legitimacy*, eds. Hilary Charlesworth and Jean-Marc Coicaud (Cambridge: Cambridge University Press, 2009), pp. 239–75; Dianne Otto, 'The Exile of Inclusion: Reflections on Gender Issues in International Law over the Last Decade', *Melbourne Journal of International Law* 10, no. 1 (2009): 25, problematizing the gender narrative reflected in Resolution 1820. Otto argues that the adoption of Resolution 1325 was itself an attempt by the Security Council to bolster its flagging legitimacy by demonstrating its dedication to the collective good,

including women. She bases this argument on the finding that Resolution 1325 does not make any attempt to address the structural causes of women's equality. In this way, '[d]e-linking gender mainstreaming from the goal of gender equality is a very effective way to remove any feminist political content': Otto, 'The Exile of Inclusion', 21. See also Maria Jansson and Maud Eduards, 'The Politics of Gender in the UN Security Council Resolutions on Women, Peace and Security', *International Feminist Journal of Politics* 18, no. 4 (2016): 590–604.

76. For example, at the tenth anniversary of Resolution 1325, the Committee on the Elimination of Discrimination Against Women issued a statement declaring that women are 'widely recognized as effective agents of peace': Committee on the Elimination of Discrimination against Women, *Statement of the Committee on the Elimination of Discrimination against Women on the 10th Anniversary of Security Council Resolution 1325 on 'Women, Peace and Security'*, 12–30, July 2010, www2.ohchr.org/english/bodies/cedaw/docs/statements/Statement_SCR_1325.pdf.
77. UN Secretary-General, 'Secretary-General Calls for Council Action to Ensure Women are Involved in Peace and Security Decisions', Press release SG/SM/7598, 24 October 2000.
78. See, for example, Carol Gilligan, *In a Different Voice: Psychological Theory and Women's Development* (Cambridge, MA: Harvard University Press, 2003); Robin West, *Caring for Justice* (New York: New York University Press, 1997).
79. See, for example, Natalie Florea Hudson, *Gender, Human Security and the United Nations: Security Language as a Political Framework for Women* (Hoboken, NJ: Taylor and Francis, 2009). Hudson, who quotes from an interview with a UN official, describes how it is essential to move human rights concerns on to the discursive terrain of security in order to get traction on such issues from politicians.
80. Anne Orford, 'Feminism, Imperialism and the Mission of International Law', *Nordic Journal of International Law* 71, no. 2 (2002): 281.
81. See, for example, UN Secretary-General, 'Calls for Council Action'; Jamie J. Hagen, 'Queering Women, Peace and Security', *International Affairs* 92, no. 2 (2016): 313–32.
82. Dianne Otto, 'A Sign of "Weakness"? Disrupting Gender Certainties in the Implementation of Security Council Resolution 1325', *Michigan Journal of Gender & Law* 13, no. 1 (2006): 122.
83. Janet Halley et al., 'From the International to the Local in Feminist Legal Responses to Rape, Prostitution/Sex Work, and Sex Trafficking: Four Studies in Contemporary Governance Feminism', *Harvard Journal of Law & Gender* 29, no. 2 (2006): 419. See also Halley, 'Governance Feminism: An Introduction'.
84. Halley, *Split Decisions*, pp. 4–5.
85. Orford, 'Feminism, Imperialism'. Orford puts forward a critique regarding the effect of international law on feminism, and feminism's effect on international law (at p. 275). See also Cyra Akila Choudhury, 'Governance Feminism's Imperial Misadventure: Progress, International Law, and the Security of Afghan Women', in *Contesting Feminisms: Gender and Islam in Asia*, ed. Huma Ahmed-Ghosh (New York: State University of New York Press, 2015), pp. 227–50.
86. Kristin Bumiller, *In an Abusive State: How Neoliberalism Appropriated the Feminist Movement against Sexual Violence* (Durham, NC: Duke University Press, 2008), pp. 1–15; Shruti Iyer, 'Taking a Break from the State: Indian Feminists in the Legal Reform Process', *Journal of International Women's Studies* 17, no. 2 (2016): 18–29.
87. Brown, *Undoing the Demos*; Margaret Thornton, 'Neoliberal Governmentality and the Retreat from Gender Equality', in *Feminisms of Discontent: Global Contestations*, ed. Ashleigh Barnes (New Delhi: Oxford University Press, 2015), pp. 71–96.
88. Halley, 'Rape at Rome'.
89. Halley, *Split Decisions*.
90. Otto, 'The Exile of Inclusion', p. 25.
91. Ibid., p. 13.

92. Hilary Charlesworth, 'Talking to Ourselves? Feminist Scholarship in International Law', in *Feminist Perspectives on Contemporary International Law: Between Resistance and Compliance?*, eds. Sari Kouvo and Zoe Pearson (Oxford: Hart Publishing, 2011), p. 18.
93. Hilary Charlesworth, 'Feminist Methods in International Law', *The American Journal of International Law* 93, no. 2 (1999): 379–94.
94. Vanessa E. Munro, 'Navigating Feminisms: At the Margins, in the Mainstreams or Elsewhere? Reflections on Charlesworth, Otomo and Pearson', in *Feminist Perspectives on Contemporary International Law: Between Resistance and Compliance?*, eds. Sari Kouvo and Zoe Pearson (Oxford: Hart Publishing, 2011), pp. 13–16. For a discussion of some of these dilemmas, see Sari Kouvo, 'Taking Women Seriously? Conflict, State-Building and Gender in Afghanistan', in *Feminist Perspectives on Contemporary International Law: Between Resistance and Compliance?*, eds. Sari Kouvo and Zoe Pearson (Oxford: Hart Publishing, 2011), pp. 159–76.

4. Alterity, gender equality and the veil

> Critique, I believe, is most powerful when it leaves open the possibility that we might also be remade in the process of engaging another's worldview, that we might come to learn things that we did not already know before we undertook the engagement.
>
> —Saba Mahmood, *Politics of Piety*[1]

This chapter elaborates on the theme of the gendered 'Other' through a twofold discussion of the ways in which human rights advocacy engages with alterity, specifically in relation to the veil. I use the term 'veil' as a generic category that includes its various manifestations – the hijab, jilbab, abaya, niqab, burqa and chador – each version of the garment encoded with particular meaning for its adherents, proponents and opponents, and serving as both topos and target of national and regional socio-politics as well as global geo-politics. However, the custom of veiling, in its manifold expressions across diverse locations, is today invariably assumed by its liberal adversaries to be an oppressive religio-cultural expression of selfhood by a monolithic Muslim 'Other'; a negative, backward practice that thoroughly subordinates Muslim women.

Chapter 3 described how gender as a category is structured in human rights law and advocacy, including the preferential approach by which inclusion or recognition is bestowed upon disenfranchised female subjects. It also highlighted how articulations of gender and freedom from violence are increasingly aligned with the neoliberal market that is shaping both the material and performative aspects of gender. I extend that discussion here by focusing on the right to gender equality in relation to a particular category of woman; that is, practitioners of the veil, within the category of gender. I delineate how engagement with the veil in human rights advocacy and law hinges on the forceful liberal premise that freedom from this practice is a universally desired end goal in the domain of gender equality, which can effectively be secured by incorporating the wearer into rights discourse. These interventions demonstrate how the human rights project is advancing a specific vision, not only of gender but also of freedom – and is, in fact, aggressively asserting itself as *the* vision of freedom unequivocally aspired to by all those who, according to the liberal paradigm, are unfree. Freedom as projected in this register presupposes that there is a specific way to be free in the world as a liberal female subject; that is, as the bearer of rights that are established through the suppression of cultural practices assumed to be an inherent obstacle to this freedom. Thus, strategies to emancipate women *from* the veil become central to this particular articulation.

The second, and related, focus of this chapter is to draw attention to the politics that inform the choice of the woman who refuses to unveil. Opponents of veiling often present the logic of false consciousness, or of cultural resistance to the assimilative impulse of rights discourse and liberal democracy, as the framework for understanding or explaining this expression of female agency. This perspective has been extensively analysed in the critical work of Saba Mahmood, Mayanthi Fernando and Joan Wallace Scott. In my discussion, I draw attention to the understanding of freedom that informs the choice of some adherents of the practice. My argument quite specifically illuminates how such alternative definitions of freedom push back against the hegemonies of rights discourse with regard to the axiomatic liberal definition of what constitutes freedom for *all* women. In the process, I expose not simply the coercive limits but also the illusion of human rights as a viable and effective freedom project.

This critical trajectory offers a reading of human rights interventions as material mechanisms for policing or erasing alternative registers of freedom, and for assuaging the fear and anxiety that such registers produce in liberal constituencies. Such panic is generated partly by the apparent social threat that alterity poses to the liberal vision, as embodied in the third avatar of the subject that I addressed in Chapter 1. It also partly arises from the unsettling prospect of having to acknowledge that the secure philosophical certainties in which the liberal image of freedom is embedded are, in fact, highly vulnerable to destabilization when they (directly) encounter radical difference and engage with apparently unintelligible non-liberal epistemologies. This chapter thus serves as a transitional moment in the book, with my argument moving from engagement with critique that reproduces and reinforces the dominant narrative of human rights as a freedom project, to a theoretical space that presents the productive possibilities of critique after laying bare the complicity of rights regimens and other discourses within the confines of the liberal fishbowl.

LAW AND THE EUROPEAN 'VEIL' CASES

As discussed in Chapter 3, male and female bodies have not only been cast as naturally different but have also consistently been displaced onto a First/Third World divide, where cultural difference, tradition and antiquity have been historically equated with backwardness and primitiveness. These assumptions about culture, gender difference and alterity continue to underpin the politics of the contemporary moment, including dominant accounts of modernity more generally, and human rights discourses of gender equality more specifically. The colonial past and its linked discourses are integral to the current understanding of the male and female 'Other' in human rights frameworks, the latter of which are viewed as the contemporary saviour of victims of barbaric traditions presented and practised as essential, natural and/or divinely ordained.[2] The projection of human rights as a freedom project designed to bring about women's liberation works alongside the assumption that traditional culture is an inherently regressive and intractable feature of the developing world, and a central obstacle to the realization of the universal right to gender equality. As discussed earlier, this assumption is actively sustained in contemporary human rights advocacy on gender equality, within which veiling is regarded as a cultural practice that always subjugates women and/or erases agency and where freedom is reflexively understood and presented in purely liberal terms – that is, freedom *from* the veil. My discussion of recent veil-related cases decided by the European Court of Human Rights, and the domestic legal responses to these decisions – particularly in relation to France – pushes back against the assumption regarding 'traditional culture' by examining the governance work undertaken in the veil cases to control and discipline a specific mode of faith-based alterity within the homogenizing logic of gender equality. By highlighting what is consciously omitted or foreclosed in these judicial responses, I create space for the possibility of a deeper conversation on the meaning of the veil, in terms of the wearer's worldview and her experience of freedom *through* the veil, and thus expose another way in which women's rights are being manipulated to serve larger neoliberal governance agendas.

The Veil Cases

The tension between human rights and alterity has explicitly played out over the past two decades in a series of decisions from the European Court of Human Rights (ECtHR) concerning the veil. One of the best known and most well-publicized cases is *Şahin v. Turkey*, in which a university lecturer in Istanbul brought a challenge under the European Convention on Human Rights (ECHR)[3] regarding the validity of a circular issued by the Vice-Chancellor of Istanbul University.[4] The circular directed that students with beards and students wearing the Islamic headscarf would be refused admission to lectures, courses and tutorials. In March 1998, the applicant was refused access to sit an exam on one of the subjects that she was studying because she was wearing the Islamic headscarf. Subsequently, on the same grounds, the university authorities refused to enrol her in a course and admit her to various lectures and exams. The faculty also issued her with a warning for contravening the university's rules on dress, and then suspended her from the university for a semester, as she had taken part in an unauthorized assembly that had gathered to protest against the warning. The applicant claimed that the circular violated several of her rights, including her right to freedom of religion under Article 9 of the ECHR, which encompassed the manifestation of religion or belief.

The Court upheld the ban on the wearing of headscarves at Istanbul University on the grounds that the impugned circular was consistent with the principles of secularism and equality in Turkey, in particular, the right to gender equality. Quite specifically, the Court held that there had been no violation of Article 9 (freedom of thought, conscience and religion, including the manifestation of religion or belief); Article 8 (right to respect for private and family life); Article 10 (freedom of expression); Article 14 (prohibition of discrimination); or Article 2 (right to education) of Protocol No. 1 to the ECHR. The circular was held to be consistent with the Turkish Constitutional Court's ruling that authorizing students to 'cover the neck and hair with a veil or headscarf for reasons of religious conviction' in universities was contrary to the Constitution.[5] The Court also stated that such interventions were designed to protect the individual not only against arbitrary interference by the state, but also from external pressure by extremist movements.[6] Implicit in this position is a reinforcement of the widely held assumption that women are *always* coerced into wearing headscarves, and that Muslim women lack agency, are invariably victims of their traditional culture and are awaiting rescue from subservience through a liberal rights intervention.

The Court accepted the government's argument that the restriction on wearing the headscarf was integral to gender equality and maintaining secularism. Given the Court's finding that gender equality was 'one of the key principles underlying the Convention',[7] and that the practice of wearing the headscarf violated this principle, there was almost no scope for Şahin to argue that the ban itself constituted sex discrimination. In her dissent, Justice Tulken pointed out both the paternalism of and the contradiction in using the logic of sexual equality to prohibit a woman from wearing the veil when, in the absence of proof to the contrary, she has freely adopted it. In *Dahlab v. Switzerland*, the same court rejected an argument that a Swiss ban on the wearing of a headscarf and other 'visible religious symbols' while engaged in teaching was based on sex discrimination.[8] The applicant argued that a man belonging to the Muslim faith could teach at the school without facing any prohibition, while she had to refrain from practising her religion; that is, that she was not allowed to wear a headscarf, although she held the same beliefs. The Court held that the ban would be just as valid for any male teacher who wore clothing that identified him as Muslim, and therefore the prohibition on Muslim women was not disparate in nature.[9]

In these cases, the Court's reasoning pits a progressive secular ideal against what in the West is generally perceived and presented as a premodern and oppressive religious order. This binary obscures the majoritarianism that is advanced in and through the discourse of secularism, and which aggressively associates gender equality with the unveiled woman. There is an overwhelming emphasis on a formal approach to equality, which holds that Muslim women who practise veiling should be treated the same as all other (that is, unveiled) women. This logic is based on two confident liberal assumptions: that *all* veiled Muslim women are oppressed by the practice; and that Muslim women's systematic observance of certain religious practices is *always* an explicit obstacle to their realization of gender equality. Rights interventions do not disrupt the normative liberal postulates about gender and culture on which concepts of gender equality are based. The cases described above exemplify how alterity is taken up in gender equality analysis through discourses in which unveiling/to be unveiled becomes an ineluctable part of the normative scaffolding of the universal right to gender equality.

The veil cases serve as confirmation of the prevalent view that regards Islam as essentially authoritarian, regressive and oppressive to women. It reproduces the deeper liberal assumption that religion in the non-Western world exists through ancient systems of entrenched conformity, its adherents bound in unquestioning obedience to revelation and exegesis, with the associated rules for human conduct laid out in foundational texts to which believers subscribe without any impulse to interrogate, debate, deconstruct or reconstruct. The legal and, at times, even social response to the traditional practice of veiling is used to homogenize, essentialize and demonize an entire religion, and to implicitly project Muslim men or proponents of such practices as illiberal, misogynistic and fundamentalist. At the same time, the veiled Muslim woman is considered as a victim of her culture or religion, as having no agency, and as being uncritical of the custom. However, the very terms of equality within liberal logic are what deny her this agency. If she chooses to wear the veil, the choice is either regarded as an outcome of false consciousness and thereby hypocritical and irrelevant, or interpreted as a belligerent act of personalized dissent that refuses to comply with the reasonable demands of liberal secular democracy. Her choice to wear the veil is stuck within this binary, and the complexity of the personal rationale behind the choice is never fully attended to. Choosing to veil rather than not to is, according to liberal constituencies, choosing incarceration over autonomy – and hence no choice at all, since a choice that polices women's sexuality and sociality, and reinscribes existent gender roles, is not a choice and contravenes the norms of liberal equality and freedom. Gender equality is defined by and aligned with majority political ideals, which are understood as chosen, and thus axiomatically associated with the autonomous, unveiled female subject.

Legal Bans and the Veil

The generic Western views about gender, culture and freedom expressed in these court decisions are also reflected in the specific legal regulation of the veil in the domestic context. France has become the epicentre of the European debates around the veil through its enactment of two controversial laws. The first, enacted in 2004, bans the wearing of religious symbols and clothing, including the Islamic headscarf, in public schools.[10] The law is based on the recommendations of the Stasi Commission Report, which stated that 'young girls are pressured into wearing religious symbols' and that '[t]he familial and social environment sometimes forces on them a choice that is not theirs'.[11] The second, enacted in 2010, banned the wearing of the burqa – a traditional garment that veils both face and body – in public. French lawmakers endorsed the position that France 'cannot accept to have in our country women who are prisoners behind netting, cut off from all social life, deprived of identity … That is not the idea that the French republic has of women's dignity'.[12]

Though couched in neutral terms, the legal ban on manifest religious symbols and veils in France has had a disproportionate impact on Muslim women. Initially, the 2004 law only prohibited overtly manifest markers of religious affiliations. However, the Ministry of Education subsequently issued a decree clarifying that 'The prohibited signs and dress are those by which the wearer is immediately recognizable in terms of his or her religion, such as the Islamic veil, whatever its name, the kippah or a crucifix of manifestly exaggerated dimensions'.[13] The legal terminology is indicative of the stark socio-political bias which underlies a ban that has come to be reified as secular and impartial. Not only do the stipulated exceptions reflect the practices of the dominant religious community, but the very fact that ostentatious symbols of faith are not permitted to be worn in public is reflective of a religious and cultural ethos where such expression of selfhood, identity and community is not a common or pervasive aspect of popular religious or cultural practice. Here the benevolent rhetoric of purported equality across different cultures and religions actually signifies 'the same as' the dominant culture/religion, and raises concerns of subordination and coercion amongst religious and/or cultural minorities.[14] The literal and psychological impact of the ban has been felt overwhelmingly by Muslim girls and young women who veil, and who have at times been compelled to attend privately run religious schools rather than remain in the state school system.[15]

In 2007, the ECtHR once again dismissed a petition claiming that the law violated the wearer's right to religious freedom under Article 9 of the ECHR. The central ground for upholding the law was based on the principle of secularism as a founding principle of the French Republic 'to which the entire population adheres and the protection of which appears to be of prime importance, in particular in schools';[16] the law was also upheld on the basis of the protection of women's rights.[17] The uninterrogated logic of this position produces outcomes that *seem* reasonable and acceptable, despite evidence to the contrary. A number of French feminists, among other opponents of veiling, have applauded such initiatives, viewing the veil as a 'visible symbol of the submission of women'.[18]

Suppressed – perhaps one could say veiled – within the judicial and feminist discussions of the veil is the question of the cultural specificity of France's policy of *laïcité* or neutral 'secularism'. Yet, despite this doctrine, Christian holidays perpetually feature in the Republican calendar; the government continues to fund hundreds of private Catholic schools, in contrast to just a handful of Muslim schools, nationwide; and the national culture is defined as 'Christian'. In addition, the principle does not apply to Alsace-Mosel, where the Napoleonic-era Concordat system of governance continues to apply, and where Catholicism, Calvinism, Lutheranism and Judaism remain officially recognized religions; religious education in one of these four tracks is obligatory for public school students in this region.[19] The state's envisioning and enshrining of the Republican citizen is not a purely neutral act. Rather, it is a demand that the 'Other' think beyond the upholding of minority difference, and conceptualize her selfhood entirely in terms of Republican French identity, that is, in alignment with majoritarian ideals. The call to think beyond difference or to surrender alterity usually ends up reinforcing the dominance of the dominant, and the conditions – wherein the hierarchies of power operate through the apparently universalizing category of 'human' – do not disappear. Removal of the overt markers of difference ensures the stability of these hierarchical arrangements, as well as the distinct understanding of exactly who is adequately and appropriately 'human' within a seemingly pluralistic liberal society. The criteria for full citizenship includes evidence of assimilation in respect of the explicit cultural norms of the majority.

In 2010 a law popularly described as the 'burqa ban' was enacted, which outlawed the public wearing of the full veil or burqa.[20] One lawmaker specifically stated that 'it is our living together based on the Spirit of the Enlightenment that is violated' by the burqa.[21] Such statements reinforce the stigma that attaches to the wearing of the veil within the liberal ethos, once again reinforcing the singular view that Islamic religious practices are subordinating, misogynistic and utterly repressive in relation to women. The position further reproduces the common societal belief that Muslim women are *always* coerced into wearing the veil – with the rhetoric of gender equality obscuring the liberal democratic state's coercive act of banning the practice. Such skewed conviction completely forecloses any possibility of accepting the rationale that some women are, in fact, *not* oppressed by the veil; that such practitioners actively desire to veil, and are freely exercising personal choice in this regard.

The 'burqa ban' was challenged in *S.A.S. v. France* as a violation of the claimant's rights under various articles of the ECHR, although the Court focused primarily upon Articles 8, 9 and 14.[22] The government's central argument was based on public safety concerns, as well as 'respect for the minimum set of values of an open and democratic society', which includes gender equality, human dignity and 'respect for the minimum requirements of life in society' or 'living together'.[23] Interestingly, the Court rejected some of these arguments, which had been successful in earlier cases. The Court did not accept the argument that the ban advanced the legitimate aims of gender equality and human dignity, partly for the reason that the practice itself was being defended by the woman wearing the burqa. The Court simply accepted that the burqa was a choice, avoiding the essentialism and paternalism of earlier cases, and that, as highlighted in Justice Tulken's dissenting judgment in the *Şahin* case, the ban disregarded the wearer's choice as well as the meaning attributed to the veil by the applicants. The Court also rejected the argument that the ban advanced human dignity, stating that there was no evidence that the women who wore the burqa were expressing a form of contempt towards others or seeking to offend the dignity of others.[24] In a similar vein, the Court rejected the public safety argument, finding it had not been established that the veil posed a general threat to public safety, and holding that the ban was therefore disproportionate.[25] Instead, the Court's decision relied upon the government's justification of 'respect for the minimum set of values of an open and democratic society' or 'living together' as a legitimate ground for restrictions on the right to manifest religion or belief under Article 9. As this ground is not explicitly articulated as such in the Convention – that is, under either Article 8(2) or 9(2)[26] – the Court interpreted it as falling within the broad 'protection of the rights and freedoms of others'.[27] Thus, even if the claimant wore the veil freely, and as an exercise of her choice and liberty of expression, the ban would still be justified on the basis of the Court's reasoning that it was incompatible with the democratic precept of 'living together'.

In upholding this justification, the Court's analysis focused on the face, stating that it plays an important role in the civility of social interactions and open interpersonal relationships. These were important markers of the community life of a society, and thus the wearing of the burqa in public was 'incompatible, in French society, with the ground rules of social communication and more broadly the requirements of "living together".'[28] The Court accepted the findings of a parliamentary commission tasked with drafting a report on the wearing of the burqa in France, which described the practice as being at odds with the values of the Republic, a denial of fraternity and 'constituting the negation of contact with others and a flagrant infringement of the French principle of living together'.[29]

This ruling privileges the concept of 'living together' over and above the right to manifest religion; hence it is a cause for concern, as it reflects the assimilationist impulse that underscores the enforcement of the ban under the right to gender equality, even though the decision was not explicitly based on this right. The Court's holding further underscores the unstated religious majoritarianism that informs the requirements of 'living together', where manifestations of belief in the form of displays of the cross, or recognition of Christian holidays in the secular calendar, or state support for Christian-denomination schools in France, remain unscrutinized yet continue to inform the principle of secularism or *laïcité*, the declared cornerstone of the French Republic. 'Living together' operates exclusively in one direction – that is, in favour of majoritarianism – and remains somewhat problematic, given that it is not a right recognized under the terms of the ECHR. Nevertheless, juridical approval of this concept demands compliance by Muslim women who are

French citizens. It does not require any simultaneous obligation on the part of the majority to work through socio-cultural prejudice and find ways to 'live together' equally with, for example, a Muslim woman for whom wearing the veil is an inherent aspect of subjectivity and a crucial signifier of her existential, ethical and spiritual commitments.

In these legal interventions, freedom is displaced onto a binary between one's particular cultural identity and the political concept of gender equality, the latter of which falls within the orbit of liberal sociality generally, and within the more 'far-fetched and vague' idea of 'living together' in particular.[30] Within this paradigm, the veil symbolizes the ultimate subordination of women, and its ban or removal is evidence of liberation and the reestablishment of a cherished secular ideal. The debate on women's autonomy and entitlements is framed by certain assumptions about freedom in the context of gender equality – as being unequivocally associated with the unveiled body, in contrast to the corresponding association of non-freedom with the veiled body. Veiling is categorized as a barbaric practice of the 'Other'; criminalization of the veil and its adherents thus becomes a justifiable response. These cases perpetuate the earlier colonial fetish with the veil, and the characterization of its removal as an act of freedom liberating oppressed Muslim women from their oppressive Muslim culture, and from oppressive Muslim men.[31]

In the contemporary moment, legal, feminist and Republican discourses collude to obscure how the proclaimed universal right to gender equality is *itself* fundamentally discriminatory and undemocratic, based on specific gender and sexual norms that unequivocally privilege some constituencies of French women over others.[32] The veiled subject can be included only without the veil, and responsibility for her political and ontological exclusion as a non-normative subject is entirely displaced onto her. In challenging her experience of discrimination, she is forced to decide between the assimilative framework of liberal universalism that will afford her political recognition, access to rights, state benefits, and so on, and the faith-based particularity of being a veiled Muslim woman – a criminalized non-subject without public agency, civic credibility or social intelligibility, and ineligible for membership within the entitled demographic of rights-bearing unveiled female citizens. Within this discriminatory ethos, adherence to the veil elicits the implicit charge of violating the precepts of gender equality along with an explicit violation of the law; thus the veil renders its wearer permanently vulnerable and marginalized in external socio-cultural terms, even while she may experience it as an expression of her internal psychological and spiritual freedom.

UNVEILING AS GOVERNANCE

In the challenges to the French bans on the veil described earlier in this chapter, the applicants sought recognition as valid citizen-subjects under French law. Yet, to reiterate Butler's argument presented in Chapter 2, recognition requires compliance with the terms of 'recognizability', which in this instance includes shedding the veil and fully exposing the face to the liberal public gaze. This logic of revealing the face – understood in terms of open social interaction and compatible with the fundamental requirements of 'living together' – which was central to the *S.A.S. v. France* decision conceals the power dynamic operating in this apparently reasonable, democratic requirement, as well as the way in which the assimilationist mandate functions as a technique of governance. The reasoning in the veil cases directly associates the personal and collective freedom of the Muslim woman with her – whether voluntarily or compulsorily – revealing her face in public. As mentioned earlier, the national conflicts around issues of veiling highlight how gender equality and freedom are axiomatically associated with the unveiled face, while the veiled face is axiomatically associated with unfreedom, repression and barbarism. Filtered through the human rights discourse, the political logic that insists on disrobing the Muslim woman continues to perpetuate the colonial fantasy that this single, essential act of unveiling will ensure her liberation from the oppressive men and oppressive practices of her oppressive culture. Penalizing her failure to do so severely constricts and distorts the emancipatory principle of gender equality by equating it, in this context, with the right of women to wear what they want in public – *except* when it is a veil. The legal mandate also fails to appreciate how the meaning of the veil, for some Muslim women, cannot simply be inscribed within liberal secular assumptions about choice and freedom. For such committed practitioners, 'the veil' is not what they simply opt to wear – a garment that can be donned or removed as required – but rather is their very mode of being, an elision of self-concept/image, interiority and identity.

A female Muslim French citizen who refuses to unveil in public, thus contravening the law, risks her right to education and to attend a secular public school, or loses her right to mobility and access, and is compelled to remain sequestered in the home. In each instance, she does not want to choose between these rights – she wants both. But the liberal democratic state, coupled with the discourse of human rights, which is largely informed by the view that veiling is a backward practice amounting to a denial of women's rights, unilaterally arrogates to itself the right to decide the terms on which a Muslim woman can enjoy her freedom – which, somewhat paradoxically, forces her to 'choose'. If she chooses incorrectly, in the case of French law, she is subject to penalties that include the payment of a fine, and she may also be unequivocally directed to participate in citizenship education. Much like the formulae of gender equality, 'living together' becomes one of the techniques for managing and disciplining this unruly, intractable, culturally unintelligible subject into the practices of 'proper' French citizenship, despite the fact that she is already and incontrovertibly a French citizen.[33] And it simultaneously belies the assumption that coercion is exclusively a feature of a religion assumed to be inherently misogynistic and authoritarian; it also illuminates how the 'secular' state's imposition of the right to gender equality can, in fact, provide epistemic clarity through being experienced by 'unrecognized' women as a form of political violence.

This coercive side of the secular state, in relation to the 'Other' woman, has taken a distinct turn in the direction of blatant sexism, Islamophobia and racism, where the issue of gender equality is no longer even superficially presented as the central concern. After a series of terrorist attacks in France, during 2015 and 2016 bans were imposed by several French municipalities and towns on the wearing of the 'burkini' – a full-body swimsuit that is like a wetsuit and covers the entire body except for the feet, hands and face – on French beaches.[34] These new sartorial regulations were forcefully and immediately implemented. Shortly after they were adopted, images emerged of armed municipal police officers attired in ballistic vests surrounding a woman on a beach in Nice. She was made to remove her attire and issued with a citation for not wearing 'an outfit respecting good morals and secularism'.[35] These bans signal a discursive shift. While the earlier bans, in 2004 and 2010, were ostensibly implemented in support of rights to gender equality, this new development makes no such pretence. Women's rights are no longer the focus. The concern is purely and simply about the identity of the French nation, where the burkini now epitomizes the threat rather than the vulnerability posed by the French Muslim women, and where the vulnerable subject is transformed into a dangerous, threatening subject. Rather than seeking to 'rescue' her through gender equality, she has become the embodiment of immorality and anti-secularism, and a distinct and clear threat to 'living together'. While legal challenges to the ban have, in some instances, resulted in it being overturned on the grounds that it violates individual freedom, the coercive political and cultural space that has enabled the 'Othering' of the French Muslim woman continues to flourish.

This coercive aspect is demonstrated in the following explicit – and more nuanced – ways. Muslims continue to be conceptualized as the embodiment of a threatening alterity, and always as incommensurable with the liberal values that are the substrate of human rights discourses. They are constantly called upon to assert or prove their European identity, whether in terms of fidelity to the nation or through overt assimilation. Even as legal citizens, they never belong, and are continually referenced in accordance with their generational affiliations rather than their formal legal status. The force of the liberal democratic state, applied in and through the rhetoric of gender equality, also reveals the precariousness of Muslim subjects in terms of their belonging, or of their recognition as humans entitled to rights. In the French veil cases the Muslim women involved were citizens, yet their position remained tenuous and ambiguous, and only assumed full meaning when recognized by the state and the majority whose identity and values constitute the apparently secular, neutral norm. In *S.A.S. v. France*, the rhetoric supporting the political idea of 'living together' categorically assumed that the veil is an obstacle to open social interaction. The way in which this idea is articulated without qualification or circumspection treats Muslims as perennially new arrivals to the Republic, instead of accepting Islam as an integral constituent of French identity, inscribed through the nation's colonial history.[36] In terms of political sovereignty, the veiled Muslim woman remains a non-recognizable, hence non-enfranchised, 'Other' – not incorporable into the liberal logic of human rights or French Republicanism. Like the categories of abjected sexual subalterns described in Chapter 2, she is either a 'failed subject' or an inappropriate one. In both instances, she remains an object of obsessive attention by the French state and human rights advocates, in anticipation that she can, via legal penalties, be rescued from her carceral status – that is, released from the compulsion to veil imposed by what liberals view as a sinister, regressive and illiberal socio-religious modality that dominates her life, thinking and culture.

The fact that challenges to French law were brought by French citizens from a minority community raises the complex question of *who* exactly constitutes the 'real' or legitimate, sovereign, rights-bearing French subject. In Scott's discussion of the veil and its meaning for French Republicanism, she argues that this obsession with the veil needs to be understood within the broader context of the emergence of what she terms as 'sexual nationalism', in which secularism and sexual freedom are equal components. She argues that sexuality has become the measure of difference, and of the distance that Muslims have to traverse if they are to become 'fully French'.[37] Scott traces the transformation of French

Republican universalism, an ideal based on abstract individualism, into an existential equivalent that is based on citizens' sexuality rights as an index of political equality. The rhetoric of sexual emancipation is then deployed in racist ways to stigmatize and depict the Muslim man as a religious fanatic who is also irredeemably misogynistic, repressed and sexist.[38] Produced through liberal nationalist and legal discourse, 'the Muslim' – particularly the Muslim man who condemns his women to the veil – is categorized and iterated as a political-social-cultural problem to be solved, rather than as a political-social-cultural subject whose problems need solving.

Thus, the liberal rights narratives of gender equality and assimilation invariably operate to demonize the culture of the besieged 'Other', and to represent 'Other' women, especially Muslim or Third World women, as exploited, violated and abused primarily in and through cultural practices considered as feudal and uncivilized, and repudiated by Western liberal democracies. Driven by a homogenizing agenda, gender equality is also complicit in the political foregrounding of a particular image of Islam – an image constructed through the liberal excoriation of or bans on veiling. This response fuels suspicion within Muslim minority and immigrant communities, which aggravates their marginalization and, at times, encourages the deeper embrace of faith-based practices as a form of resistance to assimilation. Muslim disillusionment with the state following the laws against veiling is a response to what has been described as a mode of internal exclusion where the French Republican imaginary has never considered Islam as anything but 'Other'. Yet, the practice of veiling is as much a private act as it is a political one: it is about being French while *also* being Muslim, in a public way that involves the deepest dimensions of the practitioner's selfhood. As Fernando argues, for some Muslim women who are French citizens, the veil is part of an ethical and moral commitment as well as a performance of public religiosity which is neither incommensurable nor inconsistent with their practice of French citizenship. Fernando states that it is critical to view the Muslim citizens of France as being French, that is, as authentic natives of France. Equally, she argues that it is just as critical to understand Islam as being intrinsic to the French nation, and to Republicanism, as a political principle and the Muslim citizen in France as being wholly and fully French – despite almost virulent resistance to this idea by the French state, which is obsessively constructing Muslims as a discrete category of citizen. While not recognized by the state as being 'fully French', they are accorded full recognition as 'Muslim' – a recognition that is simultaneously fractured by legal bans on the 'Muslim' practice of veiling, which is declared entirely un-French in both expression and spirit.[39]

However, the real issue here is not about minority/'Other' recognition by the state. In light of the larger thematic pursued by this book, the political responses to veiling within liberal democracies reflect the normative structure of the supposedly inclusive principles of secularism and the right to gender equality, which are exposed as exclusionary and selective – that is, undemocratic – in the moment of their encounter with alterity, in this instance represented by the veil. An invitation into 'civilized' liberal democratic space, as one of the end goals of the human rights project, is not an invitation to inhabit conditions of universal freedom and justice. Rather, it is a move that incorporates the disruptive 'Other' into a regulatory and normative order, thus ensuring that only certain types of cultural, sexual and gender arrangements are sustained while recalcitrant and/or dissident alterities continue to be stigmatized, penalized, marginalized or erased. These encounters with alterity demand a much deeper interrogation of the historical genealogies underlying the right to gender equality, and its complicity in governance – as opposed to the right being per se progressive, part of a freedom project and with the capacity to emancipate and benefit *all* women. How is this right deployed in the state's approach to managing and regulating the veiled 'Other'/her community? What role does it play in the production and management of religious subjects and the gendered 'Other', in terms of guaranteeing or protecting the rights and freedoms of the validated, 'recognizable' citizen-subject/'Other', who has been legally compelled to unveil – that is, to renounce the proscribed markers of her alterity in order to earn that recognisability?

This trajectory places into question both the Republican rhetoric of *liberté, egalité, fraternité* and the redemptive capacity of the human rights project as a whole. While conservative forces, some feminist groups and the law may all have been empowered in different ways, as a result of the veil controversies and subsequent cases, what is most evident is that Muslim women as a whole have ended up *less* enfranchised. The central casualty in this ideological stampede has been the core idea of subaltern feminist thought – that, vis-à-vis advocacy around faith-based issues, both gender and religion should be viewed as symbiotic, as collaboratively shaping women's subjectivity and identity. Liberal interventions have fractured this innate mutuality and encouraged a deep rift in the constituency by compelling women to choose between their right to gender equality and their right to freedom of expression and religion. This choice is both disingenuous and a coercive act on the part of the liberal democratic state in order to erase Muslim identity. Such interventions encourage a turn away from equality rights discourse, which is no longer associated with freedom and empowerment, but rather with surveillance and the constant scrutinization and policing of the despised and negated 'Other'.

The veil controversies illustrate the way in which equality rights discourses can reinforce deep fractures within society by producing, and promoting, the binary categories of 'Muslim' and 'woman' – the former represented as oppressive, the latter as oppressed. By consistently viewing Muslim men as inherently oppressive, and similarly viewing veiled Muslim women exclusively as victims, overt liberation from Muslim identity and its public markers, such as the veil, is uncritically projected as a desired and appropriate goal for liberal activism. Human rights advocates and feminists are, here, barely distinguishable from conservative and religious advocates, all apparently joining hands in an effort to save 'brown women from brown men'.[40] The short-sighted assumption that all veiled Muslim women in Europe will passively comply with the ban on the veil in the interest of pursuing and attaining 'recognizability' and rights completely misses the deeper relationship of exteriority and interiority – that is, the crucial place and role of veiling in the constitution of faith-based subjectivity and the formation of gender identity within a minority community. The alignment of international human rights with the anti-terrorism and global security discourse raises the question of how gender and, in this case, the focus on banning the veil has been deployed by human rights to facilitate the larger project of defending liberalism from illiberal 'Others'; that is, in what sense has the rhetoric of rights justified employing illiberal means, such as banning the veil, in support of this larger project?

SELF AND OTHER: VEILING AS SIGNIFICATION

In relation to the veil, the overwhelming emphasis of women's human rights advocacy is on a stated commitment to bringing about women's freedom from the veil – its various manifestations viewed as symbols of oppression; its signification a 'kind of body bag for the living'.[41] The practice continues to be evaluated against the rhetoric of (Western, Christian) civilization and its 'respect' for women, and includes feminist claims of 'rescuing' Muslim women from their 'barbaric' culture. When, occasionally, the beneficent and compassionate aspects of the faith are noted, it is always against criteria that distinguish the 'good' Muslim from the 'bad' Muslim.[42] The appeal to religion serves primarily as a means by which to assert the civilizational argument, wherein the righteous 'crusade' against the 'evil ones' – those visualized and inscribed as the adversarial 'Other'. What follows is an inevitable dissection and denouncement of the culture and value systems of the 'Other', including its treatment of women. The almost obsessive focus on the veil as a symbol of the discriminatory treatment of women in Islamic societies perpetuates the cultural divide along which many global conversations about culture in relation to women's rights take place.

The discussion in this chapter illustrates how freedom as schematized in the liberal paradigm is, in some respects, threatened by the phenomenon of the regularly veiled face: the wall of cloth offers the viewer ambiguity rather than certainty, prevents direct visual identification and thereby keeps the 'Other' from being instantaneously, and adequately, recognized and categorized. As discussed in Chapter 2, recognizability is the first and most crucial aspect of the process of subaltern/minority incorporation into the national body. Only when recognizability is established will legibility, social inclusion and civic entitlement follow, usually in the form of selective assimilation, open only to those individuals who demonstrate full compliance with the terms of dominant secular and gender norms. In the French cases, compliance with the terms of Republican secularism and citizenship is a prerequisite to equality. The situation is reminiscent of the practice of the French colonial state, where selective assimilation was available to those natives who were exceptional in their ability to demonstrate '(French) cultural competence'.[43] In the context of gender, Fernando discusses how the social inclusion of such exceptional individuals (here, non-white, unveiled, secular Muslim women) remains integral to the political practice of contemporary French Republicanism.[44] Having conformed to the law, the 'emancipation' of a Muslim woman is defined, and recognition bestowed, in terms of the extent to which she is able to exercise personal freedom apart from the Muslim male – who, in the liberal view, is thoroughly misogynistic, will take every chance to oppress her, will be sexually violent, and will compel her to veil, thereby denying her the chance to demonstrate or perform her femininity, sexuality and autonomy.

A similar totalizing rationale was exhibited in the context of the war, launched in March 2003, to 'liberate' the Afghan woman from the medieval vision of the Taliban. Human rights, including women's rights, provided the veneer of righteous legality for what is today categorized by all parties as an 'invasion'. Described as the 'first feminist war in all of history', the military operation was saturated with the rhetoric of gender liberation. The US-led war was presented as a gentle civilizing mission which was somehow a better option for the natives than submission to a sadistic Taliban rule that would leave the country, its minorities and its women clearly worse off.[45] Butler analyses how the representations of unveiled Afghan women welcoming US Marines paradoxically masked more than they revealed.[46] She discusses how the Western understanding of Afghan women's freedom was entirely contingent on the idea that the Marines were rescuing them from a brutal and unjust regime. The images of women pulling back their veils and smiling at the invading troops were read as indicative of native joy at the prospect of emancipation by liberal saviours, with 'Operation Infinite Justice' (as the US response to 9/11 was initially named; it was subsequently changed to 'Operation Enduring Freedom') finally effecting the rescue of those who, ostensibly, had never known what true justice means – although it seemed that they fully comprehended and materially experienced the meaning of unfreedom. Images and descriptions of such 'unfree' women joyfully and fearlessly 'throwing off their veils' and exposing their faces were myopically and mistakenly presented and read as emblematic of permanent and 'positive' autonomy. Making the face visible and open to social scrutiny is fundamentally connected to the idea of freedom as reflexively delineated in corporeal and consumerist terms, where autonomy is ultimately associated with practices such as wearing makeup, the latest fashion accessories and alluring clothing – that is, the contemporary customs of emancipated, enfranchised women.[47]

This mode of consumption nurtures and reinforces a self-image aligned with a particular schema of female autonomy scripted and propagated by the neoliberal market, regarded as the greatest enabler of individual and collective freedom. Within the liberal ethos, it is the body – and exposure of the body – with which individual autonomy and sexual equality are primarily equated. As Butler's analysis indicates, what is so consciously occluded in this Western narrative of occupation/'emancipation' is the thoroughly militarized context within which the native women are baring their faces: the devastation wreaked by the war in Afghanistan, the regrouping and reestablishment of the Taliban and the complex politics of nationalism that attach to the signifier of the veil in Afghanistan and elsewhere.[48] The full account of individual and collective suffering, and the destruction produced by the action – and inaction – of participating Western governments complicit in the perpetuation of atrocities on the ground, has not been disclosed to, and hence is not registered by, citizens of those nations.[49] Military interventions under the banner of gender liberation render invisible the unconscionable harms of war inflicted on local populations. Uprooted, damaged and destroyed, these anonymous lives are kept unrecognizable, and are therefore not grievable;[50] not legible, except as statistics in the casualty count of global jihad; not cherished, not commemorated and not consecrated by public markers that document the human cost of inhumanity.[51]

More than a decade later, the veil remains an intact practice, violence against women and other civilians continues on a staggering scale, and saviours have become indistinguishable from perpetrators. The Western military 'intervention' ultimately demonstrated the US resolve, and ability, to further pulverize an already demolished landscape and a society riven by religious division. Further, the Western propaganda effort foregrounded the veil as core evidence that Muslim women are oppressed by Muslim men, and presented the cultural practice of veiling as more injurious to Afghanistan's women than decades of civil war, terrorism, displacement and starvation.[52] There is little interrogation of the way in which liberal opposition to the veil was effortlessly co-opted into the military and human rights justification for the US bombing of Afghanistan, the related breaches of international law and the enormous civilian casualties that subsequently resulted. The tragic legacy of this violence continues with the stuttering, stretched-out withdrawal of American troops from the region. The US decision to fund the rise of the Taliban in order to combat the Russian invasion of Afghanistan in 1979, and the culpability of liberal feminist support for the rationale behind military intervention in 2001, is neither scrutinized nor critiqued, and never addressed as central to the problem. Within this arrangement, liberal feminist positions are exposed as deeply problematic. The act of unveiling projects the desirable incorporation of a modified 'Other' woman – one who sufficiently embodies liberal gender norms – into the fold of this particular strand of Western feminism. The Western act of establishing a violent presence on the ground, partly under the pretext of delivering Afghan women into a condition of socio-sexual 'liberation' from the Taliban, becomes indistinguishable from the denial not just of freedom but of life itself – denied by the warring sides to innumerable women, 'enemy non-combatants', civilians and other innocents. All these 'unrecognized' lives have become disposable cogs in the savage mechanics of invasion, occupation and warfare, featuring what has been enthusiastically described as 'the most awesome military power the world has ever known'.[53]

While the veiled body is typically associated with inequality and confinement, it is also paradoxically associated with what might be called 'negative autonomy', that is, action, empowerment and mobility. Young Muslim women raised in the liberal West have been opting to join Islamic State (IS) by travelling to Syria, embracing the veil, marrying IS militants and themselves engaging in militancy. This includes a willingness to annihilate themselves through suicide bombings, in violent assaults on the liberal or liberal-backed state oppressor and everything associated with these adversaries. The veil in this incarnation comes to be associated with a monstrous, illiberal subjectivity that is ever threatening to liberal freedom, and warrants incarceration or destruction by the security apparatus. We are still asking why some young women and men, born and brought up within secular liberal democracies, become so disaffected that they are willing to freely consider personal 'martyrdom' through death, not just as a political act of resistance, but also as the ultimate emancipation attained through serving a religious cause.[54] Nor are we able to explain why some young women from liberal backgrounds completely renounce liberal selfhood, actively opting for sexual subservience to male militants and jubilantly, almost euphorically, embracing IS life in war zones. In contrast, the local women in Raqqa, that was the self-declared capital of the IS 'caliphate', struggled to understand such outsiders' choice to enter jihad while they themselves were contemplating the near impossibility of their own escape from this savage formation and its brutal chokehold on women.[55] Studies of this issue are largely media-driven, anecdotal or vicarious, rather than being based on thorough, nuanced research and analysis. Some of these radicalized young Western women are exceptionally bright, ranked as top students in their schools, and from secure, assimilated families with material resources. False consciousness, romantic fantasies or rebellious adolescent behaviour offer a limited and unsatisfactory explanation for their choice to leave home on an apparently transformative mission to acquire what they feel is their true identity. Nor can the prosecution and penalization of such women by their home countries for the crime of affiliating with terrorist groups enhance our understanding of their choices.[56] Reductive and sensationalist accounts with dramatic titles such as 'Runaway Jihadi Brides' offer little clarity. Western attention has been largely focused on radicalization and indoctrination through online jihadist platforms, as well as the sophisticated proselytizing strategies that IS deploys to recruit these young women, with the emphasis on how this susceptible constituency is ideologically manipulated to join IS and marry IS men. These claims are conflated with a continuing and pervasive representation of Islam as a violent and misogynistic faith that is inherently oppressive in its treatment of women. There is little critical inquiry into *why* the freedoms offered by liberal democratic states are experienced as illusory, futile or alienating by these young citizens. Such freedoms' failure to hold any meaning for these citizens enables the forsaken entitlements to then be antithetically implicated in personal choices, such as choices made by women who 'freely' renounce their liberal context and families, commit to jihad and join the ranks of the IS as fighters, servitors and wives – choices which are anathema/remain incomprehensible to adherents and proponents of the liberal concept of freedom.

The suggestion here is not that liberal values are to blame for the ongoing suffering and violence; rather, it is that there is a dark side to these values that is partly constitutive of the liberal project, and deeply implicated in the unfreedom of 'Others'. This acknowledgement must form part of any critical analysis of the destructive choices made by women who join IS, or who seek to find freedom outside of the liberal paradigm through other avenues of jihad. Rights critiques must endeavour to identify the root cause for the profound disaffection that encourages these young women to reject the 'liberal' way of life and instead choose lethal alternatives as a means for acquiring selfhood and community. Yet, calls for deeper reflection on these problems are often equated with misguided support for/refusal to condemn 'Islamic' tyranny, and unfairly viewed as validating illiberalism. And statements by political leaders – in the wake of terrorist attacks directed at the heart of liberal democracies, whether in New York, London, Paris or Brussels – invariably focus on a narrative of attacks on 'our' way of life, 'our' freedoms and 'our' values, thus reproducing and affirming the binary of liberal 'us' and illiberal 'them'. This rhetoric seeks not only to distance but also to exculpate the West from its core role in the violence that is also partly constitutive of the aforementioned freedoms and values.

As discussed in Chapter 1, the contemporary moment has witnessed a strong resurgence in calls for a return to European roots and Western civilizational values backed by a vast and lethal Western military arsenal, in relation to which waging wars for democracy and liberal values – against rebellious 'uncivilized' and unfree constituencies – has become a legitimate liberal end goal.[57] Demographic groups characterized as non-liberal, unreasonable, obstinate 'Others' are coerced, conditioned, groomed and governed into conforming with a particular array of globalized aspirations and pursuits, which purportedly make 'them' just like 'us' – thereby intelligible and consensual, and no longer a threat to liberal hegemony. *All* understandings of freedom that depart from the liberal trajectory are immediately, inevitably, axiomatically understood as conditions of unfreedom. And any substantive challenge to the liberal definition of freedom is, in turn, defined by liberal ideologues as opposition to freedom itself, and thus incontrovertibly cast as alignment with 'them' and 'their' illiberal worldview.

FREEDOM *THROUGH* THE VEIL

Returning to the particular political conflict surrounding the veil, and how the legal cases discussed either ignore or erase the choice to wear the veil that is exercised by practitioners, it is a regrettable fact that such outcomes are informed by a particular image of the veiled woman which has come to inhabit our imaginations in a way that is totalizing of Islamic culture and its treatment of women. The complex relationship between practitioners of veiling and the veil, and their capacity to realize freedom *through* the veil, are largely erased in such an account. Agitations by Muslim women to retain the right to wear the veil in its partial and full forms – whether it is the hijab, the niqab or the burqa – and declarations by many that they will either defy the ban and accept the accompanying penalties, or remove themselves from public spaces rather than relinquish the right to wear the veil, need to be understood through two different sets of registers. The first is the broader normative and discursive struggle that is being waged in and through equality rights discourse, wherein the liberal democratic state constantly seeks to constitute the unveiled female subject as the *only* legitimate female subject. The second emphasizes the accumulation of more rights as the *only* path by which Muslim women can secure the supposed 'end goal' of freedom.

There is broad consensus, but no fixed opinion, as to the functions of the veil among those who defend it or wear it. For some practitioners and proponents, it reflects an orthodox worldview and is considered symbolic of personal honour, as well as providing an effective mechanism against the socio-sexual tempting of men. It is a public badge of individual and collective identity and affiliation, and, more significantly, in some countries it has been a highly empowering and a crucial political symbol for women. In Iran, it was a sign of rebellion and rejection in relation to the Shah's regime and Western imperialism. In Turkey, it signified resistance to the accelerated and coercive imposition of modernity. Among some immigrant communities in France, it represents an exclusive cultural space and an overt repudiation of the assimilative urges of the liberal democratic state.

Moreover, while human rights interventions occlude the violence that is conducted in the name of rescuing or freeing women *from* the veil, gender analysis rarely considers the role of the veil in enabling the freedom of the wearer – that is, the fact that *some* women specifically and actively seek freedom *through* the practice. For example, in the context of her ground-breaking work with the piety movement among the mosque women in Egypt, Saba Mahmood has carefully explored the relationship between the veil and the wearer's subjectivity.[58] The veil is integrally connected with the wearer's inner journey to greater self-awareness in all areas of life; thus, the veil signifies an emancipatory relationship. For such practitioners, the idea of human freedom lies in ethical and faith-based conceptions of the self/subject that do not have their source/cannot be inscribed within the liberal imaginary. Mahmood's work upends the certainties of liberal secular thought through the presentation of alternative lifeworlds, where women are not duped into choosing to veil, nor awaiting rescue from its confinements, nor embracing it exclusively as a form of resistance. For some adherents the practice affirms a particular modality of religious devotion based on piety and, in the process, points to the limits not just of liberal conceptions of women's agency, but also of feminist positions which prescribe the form that agency should always take – that is, freedom from the veil.

For committed practitioners, the veil may be constitutive of both the wearer's Muslim identity and her gender identity, thus reflecting a worldview or personal ethic that cannot be subordinated, framed or dissected by the liberal imaginary. Hence, it remains unintelligible from the liberal perspective. However, the political intractability and social incomprehensibility of the position that claims veiling as a practice of freedom is generated by the very terms of gender equality which are incapable of understanding the veiled Muslim woman, and Islam more generally, as anything but threateningly different, irrational and an embodiment of unfreedom. By this logic, in order to be seen as socially reasonable and treated as legible/fully enfranchised within the liberal paradigm, the veiled woman must first be 'recognizable' as a subject worthy of political inclusion and equal rights – that is, she must first compel that recognition through the act of unveiling.

This adversarial logic places into question human rights interventions based on the premise that *all* veiled women require liberation from the practice. Analysis of the Western encounter with the veiled woman does not address the liberal fear of the practitioner's adherence to ideas of freedom that cannot be explained within the liberal universe. The veiled 'Other' is expressing a self-directed choice integral to her interiority, piety and ideals, and her way of being in the world. This manifestation of a broad conception of self, rooted in and accessing a different knowledge system, generates considerable discomfort and consternation for liberal constituencies locked into a narrow and hostile misreading of a culture that seems so profoundly irrational and regressive. The veil, in this instance, involves the relationship between an internal desire to be free through devotional attitude and principled conduct, and an external mirroring of this through one's motives and acts as a social being. This more complex, commodious and flexible enunciation of the self cannot be restricted to the paradigm of freedom found within the liberal fishbowl, and therefore remains unrecognized within the legal terrain on which the fraught political discussion of the veil has occurred.

The practitioner's claiming of the veil as a *self-chosen* instrument of freedom, rather than as a traditional habit or custom inherited and adhered to by default, cannot be shackled within the terms of a liberal equality discourse or a familiar politics of resistance; thus, the practice remains elusive and enigmatic, and the practitioners literally and socially inscrutable. The veiled woman moves beyond both the grasp and the comprehension of advocates of gender equality when she asserts her choice on terms that *to her* are totally valid and affirming, as a regular devotional act within the sphere of Muslim religiosity. Her choice is exercised not only outside of the normative prescriptions of gender equality, but also outside the epistemic fishbowl of human rights and its limited conceptions of freedom. And it is this aspect – either jaggedly, vaguely and partially understood, or not understood at all – that produces such anxiety within the human rights dispensation. Alternative expressions of freedom can seem to present a profoundly sinister threat to the hubris of a liberal project that regards itself as universal, axiomatic, singular, righteous and virtuous – the one most capable of emancipating and bringing freedom to the disenfranchised and unfree.

FREEDOM FROM THE VEIL, *FOR WHOM* … ?

Just as one might ask, with reference to Chapter 2, whether the current paradigm of international gay advocacy is hospitable and applicable to *all* queer constituencies, one might also ask whether the current model of rights-enabled gender equality, in relation to alterity, is really about equality and freedom for *all* women. My critique confronts the political rhetoric which suggests that only *some* kinds of women are worth knowing, seeing and 'living together' with, and therefore fit to be entitled citizens or humans. At this point, the key issue in my inquiry is not why some women refuse to renounce the veil as a way of life; rather, it is the question of *who* is actually being 'liberated' from the veil through its legal proscription, as in France, and what larger governance/market projects are being served.

As a stark disruption to the visual field, the veil is simultaneously equated with disruption to social equilibrium and normative patterns of civic, 'civilized' life and 'living together'. In the context of the French bans, it is not just the wearers for whom the veil is intrinsic to both interior and exterior life, but also the majority population. The bans provide this latter group with a degree of 'liberation' – from the undesirable sight of the veil in public, from the garment's signification as the ambivalent interface of liberalism's direct encounter with difference, and from the veil's capacity to trigger individual and collective phobic responses. This reading of the bans inverts the supposedly benevolent rationale of a nation emancipating its oppressed female 'Other' citizens through the processes of liberal legality and human rights. Any act – including advocacy and scholarly critique – justifying the bans or demanding the removal of the veil on the grounds of gender equality and as a defence of women's human rights almost without exception presumes to 'know' what is good for the veiled woman. This knowledge posits that optional unveiling under social pressure, or mandatory unveiling imposed by law, *is* what is best for her; that veiling is inherently oppressive and unjust, and represents a practice that incarcerates the female body and spirit. On what is such apparently certain 'knowledge' actually based? Does the state's political act of proscribing a particular expression of subjectivity, or of erasing a particular mode of public difference somehow enable French citizens to better tolerate, accept and 'know' the Muslim female 'Other'? Will the compulsory unveiling of the Muslim woman somehow enable the French public to socially and psychologically – not just visually – experience her community as their equal in every way?

The discussion suggests that there is an urgent need for critical engagement with the complex ways in which gender equality and human rights can be deployed as techniques of governance and informed by Christian majoritarianism. The right to gender equality *itself* needs to be more rigorously scrutinized, and its complicity in the production of some of the very binaries and exclusions that it ostensibly seeks to remove needs to be more fully exposed. The antidote to gender inequality does not lie in greater political inclusion coupled with a constant attack on the unruly, obdurate, marginalized 'Other', but rather in rigorously probing the ways in which the logic of gender equality is used as a mechanism for the targeting, policing and penalizing of alterity within the wider social goals of homogenization and orderly assimilation. We require a critical approach in which 'culture' is no longer constantly placed in the dock and singled out as culpable. Such engagement would displace the fatigued and unhelpful binary that sets up the practices of Muslim women, or women in religious minority communities, in opposition to human rights, and in particular the right to gender equality. It would also force deeper questioning of the way in which women's right to equality is utilized to demonize Muslim men. Fresh critique can illuminate how cultures rooted in non-liberal worldviews are not necessarily a negative attribute of the developing world, or of Islam. It will also provide evidence of how human rights and gender equality are, in fact, so saturated in culture that no intervention would be successful in expanding freedom unless culture is given proper weight and placement in strategies to bring about freedom.

This sort of approach could produce a more enabling and constructive dialogue on women's human rights, especially concerning the rights of Muslim women, than has been permitted by reactive scholarship and the current static and paralyzing debates on universality, civilizational superiority and cultural relativism. This theoretical challenge would compel human rights scholars to think more incisively about the relationship between well-intentioned human rights advocacy and the conservative and regulatory urges that it produces in the area of gender equality, as well as help to unharness human rights from the market and from the civilizing mission. It would also compel an interrogation of the redemptive claims and capacities of human rights, and present gender advocacy with an opportunity to – as stated by Mahmood in this chapter's epigraph – 'be remade' through engaging with another worldview. This reengagement involves a willingness to accept one's own vision as limited, as well as a willingness to foreground the motivations and choices of specific disempowered populations rather than primarily to seek the analytical confirmation of one's own assumptions. It is also about addressing the deeper epistemological veiling, which projects liberal subjectivity as all-encompassing through a refusal to consider other modes of being as valid and worthy. The space for such self-interrogation partly manifests once the concept of human freedom is no longer exclusively aligned with the pursuit of *more* rights and *more* law. The choice to wear the veil, as a means of facilitating the freedom of the wearer, pushes back against a liberal tradition that regards itself as axiomatically and universally identified with the ideal of freedom. When freedom is framed within an alternative – that is, non-liberal – register, human rights can no longer claim a monopoly over the philosophical terrain. It might even be said that, through such alternative framings, the very legitimacy of human rights as a freedom project is placed into crisis.

At a deeper, philosophical level, the act of removing the veiled woman from the public visual field – either via a ban or in the name of gender equality, liberal sociality and democratic culture – amounts to consciously abjuring any chance to know her further, to genuinely and productively engage with the epistemological challenge that she presents. This exclusionary logic also applies to other marginalized, penalized, illegible subaltern bodies considered ideologically problematic and socially disruptive for multiple reasons, as discussed in Chapters 2 and 3. The continuing abjection and stigmatization of such undesirable bodies is a rebuke of the emancipation-and-equality claims of rights discourses, and a potent reminder of the skewed trajectories of rights interventions. Political bans and censorship, while reducing freedom for this unintelligible 'Other' by legally enforcing her removal from the public space, also simultaneously reduce the freedom of liberal subjects, by denying *them* the opportunity to scrutinize their own prejudices, reactive inscriptions and self-validating liberal conceits in relation to the despised 'Other' and to take responsibility for these discriminatory interior processes. The difficult and necessary act of such self-scrutiny is what can transform ordinary 'understanding' into 'discernment' – an alternative mode of observing, perceiving, processing and knowing oneself and one's 'other/s' – which is my larger thematic, and which is addressed in the following chapters of this book.

NOTES

1. Saba Mahmood, *Politics of Piety: The Islamic Revival and the Feminist Subject* (Princeton, NJ: Princeton University Press, 2005), pp. 36–7.
2. Mutua, 'Savages, Victims, and Saviors; Mutua, *Human Rights Standards*.
3. Convention for the Protection of Human Rights and Fundamental Freedoms (European Convention on Human Rights, as amended), 4 November 1950, 213 UNTS 221 (ECHR).
4. *Leyla Şahin v. Turkey* (2005) 41 EHRR 8. See Carolyn Evans, 'The "Islamic Scarf" in the European Court of Human Rights', *Melbourne Journal of International Law* 7, no. 1 (2006): 52–73 for a critique of the ECtHR decisions on the banning of the veil.
5. *Şahin*, 41 EHRR 8 at [78].
6. *Şahin*, 41 EHRR 8 at [109]. See Karima Bennoune, 'Secularism and Human Rights: A Contextual Analysis of Headscarves, Religious Expression, and Women's Equality under International Law', *Columbia Journal of Transnational Law* 45, no. 2 (2007): 367–426 for a feminist argument that supports this finding.
7. *Şahin*, 41 EHRR 8 at [107]; see also [114]–[115], affirming the finding of the Administrative Court. The Court did not address the applicant's argument that she chose to wear the headscarf and that her aim was not to pressure other women into wearing the headscarf.
8. *Dahlab v. Switzerland*, 2001-V ECtHR 447, 464.
9. The holding in Dahlab was reaffirmed in the Şahin case, as well as in *Dogru v. France* where the same court upheld the 2004 French law (discussed below) banning the wearing of headscarves in French public schools: *Dogru v. France* (2009) 49 EHRR 8. See also *Ebrahimian v. France*, App. 64846/11 ECtHR 2015, upholding the secular (read: neutral) workplace rule on the unveiled dress code over the applicant's interest in not having the expression of her religious beliefs curtailed.
10. On 15 March 2004, the French Parliament enacted Law No. 2004-228, and inserted a new article (L. 141-5-1) in the Education Code which provides: 'In State primary and secondary schools, the wearing of signs or dress by which pupils overtly manifest a religious affiliation is prohibited. The school rules shall state that the institution of disciplinary proceedings shall be preceded by dialogue with the pupil': Loi n° 2004-228 du 15 mars 2004 encadrant, en application du principe de laïcité, le port de signes ou de

tenues manifestant une appartenance religieuse dans les écoles, collèges et lycées publics, *Journal Officiel de la République Française [JO] [Official Gazette of France]*, 17 March 2004, 5190.

11. Susanna Mancini, 'The Power of Symbols and Symbols as Power: Secularism and Religion as Guarantors of Cultural Convergence', *Cardozo Law Review* 30, no. 6 (2009): 2648, quoting from the Stasi Commission's report (Commission de Reflexion sur l'application du Principe de Laïcite dans la Republique, *Rapport au President de la Republique*, 11 December 2003, www.ladocumentationfrancaise.fr/var/storage/rapports-publics/034000725.pdf).
12. Former French president Nicolas Sarkozy, quoted in Vaiju Naravane, 'The Burqa Debate Splits France', *The Hindu*, 14 July 2009, www.thehindu.com/todays-paper/tp-international/The-burqa-debate-splits-France/article16555357.ece. For a comprehensive discussion of both laws, see Melanie Adrian, *Religious Freedom at Risk: The EU, French Schools, and Why the Veil Was Banned* (Cham: Springer International Publishing, 2016).
13. Mancini, 'The Power of Symbols', 2646, quoting from Circulaire No. 2004-084 of 18 May 2004, *Journal Officiel de la République Française [JO] [Official Gazette of France]*, 22 May 2004. For a specific challenge to the display of crucifixes in school classrooms as a violation of Article 9 (ECHR), see *Lautsi v. Italy*, where the Grand Chamber of the ECtHR upheld the Administrative Tribunal's ruling and finding that the right of Italian public schools to display the crucifix in classrooms could not be regarded exclusively as a religious symbol, but was also a 'symbol of a value system: liberty, equality, human dignity and religious toleration, and accordingly also of a secular nature of the State': *Lautsi v. Italy* (2012) 54 EHRR 3 [15].
14. See Mancini, who argues that, in the jurisprudence of the ECtHR, Christian norms are taken to reflect the neutral standard and Islam provides the irreconcilable other: Mancini, 'The Power of Symbols', 2629. See also Carlo Invernizzi-Accetti, 'Is the European Union Secular? Christian Democracy in the European Treaties and Jurisprudence', *Comparative European Politics*, 24 March 2017, doi: 10.1057/s41295-017-0091-0.
15. At the same time, it has been reported that some Muslim women have experienced the ban as liberating: Dominic McGoldrick, *Human Rights and Religion: The Islamic Headscarf Debate in Europe* (Oxford: Hart Publishing, 2006).
16. *Dogru*, 49 EHRR 8 at [72].
17. Through reference to *Şahin*: Ibid., [66].
18. 'Le magazine Elle lance un appel contre le voile', *Elle*, 5 December 2003.
19. Murat Akan, '*Diversité*: Challenging or Constituting *Laïcité*?' *French Cultural Studies* 28, no. 1 (2017): 123–37; Murat Akan, *The Politics of Secularism: Religion, Diversity, and Institutional Change in France and Turkey* (New York: Columbia University Press, 2017).
20. Loi n° 2010-1192 du 11 octobre 2010 interdisant la dissimulation du visage dans l'espace public, *Journal Officiel de la République Française [J.O.] [Official Gazette of France]*, 12 October 2010, 18344. For a detailed philosophical discussion on the headscarf and burqa, see Alia Al-Saji, 'The Racialization of Muslim Veils: A Philosophical Analysis', *Philosophy and Social Criticism* 36, no. 8 (2010): 875–902.
21. Translation from Susanna Mancini, 'The Tempting of Europe, the Political Seduction of the Cross: A Schmittian Reading of Christianity and Islam in European Constitutionalism', in *Constitutional Secularism in an Age of Religious Revival*, eds. Susanna Mancini and Michel Rosenfeld (Oxford: Oxford University Press, 2014), p. 114 n 19, quoting from Assemblée Nationale, Rapport d'information no. 2262, 'Au nom de la mission d'information sur la pratique du port du voile intégral sur le territoire national, 26 janvier 2010', 14.
22. *S.A.S. v. France* (2015) 60 EHRR 11. The Court completely dismissed the claims brought under Articles 3 (prohibition of torture), 10 (freedom of expression) and 11 (freedom of assembly).
23. Ibid., [82]. See also [116] and [121].
24. Ibid., [120].
25. Ibid., [139].

26. Article 8 (ECHR) provides for the respect of family and private life, subject to 8(2), which states: 'There shall be no interference by a public authority with the exercise of this right except such as is in accordance with the law and is necessary in a democratic society in the interests of national security, public safety or the economic well-being of the country, for the prevention of disorder or crime, for the protection of health or morals, or for the protection of the rights and freedoms of others.' Article 9 protects freedom of thought, conscience and religion, subject to 9(2), which states: 'Freedom to manifest one's religion or beliefs shall be subject only to such limitations as are prescribed by law and are necessary in a democratic society in the interests of public safety, for the protection of public order, health or morals, or for the protection of the rights and freedoms of others.'
27. *S.A.S.*, 60 EHRR 11 at [117]; see also [121]–[122]. Similar arguments were presented by Belgium in a challenge to the state's ban on the full face veil: *Belcacemi v. Belgium*, App. 37798/13 ECtHR 2017.
28. *S.A.S.*, 60 EHRR 11 at [153].
29. Ibid., [17].
30. Ibid., [OI-5] (Joint Partly Dissenting Opinion of Judges Nußberger and Jäderblom). For a critique of the notion of 'living together', see Sune Lægaard, 'Burqa Ban, Freedom of Religion and "Living Together"', *Human Rights Review* 16, no. 3 (2015): 203–19. See further Ilias Trispiotis, 'Two Interpretations of "Living Together" in European Human Rights Law', *The Cambridge Law Journal* 75, no. 3 (2016): 580–607.
31. Franz Fanon, *A Dying Colonialism*, trans. Haakon Chevalier (New York: Grove Press, 1965), pp. 36–8; see also Daniel Gordon, '"Civilization" and the Self-Critical Tradition', *Society* 54, no. 2 (2017): 106–23.
32. See generally Alessandro Ferrari and Sabrina Pastorelli, eds., *The Burqa Affair Across Europe: Between Public and Private Space* (Farnham: Ashgate, 2013), providing a comparative perspective on the socio-legal and human rights aspects of the response to the burqa across Europe. Also see Günter Frankenberg, 'The Innocence of Method – Unveiled: Comparison as an Ethical and Political Act', *Journal of Comparative Law* 9, no. 2 (2014): 222–58, examining the political and ethical consequences resulting from the proclaimed neutral, scientific methodological device of comparison, as revealed through various legal and juridical responses to the veil.
33. Mayanthi L. Fernando, *The Republic Unsettled: Muslim French and the Contradictions of Secularism* (Durham, NC: Duke University Press, 2014), p. 11. See also Mayanthi L. Fernando, 'The Unpredictable Imagination of Muslim French: Citizenship, Public Religiosity, and Political Possibility in France', in *Muslim Youth and the 9/11 Generation*, eds. Adeline Masquelier and Benjamin F. Soares (Santa Fe: School for Advanced Research Press; Albuquerque: University of New Mexico Press, 2016), pp. 123–50, discussing how the Muslim French subject defines her Muslimness as always already French.
34. The reasons articulated in support of the burkini bans included that it was inappropriate as swimwear, did not respect the hygiene and security of other bathers on the public beaches, and was incompatible with the 'good morals and secularism' of France. There was almost no feminist opposition to the bans: Huda Jawad, 'The Burkhini Ban Is Misogynistic – and Western Feminists Are Turning a Blind Eye', *Independent*, 13 August 2016, www.independent.co.uk/voices/burkini-cannes-islamophobia-banning-the-burkini-is-misogynistic-and-western-feminists-are-turning-a-a7188806.html. See also Agence-France Presse, 'Mayor of Cannes Bans Burkinis on Resort Beaches', *The Guardian*, 12 August 2016, www.theguardian.com/world/2016/aug/11/cannes-mayor-bans-burqinis-beachwear-must-respect-secularism.
35. Ben Quinn, 'French Police Make Woman Remove Clothing on Nice Beach Following Burkini Ban', *The Guardian*, 24 August 2016, www.theguardian.com/world/2016/aug/24/french-police-make-woman-remove-burkini-on-nice-beach. It is irrelevant that the woman was, in fact, a French citizen.
36. Fernando, *Republic Unsettled*, p. 96.
37. Joan Wallach Scott, *The Politics of the Veil* (Princeton, NJ: Princeton University Press, 2007), p. 83. See also Sara R. Farris, *In the Name of Women's Rights: The Rise of*

Femonationalism (Durham, NC: Duke University Press, 2017), who introduces the term 'femonationalism' to explain the use of gender equality as a technique for stigmatizing Muslim men and encouraging anti-Islam and anti-immigrant campaigns, and to understand the intersection among nationalists, feminists and neoliberals in different European countries, including France.

38. Scott, *Politics of the Veil*, pp. 162–6.
39. Fernando, 'The Unpredictable Imagination'.
40. Spivak, 'Can the Subaltern Speak?', p. 33.
41. Richard Lacayo, 'Lifting the Veil', *Time*, 3 December 2001, 36.
42. Mahmood Mamdani, 'Good Muslim, Bad Muslim: A Political Perspective on Culture and Terrorism', *American Anthropologist* 104, no. 3 (2002): 766–75. See also Sharif Gemie, 'In Search of the Good Muslim: French Muslims, the French State, and the Politics of Identity', in *The State of Social Progress of Islamic Societies: Social, Economic, Political, and Ideological Challenges*, eds. Habib Tiliouine and Richard J. Estes (Cham: Springer International Publishing, 2016), pp. 331–2.
43. Gary Wilder, *The French Imperial Nation-State: Negritude & Colonial Humanism Between the Two World Wars* (Chicago: University of Chicago Press, 2005), p. 130.
44. Fernando, *Republic Unsettled*. Fernando discusses how individuals such as Ayaan Hirsh Ali in Holland, Necla Kelek in Germany and Irshad Manji in North America exemplify this kind of 'secular' or 'ex-Muslim' individual, as do Loubna Meliane and Fadela Amara in France, who became vociferous supporters of the ban (at pp. 187–94). For a discussion on the relationship between freedom, religion, secularism, sexuality and gender, see Christine M. Jacobsen, Mayanthi Fernando and Janet Jakobsen, 'Gender, Sex and Religious Freedom in the Context of Secular Law', *Feminist Review*, no. 113 (2016): 93–102.
45. Paul Berman, *Terrorism and Liberalism* (New York: W.W. Norton & Company, 2003), p. 195.
46. Butler, *Precarious Life*, pp. 131–4, 143.
47. See Mimi Thi Nguyen, 'The Biopower of Beauty: Humanitarian Imperialisms and Global Feminisms in an Age of Terror', *Signs* 36, no. 2 (2011): 359–83; Bracke, 'Is the Subaltern Resilient?'; Sujatha Fernandes, 'Stories and Statecraft: Afghan Women's Narratives and the Construction of Western Freedoms', *Signs* 42, no. 3 (2017): 643–67.
48. Butler, *Precarious Life*, p. 143.
49. 'Anti-Terror Campaign Cloaking Human Rights Abuse', *Human Rights Watch*, 16 January 2002, www.hrw.org/news/2002/01/16/anti-terror-campaign-cloaking-human-rights-abuse.
50. Butler, *Frames of War*.
51. Scott Veitch, *Law and Irresponsibility: On the Legitimation of Human Suffering* (Abingdon: Routledge-Cavendish, 2007), p. 17.
52. Charles Hirschkind and Saba Mahmood, 'Feminism, the Taliban, and Politics of Counter-Insurgency', *Anthropological Quarterly* 75, no. 2 (2002): 339–54; Nermeen Shaikh, 'Saba Mahmood', in *The Present as History: Critical Perspectives on Contemporary Global Power* (New York: Columbia University Press, 2007), p. 167.
53. Michael Ignatieff, 'The American Empire: The Burden', *The New York Times Magazine*, 5 January 2003, www.nytimes.com/2003/01/05/magazine/the-american-empire-the-burden.html.
54. Achille Mbembe, 'Necropolitics', trans. Libby Meintjes, *Public Culture* 15, no. 1 (2003): 11–40; Talal Asad, *On Suicide Bombing* (New York: Columbia University Press, 2007); Stewart Motha, 'Liberal Cults, Suicide Bombers, and Other Theological Dilemmas', *Law, Culture and the Humanities* 5, no. 2 (2009): 228–46.
55. Dallin Van Leuven, Dyan Mazurana and Rachel Gordon, 'Analysing the Recruitment and Use of Foreign Men and Women in ISIL through a Gender Perspective', in *Foreign Fighters under International Law and Beyond*, eds. Andrea de Guttry, Francesca Capone, and Christophe Paulussen (The Hague: T.M.C. Asser Press, 2016), pp. 97–120; Azadeh Moaveni, 'ISIS Women and Enforcers in Syria Recount Collaboration, Anguish and Escape', *The New York Times*, 21 November 2015, www.nytimes.com/2015/11/22/world/

middleeast/isis-wives-and-enforcers-in-syria-recount-collaboration-anguish-and-escape.html?_r=0; Rafia Zakaria, 'Women and Islamic Militancy', *Dissent* 62, no. 1 (2015): 118–25.

56. Caroline Davies, 'Girl Becomes First Briton Convicted of Trying to Join Fight against Islamic State in Syria', *The Guardian*, 21 November 2015, www.theguardian.com/uk-news/2015/nov/20/girl-becomes-first-briton-convicted-of-trying-to-join-fight-against-islamic-state-in-syria. See Tania Saeed, *Islamophobia and Securitization: Religion, Ethnicity and the Female Voice* (Basingstoke: Palgrave Macmillan, 2016), pp. 57–83.
57. Nick Cohen, *What's Left?: How Liberals Lost Their Way* (London: Fourth Estate, 2007), pp. 314–15; Ignatieff, 'American Empire'.
58. Mahmood, *Politics of Piety*. See also Inés Valdez, 'Non-domination or Practices of Freedom? French Muslim Women, Foucault, and the Full Veil Ban', *American Political Science Review* 110, no. 1 (2016): 18–30; Amina Jamal, 'Piety, Transgression, and the Feminist Debate on Muslim Women: Resituating the Victim-Subject of Honor-Related Violence from a Transnational Lens', *Signs* 41, no. 1 (2015): 55–79, who proposes the notion of transgressive piety, which problematizes the association of freedom with secularism, and violence with Islam. For critical engagement with Mahmood's argument, see William Clare Roberts, 'The Idea of Emancipation after Postcolonial Theory', *Interventions: International Journal of Postcolonial Studies* 19, no. 6 (2017): 747–63; Rosa Vasilaki, 'The Politics of Postsecular Feminism', *Theory, Culture & Society* 33, no. 2 (2016): 103–23.

5. Despair, redemption and the turn away from human rights

> [I]t's frightening when things you love appear suddenly changed from what you have always known.
>
> —Barbara Kingsolver, *The Poisonwood Bible*[1]

> Normative forms of self-recognition needed to be peeled away from the desires that brought one to *that* way of being *again*.
>
> —Lauren Berlant, *Starved*[2]

In the preceding three chapters, the work of human rights has been addressed in relation to 'precarious desires' – as they were termed in Chapter 2 – through LGBT activism, or through women's human rights interventions on violence and equality. The analysis illustrates how human rights function against a hierarchy of who and what 'human' is constituted by, and also considers the use of normative and material criteria to categorize people according to varying levels of 'humanness' – the superhuman, the lesser human and the non-human. Gender, sexuality, religion, race and market parameters all serve the process of delineating and reifying a specific meaning of 'human', in addition to determining the portions, dimensions and cartographies of freedom and happiness to be bestowed upon the different classes of humans. These preferential inscriptions become the core method of distinguishing between humans who are socially and politically avowed, and have recognition conferred upon them, and those who are overtly or covertly disavowed, and negated. The analysis thus questions the meaning and efficacy of human rights as a freedom project – in liberal terms, a project to secure and uphold the rights of *all* humans.

As illustrated in the preceding chapters, freedom and its sub-elements – happiness and the good life – operate in and through human rights to normalize and ratify the normative categories of gender and sexuality, rather than to unsettle and expand them. In terms of the broader thematic, this is evident in, for instance, the legalization of same-sex marriage, the reiteration/affirmation of strict sexuality and gender categories structured along a male/female binary or the insistence that a female body which is unveiled in public space and civic sociality is the only appropriate and 'normal' one. In light of this, can human rights interventions ever be thoroughly utilized by radical or subversive identities, or arguments, to perform a genuinely counter-hegemonic role for the disenfranchised? Can precarious desires be recognized without in the process consolidating the state and market's ability to define the terms and contours of these desires? The analysis points to the answer being an explicit *no*. Human rights are interventions that inevitably align with a specific normative order, where populations that comply secure recognition and sovereignty while those that do not are deemed disruptive and subjected to various kinds of injustice, illegibility and abjection.

As demonstrated through my argument in preceding chapters, human rights and their normative prescriptions cannot serve as an effective template for the procurement of lasting freedom. In this chapter, I further argue that human rights in fact need to be uncoupled from the aspiration for such freedom. While continuing to engage with human rights is necessary, particularly as they are so thoroughly implicated in power and materially impact on innumerable, diverse constituencies, we also need to step back from the cherished ideal of human rights as a freedom project and reflect, in depth, on whether there is another modality – an imaginable, possible and liveable approach; an alternative, inclusive paradigm – for rendering and keeping the human subject affirmed and freed.

However, there is enormous reluctance, on the part of activists and theorists, to let go of the rights project as a redemptive and hopeful pursuit that will enable such freedom. There has been so much political faith, hope and passion invested in the human rights endeavour that to turn away from it for any reason would seem like an overwhelmingly nihilistic and defeatist move. In this chapter, I specifically focus on the work of three scholars – Costas Douzinas, Boaventura de Sousa Santos and Wendy Brown – to illustrate how such reluctance to step back from the rights modality manifests in critical and counter-hegemonic human rights scholarship. The discussion illustrates how, after their respective critiques, Douzinas and de Sousa Santos take a curious turn – not away from but back into the affirmation of human rights as a freedom project – and, as in the case of Brown, find solutions within a return to a system of 'bare' democracy where 'the people', meaning *all* people, rule in consensus and collaboration. This theoretical recursion is configured as pragmatic reform, renewal and reinvestment in human rights, thus persisting with a commitment to rights deployment as a mechanism for procuring lasting freedom. At one level, these critical re-postulations open up the rights discourse to different readings, and invoke its potential for different future uses, meanings and possibilities.[3] However, freedom is not among those uses. Such efforts do not confront the illusion that underlies the despair and scepticism overtaking progressive politics as its adherents acknowledge that, in terms of delivering on the promise of freedom, human rights have indubitably proved to be a grievous illusion – one that should prompt a turn away from the human rights schema, and towards the exploration of alternative conceptualizations of freedom. In metaphorical terms, what is required is a realization that human rights have been mistaken for freedom, just as the rope has been mistaken for a snake. The snake becomes the illusion of freedom – and all that flows from this illusion or error in perception is itself a part of the error. Running away from or attacking the snake does not correct the error that there is no snake there. These efforts cannot move us in the direction of freedom. As I explore in greater detail in Chapters 6 and 7, freedom rests in freedom from the error, and cannot be secured through the error.

Recent feminist and queer scholarship in affect theory has addressed this crisis to some extent by complicating how freedom and unfreedom are experienced in everyday life, an aspect mostly overlooked in epistemological critiques. Scholars of affect usefully write the body back into theory through an emphasis on the intimate, immediate and granular dimensions of daily existence. Affect theory posits a struggling, precarious subject who continually lives and arduously strives in a state of 'cruel optimism' – that is, faith in the idea of the good life and happiness, which never materializes and is in fact not attainable through such striving.[4] In human rights terms, this translates into how the subject remains invested in the reassuring illusion of rights as salvific. However, analysis of affect does not explore the consequences of turning away from this illusion. This chapter concludes with a discussion on how the 'turn away' option becomes a viable alternative, but only when the subject is able to fully confront the despair, anxiety and instability generated by the surrender of the illusion. This difficult process requires recognizing as erroneous the deeply embedded and continually reinforced perception – held as a cherished and irrefutable truth – that meaningful and sustained freedom for both enfranchised and disenfranchised constituencies is realizable *only* through the unquestioned embrace of human rights. Read in philosophical terms, the act of turning away, when fully and fearlessly undertaken, reflects not only the abjuration of a failed model but also a metaphysical repudiation – that is, a repudiation of illusion itself. I explore this aspect of awareness/self-awareness in the final chapter of the book.

REFORM, RENEWAL AND REINVESTMENT

The general and political understanding of human rights as exclusively a discourse of emancipation, which marks the shift of society from a primitive to a more evolved form, has been placed into question by contemporary critiques of human rights. The scholarship has engaged with the 'dark side' of the project at both a material and a theoretical level, and includes: exposing the unequal, colonial, patriarchal and bourgeois hierarchies that mutually uphold, and are upheld by, the project;[5] centring popular, bottom-up movements that resist, invert and subvert hegemonic accounts of human rights;[6] and foregrounding postcolonial critiques that examine the ways in which the colonial encounter continues to inform the postcolonial present, and in particular how human rights advocacy addresses the political inscription of alterity and difference.[7] The critiques have also scrutinized the discursive aspects of human rights: how rights rhetoric is thoroughly implicated in power relations and operates as a governance and normative project.[8]

These critiques have given rise to a renewed kind of faith – strategic and political, as well as pragmatic – in the human rights project. The critiques insist that human rights discourse has little to do with the actual freedom of the disempowered; that the freedom and entitlement promised by rights remain largely illusory. Acknowledgement of the profound failure of the rights project is not sufficient to quell the panic that manifests when the option of renouncing one's intellectual relationship with human rights as a freedom project is presented through valid counter-critique. Having problematized the liberatory role (and essentialist conceit) of human rights, the critique then pulls back from the brink and seeks to retrieve the transformative vestiges of human rights.[9] For example, Kennedy recognizes how human rights occupy and dominate the space of emancipatory possibilities, thus crowding out other discourses; also, that rights variously serve as a 'vehicle of empire rather than an antidote to empire'.[10] He argues that the naïve faith placed in human rights by its advocates must give way to hard-nosed pragmatism and a specific avowal of the civilizing and world-making power of human rights. Kennedy uses the counter-critique as a way to turn back to human rights, cajoling human rights advocates to become partners in ruler-ship, to embrace the exercise of power and to develop a 'responsible exercise of human freedom'.[11] The pitch for a critical redemption of human rights, through what Golder describes as 'muscular pragmatism', does not surrender the ideals of human rights as a freedom project, but demands a responsible exercise of that freedom through a particular deployment of power.[12] It is an argument intended to defend the value of human rights by reaffirming their salvific potential – where 'critical reflection' gives way to a pragmatic renewal and repetition, which contrasts with Ignatieff's ostensibly 'minimalist' pragmatism discussed in Chapter 1.[13]

Through a synoptic analysis of the work of three influential critical scholars who seek to recuperate human rights in the service of freedom – Douzinas, Santos and Brown – I describe the inevitability of this turn back to the liberal fishbowl, a recursion that is a marked feature of counter-hegemonic and critical human rights scholarship. Douzinas resolutely affirms the existence of freedom as an ideology – in the form that originally characterized the human rights project – and advocates for its redemption in this respect. Santos is more circumspect, having developed an argument that is willing to move beyond the liberal paradigm to account for other, non-liberal and progressive theological articulations of freedom and human dignity. And while Wendy Brown acknowledges the equivocations and ambivalences of human rights, her work explicitly identifies a reclaiming of the demos and *homo politicus* as the desirable path through the critical and political impasse.

Douzinas traces the way in which postmodern technologies of power operate through human rights, that is, how the philosophies of human rights and cosmopolitanism overtly and covertly function as strategies and tools of empire.[14] In critiquing actions such as the US-led wars in Afghanistan and Iraq, both justified in part by support for the human rights of the oppressed (most notably the Muslim woman), Douzinas argues that human rights have been appropriated as part of the *justa causa* for these allegedly humanitarian wars.[15] He does not see how human rights can be effective tools against state oppression while they are deployed in the service of international aggression under the guise of humanitarian intervention, thus serving as 'the ideological gloss of an emerging empire'.[16] He breaks with Kennedy's view that the answer rests in international humanitarians abandoning their tentative position on the margins of decision making and getting more directly, and authoritatively, involved in the business of governance. For Douzinas, this is a profoundly conservative move that expands the writ of American imperialism.[17] He pursues a theoretical return to the 'essence' in human rights, based purely on the idea of freedom – which does not resonate in the slightest with the interests and tactics of empire – thus rendering the project of human rights as one that is inherently redeemable and worthy of pursuit. He goes so far as to call upon 'good people' to 'defend rights against attacks by fearful and fear-exploiting governments', as well as against political proponents such as Ignatieff who have sacrificed the cardinal principles of liberalism.[18] As mentioned earlier, Ignatieff has supported a 'benign imperialism', or what he calls 'Empire lite', as 'the only way of protecting human rights and humanitarian values in a brutal world'.[19]

Douzinas argues that in the contemporary moment, global neoliberal capitalism and human rights have similar trajectories, which cause the two modalities to merge into the single project of liberal hegemony.[20] He draws a distinction between human rights that are subjective and those that are institutional,[21] with the latter being used to serve the interests of the sovereign state and status quo by the judicial apparatus and policy-makers rather than to provide justice, legibility and protection for rights claimants. He argues in favour of uncoupling human rights from its institutional alignments, as well as reclaiming the essential redemptive capacities of human rights as the fuel of resistance and struggle. In contexts where rights have been appropriated by governments and bureaucracies, the return to a subjective – as distinct from an institutional – understanding of human rights may restore an innate, suppressed, subverted radicalism to the core of the project. This is a call for an egalitarian 'cosmopolitanism to come', which puts the tools of human rights in the hands of those actively engaged in resistance and unified against domination.[22]

Douzinas seeks to recover the transcendent position and the nobler aspirations of human rights – the subjective aspect that functions as a radical force in any context of struggle and any methodology of intervention. He argues in favour of reactivating 'radical natural law', that is, the tradition of rebellion and dissent in human rights. This urging is, in some ways, a return to the utopian configuration posited by idealists eager to save human rights from certain death. Douzinas' plea focuses on the emancipatory content of human rights as a tool for dismantling oppression, an approach that he argues is superior to the options, often based in violence, found within existent alternatives. He rather startlingly confines his list of such alternatives to two phenomena: ethnic nationalism and religious fundamentalism. He acknowledges the 'dark' – self-interested, self-referential, solipsistic – side of human rights, which is complicit in, and facilitates, an illusory world of contradictory justifications by various actors and stakeholders. Douzinas suggests that the negative dimensions of human rights can be overcome through an appeal not to the idealistic norms of human rights, but to the values and principles of ethical governance: 'Every time a poor, oppressed, tortured person uses the language of rights – because no other is currently available – to protest, resist, fight, she draws from and connects with the most honourable metaphysics, morality and politics of the Western world'.[23]

Douzinas' reinvestment in a transcendent idea of human rights is thoroughly infused with a seductive nostalgia – a desire to return to some earlier moment when human rights were indeed a revolutionary schema to be deployed for actualizing freedom. It is a position that continues to treat rights as a consolidated defence against abuses of state power, rather than considering them as techniques of surveillance, discipline and control of individual life. As I have already demonstrated in the three preceding chapters, this idealized conceptualization of human rights does not hold up to critical scrutiny. *What* exactly constitutes the notion of freedom that informs this popular conception of rights as inherently radical and rebellious? The call for a return to some hypothetical, pure, originary moment of individual and collective self-assertion distances human rights from the stark and difficult truths of their colonial genealogies, from which a cascade of traumatic suffering continues to erupt, even while the liberal agents of empire have adeptly changed tactics and assumed a new guise. Such critique does not automatically purge the dark aspect of the rights schema or leave in place the scaffolding of a cleansed, expansive, equitable project committed to procuring authentic freedom for *all* constituencies.

Santos also seeks to reconstruct human rights as a freedom project, but through an approach that is somewhat different theoretically.[24] He recognizes how the concept of individual autonomy has come to be firmly embedded as a crucial variable in the 'planetary marketplace', the modality which now determines power relations in society. In this neoliberal formulation, humans are equated to commodities that can be traded and transacted; the script of *homo economicus* is treated as the primary site of human value, and any other assertions of human dignity are viewed as unprofitable, thereby unworthy of consideration. While neoliberal globalization is theoretically grounded in democracy, human rights and the rule of law, in actual fact mass violations of human rights continue to be tolerated and regarded as almost commonplace within this paradigm. Santos argues that the only way to counter both the material injustices and the political apathy that augments them is to develop a more dynamic approach to human rights alongside political theologies that include faith-based mobilization and the use of indigenous practices. For Santos, these dual trajectories need not be adversarial; he reveals the internal diversity present in both, and identifies how the 'translational zones of contact' between human rights and such theologies can indeed, through appropriate elision, yield the energies required for radical social transformation. The pluralist and progressive features of political theologies, which critique the ways in which religious prejudice, sexism and homophobia influence policy-makers, are based on new concepts of redemption. These need to be combined with grassroots counter-hegemonic human rights struggles in order to secure the development of a radical politics of social transformation and the realization of human dignity.

Santos presents the conventional account of human rights as an influential expression of human dignity and a dominant discourse of emancipation, and then exposes its coercive and collusive aspects. This 'hegemonic liberal, imperialist human rights complex'[25] consolidates and legitimates oppression, leaving open to question whether human rights can serve as subversive tools or be used in authentically counter-hegemonic ways.[26] Santos seeks to excavate the emancipatory core of human rights for the purpose of re-envisioning and repurposing human rights as both an epistemological and an ethical resource in material struggles for freedom. Like Douzinas, Baxi and others, his approach reclaims a counter-hegemonic position for human rights, which consists of non-hierarchical, grassroots people's struggles and movements aimed at reducing socio-economic inequalities and transforming existent power relations. He argues that these struggles can effectively challenge liberal ideology and provide 'oppositional ideals of a good society born from the struggles themselves'.[27]

However, Santos also sees a productive role for religion in this mode of counter-hegemonic politics. Oppressive regimes in the Global South have encountered resistance from collective action, such as indigenous movements in Latin America, peasant movements in Africa and Asia and contemporary Islamic insurgencies. These mobilizations have not been formulated purely in terms of human rights, but are often grounded in cultural, historical and religious ideals: their cultural and political references are non-Western,[28] and their faith-based and political theologies have provided alternative understandings of how to defend human dignity – local constellations and formulations that, at times, contradict the hegemonies of the liberal fishbowl in which human rights is based. Focusing on the Semitic religions (Christianity, Islam and Judaism), Santos recognizes the counter-hegemonic potential of the progressive thought present in each of these traditions. These include the presence of feminist theologies which critique the patriarchal structures and sexism of religion.[29] They also offer re-readings of cultural narratives to provide space for an alternative sexual politics that supports sexual rights and homosexuality. For example, in various African contexts and countries, approaches such as these can challenge the traditional characterization and rejection of homosexuality as 'un-African', a conceptualization that is reminiscent of its status as a depraved 'Western import' within the apparently pristine, virtuous scheme of 'Indian cultural values', as discussed in Chapter 2. Progressive indigenous mobilizations can thus use the logic of rights to confront the legacies of colonialism and the contemporary proselytizing of homophobia through fundamentalist Christianity, the latter of which is often supported by powerful Western conservative churches that provide aid to various African states and, through this medium, exacerbate existing anti-gay public opinion and legislation.[30]

Cultural re-readings applied to local traditions of dissent have also provided necessary critiques of capitalism and empire, while focusing on the need for structural reform to enable the collective liberation of abject, impoverished, illegible constituencies from home-grown bigotries and inequities as well as from Western imperialism.[31] Santos' reconstructive approach – a 'post-secularist conception of human rights' – emphasizes the incompleteness of different epistemologies and discourses, and the usefulness of weaving these partial strands into a broad ecology of varied indigenous knowledge systems that could be deployed to legitimize local struggles for securing human dignity.[32] In rethinking human rights as a freedom project, Santos demonstrates a greater willingness to draw upon the epistemological space *outside* of the liberal rights heuristic.[33] Simultaneously, he links this critical search to grassroots mobilizations and, like Douzinas, assumes that there is a revolutionary capacity embedded at the ideological and emotional core of human rights which can be recovered through appropriate intervention. Santos' framing of these narratives of struggle is richly contextual and inclusive, but is still primarily dependent upon the scaffolding of human rights for its overall visibility and legibility. It does not answer the fundamental question of *what* underpins the deep and persistent theoretical desire to redeem the liberal paradigm of human rights by re-inscribing it as an inherently revolutionary or progressive pursuit, and one with the inherent potential to emancipate the disenfranchised.

Wendy Brown's arguments, referred to in Chapter 1 of this book, unmask the defence of human rights – especially by theorists who take the 'liberalism of fear' position – as nothing more than a defence of the neoliberal market and capitalist democracy. I return here to Brown's argument about the paradoxes of rights, which asserts that human rights – although a supposed conduit for personal and collective autonomy – are deeply implicated in the political, operate within hegemonic discursive and normative parameters, and thus are not exercised freely.[34] Her subsequent work elaborates upon this political contextualization and argues that, within neoliberalism, economics has become the sole rationale and measure for all actions and activities in everyday life.[35] Like

Santos, she asserts that we are witnessing the formation of an exploitative, technocratic 'planetary marketplace' that is increasingly governing all aspects of our existence: we observe the substitution of *homo politicus* (or any other interpellation of the human) with *homo economicus*, whose subjectivity is *itself* rendered an abstract commodity, ever available to be entirely and ceaselessly, profitably mapped and assessed by market forces along a demand-and-supply grid.

With respect to gender, the market heralds the arrival of a particular form of female sovereignty, privilege and agency: what can be termed as the *femme economicus*, a subject who appears to be 'free', or at least freer than her previous incarnations, but who is in fact thoroughly constituted within the parameters of neoliberal political rationality. She is partly a product of the intensely marketized space wherein the imaging of women's freedom is relentlessly aligned with her potential and/or presence as an empowered economic actor, rather than with subversive expressions of gender or sexuality. While this new, more enfranchised generation is invested in competing, consuming and actively living out what they are entitled to without social censorship or interference by a bloated state apparatus – as is particularly true in emerging economies – and effectively utilizing their credentials as consumer citizens and individuals,[36] it continues to appeal to the state to ensure the stability and security that facilitates the exercise of this very freedom. This conceptualization of freedom embeds a reification of the self-sufficient individual who is able to acquire social capital through successful competition in the marketplace; further, it reifies the terrain whereupon the *femme economicus* may exercise, experience and enjoy these freedoms – the field of global capital, where neoliberal rationality has crafted a new morphology of aspiration through a skilled elision of international and local allures. This public mode of gender autonomy is intrinsic to the emerging model of privileged neoliberal citizenship and the cosmopolitan conception of the 'good life'. And it simultaneously valorizes the seductive illusion that the market is a space of 'free' choice; an unlimited, innately benevolent, flexible field for the 'free' exercise of 'free' subjectivity.

Building upon Foucault's lectures on neoliberalism as a 'political rationality', Brown discusses how power is dispersed and functions through a number of non-state actors. Within this rationale, concepts such as 'good governance', 'best practices' and 'benchmarking' all primarily become techniques for extending market principles into every aspect of daily life, from education and the right to free speech, to health and caregiving. These mechanisms reduce life to strategic problem solving and programme implementation at the cost of authentic debate and deliberation on justice, values and respect for different visions of the 'good life'.[37] Stakeholder guidelines, technical knowledge and facilitation methodologies come to replace interest groups, law, traditions and protocols that offer (a democratic) space for representation and engagement.[38] The primary objective of these varied economic mechanisms is to maximize consumer participation and access in a competitive marketplace. While these market modalities are cast as anti-political and as an essential materialization of freedom of choice and self-governance, they in fact function to overtly and covertly bring the political order under the dominance of a neoliberal market regime and business model.[39] The issues of justice, welfare and social and economic equality are displaced by the purposive securing of a healthy investment climate, a competitive market and economic growth. Having been objectified as commercial 'targets', rights-bearing subjects and the rights that they bear are thoroughly recast into an economic register.[40]

Focusing on the Euro-Atlantic world, Brown argues that as a generic category, *homo economicus* is relentlessly appropriating the space of political action. These consumption-oriented mimetic selves are not pursuing their own interest and well being through an inherent agency. Rather, such selfhood is *produced* through the neoliberal market, which then mandates that the subjects thus engendered must become self-investing human capital tethered to the project of macro-economic growth and credit enhancement – that is, fully aligned with the neoliberal project.[41] This coercion leaves no room for the individual to nurture and enact an alternative vision of self, or craft a life and future as he or she sees fit. The extractive, homogenizing trajectory of the market ensures a stark narrowing of the general political space and a slow erasure of the cartography of dissent.

Brown identifies the devastating implications of this shift for the *demos* – a shift that also portends the ultimate demise of *homo politicus*, for this surrender to insatiable economic aggression is accompanied by an equally voracious exhaustion and despair that currently pervades the ethos of Western civilization. Her argument is linked to her work on the way in which human rights are part of a configuration of governmentality that inexorably ratifies the existing social, economic and political constraints within which freedom is pursued. For Brown, mismanaged and/or manipulated rights can be redeemed by a conscious return to/resurrection of the demos, where there is an inherent assumption of politics as meaning 'rule by the people'. She clarifies that her call for retrieving the demos is not a defence of liberal democracy, which, as she argues, often uses the ideals of personhood, freedom and equality as tools to perpetuate class domination, produce racial and sexual exclusions and promote colonial and imperialist practices.[42] She asserts that democracy as such has no specified content: it is not a positive political value, but is instead a negative assertion that people should not be ruled by others and that the people themselves, rather than their economic inscription, will decide their existence and future. Critique that tries to recuperate the demos is a minimalist account of democracy as an open, inclusive system that can be filled with both good and bad content. According to this theorization, the role of the demos at least provides the language and framework through which people can be accountable to the present and make their future, as well as being able to help contest and contain anti-democratic forces that may otherwise claim these futures.[43]

Brown's dissection of neoliberalism and her analysis of the ways in which the tools of human rights are used to defend and facilitate this agenda are important contributions to critical discourse. However, apart from calling for the recapture of political autonomy and a return to the idea of democracy based on people deciding the 'fundamentals and coordinates of their common existence', Brown does not elaborate on how we should counter the current sense of despair.[44] She leaves open the question as to what futures are being envisaged and how they are being shaped, beyond the familiar, predictable and hopeful scripts of political reform and resistance. Further, the idealistic recuperation of the demos as the way forward or out of the current despair and theoretical paralysis, and the way in which this recuperation serves to consolidate a political space of greater justice and equity, again seems to reflect a bid to resurrect or reinvest in a liberal project that has historically been based on exclusions and abjections. The bare, egalitarian framing and participatory ethic of the demos are invariably linked to privileged ideologies and normative agendas, as Brown so deftly demonstrates in her analysis of Ignatieff's 'minimalist pragmatism' approach to human rights, discussed in Chapter 1. In her discussion of liberal democracy, Brown acknowledges these linkages and the exclusions against which liberal democracy operates, but argues that it has the potential to exceed this particular narrative. The idea that the demos should rule places constraints on exclusive rule by the few, incites political action from below and is directed at addressing the concerns of 'ordinary lives'. These features are jeopardized by neoliberalism, which extinguishes the very idea of the agency of demos through overt and covert manipulation of the public – viewed primarily as economic units, consumers and forms of capital – in accordance with the profiteering vision, terms and practices of the market.

Having said this, Brown does indeed appear to mourn the incontrovertible loss of the liberal democratic register to a market register.[45]

Interestingly, she considers this mutation – the wholesale economic scripting of democracy – as the factor that will 'finally kill it'.[46] This claim seems to be based on an assumption that racial colonialism, capitalist hegemony and/or religious majoritarianism, which have all been globally advanced through the rubric of democracy, are somehow fundamentally *less* voracious and detrimental than market forces. It is hard not to conclude that this fear of market hegemony is informed by the fact that the demos is indeed under threat in the Euro-Atlantic world, and that this threat in the form of a further reification of neoliberal political rationality is palpable and imminent. And it is unclear how such an argument would discourage the massive, destructive, militaristic projects disguised as hopeful humanitarian endeavours to implement democracy and the rule of law, such as the kind initiated by the West in Afghanistan in 2001 and Iraq in 2003. How would 'rule by the people', combined with a more complex analysis of the paradoxes of human rights, deter interventions/invasions based on a messianic complex, or for economic gain, or inflicted on non-liberal 'Others' as a necessary, emancipatory, 'civilizing mission'?

My brief analysis of these different descriptions and options by scholars who have been at the forefront of human rights critique, including as a freedom project, is simultaneously an exploration of the larger structural and normative postulates that limit theorizations to the liberal imaginary. It also illustrates how such scholars themselves fall short of articulating the kind of robust and radical alternatives that are essential if we are to confront the profound despair that torments the politics of human rights in the contemporary moment. We have acknowledged through critiques that the existing discursive frameworks of human rights are no longer able to secure what we desire; that is, meaningful freedom. In each case, the theoretical alternatives presented are located mainly *within* the very fishbowl that has proved constrictive, illusory, exclusionary and claustrophobic. Various narratives of renewal or hopeful reinvestment in, or realignment of, the project do not address the fundamental truth that produces the distress and political despair present within human rights advocacy and scholarship – namely, that the desire for freedom and meaningful happiness *cannot* be met by human rights, even through a revisionary, inclusive and open reengagement with it. A hopeful reinvestment in human rights should and must be pursued, but not because it is seen as *the* modality through which freedom can be procured and upheld. I argue that we require new, audacious and dynamic insights into the problem – an epistemological shift that will necessarily be unsettling, since it requires that critical inquiry be extended into philosophical spaces *beyond* the familiar and comfortable.

My argument in this book is that today, human rights are deployed as a potent form of seduction into a particular type of normativity and a specific mode of governance, rather than utilized as instruments that are reliably, systematically and genuinely productive of lasting freedom. With regard to both critique and advocacy, the gravitational pull of normativity insists on answers being found within a liberal constellation that channels interventions in a specific manner, and which has not proved emancipatory except in a transient, limited and exclusive way. Sexual violence and sexual exploitation have not been eradicated despite decades of activism, resolutions, hectic activity at the UN and the establishment of a formidable agency in the form of UN Women and its accompanying repertoire of declarations and conferences. The dynamic dissonance of the grassroots movements that have driven rights claims has been flattened by the human rights apparatus into an array of carceral measures, a focus on law and order and criminal justice, and an expanded security discourse. The state panopticon's ingestion of protest takes us even further away from the urgent task of addressing the structural causes of violence and restriction of freedom, but also, more significantly, distances us from the very possibility of freedom.

Meanwhile, contemporary critique rarely enquires into the logic through which gender categories remain rigid, normalized and naturalized through the governance processes of the neoliberal market and consumer lifestyles purportedly based on 'free' choice. Within these parameters, the supposedly deviant individuals are those who refuse to assimilate – through, for example, defying the ban on wearing a proscribed garment – and who are stigmatized and penalized in various ways for asserting their own freedom to choose. A similar pathologization is undertaken with regard to minority men, who are objectified and essentialized by being considered inherently culturally and racially prone to violence and discriminatory treatment towards women, and also with regard to queer subalterns or the queerly queer, who do not conform to mainstream trends within the domains of sexual/gender identity. However, in spite of discrediting the script of human rights as a mechanism for securing freedom, critique has not discouraged or shifted the faith placed in the immense possibilities available within rights frameworks, even while it has not encouraged any significant exploration of other lifeworlds or alternative ways of being free *outside* the vocabulary of human rights and its formulaic regimen of 'normativity'.

The critique and counter-critique of human rights can take us only so far. In symbolic terms, it might be said that critique is the liberal snake sloughing its skin, literally 'turning' inside out. This slow, systematic process of inversion enables the emergence of a new layer – a counter-critique that replaces what is now cast off as a spectral husk. Yet, as I argue in the later chapters of this book, any renewal of the rights project requires much more than mere mechanical discarding/contingent re-theorizing of existent rights discourse – it necessitates a deeper epistemic inquiry. It is simply not enough to observe and critique the skewed and paralyzed current dispensation of human rights – we also need to address the question of *where* we should turn, now that the rights project arising from the hegemonic liberal episteme and holding out so much promise of freedom has proved illusory? Regardless of the specificity of our critical/counter-critical approaches, we cannot deny the evidence – that human rights today appear to be a chronically disabled mechanism that repeatedly reneges on its assurances to the disenfranchised. The human rights project is helplessly knotted within the loops of its own rhetoric, amplified through the allegations, testimonials and rhetorical condemnation periodically reiterated at UN conclaves regarding the ongoing 'problem' of global violence.

THE REPARATIVE TURN

The analytic turn back to the liberal fishbowl – signalled by counter-hegemonic and critical human rights scholarship that proposes reform, renewal and reinvention in rights discourses and their deployment – illustrates a layered ideological reluctance to negate the value of human rights, worthy in and of themselves, as an effective freedom project. And yet, critical exploration of alternative options is essential, given the limited repertoire of emancipatory strategies that are offered by the rights schema. In this section, I consider whether the search for freedom through some aspects of feminist affect theory may be useful in the aftermath of the contemporary epistemological critique of human rights. The discussion is not intended to provide a comprehensive overview of what is a vast and burgeoning scholarship, but rather to specifically highlight whether and how affect may be utilized as an effective methodology for deeper scrutiny of this theme.

Affect theory expresses concern over postmodern and feminist epistemological critiques that have not only produced suspicion and paranoia about all categories and concepts that once held out a promise of freedom, happiness and the good life, but have also obscured the ways in which life is actually lived. 'Affect' itself is a contested, multivalent term. While it is predominantly understood in the scholarship as presenting a new ontology, it has also been attributed a spectral presence and viewed as a technology that exposes the porosity of the subject and constitutes another form of knowing and of being.[47] My focus here is on the shared preoccupation, in these competing positions, with the granular quality of daily life, of the intimacies and immediacies of ordinary experience that cohere into a supportive and politically salient body of knowledge.

Affect theory has emerged partly in response to contemporary critiques that have left us with either a dystopian vision, pessimistic projections or a sense of futurity marked by paralysis and despair. A powerful feature of affect theory is its resistance to the simple binaries of epistemological critique based on subversion versus hegemony, resistance versus power. Instead, affect focuses on the 'connective tissue' and 'relational modes' rather than on oppositions. It favours re-description over critique; it emphasizes the creative act as a way in which to respond effectively to the conditions of the political present.[48] Centring affect and de-centring the emphasis on structural restraints draws attention to the ways in which a subject survives, and makes choices, and possesses some control over her future – that is, how she actively shapes what can be termed as affective freedom. When viewed as separate from social structures, affect represents a way forward through its capacity to restructure social meaning.[49] By taking this ontological and intimate turn in the midst of current theoretical gloom and paralysis, affect theory offers a more complex, personalized reading of hope and freedom. It represents a broad range of different and, at times, contradictory views on how this ontological turn relates to epistemological critiques and the search for freedom in ways that, as I argue in the rest of this section, are also relevant to human rights critiques.[50]

As a strong exponent of affect theory, Eve Sedgwick argued that epistemological critique with an anti-essentialist focus provided a 'paranoid reading' of the world in which we live. Paranoid reading is defined as a position of theoretical omniscience where there are no surprises; it marginalizes or discounts alternatives that seek a more intimate and flexible relationship with their object of study.[51] Epistemological critique has not provided either a blueprint for ethical practice or adequate guidance for appropriate intervention in the direction of freedom. It remains primarily preoccupied with exposure, and is founded on the mistaken assumption that making something visible as the problem is only a short step away from finding the solution.[52] For Sedgwick, the privileging of an epistemic approach that pays relentless attention to the formal structures of truth and knowledge not only obscures our personal experience of those structures, but also becomes uninventive and static.[53]

Sedgwick's critique of paranoid reading marks a crucial shift from the prioritizing of epistemology in her earlier work.[54] The shift is partly influenced by her explorations of non-dualist thinking in Tibetan Mahayana Buddhism, an aspect discussed in detail in Chapter 6.[55] My focus here is on Sedgwick's 'reparative turn', which identifies the different ways in which less enfranchised and illegible communities empower themselves through building small worlds of nourishment and finding unconventional ways to affirm themselves within a dominant culture that has not always been, or is not, supportive of them.[56] Sedgwick focuses on how the intimate, proximate and present provides a more textured and deeper understanding of the world in which we live.[57] She sets out how to recuperate possibility from a world that is damaged and destroyed by writing the body back into theory, narrating the subjective experiences of structures of truth and knowledge and highlighting the importance of interpersonal relationships in processes of subject formation and identity. She uses affect to develop a more complex and inclusive delineation of human agency as an instrument in the pursuit of affective freedom. Affect is understood as an autonomous free radical that is unpredictable and attaches randomly to anything, producing a distinct archive of experience.

The argument in favour of affective freedom is an important one, for, unlike critique, it moves in the direction of definite possibility. At the same time, the assumption that affect is random or an entirely unpredictable realm of possibility needs to be problematized. It is not an autonomous manifestation, but one that is conditioned by the structural constraints within which it is experienced. For this reason, it is not always liberating, and can operate to strengthen rather than challenge deeply entrenched sexed, gendered and raced dialectics of aggression and submission. Ahmed, for example, argues that in affective economies, emotions do not positively reside within the subject; rather, they *mediate* the individual and the collective, and the psychic and social worlds, to bind or sever subjects.[58] Emotions circulate and travel within and across cultures, and allow different bodies and objects to take shape.

The link between affect, power and the possibility of freedom through a focus on the intimate has been highlighted in Fanon's attention to shame, as well as his consideration of how specific bodies, namely the black body, are designated to carry the weight of affect and the ways in which power is implicated in the distribution of such weight.[59] The affect of shame powerfully modulates the ways in which racism constructs colonial black subjectivity and reifies a particular experience of knowing and being. Fanon theorizes affect to be constituted epistemically and inclusively through colonialism, a Manichean system that functions from the level of the abstract and intellectual to the level of the somatic and intimate.[60] His argument reflects how abjection – the process of being purged, ostracized, cast out – functions as both social relation and ontology of the dominated subject. Cultural and political forces construct the subject's immediate external position as well as the intimate sites of the subject's life, thereby producing a sense of inferiority and precariousness. These forces further negate the subject by disenabling the indigenous inscription of either history or memory. For Fanon, freedom lies in the complete rejection of the aggregates, imprints and residues of the colonial past; thus decolonization, in affective terms, is achieved through the mobilization of cultural and political violence, which includes confronting and utilizing the energies of racial rage and grievance for the purposes of emancipation.[61] Affect can thus be the site of internal and external radicalism, resistance and transformation, but, as a mode of subjectivity, it is always in a symbiotic relationship with the normative and social construction.

A further example of how the affect of shame *cannot* be untangled from its discursive and normative features is in relation to gender and sexuality, where some female bodies carry more shame than others, and are more severely penalized for inappropriate sexual conduct.[62] In postcolonial feminist scholarship, a famous example is found in the Bengali writer Mahasweta Devi's allegorical short story *Draupadi*.[63] The main protagonist, Dopdi – her name being a colloquial form of Draupadi, a royal character in the mythological Indian epic *Mahabharata*, a core text in the Hindu spiritual and literary canon – is a poor, low-caste woman and a tribal revolutionary wanted by the Indian army. After she is captured, gang-raped and then stripped in public by army officers, Dopdi refuses to be clothed again and marches towards the army general, intending to shame her violators into contrition through the deliberate exhibition of her bloody naked body. She uses this moment of profound abjection to produce a fearless defining enactment of symbolic resistance to multiple oppressions: deploying the affect of shame, she forcefully transforms the vulnerable, helpless and violated subaltern body, an erotic object that has been sadistically objectified and abused, into the powerful instrument of a subversive subject capable of retaliation and revenge. Dopdi counters her brutalization by using that very trauma to overwhelm the perpetrators of that violence through shame and to extend her self-enunciation by amplifying the horror as expansively, as publicly and as directly as she can. This assertion of subjectivity by an utterly disempowered woman is radical at the level of both ontology and epistemology: Dopdi experiences her true being through a heroic, uniquely personal act that is also absolutely political.[64]

Mahasweta Devi similarly scrutinized the empowering use of shame through a female figure in her short story *Rudali* (lit. 'the crier/the lamenter/the mourner'). This term is used to identify women of a low caste in Northern India (particularly in the western state of Rajasthan) who perform mourning dances and songs at the funerals of upper-caste men through a full-body performance of weeping, wailing and singing praises of the dead, 'rolling on the ground and beating one's head … and beating one's breast'.[65] The description of the ritualized public expression of grief is a narrative comment on class and gender hierarchies, where such emotional articulation at funerals is considered shameful and unacceptable for women of wealthy families, who compete furiously to throw lavish ceremonials, and spend large amounts on hiring the most talented *rudali* to mourn at these events.[66] Respected for neither their performing skill nor their necessary role in socio-religious ceremonials, the *rudali* is accorded the status of a prostitute; at the same time, she subverts gender norms through an intense, physically uninhibited yet superbly controlled public display of emotions that bourgeois women are conventionally expected to keep private.

Devi's short story was also made into a film and in this version of the narrative, Sanichari, a poor widow whose son has abandoned her, is unable to express grief as her 'sorrow has hardened in [her] heart like wax'.[67] She transforms into a *rudali* at the end of the film because her body is simply no longer able to contain the grief from all the tragedy that she has experienced in her life. Her mourning performance of breast beating, head tossing and uncontrollable keening provides not only emotional release but also public confirmation of how this particular affect-based cultural script inverts the hierarchical imperatives of gender and class, as well as caste – the deprived woman has the privilege of free expression, while the privileged woman is deprived of this freedom.

The literary and celluloid examples presented here reveal how the emancipatory possibilities of affect cannot be realized without the normative social construction also being simultaneously and rigorously addressed. The discussion indicates how paranoia and reparation are co-constitutive trajectories.[68] It is, after all, 'paranoid reading' that clears a space for alternatives to emerge – reparative reading being one such possibility.[69] Affect theory offers an intimate account of how the practices of freedom are found in everyday life rather than in discourse or critique, even though critique is what opens up this space for investigation into the intimate and scrutinizes the modes of freedom that become available through the resources of affect. At the same time, these resources may continue to perpetuate what has been termed 'cruel optimism' – the hope, deeply fed and deeply held by precarious populations, that their suffering may be alleviated and a 'better' life actualized, and preserved, through the existent material and social apparatus.

'CRUEL OPTIMISM' AND ITS DEFERRAL OF FREEDOM

The turn to affect is useful in terms of theorizing the desire of the subject, within the liberal fishbowl, to remain committed to a way of life that includes viewing human rights as a valid freedom project, despite knowing that they cannot give us what we want. The desire or need to retain faith in systems and interventions in which so much hope has been invested can be partly explained through what Lauren Berlant calls 'cruel optimism'.[70] Focusing on post-Cold War Europe and the United States, in the context of social structures that are being dismantled, reshaped and recalibrated through neoliberalism, Berlant queries how the subject 'lives on' amid the drastic collapse of familiar, bounded fields of reference. She focuses on the role of affective relations as a way of coping with crisis, and considers the precarious subject's survival through the development of life-practices based upon the concept of cruel optimism – a 'relation of attachment to compromised conditions of possibility'.[71] While the attachments are optimistic, they are also cruel, as the subject desires objects that are actually a hindrance to her flourishing. Despite continual erosion of the self and of possibility, the optimistic precarious subject maintains their faith in the illusion or the fantasy of attaining the 'good life' by maximizing their efforts within a circumscribed existential domain where precarity is the uncontested, affective, everyday condition of the present.

Berlant demonstrates the link between affect and normativity in our neoliberal times, and describes how the demographic trapped at the economic bottom continues to cling to fantasies of meritocracy and being worthy of progress. These fantasies are linked to the practices of intimacy in the home, in the family and in the consumer world. Aspirational normativity animates and infuses living on in the present, where agency is found in the maintenance rather than in the making of life.[72] It is a kind of 'slow death' – that is, the 'physical wearing out of a population and the deterioration of people in that population that is very nearly a defining condition of their experience and historical existence'.[73] The experience of an intractable and abrasive dissonance between one's material reality and the social descriptions of what one might become, and be, through the right kind of consumer participation can be paralyzing – but it can also serve as the catalyst for a type of life building that is forged through affective solidarities. It is this productive, dynamic aspect of affect that generates community, inclusive politics and alternative values.

Importantly, the irreversible waning of the 'good life', in terms of materialism, economic security and consumerism for some constituencies, has *not* in fact led to the defeat or surrender of faith in the fantasy that an improved condition is indeed realizable.[74] 'Affective attachment' to the good life serves as an aspirational fulcrum for what is, for so many, an incontrovertibly *bad* life – one that arises from the ordinary conditions of living in the present and relentlessly wears down the subject, who nevertheless continues to find her conditions of possibility within it.[75] The precarious subject lives on temporarily as if this existential oppression is transient rather than permanent, and continues to invest hope in a normative fantasy of the 'good life' long after it 'no longer makes sense'.[76]

Cruel optimism offers an astute diagnosis that assists us in understanding the persistent faith in rights and the persistence of the illusion that the pursuit and accumulation of more rights will offer more freedom, despite material evidence to the contrary. The continuing longing for, or attachment to, human rights as a reliable modality of empowerment may not be in the precarious subject's best interest. Yet, she remains intimately aligned with the idea of human rights, despite their failure to deliver on their promises. In her thinking, rights continue to be an important way in which to negotiate the world and her place within it; they underpin both her navigation of crisis and her imaginings of freedom. This adherence arises from a fear that losing rights may bring about irreparable destruction or utter hopelessness: '(I)t is awkward and it is threatening to detach from what is already not working.'[77] The precarious subject expects her pursuit and realization of human rights to ensure a social belonging that brings a sense of physical and emotional relief, security and rest. This optimistic attachment to the object of human rights is experienced as cruel when it repeatedly and coercively reneges on its assurances. Cruel optimism describes the relationship between actual unfreedom and hypothetical freedom; it is a non-teleological, dystopian yet inclusive theorization of experience, explaining how the precarious subject endures the intolerable. The concept does not deny the subject's vital sense of hope, but neither does it make a case for the subject to remain invested in an illusory understanding of freedom, happiness and the good life.

CONFRONTING THE DESPAIR

Human rights invoke despair and cruel optimism in equal measure, as they promise an end that is invariably not realizable – and yet they are not something easily surrendered. The subject's attachment to human rights is born from a desire to sustain oneself and one's autonomy, even when the concept of human rights as a freedom project has failed or is set up to fail. Nevertheless, the focus on affect – that is, a turning to the intimate, to the daily experience of the precarious present – does not offer space to address the epistemic *causes* of the theoretical impasse. The grim truth is that, on some level, our rights-related liberal projects are on life support and further palliation is pointless; the experience of their failure cannot be remedied or justified by the precarious subject tenaciously pursuing the path of 'cruel optimism'. We continue to cling to these inept frameworks and the possibility that they might at least reduce human suffering by infinitesimal degrees, even if they do not uphold their emancipatory pledge. The pain of acute epistemic disillusion must be confronted and embraced, for this very affliction is what can push us into a more reflective space and provoke a willingness to explore possibilities of conceptualizing freedom in alternative registers; that is, other than via the liberal paradigm.

The 'affliction' that generates a sense of epistemic failure and disillusionment has been likened to *acedia* or a spiritual crisis.[78] It is more than a feeling of deep melancholia, sadness or depression experienced when things go wrong in the existential present. The term is invoked to characterize the particular, intense, metaphysical torment experienced when the epistemological foundations of a project are placed into severe, continuous, corrosive crisis, and appear irredeemable and bereft of options.[79] In the context of human rights, this despair rests not in the recognition that the rights project seems incontrovertibly broken, since we still cling to the hope that it can be glued back together again. Rather, the source of despair is the acute realization that human rights simply *cannot* fulfil their promise of emancipating and empowering the disenfranchised subject. While despair may generate yearning for a nostalgic past, when politics appeared more potent and social justice agendas more achievable,[80] this does not alleviate the anguish caused by recognition that the project is not capable of embodying the ideals and serving the purposes that were originally envisaged as its goal – ultimate freedom and happiness for *all* constituencies. The analysis acknowledges that disillusion and disaffection are inherent dimensions of political life.[81] However, this despair should not inevitably be equated with defeat and resignation – it can also be the catalyst for a genuinely productive search to determine how long-term beneficial change can be brought about through new parameters of intervention. In other words, despair need not be confined to a predictable rechannelling through reform, renewal, and reinvestment of the same fatigued human rights strategies that have repeatedly proved incapable of delivering upon the promise of freedom, and which continue to reproduce normative legibility, agency and entitlement. However, the proposition of more equitable, inclusive models or alternative strategies requires political will and commitment of a different order and magnitude than can be offered by a predictable reconfiguration, and re-narration, of the human rights project which changes little on the ground; nor can this be offered by the theoretical and methodological focus on affect, a flexible construct that foregrounds subjectivity but ultimately fails the subject.

Thus, in and of themselves, human rights can grossly hinder human flourishing and the realization of freedom; in other words, the very object which liberal scholars deemed so necessary for human flourishing instead becomes precisely the opposite. By identifying and articulating the despair produced through recognition of the failure of human rights as a freedom project, we also come to an unsettling deeper recognition – that we remain intractably constituted through a specific epistemological universe, its instruments and its operations. We come to see how our interventions, including the diagnosis offered by feminist affect theory, surrender to the inevitability of that universe with regard to principles, functions, relationships and outcomes. When we are so fully colonized into a specific way of thinking and being in the world, our efforts at reform/renewal/reinvention, and our commitment to a 'cruel optimism', become the only way in which to continue our existence. This approach is unable to conceptualize freedom in terms other than the sanctioned constellations within the liberal fishbowl.

I argue that understanding this epistemic and material despair can generate an alternative way in which to think about and approach freedom – that is, *other* than as a legal, progressive or futuristic human rights project. I return again to the metaphor invoked in the Introduction: the rope-snake, found in non-dualist philosophical thought. The rope is mistaken for the snake or may even be mistaken for a garland – but what is important is the fact that it is mistaken, not what it is mistaken for. The metaphor implies that mistaking the rope for a snake is what will determine the actions or strategies that then follow by way of response to this profound misperception. How does one rectify the mistake/remove the illusion? It cannot be resolved through an action, such as examining every detail of the snake to deduce its genus and characteristics, or trying to identify the garland's flowers and inhaling its fragrance. The error can only be resolved through the subjective process of discernment; that is, the correct recognition of both external *and* internal objects and states. Such awareness, developed through practices of self-scrutiny, brings a deep, intimate clarity free of contradiction, distortion or equivocation in relation to either the observer or what is observed. There is no relating to the appearance as if it were reality, to falsehood as if it were truth – to what is not, as if it were what is.

Human rights are not in and of themselves illusory. They do materially protect and benefit those who receive them, even while they channel claimants into specific market processes; they do empower and entitle, although preferentially and partially. Within rights discourse, affect theory usefully illustrates how the critical response to inequity, either through theorizing political disillusion or through deconstructing methodological failure, is severely inadequate, since meaningful intervention must be an existential experience that is grounded at the level of the daily, the granular, the intimate. However, this approach is also limited by its reliance upon the senses, the body, and the body's unreliable ontological spectra. A critical step back from the liberal episteme, as well as from affect, enables a range of other non-liberal possibilities to manifest and come into play. Any theoretical focus on the present crisis in human rights and on the question of whether there is any other valid way to become free and stay free, or whether we possess options other than a commitment to the debilitating dynamic of 'cruel optimism', requires a conscious and committed turn away from the rationale and rhetoric engendered within the liberal fishbowl.

Like the false 'snake' imposed on the true 'rope', the fundamental misperception of liberal ideologues – their conviction that human rights are the axiomatic template, and singular means, to empower the dispossessed and deliver them into lasting freedom – is a profound illusion, a mistaking of what is not for what is. Founded on this primary error – assumed by the liberal knower to be correct knowledge – the liberal discourse of rights does *not* contain solutions to injustice and inequity; rather, it is a part of the problem. The total alignment of human rights with the liberal idea and goal of freedom prevents us from seeking options outside of, autonomous of, or parallel to the fishbowl. To contemplate a serious engagement with alternate registers, in which freedom is experienced and understood by very large and diverse populations of the disempowered – or even to contemplate the possibility of such engagement – it is necessary to renounce the cherished notion that lasting freedom can be experienced *only* within and on liberal terms. Critiques rooted in the liberal episteme tend to reflexively perceive, judge and often reject non-liberal concepts and practices of freedom as inherently illiberal. As discussed earlier in this chapter, ideological resistance to liberal hegemony has provoked alternative theorizations – Santos, for instance, discusses the possibilities of pluralist and progressive political theologies that articulate understandings of human dignity outside of rights discourse, although he also sees these articulations as linked to or compatible with counter-hegemonic human rights struggles. I push the argument further by stating that human rights are thoroughly and incontrovertibly implicated in structures and methods of governance and normativity, and do *not* have the capacity to generate meaningful freedom. It is essential to understand freedom on its own terms, and not either accept alternative accounts as valid, or dismiss them as invalid depending upon their similarity to or difference from the account of freedom propagated within and from the fishbowl – the singular narrative prioritized and valorized in rights discourses.

A conscious critical dissociation of human rights from the liberal concept of freedom does not mean that social justice or progressive politics would no longer be possible. Rather, it means that we need to understand and engage with human rights, not as a universalized freedom project, but primarily as a governance project that is wholly implicated in structures and hierarchies of power – that is, with rights *themselves* serving as sources of profound inequity and injustice, and as instruments of suffering. The act of 'discerning' their essential finitude involves simultaneously repudiating both the surface and the substrate of rights in their contemporary guise – that is, not further condoning the deceptive rubric of promised emancipation or the jaded assertions of idealistic passion. One can then understand exactly what rights are: a conditional, preferential, discriminatory heuristic that is differentially procured, bestowed, valorized and upheld in the name of freedom. This recognition will keep us from reflexively investing/reinvesting in them to the point that they obscure what is real, or render it impossible for both the givers and receivers of rights to think outside the liberal fishbowl in their search for meaningful freedom.

NOTES

1. Barbara Kingsolver, *The Poisonwood Bible* (New York: Harper Flamingo, 1998), p. 236.
2. Lauren Berlant, 'Starved', *South Atlantic Quarterly* 106, no. 3 (2007): 435.
3. See, for example, Golder, *Foucault and the Politics of Rights*.
4. Berlant, *Cruel Optimism*.
5. Mutua, *Human Rights Standards*; Boaventura de Sousa Santos and César A. Rodríquez-Garavito, 'Law, Politics, and the Subaltern in Counter-Hegemonic Globalization', in *Law*

and Globalization from Below: Towards a Cosmopolitan Legacy, eds. Boaventura de Sousa Santos and César A. Rodríquez-Garavito (Cambridge: Cambridge University Press, 2005), pp. 1–26.

6. Balakrishnan Rajagopal, *International Law from Below: Development, Social Movements and Third World Resistance* (Cambridge: Cambridge University Press, 2003); Baxi, *The Future of Human Rights.*
7. Mutua, *Human Rights Standards*; Anghie, *Imperialism, Sovereignty, and the Making of International Law*; Anghie, 'International Human Rights Law'.
8. Brown, '"The most we can hope for ..."'; Douzinas, *End of Human Rights*; Engle, 'Anti-Impunity'; Kennedy, 'The International Human Rights Movement'; Anne Orford, *Reading Humanitarian Intervention: Human Rights and the Use of Force in International Law* (Cambridge: Cambridge University Press, 2003); Günter Frankenberg, 'Human Rights and the Belief in a Just World', *International Journal of Constitutional Law* 12, no. 1 (2014): 222–58. See also Perugini and Gordon, *Human Right to Dominate.*
9. Sundhya Pahuja, 'This Is the World: Have Faith' (Review: Shelley Wright, *International Human Rights, Decolonisation and Globalisation: Becoming Human.* London and New York: Routledge, 2001), *European Journal of International Law* 15, no. 2 (2004): 381–94. For an argument that takes the critique in a more productive direction by linking it to a radical democratic tradition, see McNeilly, 'After the Critique of Rights'.
10. David Kennedy, 'Reassessing International Humanitarianism: The Dark Sides', in *International Law and Its Others*, ed. Anne Orford (Cambridge: Cambridge University Press, 2006), p. 133.
11. David Kennedy, 'The International Human Rights Regime: Still Part of the Problem?' in *Examining Critical Perspectives on Human Rights*, eds. Rob Dickinson et al. (Cambridge: Cambridge University Press, 2012), p. 33.
12. Golder discusses this redemptive move in the context of the work of two other scholars, Anne Orford and Makau Mutua. See Golder, 'Beyond Redemption?'. I follow a similar line of analysis primarily to exemplify how critique is not able to look beyond the liberal fishbowl in its search for freedom.
13. Golder, 'Beyond Redemption?'
14. Costas Douzinas, *Human Rights and Empire: The Political Philosophy of Cosmopolitanism* (Abingdon: Routledge-Cavendish, 2007). See also Douzinas, *End of Human Rights*; Costas Douzinas, *The Radical Philosophy of Rights* (Abingdon: Routledge, 2018).
15. Douzinas, *Human Rights and Empire*, p. 178.
16. Ibid., p. 7.
17. Ibid., p. 224.
18. Ibid., p. 6.
19. Ibid., p. 139.
20. Ibid., p. 293.
21. For a similar argument, see Hopegood, *Endtimes of Human Rights.*
22. Douzinas, *Human Rights and Empire*, p. 291.
23. Ibid., p. 33.
24. Boaventura de Sousa Santos, *If God Were a Human Rights Activist* (Stanford, CA: Stanford University Press, 2015).
25. Ibid., p. 47.
26. Ibid., p. 1.
27. Ibid., p. 13.
28. Ibid., p. 8. See also Boaventura de Sousa Santos, *Epistemologies of the South: Justice against Epistemicide* (Boulder, CO: Paradigm Publishers, 2014); José-Manuel Barreto, 'Epistemologies of the South and Human Rights: Santos and the Quest for Global and Cognitive Justice', *Indiana Journal of Global Legal Studies* 21, no. 2 (2014): 395–422. For another example focused specifically on reconciling human rights with Islamic jurisprudence, see Abdullahi A. An-Na'im, *Toward an Islamic Reformation: Civil Liberties, Human Rights, and International Law* (Syracuse, NY: Syracuse University Press, 1996).

29. Santos discusses the reading of foundational texts that may be emancipatory for women. For example, in Islam, Santos, *If God Were a Human Rights Activist*, cf. Margot Bardan, *Feminism in Islam: Secular and Religious Convergences* (Oxford: Oneworld, 2009); Amina Wadud, *Inside the Gender Jihad: Women's Reform in Islam* (Oxford: Oneworld, 2006).
30. Santos, *If God were a Human Rights Activist*, pp. 38–9. See, for example, Sylvia Tamale, 'A Human Rights Impact Assessment of the Ugandan Anti-Homosexuality Bill 2009', *The Equal Rights Review* 4 (2009): 49–57.
31. Jung Mo Sung, *The Subject, Capitalism, and Religion: Horizons of Hope in Complex Societies* (New York: Palgrave Macmillan, 2011); Hamid Dabashi, *Islamic Liberation Theology: Resisting the Empire* (New York: Routledge, 2008). See generally Catherine Keller, Michael Nausner and Mayra Rivera, eds., *Postcolonial Theologies: Divinity and Empire* (St Louis, MO: Chalice Press, 2004).
32. Santos, *If God were a Human Rights Activist*, pp. 63–82.
33. See further Santos, *Epistemologies of the South.*
34. Wendy Brown, 'Suffering the Paradoxes of Rights', in *Left Legalism/Left Critique*, eds. Wendy Brown and Janet Halley (Durham, NC: Duke University Press, 2002), pp. 420–4.
35. Brown, *Undoing the Demos.*
36. Anne M. Cronin, 'Consumerism and "Compulsory Individuality": Women, Will and Potential', in *Transformations: Thinking through Feminism*, eds. Sara Ahmed et al. (London: Routledge, 2000), pp. 273–87; Brown, 'Sacrificial Citizenship'.
37. Brown, *Undoing the Demos*, p. 127.
38. Ibid., p. 129.
39. For an excellent example of this, see Brown's discussion on the transformation of Iraqi agricultural practices in a post-Saddam era: Ibid., pp. 142–50.
40. Ibid., p. 154. See also Marks, *Four Human Rights Myths.*
41. Brown, *Undoing the Demos*, p. 84.
42. Ibid., p. 202.
43. Ibid., p. 210.
44. Ibid., p. 209.
45. Ibid., p. 208.
46. Ibid., p. 209.
47. Ranjana Khanna, 'Touching, Unbelonging, and the Absence of Affect', *Feminist Theory* 13, no. 2 (2012): 213–32.
48. Robyn Wiegman, 'The Times We're In: Queer Feminist Criticism and the Reparative "Turn"', *Feminist Theory* 15, no. 1 (2014): 16. At the same time, Wiegman's main point is to problematize the 'reparative turn' in affect scholarship, and also point to the commonalities between its practice and that of paranoid criticism or the hermeneutics of suspicion.
49. Brian Massumi, 'The Autonomy of Affect', in *Deleuze: A Critical Reader*, ed. Paul Patton (Oxford: Blackwell, 1996), pp. 217–39; Eve Kosofsky Sedgwick, 'Paranoid Reading and Reparative Reading, Or, You're So Paranoid, You Probably Think This Essay Is About You', in Eve Kosofsky Sedgwick, *Touching Feeling: Affect, Pedagogy, Performativity* (Durham, NC: Duke University Press, 2003), pp. 123–51. See also Elizabeth Weed, 'Gender and the Lure of Postcritical', *Differences* 27, no. 2 (2016): 153–77.
50. My discussion does not address the charges of essentialism and the theoretical overprivileging of the individual levelled at affect. For an overview of these debates and responses, see Carolyn Pedwell and Anne Whitehead, 'Affecting Feminism: Questions of Feeling in Feminist Theory', *Feminist Theory* 13, no. 2 (2012): 115–29.
51. Eve Kosofsky Sedgwick, 'Introduction: Queerer than Fiction', *Studies in the Novel* 28, no. 3 (1996): 279; Sedgwick, 'Paranoid Reading', p. 130. For other feminist scholars who situate themselves within the reparative turn and centre the temporal frameworks of the everydayness of life, see Elizabeth Freeman, *Time Binds: Queer Temporalities, Queer Histories* (Durham, NC: Duke University Press, 2010); Ann Cvetkovich, *An Archive of Feelings: Trauma, Sexuality, and Lesbian Public Cultures* (Durham, NC: Duke University Press, 2003); Heather Love, *Feeling Backward: Loss and the Politics of Queer History*

(Cambridge, MA: Harvard University Press, 2007); Ahmed, *The Promise of Happiness*; Halberstam, *Queer Art of Failure*. Freeman, for example, examines pleasure and the erotic through a non-teleological lens and a focus on 'minor visual works by minor artists' (at p.xvii). Through this, she gives visibility to other possibilities of living when the bigger revolutions appear to have failed: Freeman, *Time Binds*. Similarly, Love draws upon the long tradition of scholarship on queer negativity, such as Lee Edelman's 2004 text *No Future*, to discuss the experiences of failure or 'ruined or failed sociality', emphasizing the descriptive over the critical: Love, *Feeling Backward*; Lee Edelman, *No Future: Queer Theory and the Death Drive* (Durham, NC: Duke University Press, 2004).

52. Sedgwick, 'Paranoid Reading', p. 139.
53. Eve Kosofsky Sedgwick, 'Introduction', in *Touching Feeling*, p. 17.
54. Eve Kosofsky Sedgwick, *Between Men: English Literature and Male Homosocial Desire*, 30th anniv. ed. (1985; repr., New York: Columbia University Press, 2016); Sedgwick, *Epistemology of the Closet*.
55. Eve Kosofsky Sedgwick, 'Pedagogy of Buddhism', in *Touching Feeling*, pp. 165–6.
56. Wiegman, 'The Times We're In', p. 8.
57. Sedgwick draws on the work of psychologist/personality theorist Silvan Tomkins: Silvan S. Tomkins, *Affect, Imagery, Consciousness*, 4 vols. (New York: Springer, 1963).
58. Sara Ahmed, 'Affective Economies', *Social Text 79* 22, no. 2 (2004): 119.
59. Frantz Fanon, 'The Fact of Blackness', in *The Post-Colonial Studies Reader*, eds. Bill Ashcroft, Gareth Griffiths and Helen Tiffin (1952; repr., London: Routledge, 2003), pp. 323–26; Clare Hemmings, 'Invoking Affect: Cultural Theory and the Ontological Turn', *Cultural Studies* 19, no. 5 (2005): 561. See also Clare Hemmings, 'Affective Solidarity: Feminist Reflexivity and Political Transformation', *Feminist Theory* 13, no. 2 (2012): 147–61. See also Dia Da Costa, 'Cruel Pessimism and Waiting for Belonging: Towards a Global Political Economy of Affect', *Cultural Studies* 30, no. 1 (2016): 1–23.
60. Frantz Fanon, *The Wretched of the Earth*, trans. Constance Farrington (New York: Grove Press, 1966); On racial affect and how the body is placed along racially defined lines, see also Sara Ahmed, 'Embodying Strangers', in *Body Matters: Feminism, Textuality, Corporeality*, eds. Avril Horner and Angela Keane (Manchester: Manchester University Press, 2000), pp. 85–96.
61. Fanon, *The Wretched of the Earth*, pp. 32–5, 178–80.
62. Sara Ahmed, *The Cultural Politics of Emotions* (Edinburgh: Edinburgh University Press, 2004); Sally Munt, *Queer Attachments: The Cultural Politics of Shame* (Aldershot: Ashgate, 2008); Elspeth Probyn, *Blush: Faces of Shame* (Minneapolis: University of Minnesota Press, 2005).
63. Mahasweta Devi, 'Draupadi', in *In Other Worlds: Essays in Cultural Politics*, Gayatri Chakravorty Spivak (Abingdon: Routledge, 1998). See also Shweta Choudhary, 'Unarmed Mutiny of Draupadi in Mahashweta Devi's Draupadi', *Language in India* 16, no. 1 (2016): 245–61. Affective frameworks, including the experience of shame, have featured prominently in postcolonial scholarship on gender and communitarian violence, especially in the context of the bloody partition of 1947, through which the two independent states of India and Pakistan emerged as separate entities having secured freedom from colonial rule (a process that involved the mass migration of Hindus, Muslims and Sikhs), and the 1984 riots in Delhi following the assassination of Prime Minister Indira Gandhi by her Sikh bodyguards: see Veena Das, *Life and Words: Violence and the Descent into the Ordinary* (Berkeley, CA: University of California Press, 2007). See generally Debra A. Castillo and Kavita Panjabi, eds., *Cartographies of Affect: Across Borders in South Asia and the Americas* (Delhi: Worldview, 2011).
64. The famous *Mahabharata* scene involves the public humiliation of the highborn queen Draupadi by Duryodhana, the greedy, malevolent cousin of the five Pandava princes who have allowed her, their common wife – along with themselves and all their property and possessions – to be gambled away in a game of dice rigged by Duryodhana. He then declares them his slaves and their wife his maid, who now has to serve him in all ways. His brutish younger brother, Dushasana, drags Draupadi by her hair out of her private

chambers and into the crowded court, and proceeds to pull her sari off her body. Helpless, the traumatized Draupadi prays to Lord Krishna, in whom she has intense faith, and through divine intervention the garment miraculously extends into an infinite flow; the lustful prince eventually collapses in fury and frustration under the weight of cloth without end. Draupadi, born of sacrificial fire with her warrior twin brother, is capable of great ferocity; she shames everyone present, passionately berating them for their cowardice and for being mute bystanders to her terrible abjection. She takes a terrifying vow that she will now bind her hair (customary for all 'respectable' women) only with Dushasana's entrails, after washing it with his blood. In contrast to the classical, royal Draupadi, who is rescued via the logic of the supernatural, the modern, subaltern Dopdi intervenes on her own behalf.

65. Mahashweta Devi and Usha Ganguli, *Rudali: From Fiction to Performance*, trans. Anjum Katyal (Calcutta: Seagull Books, 1997), p. 75.
66. Ibid., pp. 74–5.
67. *Rudaali*, Film, Directed by Kalpana Lajmi (India: Doordarshan/National Film Development Corporation of India, 1993).
68. Wiegman, 'The Times We're In'; Hemmings, 'Invoking Affect'.
69. For an important feminist critique and emerging debate on the possibilities of queer theory outside of its predilection for anti-normativity, and how this may open up space to consider the dynamic and non-static character of norms, see Wiegman and Wilson, 'Introduction: Antinormativity's Queer Conventions'. See further Ruti Mari, *The Ethics of Opting Out: Queer Theory's Defiant Subjects* (New York: Columbia University Press, 2017).
70. Berlant, *Cruel Optimism*.
71. Ibid., p. 24.
72. Lauren Berlant, 'Slow Death (Sovereignty, Obesity, Lateral Agency)', *Critical Inquiry* 33, no. 4 (2007): 759.
73. Ibid., p. 754.
74. Berlant, *Cruel Optimism*, p. 3.
75. Ibid., pp. 27–8.
76. Ibid., p. 13.
77. Ibid., p. 263.
78. Ann Cvetkovich, *Depression: A Public Feeling* (Durham, NC: Duke University Press, 2012). *Acedia* is an antiquated Latin term that signifies 'weariness or distress of heart', and describes the powerful affective constellation experienced by the desert monk who is distracted from his meditation, and contemplation, of the divine purity that is to be achieved in silence and isolation: Ibid., p. 85.
79. Cvetkovich uses this description of spiritual despair to draw a parallel with the experiences of both activists and academics who feel a profound and crippling loss of faith in light of the failure of political projects that once held out so much hope and possibility. For examples of other contemporary scholars who have used the concept of *acedia* see Giorgio Agamben, *Stanzas Word and Phantasm in Western Culture*, trans. Ronald L. Martinez (Minneapolis: University of Minnesota Press, 1993); David L. Eng and David Kazanjian, eds., *Loss: The Politics of Mourning* (Berkeley, CA: University of California Press, 2003), pp. 12–14.
80. Brown describes this kind of yearning as the psychological process of a Left 'that has become more attached to its impossibility than to its potential fruitfulness, a Left that is most at home dwelling not in hopefulness but in its own marginality and failure': Wendy Brown, 'Resisting Left Melancholia', in *Loss*, pp. 463–4.
81. See, for example, Love, *Feeling Backward*; Michael D. Snediker, *Queer Optimism: Lyric Personhood and Other Felicitous Persuasions* (Minneapolis: University of Minnesota Press, 2009); Eng and Kazanjian, *Loss*; Butler, 'Afterword', in *Loss*, pp. 467–73.

6. Seeking freedom through alternative registers

As the archaeology of our thought easily shows, man [sic] is an invention of recent date. And one perhaps nearing its end.

If those arrangements were to disappear as they appeared, … then one can certainly wager that man would be erased, like a face drawn in sand at the edge of the sea.

—Michel Foucault, *The Order of Things: An Archaeology of the Human Sciences*[1]

Foucault's controversial quote – here serving as this chapter's thematic epigraph – is often read as his theoretical signalling of the death of the subject, and hence an annulment of the ground for interventionist politics, especially in regard to disenfranchised and marginalized groups. However, as thematically explored in this and the preceding chapters, Foucault's claim indicates the ultimate demise of a particular conception of liberal subjectivity – universalized, sovereign and transcendental – rather than an annihilation of the subject itself. I use this reference to stage an inquiry into the possibility of heralding a new type of subject: neither one that is fettered nor constrained through the technologies of domination, nor one that exemplifies the fiction of an entirely autonomous subject – that is, one who occupies a space outside of discourse. This chapter examines the possibilities of redefining freedom by drawing upon non-liberal epistemologies and histories, by partly locating lasting freedom in freedom from the transcendental liberal subject through a self-reflective turn inwards and by centring the relationship between the self and the turn inwards as the fundamental requirement for shaping such freedom.

Individuals or communities in postcolonial states who are denied recognition or legal status invariably struggle to claim recognition through human rights in the hope that such recognition will give them access to a range of individual and collective entitlements. But, as I have argued, the pursuit of freedom through the accumulation of more rights always has political effects that are invariably aligned with a specific – that is, liberal – understanding of how to be in the world, and of how to be free by materializing aspirations for 'the good life', coupled with a specific mandate regarding the inscription and implementation of this worldview and its promise of happiness. Rights-bestowed recognition and entitlements are assured only if certain gender, sexual and cultural norms are adopted and secured, this being the coercive side of a liberal political project that invariably represents itself as the absolute embodiment of political and personal freedom.

Yet the belief in and pursuit of human rights as a benefic endeavour remains constant, despite the normative hegemonies of the project and evidence of the grievous failure of rights regimens on the ground. In the current scenario of global crisis, we may have to accept this condition and its inherent tensions where the experience of living under the governing norms of human rights continues to inform gender rights advocacy, engagements with alterity and the recognition of precarious desires. At the same time, this necessary ongoing commitment to rights should not prevent us from considering a more radical shift that involves a turn *away* from the attachment to human rights as a freedom project. The desire for freedom needs to be delinked from human rights – a move that would necessarily create space for other registers within which to think about the measures for achieving meaningful freedom, that is, a modality or modalities of emancipation *not* contingent upon structures of governance. The question to consider is whether there is a substantive way to think about this moment of epistemic crisis by, for instance, drawing upon a logic external to the Euro-Atlantic liberal tradition and the normative order upon which it is based – an order to which we have a powerful attachment, and which is assumed to be axiomatic. What alternative epistemological and metaphysical possibilities emerge as we inexorably come closer and closer to a point at which, as posited in the epigraph to this chapter, 'one can certainly wager that man would be erased, like a face drawn in sand at the edge of the sea'?[2] Is this contemporary impasse actually a rare moment of ideological stasis, when we can turn to non-liberal, not illiberal, ways of being that are more closely attuned to what we want – namely, freedom – and that do not slip into the trap of cultural relativism?

As stated at the outset, a central task of this book is to lend more visibility to those traditions and vocabularies that arise from other – that is, non-liberal – sources, and thus to provide alternative philosophical substrates in which to ground the concept of freedom. Yet I remain concerned at the intellectual and emotional reactivity produced in the realms of both critique and advocacy by any such proposal to engage with alternative registers. What is the true nature of this particular fear? Why is the response to such proposals so severe, negative, dismissive and, at times, actively hostile? It may be that *this* is the very fear that 'destroys' freedom – my interpretation here being distinct from Shklar's theorization discussed in Chapter 1. I suggest that what needs to be addressed is not the general threat of what might materialize if we do turn away from human rights *as a freedom project*, but rather the particular epistemic anxiety that continues to proliferate and circulate within the fishbowl at the slightest suggestion that we look elsewhere for alternatives to the current structure of the liberal rights paradigm.

As discussed in Chapter 5, I argue that this fear underscores the critiques of human rights that morph into a hopeful reinvestment in human rights as a viable, effective project of freedom or as containing a core benevolence and progressiveness that can be excavated or retrieved by counter-hegemonic movements, or those critiques that reclaim the exalted and original conceptualization of rights and its emancipatory role in the world. These efforts reflect not only a failure of theorization, enunciation and imagination, but also a deep-rooted reluctance to turn away from a project that has held out the promise of so much possibility for genuine transformation. The turn to reform and renewal equates to further investment in a project that has already failed – such recursion is *itself* a nihilistic move that can take us nowhere; nor can it change the conditions in which we find ourselves today. Contemporary critiques have revealed not only that human rights are still intimately bonded with the structures of domination laid in place by the colonial past but also that, under this rubric, gender and sexuality are constantly reproduced within the logic of advocacy as stable categories that apparently need not undergo any transformation in our pursuit of freedom. This reading of rights does not imply that they are of no value. Rather, the suggestion is that, while these engagements may identify and affirm specific forms of recognition for subjects who have been violated and silenced by experiences of marginalization and invisibility, the stitching together of all these transient phases of attenuated suffering is not in and of itself constitutive of lasting freedom.

The tenor of counter-hegemonic critique suggests a deeper epistemological crisis that cannot be remedied through renewal or reform, or a superficial restructuring of the rights heuristic. This crisis needs to be urgently confronted, and it demands nothing less than a search for freedom that is consciously delinked and released from the epistemic fishbowl of human rights. Such a move imagines human freedom outside of the vocabulary of human rights, and requires engagement with modes of thinking where freedom is conceived not simply as a linear, evolutionary march through time – that is, from good to better to still better – or where the subject is either aligned exclusively with liberal individualism or understood as constituted through discourse. This turn towards alternative registers provides critical thinkers with the larger discursive frame that has so far eluded them – the frame within which to situate their critiques after successfully provincializing the tools of Western modernity and liberalism, and exposing these as incomplete and limited.[3] It simultaneously challenges pervasive assumptions that non-liberal epistemologies, especially those emerging from the non-West/postcolonial context, have nothing to offer those scholars, including feminist and queer theorists, who have arrived at a point of intellectual despair and futility. As Dabashi forcefully argues, we need to stop asking: 'Can non-Europeans think?'[4] The answer, in no uncertain terms, is: 'Yes, we can!' Unfortunately, non-liberal, non-Western philosophical traditions have invariably been regarded as either exotic or rooted in religion (inevitably regarded as fundamentalist or conservative), or have been otherwise rejected on the ground that these traditions have been appropriated by states to serve nationalist and faith-based right-wing agendas. These ideological biases are neither accurate nor productive; nor do they encourage scholars to theorize beyond the parameters of the fishbowl.

In Chapter 5, I argued that feminist affect theory offers a possible way to address the dilemma confronting feminist and human rights advocacy and scholarship in three respects. First, it articulates an understanding of how subjects continue to 'live on' even when the promise of freedom remains elusive or no longer realizable within existing frameworks. Second, it provides another starting point from which to understand experiences of freedom and unfreedom in a more layered, textured and nuanced way – an approach that draws attention to the interiority of the subject. This seems impossible within epistemological critiques where suspicion, as opposed to possibility, underpins the core analysis. Third, when affect theory's exposition of the logic of 'cruel optimism' is applied to human rights, it offers an opportunity to explore freedom by turning towards and examining culturally oriented and subjective trajectories that are autonomous of the fishbowl. Yet, beyond the affect schema, one question still remains: What epistemic terrain might present itself to the critical gaze when we undertake a complete turn away from human rights as the primary mechanism for securing freedom?

Any critical response mandates the exploration of freedom outside of human rights, including amplification of the counter-hegemonic potential as well as the non-liberal epistemological dimensions of freedom. It foregrounds the crucial need to think more deeply about freedom in a post-liberal human rights future, while at the same time re-scrutinizing the pivotal role of human rights in that future. This shift moves beyond the current critical strategy of hopeful reinvestment in human rights, which suggests that there are no better ways of thinking about freedom and happiness beyond the liberal episteme. Such a turn away from human rights does not imply the onset of reflexive panic, nihilism or alienation. I argue that losses and disappearances are, in fact, productive and encourage the necessary repudiation of the axiomatic elision of human rights with freedom, as well as stimulating a 'turn towards' the possibility that self-sustaining, self-replenishing enunciations of lasting freedom may already be available elsewhere.

It is important to emphasize that such a move is neither an act of false consciousness nor a move towards cultural relativism and the wholesale rejection of a 'Western' project. Rather, it marks a genuine search for a modality of freedom that transcends these charges as well as the epistemic structures and politicized categories in which they are rooted. If we are to take seriously the claim of critique as productive, and not just as producing paranoia or as a recursive engagement born of anxiety regarding the project of human rights, then there is certainly an urgent need to explore epistemic options outside the fishbowl. Such a quest may require seeking out non-liberal forms of freedom that have their own inscriptions of autonomy and subjectivity, and which may be used as frameworks for deeper reflection. It also requires an intellectual acceptance of the fact that non-liberal alternatives have a great deal to offer theorists, including feminist and queer scholars, whose critiques can go no further, and where resolutions are invariably sought within the liberal paradigm. In this chapter and Chapter 7, I undertake a specific inquiry into alternative registers of being and becoming free in the world. Removed from the asphyxiating parameters of liberal legality and the inexorable pursuit of more rights, freedom becomes a defiant and elusive concept whose rich possibilities can be more fully explored by paying attention to the way individual and social liberation is conceptualized within non-liberal imaginaries.

While the possibility of developing non-liberal alternatives is available in both Western and non-Western contexts, I draw exclusively upon non-Western contexts in this discussion. In this chapter, my initial focus is on a specific aspect of the work of two prominent Western critical scholars, Eve Sedgwick and Michel Foucault, whose later thought narrates how freedom might be conceived through inquiry into culturally influential schemas of personal and collective emancipation, which exist as living, flourishing traditions beyond the fishbowl. Sedgwick's critical assessment of subjectivity and freedom through the non-dualistic rationale of Tibetan (Mahayana) Buddhism, and Foucault's notion of selfhood and 'political spirituality' drawn from the context of the Iranian revolution, both exemplify how the turn away from the liberal paradigm of human rights does not send the subject spiralling into a fearsome epistemic vortex or void, nor does it inevitably encourage or align with the insular claims of religious doctrinaires or orthodox ideologues. Instead, both scholars embrace the exploration of other possibilities of freedom, theoretically distancing themselves from concepts that are exclusively inscribed within a liberal universe, thereby affirming the radical transformative potential inherent in alternative readings.

The intellectual turns – including towards the non-liberal epistemes mentioned above – of these two scholars, ranked among the central deities of critical inquiry and feminist and queer theory, need to be taken very seriously. In this respect, I have selected their 'minor' work for analysis to explicate this point. It is not my intention to privilege or conduct an exegesis of the work of Western critical intellectuals as a means of validating my own theoretical position, that is, my invocation of non-liberal trajectories. I have chosen to analyse the work of these two canonical figures from the Western academy primarily to demonstrate how their scholarship on non-liberal enunciations are marginalized, and frequently considered as inconsequential, aberrational or simply mistaken. This reductive opinion typifies the liberal hubris that overlooks its own limitations, internal contradictions and exclusions even as it dismisses other knowledge systems. At the same time, these two thinkers represent a rare and remarkable quality among progressive thinkers: the willingness to revise and rethink their own work, including moving beyond the liberal fishbowl in search of answers.

My discussion also addresses the need to expand the definition of freedom by thinking more deeply about technologies of the self and how to be in the world – a theme explored towards the end of this chapter through an example drawn from the history and literature of Persian Sufism. The inquiry sets the stage for not only 'taking a break' from Anglo-American feminism, as proposed in Chapter 3, but also for turning away from liberal freedom. I follow the critiques in the direction of alternative non-liberal and non-Western registers, which set out other ways in which to understand as well as pursue freedom. I delineate this movement more fully in Chapter 7, using two non-Western texts to provide a brief account of Adi Śaṅkara's enunciations on *Advaita* – a major subcontinental epistemology of non-dualism – as an entry point to what is urgently required: specifically, a thorough reorientation and restructuring of our notions of subjectivity and freedom.

EVE SEDGWICK AND THE TURN TO BUDDHISM

Eve Sedgwick, whose scholarship I discussed in Chapter 5 in relation to feminist affect theory, was strongly averse to the 'paranoid' approach within critical thought – that is, an approach in which intellectual suspicion and assumptions of conspiracy served as theoretical pivots. While her earlier, highly acclaimed work on queer theory was firmly located within the tradition of deconstruction and critical theory, which she continued to value, Sedgwick subsequently advocated reparative readings as a means by which to capture the intimate and expressive experiences of the subject as a valid form of self- and social knowledge – experiences otherwise generally neglected in critical scholarship. For Sedgwick, reparative readings could illuminate the immediate and personalized aspects of life in a way that rendered visible those subjects who were neither grievable, recognizable, legible or valued in justice and rights terms, and who nevertheless somehow, *without* recourse to rights or law, found ways to empower themselves in personal terms.

Sedgwick's intellectual engagements with deconstructionism and affect theory brought her to another important turn in her own intellectual and personal life – a deep involvement with Mahayana Buddhism, the school of philosophy and religio-cultural practice developed in, and primarily associated with, Tibet.[5] This turn added a complex layer to Sedgwick's scholarship as well as her life, triggering an important inquiry into understanding the place and role of knowledge in schemas of self-awareness. This crucial prioritizing of interiority is more fully elaborated in a short unfinished essay in which she wrote about the difference between what is true and what is realized.[6] The essay was prompted in part by her observation that several of her contemporaries had begun exploring some form of Buddhist practice or thought. While she offers only a limited explanation for this, stating that such encounters reflect a zeitgeist as well as an intertwining with the emotional and spiritual destinies of these scholars, she explains that her openness to the idea of non-dualism – as articulated in Mahayana epistemology – was partly informed by her alignment with American deconstructionism, which was premised on dismantling the tacit dualisms that structured Western intellectual thought. In Sedgwick's words, 'Deconstruction is the theory, Buddhism is the practice'.[7] This has enormous significance in two respects. First, it reflects how deconstruction – an outcome of the Western canon – can be effectively and confidently taken beyond the epistemic fishbowl of the liberal imaginary. Sedgwick consciously breaks with this tradition and reorients her process towards a non-liberal modality. Second, it directs Sedgwick's own intellectual momentum along a fresh trajectory. While she lamented the paranoid or symptomatic critique, which influenced her turn to affect and its potent intimacies and immediacies, she used precisely those critical aspects to productively scrutinize the epistemology of non-dualism through the aperture of Tibetan Buddhist thought.

As Sedgwick increasingly comes to recognize that her new theoretical focus on 'knowing how to be' emerges from an alternative epistemological location, namely Mahayana Buddhism, she questions the accuracy of her initial distinction between epistemology and practice. She makes a courageous confession that her earlier ideas were intellectually inadequate, and concludes that the 'stuttering, exclusive perseveration of epistemological propositions in contemporary critical theory reads as a stubborn hysterical defense' that 'can't stop claiming mastery of reality'.[8] Whether this appears in the form of 'anti-essentialist hypervigilance' or 'the moralizing Marxist insistence that someone else is evading a true recognition of materiality', for Sedgwick these critical objections are threadbare epistemological fixations that are both paralyzing and accusatory.[9] The almost excoriating tenor of her description of Western epistemology marks her own realization of its intellectual finitude, regardless of the form it takes and its fields of inquiry, and is evidence of her own drive to search beyond this horizon.

While it is not possible to assess the depth of Sedgwick's understanding of Mahayana epistemology except to the extent that it is set out in her work, two distinct features of this episteme crucially influence her theoretical re-narration of the concepts of subjectivity and freedom. The first is a reiteration of the notion that discontinuity (material transience) takes place within continuity (consciousness). The subject is not a form that is distinct from consciousness: the subject is nothing more and nothing less than a modality of profound and complete interconnectedness, an inextricable aspect of a continuum of awareness that infuses and animates all of existence. Consciousness is understood as the seamless, limitless interrelatedness of all phenomena, and freedom is the authentic experience of this *absolute* interdependence. The focus on transcendent consciousness, as opposed to foregrounding the perishable corpus, decentres any epistemic claim that the individuated material mind/body is the primary knower and perpetuator of events. Instead, emphasis is laid upon the temporality of the mind/body. It is freedom from this duality that constitutes meaningful freedom. The second feature of Buddhist thought affirmed in Sedgwick's writing is the logic of causality, the fact that nothing is random – all internal and external events are the outcome of innumerable ontological variables in innumerable permutations, continually influencing and transforming each other in a universalized cause-and-effect relationship. This axiom is also emancipatory, in that it effectively mitigates the feelings of extreme injustice elicited when randomness is offered as an explanation for individual and/or collective existential suffering. These two doctrines produce a tension with the affect schema, which not only writes the body back into theory but also emphasizes the randomness of events – the unexpected, singular and unusual. The embrace of causality also represents an important shift in Sedgwick's earlier commitment to randomness in her work on feminist affect.

The Buddha was agnostic, thus Buddhist doctrine completely abjures the notion of a divine Creator – and just as thoroughly rejects the idea of autonomous selfhood. The Buddhist formulation of what constitutes 'being' is based on a de-individuated self-and-other relationship. The subject is no longer reactively, dialectically bound within duality, but is an empty continuum – empty being not a metaphysical void, but gravid, in which the beginning and end of all emotions and materiality take place. It is described as the 'sky-like nature of mind, where clouds can scoot across it, but it still remains just the sky. When your mind is occupied in conversations among bits of you, *where* is the conversation happening?'[10] This modality of selfhood as a continuum is radically different from that of the constituted Cartesian subject who 'is'/comes into being *because* she can 'think' – that is, a selfhood that originates through the willed act of a conditioned finite individual thinker. It is also sharply different from a critical position which posits that there is no 'doer behind the deed', and never fully answers the question: in that case, where does subjectivity reside?[11] Within Buddhist logic, the discontinuities of life and embodiment take place within an 'empty' continuum; the direct experience of 'emptiness' – that is, the absolute interdependence of all similarly transient phenomena – constitutes freedom.

The epistemology of Tibetan Buddhism is based on direct realization – an experiential, unmediated insight that is unified, irreversible and, most crucially, not based on belief or speculation. Such moments of complete awareness are beyond analogy, as well as beyond doubt; they are always felt as immediate, intimate and verifiable. And time – in the form of past, present, future, and confined within the period between the birth and death of the physical body – does not impinge on this experience. Consciousness in Buddhist epistemology continues before the birth as well as after the death of the material form, and subjectivity resides in this continuity. When asked if she really believed in reincarnation, Sedgwick responded that, for her, the idea of reincarnation – and the cause-and-effect theory on which it was based – provided her with a deeper and broader existential narrative, since the uninterrupted cyclical experience of rebirth was based on the belief that the death of the corpus did not bring about the death of consciousness.[12] In this sense, she contrasts the density and richness of Buddhist thought with what she describes as the 'shrunken impoverishment of any Western psychology of knowledge and realization, whether empiricist *or* postmodern'.[13]

Although Sedgwick was drawn to Buddhism before being diagnosed with metastatic cancer, her attraction to the philosophy intensified after this point. In Tibetan Buddhism, the state of dying is only one of a group of states called *bardos*, or gaps or periods in which the possibility of realization is available through understanding death itself. The gap following death – that is, the liminal state between death and rebirth – is the *bardo* of reality, where consciousness is not connected to the material body. It is this *bardo* that preoccupied Sedgwick in the final years of her life. Engaging with this process aligns the subject in the midst of experiencing the dissolution of her body and its affiliated identity with non-material conciousness. It provided Sedgwick with a more expansive understanding of the self, a delineation absent in the logic of liberalism and in deconstructive accounts of the subject.[14] She devoted less time to writing after her diagnosis, instead turning to art as well as Buddhist teachings as a path to understanding the metaphysics of illness and dying. These preoccupations served to constitute and mediate both her cognitive and relational worlds.

While Sedgwick's turn to Buddhism is largely treated as a footnote by scholars who prefer her better known work on queer theory and feminist affect, it is noteworthy that the shift became central to her thinking about how 'to be' in the world at a point when the search for meaning in her own life had become urgent. Deploying a non-dualistic epistemology to negotiate the sense of arbitrariness and injustice that the cancer experience can inflict on a life, Sedgwick's analysis makes it clear that she did not find philosophical resolution either within the liberal tradition or within critical scholars' analysis of that tradition. The turn to affect provided her with the opportunity to speak about the everydayness of life, including her struggles with cancer, the treatment and associated therapies. Yet, it failed to offer sufficient clarity or consolation for a woman and a scholar who was constantly inquiring, seeking and willing to revise and rethink her theoretical positions – and who, in the face of her impending mortality, was forced to revaluate her life's work. These committed personal efforts, which enabled her to courageously undo some of the 'painful epistemological/psychological knots' relating to sickness and death, are vital to understanding the change in her intellectual trajectory.[15]

The Buddhist perspective provided Sedgwick with a means through which to both build a feminist liberatory politics and resolve her own sense of affliction. Sedgwick's intellectual shift demonstrates the emancipatory potential residing in the decision to surrender the parameters of liberal thought and epistemology, in spite of fear and anxiety regarding what might manifest in its place. It simultaneously disproves the liberal conceit that there is nothing beyond the fishbowl that can help the subject out of her current predicament. The radical nature of Sedgwick's philosophical turn requires further investigation by those engaged in critiquing the rights project – critique that acknowledges the limitations of human rights as a progressive end goal, and exposes their promise of freedom and social justice as largely failing to transform the lives of vulnerable subalterns everywhere. My assertion here is not that human rights have outlived their usefulness, but rather that we must accept the theoretical impasse at which we have arrived – one that offers acute confirmation of the fact that, as a modality of freedom, human rights *cannot* give us what we want, even though, as outlined earlier, they remain something we cannot *not* want.

MICHEL FOUCAULT AND 'POLITICAL SPIRITUALITY'

An equally provocative intellectual turn is found in the work of Michel Foucault, who was preoccupied in the last few years of his life with rethinking the project of revolution, including in the context of the Iranian revolution. In this section, I illuminate how Foucault's writing on the Iranian revolution – translated and reproduced in its entirety in Afary and Anderson – can be useful for rethinking the Euro-Atlantic discourse on freedom in terms of how this concept is manifested outside the liberal fishbowl.[16] I focus in particular on Foucault's idea of 'political spirituality' and how it relates to his explorations into the technologies of the self.[17]

The Iranian revolution involved a spectacular regime change that saw the end of the rule of Muhammad Reza Shah Pahlavi, who had been installed as the authoritarian head of state in 1953, after a British- and American-backed coup toppled the democratically elected leader Mohammad Mossadaq. From 1977 to 1979, Foucault was commissioned as a special correspondent for *Corriere della sera*, a respected Italian newspaper, to write a series of articles on the Iranian revolution – the extraordinary public tumult, the establishment of an Islamist regime in

1979 and the elevation of influential senior Shia cleric Ayatollah Ruhollah Khomeini to the position of Supreme Leader.[18] Foucault made two visits to the country in 1978, and also met with Khomeini while the latter was still in exile. Reporting enthusiastically about the political upheaval in Iran, Foucault witnessed the mass action of unarmed people challenging the militarized, corrupt, US-backed regime of the Shah, whose ruthlessness was reinforced by the SAVAK, a brutal national security force that terrorized the public and committed countless atrocities against dissenters.

In accordance with his position that the modality of political resistance does not move in a linear, progressive direction, Foucault distinguished the Iranian revolution from those witnessed in Europe and articulated by European philosophers, which were limited to the structures of good government and a narrow focus on the state.[19] He argued that industrial capitalism emerged out of the hopes and aspirations of this form of revolution, describing it as ‘the harshest, most savage, most selfish, most dishonest, oppressive society one could possibly imagine’.[20] He also rejected the other form of revolution – the socialist and communist movements of the twentieth century, which had ultimately produced the violence of totalitarian communism. Having concluded that humanity was at ‘point zero’ insofar as political thought was concerned, he sought to re-theorize every type of philosophical and political ideology that had contributed to oppression.[21] Foucault did not reject the idea of revolution itself but sought an alternative logic by which to rethink, and re-conceptualize, it as a phenomenon which enabled both internal and external change, and which revolved around the emergence of what he theorized as a new ‘political spirituality’, based partly on a more nuanced understanding of subjectivity and the self, and on the revolutionary aspects of Shia Islam.

Foucault found the requisite transformative potential of revolution within the ideas of Shi’ism, particularly those that featured prominently in the early stages of the Iranian revolution, and which derived their ideological source from the sermons on social justice found in the doctrine of Twelver-Shi’ism. Constituting the largest branch of Shia Islam, this theological school represents the official religion in Iran and holds the view that after the death of the Prophet Muhammad, only his direct descendants were the legitimate Imams (rightful leaders) of Muslims.[22] They recognized Ali, the son-in-law of the Prophet, as the first rightful Imam; thereafter his two sons, Hassan and Hussein; and subsequently the nine descendants of the line of Ali. The Twelvers believe that there is no longer a living Imam, and that the last Imam entered a second occultation to avoid death at the hands of the Sunni caliphate. The 'Hidden' Twelfth Imam will return as the Mahdi, a messianic figure who will bring about social justice and peace. Thus, unquestioned belief in the 'justice to come' is central to this tradition. These sacralized ideas of earthly social justice and transcendental justice to come were prominent in the influential writings of the revolutionary Iranian thinker Ali Shari'ati, a leftist, anti-clerical intellectual. Shari'ati, who died two years before the revolution, provided a radical rereading of Shia identity and activism, and presented Shia identity as one that actively revolts against injustice and oppression.[23] Shari'ati's ideas of revolution recast Shi'ism as a perpetual struggle against oppression, described by him as *Alavid* Shi'ism, or the Shi'ism of action and resistance.[24] This form of resistance not only required the overthrow of capitalism and colonialism and the necessary failure of government, but also focused on practices that enabled the transformation of one's very being – living an ethical life here and now, in preparation for the radical future or 'justice to come' that would be established when the Mahdi returned, as projected in Shia eschatology.[25] Shari'ati's ideas establish that until the arrival of the Twelfth Imam there will be no ideal justice, but instead a constant struggle against oppressive power in the name of a 'justice to come', which further serves as an inspiration 'to begin to live differently'.[26]

Shari'ati's idea of revolution did not focus on the state or institutionalized religion, but sought to 'construct another political thought, another political imagination, and teach anew the vision of a future'.[27] It was not just a political project but also a way of living – one that primarily focused on ethical life practices in the existential moment rather than on good government through the state, or social justice implemented only through the revolutionary overthrow of ideologically suspect institutions. It put forth a completely different articulation of subjectivity that 'break[s] with conventions, habits, and values of society'.[28]

Foucault's scrutiny of the Iranian revolution and his engagement with the ideas of Shari'ati – who viewed Islam as a contested discourse[29] – reflect his continued interest in historical investigation and, in this context, the way in which the subject comes to be constituted.[30] He remained theoretically preoccupied with the dynamics of selfhood and identity formation throughout his life. Foucault's recognition, in his early work, that the subject is acted upon by power relations meant that resistance required a form of subjectivity that was unprecedented.[31] His later work on the technologies of the self reflects a more intense engagement with that aspect of subjectivity.[32]

Cornell and Seely connect this relationship between new forms of subjectivity and revolution with Foucault's discussion of 'political spirituality' as a schema of freedom.[33] They argue that his interest in the care of the self, when read alongside his interest in the Iranian revolution, was what he 'had in mind' when calling for new arrangements of our 'bodies and pleasures' – thus representing a call for the reimagining of politics, rather than a call for the development of '"queer" forms of sex and desire'.[34] Freedom and care of the self require a different way of being within oneself and with others, a different way of thinking about the truth and a different way of literalizing one's understanding of, and commitment to, one's true self and one's relationships, which Cornell and Seely argue can be found in the idea of political spirituality. For Foucault, the ideas of Shari'ati and revolution proposed a way in which to reimagine the 'fundamental modes of thought and being' in the future,[35] which moved beyond liberal humanism and remained distinct from the establishment of an Islamic government. He addresses the possibilities of 'being' through attention to self-concepts and practices of self-care, which were not only revolutionary but also integrally connected to meaningful freedom.[36] What is especially noticeable is Foucault's attraction to, and view of, revolution as an attempt to open a spiritual dimension in politics, that is, to introduce issues around 'being' into the political framework, not because he embraced or supported a theocracy, but because he sought to explore a revolutionary phenomenon in contemporary times – a notion that was unfamiliar to a liberal logic, and thereby produced liberal unease.[37] The influence of the Iranian revolutionary – specifically the ideas of Shari'ati – upon Foucault's later studies regarding the inner self remain inescapable, despite the lack of scholarly acknowledgement in this respect.

While there is little elaboration regarding the idea of *political* spirituality in his work, Foucault defines spirituality as 'the subject's attainment of a certain mode of being and the transformations that the subject must carry out on itself to attain this mode of being'.[38] Foucault's understanding of spirituality is further elaborated in *The Hermeneutics of the Subject*,[39] where he questions why the concern with the self seems to have almost vanished in the modern era. Among the explanations that he provides is the division rendered by the separation of philosophy from spirituality as a result of the 'Cartesian moment',[40] where the starting point of philosophy becomes the thinking subject. The 'Cartesian moment' becomes a definitive one in terms of obscuring or marginalizing interest in the self and the focus on 'care of the self', marking a break with spiritual inquiry. With the Cartesian moment, the subject's being is no longer placed into question and the individual inquirer, rather than the object of inquiry, becomes the epistemic starting point.[41] The end result, Foucault argues, is that 'access to truth, whose sole condition is henceforth knowledge, will find reward and fulfilment in nothing else but the indefinite development of knowledge'.[42] In other words, knowledge alone is viewed as giving access to the truth/true being/freedom, where the philosopher, scientist or seeker of truth can recognize it and access it exclusively through the activity of knowing, without any need for self-transformation or alteration of the subject.

In contrast, spirituality focuses on the subject's very being; in this modality, access to freedom is only possible through the transformation of the self, as opposed to postulating the subject as having a right of access to the truth/freedom or inherently possessing this capability. In Foucault's analysis, being a thinking subject is not what justifies access to the truth. He argues that an act of knowledge can never give access to the truth/true being/freedom per se, and must be accompanied by the transformation of the subject, which he clearly distinguishes from the 'individual'.[43] In other words, the subject must come into truth/true being/freedom through transformative practices of self-inquiry, as opposed to an assumption that the thinking self, through its intellectual operations, has a right of access to the truth. Once the being of the subject is transformed and access to the truth opens up, there are profound further effects – described by Foucault as the 'rebound effect' – on the subject of the truth she knows, which transfigures her being.[44] 'Political spirituality' is therefore a term that forces a confrontation between liberal individualism and the *a priori* subject, thus asserting the impossibility of freedom within this paradigm.

At one level, it seems extraordinary that Foucault would deploy a term such as 'political spirituality', since he was well aware of the suspicion with which it might be received – especially in France, a nation steeped in a republican secular tradition. However, given that Foucault's work was committed to a different, and invariably subversive, way of seeing and being, political spirituality can be interpreted as an effort to seek out a new politics of truth. The term cannot be understood from within a liberal paradigm based on a hegemonic notion of the sovereign subject, with freedom as an external pursuit – a frayed conventional analysis that Foucault had clearly rejected. I hold instead that his idea of political spirituality marks an epistemological – not just a political – rupture with liberalism and indicates an intellectual and personal commitment to other ways of thinking and being, which include advancing practices of self-discipline grounded in the modality of evolving self-awareness.[45]

Foucault's preoccupation with the technologies of the self continued to inform his work until his death,[46] and underpinned his analysis of freedom practices that were not trapped within the two core dualisms that pervade liberal thought – the Cartesian mind–body split, and the socio-political separation of the public/collective from the private/personal realm. His increased preoccupation with the technologies of the self, as well as ethical self-care in relation to the metaphysics of being, did not mark a shift back to the idea of a liberal subject and an individualist ontology.[47] Rather, it was a more granulated critical understanding of how subjects oriented themselves in the world.

Left-leaning and feminist scholars have been resistant to Foucault's engagement with religion and spirituality, often castigating, dismissing or ignoring this aspect of his work, which so directly challenges the liberal freedom in a fishbowl.[48] Feminists have instead reprimanded Foucault for his failure to address what they have claimed are oppressive practices of religious Islam regarding women, such as the veil.[49] In the process, not only have they constructed Islam more generally as a dogmatic, ahistorical, monolithic and deeply conservative force, but they have also viewed the Iranian revolution as reactionary and fascistic. These positions contrasted starkly with the subversive and radical strands unearthed by Foucault in his more nuanced engagements with Shi'ism, and in his articulation of political spirituality. And, as Ghamari-Tabrizi argues, the interventions of Western feminists at the time of the Iranian revolution completely eclipsed the subjectivity and capability of Iranian women who had articulated their needs and demands – against both a conservative Islamic orthodoxy and the liberal colonial frameworks of femininity that flourished under the Shah – with clarity, and the comprehension that women's issues were inseparable from social justice and an anti-imperial agenda.[50]

Following the establishment of a fundamentalist regime under Khomeini, which proved swiftly to be as ruthless as the Shah's government, Foucault's analysis of the Iranian revolution was excoriated by the Western academy. It was regarded not only as providing cultural relativist cover for the reactionary, autocratic Islamists but also as a major miscalculation or gross folly on his part, and has barely been cited in critical scholarship.[51] Foucault's subsequent critiques of the Islamic regime's human rights violations are read by some scholars as not only signifying his re-embrace of liberal individualism and the tradition of the Enlightenment, but also a veiled apology for this earlier perspective.[52]

However, in view of my discussion, it is important to situate Foucault's work on the Iranian revolution, including his subsequent critique of it, in the context of both his critical engagement with human rights (as seen in his later work) and the non-liberal influences on his intellectual thought, including those stemming from postcolonial spaces. Given Foucault's commitment to exposing the disciplinary, regulatory and governing capacities of the liberal project, a simplistic and reductive reading of his work on 'the new politics of rights' as re-embracing liberal individualism is unreliable and misreads his central argument.[53] Far from re-embracing the central concept of the pre-given liberal subject, Foucault's deployment of rights discourses is consistent with his resistance to a metaphysical closure of the human subject by liberal humanism, and to rights as a form of protection for the pre-given liberal subject.[54] It is a rejection of juridical formulations concerning subjective freedom, where freedom is neither a 'ready-made region' that has to be respected through rights, nor the property of the individual subject.[55]

Non-liberal trajectories and spaces had a significant impact on Foucault's increasing scholarly focus on the self. These influences derived from different philosophical schools and religious traditions, such as Christianity and Zen Buddhism.[56] During a visit to Japan in 1978, where Foucault demonstrated an interest in Zen Buddhism, he commented:

> The crisis of Western thought is identical to the end of imperialism ... There is no philosopher who marks out this period. For it is the end of the era of Western philosophy. Thus, if philosophy of the future exists, it must be born outside of Europe or equally born in consequence of meetings and impacts between Europe and Non-Europe.[57]

Foucault's fascination with Shi'ite historical narratives of martyrdom and with cultural rituals of penitence needs to be located *within* his openness to other ways of being, interest in other lifeworlds, as well as his subsequent preoccupation with the technologies of the self. Given this context, Foucault's work on the Iranian revolution clearly cannot be read as an endorsement of clerical rule or of authoritarian theocracy.[58] Instead, it reflects a continuation of his interest in exploring an anarchic understanding of the self, and of being, as an effective instrument of freedom, with reference to non-liberal forms of personal and political transformation.

I conclude this section by invoking Foucault's extensive discussion of sexuality – a core thematic of his oeuvre that continues to influence critical discourse today. Cornell and Seely refer to Foucault's rejection of the 'repressive hypothesis' of sexuality and place emphasis upon his argument that there is a compulsion in Western thought to sexualize all relations – where subjects are viewed and treated above all else as deeply conditioned libidinal units obsessed with sex and sexuality as the primary signifier and affirmation of embodied existence. Foucault's focus on the ethic of self-care may be read as a rejection of this libidinal model in favour of one that can bring about transformation in subjectivity – what might be termed internal revolution – and what we might become in the world; a model in which sexuality is not the defining feature of our being.[59] His theoretical emphasis and the concept of political spirituality are integrally linked to his abiding interest in living differently in the world. This includes embracing the possibility of epistemic alignment with non-liberal articulations of freedom and, through such alignment, potentially engaging with alternative inscriptions of human flourishing.

INSCRIPTIONS OF ILLEGIBLE FREEDOM

In his lecture that seeks to understand the kinds of questions instigated by critique, entitled 'What Is Critique', Foucault starkly enquires 'what am I then?' in order to problematize the philosophical/political relationship between 'being' and 'becoming'.[60] If the subject is at one with, and, at the same time constituted by power – and power acts upon the subject, suggesting that the subject is there to be acted upon prior to the power that ostensibly constitutes it – then the nature of the 'I' who falls outside these norms becomes a compelling issue. Butler describes the space that falls outside these norms as terrain that may not be recognizable, a domain of ourselves that we live 'without recognizing' – that is disavowed or abjected, as discussed in Chapter 2. It is that part '[f]or which we have no vocabulary, but which we endure without quite knowing', and, as she presciently points out, it can clearly be a 'source of suffering' – but it also represents a sign of distance from regulatory norms, and suggests a 'site for new possibility'.[61] The constitutive paradox emerging from the claim that the singular subject is both pre-supposed as well as induced provokes a deeper exploration of the posited self or being that is autonomous of such constitution.

This inquiry can move in multiple directions. My earlier discussion on the feminist turn towards affect as a valid source of knowledge affords an opportunity to elaborate upon the epistemological scope of this turn inwards, towards the intimate. It pushes beyond the theorization of 'cruel optimism' which, while clearly helpful in foregrounding granular truths, remains a static analysis. Ultimately, this analysis needs to move in a direction that resolves the suffering inevitably produced by processes of cruel optimism. This is the central preoccupation of the non-liberal epistemological explorations discussed earlier. It is neither a theological search of the kind that Santos examines in the context of Semitic religions, as described in Chapter 5; nor a culturally relativist, conservative turn found, for example, in the Islamist politics discussed in Chapter

4; nor the reactive strategizing of contemporary anti-Western nationalist movements. It is found in alternative conceptions of freedom, that is, freedom as an experience not accessible through the Cartesian subject and its reified equation of thought with the 'I'. In other words, these alternative trajectories indicate modalities of freedom that are located beyond the parameters of the liberal fishbowl.

Such freedom may be an experience of dispassion. This does not necessarily mean an absence of passion, as shown in the remainder of this section, where I discuss a deeply symbolic illustration of this turn towards other registers, and specifically the exploration of freedom and the self in Persian Sufism: a digital work by Shirin Neshat, a contemporary Iranian-born artist based in New York. Neshat's evocative black-and-white video installation *Overruled* (2012), which focuses on the theme of juridical and cultural transgression, features a courtroom scene with several men sitting behind a long table strewn with books. Visually, the scene has a close affinity with the Last Supper in Christian iconography. The central figure in this depiction is a judge who, along with his colleagues, is determining the fate of two defendants – a young man and woman who are kneeling silently on the left and right sides of the screen, respectively, and facing the viewing audience. The issue before the Court concerns the defendants' recitation of the poetry of Jalaluddin Rumi, a thirteenth-century Persian Sufi poet and mystic. The video begins with the judge declaring that, in general terms, poetry in any society is invaluable, creative and productive. He then, in a somewhat sinister fashion, emphasizes the need for caution regarding poetry that is subversive, corrupting and undermining of social values and social cohesion. The defendants are assailed for reciting Rumi's Sufi poetry, which powerfully expresses the themes of rage and love in a tenor that is both erotic and political. When called upon to defend themselves, the defendants respond somewhat defiantly with a haunting and soulful rendition of Rumi's verses in song. Through an intensely affective subtext, this audio-visual allegory challenges the normative postulates of subjectivity – of being and being free.

The well-born Rumi was an Islamic jurist and scholar who lived in the town of Konya in present-day Turkey. A serious intellectual and teacher, he was highly respected within his community until he crossed paths with the much older Shams Tabrizi, an itinerant spiritual wanderer and dervish from Afghanistan who became his beloved companion and guide. Theirs was a passionate relationship, representing the profound communion between teacher and disciple found throughout spiritual literature and hagiography, and which transcends the finite 'I' and personalized loving.[62] When Shams abruptly disappeared, allegedly killed by disciples of

Rumi who were jealous of the intense and unique bond between the two men, the devastated Rumi became a dervish, and poured his anguish into more than 70,000 verses of poetry – considered one of the treasures of Persian Sufi literature and culture.[63] Some of the poetry is pure lament, the metaphors arising from the visceral need and impulse to grieve the loss of Shams – a cathartic flow channelled into a culturally sanctioned performance comparable with that of the *rudali* figure discussed in Chapter 5. Rumi mourns in a deeply affective register, his emotional cascade a tormented purging of the afflicted ego and infused with the soaring cadences of ecstatic release. For instance: 'Love has taken away my practices/and filled me with poetry … I had to clap and sing./I used to be respectable and chaste and stable,/but who can stand in this strong wind/and remember those things?'[64] He continues: 'I saw you and became empty./This emptiness, more beautiful than existence,/it obliterates existence, and yet when it comes,/existence thrives and creates more existence!'[65] While these lines are at one level intensely personal, at a deeper level, Rumi's verses narrate the experience of freedom from the finitude of embodiment and identity through communion with the 'Beloved Friend', a frequent term of address in this exalted mode of relationship. The energy of such liberation finds physical expression in the ecstatic dance of the dervish, an act of meditative worship that is a central symbol in Sufi philosophy and aesthetics.[66]

Overruled also partly draws its inspiration from the historical trial of Mansur Al-Hallaj, an ascetic Persian Sufi who lived in the late ninth century in present-day Iraq. Al-Hallaj was a mystic poet and writer as well as a dervish; he reportedly travelled as far as India and China, and his works focused on the theme of meditation and becoming one with the self.[67] The idea of the oneness of absolute existence (*wahdat al-wajood*)[68] involves a surrender of identification with the outward body or form, and the experience of unity of being through the absolute dissolution of one's sense of individuated personhood/merging into the presence of God. This freedom is what Al-Hallaj celebrated through his famous declaration *Ana al-Haq* ('I am the truth'). The Abbasid rulers of the time saw Al-Hallaj's statement as a theological claim to divinity, an utterance that violated the central credo of Islam – 'There is no God but Allah and Muhammad is His Prophet' – which threatened the authority of both the state and the orthodox clerical establishment. He was arrested for blasphemy and his refusal to recant ultimately led to his gruesome torture and crucifixion in 922 CE, with a large crowd witnessing the sadistic atrocities perpetrated upon him. The cultural narratives of Al-Hallaj's martyrdom all agree that the agonies of unspeakable torture were 'overruled' by his spiritual tenacity.[69]

In her discussion of Neshat's visual representations more generally, Khanna identifies how the energy of affect extends beyond what is directly observed or encountered: it is a 'spectral presence of another form of knowing, and another way of being, one that may be otherwise than being'.[70] This 'otherwise than' is the space that requires elaboration. When understood in terms of non-dualism, where there is no subject/object distinction and all binaries resolve, this modality of metaphysical excess becomes a valid instrument for understanding freedom. I draw attention to Neshat's allegory specifically because it presents what appears to be an aporetic relationship between the orthodox enunciation of freedom that is followed in law – namely, individual and social liberty mandated, regulated, normatively bound and contained – and a non-dualistic definition of freedom that has its locus in a different episteme; in the case of Al-Hallaj, this freedom transcends all epistemes and the category of epistemology itself. It may be that within a liberal logic, this alternative understanding is about 'religion' and thus belongs to the private realm, with no place or role in the public sphere. However, the theme of *Overruled* is not the scope and parameters of the public right to free speech, including what the theocratic state views as blasphemy, apostasy and heresy. Rather, it is about the incommensurability between freedom as defined purely within the absolute terms of formal law, rights and the unyielding prohibitions of the courtroom, and the expression of freedom through the act of reciting creative works associated with the freedom of transcendence. Rumi's verse is irradiated with unique analogies for such liberation.[71]

In other words, *Overruled* is about the experience of freedom that becomes possible only when one is free *of* the prescribed legal space; it is not about the aspiration to procure freedom *through* this finite space. The very fact that a musical rendition of Rumi's poetry becomes the defendants' response to the state's charge against them reinforces the intractable disjuncture between orthodox and heterodox understandings of being, and of being free. It is not the *act* of exercising the right to free speech through reciting poetry in defiance of the law that is impugned here. Rather, it is the poetry's metaphysical *content*, Rumi's lyrical imaging of the transcendental freedom, which 'overrules' all finitude that is considered truly undesirable, profane and subversive by the state and religious orthodoxy. Such expressions warrant efforts at eradication, with the proponent being incarcerated or annihilated, rendered unrecognizable and ungrievable.

I use the example and analysis of *Overruled* to transition into a more elaborate discussion, in Chapter 7, on the theme of what a non-liberal (not illiberal) search for freedom – that is, one outside of a liberal-based human rights paradigm – might look like, and whether any reconciliation between these two conceptual trajectories is possible, desirable or even necessary. To remain intellectually committed to a liberal mode became impossible for scholars such as Sedgwick, who turned to affect as well as Mahayana epistemology, and Foucault, whose interest in the transformative ethics and technologies of self-care saw him venture into the faith-based cartography of Shi'ism, martyrdom and revolution. This turn to a contemplative and philosophical space cannot be captured within a liberal constellation, and explores the vast epistemic terrain available once the limits of the fishbowl are acknowledged. It is a turn away from the exclusionary terms on which legal recognition or entitlement is granted, and towards non-liberal epistemologies that orient the energies of heart and mind in another direction.

This core shift may indeed produce a dissonant, frictive form of tectonics between the liberal and the non-liberal approaches to freedom. I have argued that, for the traumatized and stigmatized subaltern subject, human rights may offer space for respectability, entitlement and a pragmatic alignment with dominant norms, such recognition being contingent upon attachment to another order of unfreedom – the coercive normative order – but which remains preferable to non-recognition and non-attachment. Freedom thus functions as a governance project – one that regulates the terms on which entry into the human rights stratosphere is permitted. In this respect, the rights dispensation cannot offer the freedom sought by the proponents of radical politics and those subjects who, as discussed in earlier chapters, remain precarious. All critical efforts to negotiate the impasse must confront two fundamental questions: How can freedom that is completely defined, tethered and contained within the epistemic fishbowl of liberalism, and the globally proliferating coercions of neoliberal rationality, possibly be *actual* freedom? Who is freed through this hegemonic modality – by whom, for what, from what, and into what?

THE CALL OF/FOR EPISTEMIC ALTERITY

The discussion in this chapter reveals how non-liberal conceptions of freedom oblige us not only to problematize the discourse of human rights, but also to think beyond the static and linear vision of freedom on which the rights project is based – that is, freedom as teleological, external, to be pursued, claimed and owned invariably in the form of more rights; their bestowal contingent upon the systematic governance and regulation of recipients, some of whom are deemed worthy of liberal enfranchisement while others are not.

I have earlier provided particular examples of the liberal resistance to alternative conceptualization – Chapter 4, for example, takes up the theme of the Western response to the veil in the contemporary moment, and narrates how this public manifestation of Muslim religiosity is framed either as false consciousness or as a threat to the secular premise of the liberal democratic state. In these instances, alternative conceptions of being in the world and expressions of freedom generated through a non-liberal set of registers threaten the core of a tradition historically based on the idea that it and it alone is the appropriate universal mechanism for procuring sovereignty and freedom. The aggravated Western reactivity to other epistemes is generated partly because these are perceived as a direct threat to liberal hegemony. More significantly, this reaction also arises because esoteric and heterodox assertions of expressions of freedom incontrovertibly expose the illusion of human rights as a universal, virtuous and beneficial freedom project.

The non-liberal intellectual pursuits of progressive thinkers such as Sedgwick and Foucault, directed towards alternative registers, have received scant attention despite being significant turning points in their respective theoretical journeys; however, they reveal a rare intellectual fearlessness among feminist, left and critical scholars in pursuing these alternative registers. The idea that there are other ways of being, and of being free outside of the liberal canon, does not only suffer from academic invisibility and non-recognition; the very existence of such positions is deemed to pose a threat to the liberal episteme and establishment in their entirety. At times, this anxiety transforms into an overt or covert censorship, marginalizing or expunging other schemas from Western discourse. And when we consider the complex history of any reified canon or system and its transgressors – as ideologically disparate as the Buddha, Al-Hallaj and Foucault – it is evident that the deep intellectual distrust, suspicion and fear of epistemic alterity, and the subjugation or stigmatization of other paradigms, is not a sporadic event but a regular pattern.

A committed investigation into the concepts of freedom delineated in alternate epistemological registers would enable us to reshape the social meaning of emancipation, and discover how it can be experienced in ways other than primarily through a human rights incarnation. The redefinition of freedom needs to come about through theorizing individual and collective liberation *beyond* the bounds of liberal individualism. This challenges the idea of freedom as something linked to emancipatory rights exported from the west to the east and from the north to the south, or from the rational sovereign subject to the unruly, abjected and/or regressive 'Other'. I am not simply proposing a more complex and more hospitable understanding of the frameworks of freedom. We need a more radical move – one that, prior to anything else, requires us to renounce the axiomatic assumption that non-liberal spaces, especially in the non-West, have nothing to offer those who have reached the end point of critique and invariably return, tentatively or forcefully, to the liberal fishbowl. This recursion is rooted in the fear that opening up to alternative philosophical possibilities will trigger a disorienting, cognitively intimidating epistemic free-fall. The only way to counter such anxiety is to begin an exploration of the emancipatory paths available outside liberal discourses, and outside liberal modalities of governance normally addressed within critical, feminist and queer legal scholarship. The transformative potential of such alternative spaces warrants a more robust dialogue – one that would ideally produce more equitable, positive possibilities for lasting freedom than have hitherto been either permissible or imaginable.

NOTES

1. Michel Foucault, *The Order of Things: An Archaeology of the Human Sciences*, ed. R.D. Laing (New York: Pantheon Books, 1970), p. 387.
2. Ibid.
3. Spivak, 'Can the Subaltern Speak?', pp. 28–37, who critiques the argument that the 'subaltern' constituted an autonomous domain whose agency could be recovered independently of the politics of the elite. She argues that the search for a pure space is impossible; that it does not account for the epistemic violence which makes retrieval impossible, and which enables the subaltern to speak only through the dominant circuits of power via a discourse that is inherently gendered, sexed and racialized. See also Partha Chatterjee, 'Postcolonialism and the New Imperialism', in *The Present as History: Critical Perspectives on Contemporary Global Power*, ed. Nermeen Shaikh (New York: Columbia University Press, 2007), p. 87; Dipesh Chakrabarty, 'Radical Histories and Question of Enlightenment Rationalism: Some Recent Critiques of *Subaltern Studies*', *Economic and Political Weekly* 30, no. 14 (1995): 753; Dhawan, 'Affirmative Sabotage of the Master's Tools, pp. 63, 69. On rethinking the subaltern through an alternative understanding that is relational, intersectional and dynamic, see Alf Gunvald Nilsen and Srila Roy, 'Introduction', in *New Subaltern Politics: Reconceptualizing Hegemony and Resistance in Contemporary India* (New Delhi: Oxford University Press, 2015), pp. 1–26. My argument in favour of alternative registers seeks to find firmer ground from which to articulate this voice, while also avoiding the traps of essentialism that might accompany the turn to a non-liberal episteme
4. Hamid Dabashi, *Can Non-Europeans Think?* (London: Zed Books, 2015). See also Nikita Dhawan, 'Can Non-Europeans Philosophize? Transnational Literacy and Planetary Ethics in a Global Age', *Hypatia* 32, no. 3 (2017): 488–505, addressing the legacies of European Enlightenment for the postcolonial world, which includes the normative violence exerted and the continuing de-legitimization of non-European postcolonial thought and philosophy.
5. Sedgwick, 'Pedagogy of Buddhism', pp. 153–81.

6. Eve Kosofsky Sedgwick, 'Making Things, Practicing Emptiness', in *The Weather in Proust*, ed. Jonathan Goldberg (Durham, NC: Duke University Press, 2011), pp. 69–122. See also Eve Kosofsky Sedgwick, 'Reality and Realization', in *The Weather in Proust*, pp. 206–15.
7. Sedgwick, 'Making Things', p. 75.
8. Sedgwick, 'Reality and Realization', pp. 212–13.
9. Ibid.
10. Eve Kosofsky Sedgwick and Michael D. Snediker, 'Queer Little Gods: A Conversation', *The Massachusetts Review* 49, nos. 1/2 (2008): 198.
11. A critique levied at postmodern feminist scholarship, specifically, Butler's earlier work articulating the agency of the subject as an effect of subordination and prohibition, and locating it in a performative subversion of norms. See, for example, Butler, *Gender Trouble*.
12. Sedgwick, 'Pedagogy of Buddhism', pp. 173, 177.
13. Sedgwick, 'Realization and Reality', p. 212.
14. Sedgwick, 'Pedagogy of Buddhism', p. 177, discussing the capaciousness of the framework of rebirth.
15. Ibid., p. 178.
16. I will continue to refer to this text as source material. There have been several critiques of Afary and Anderson's understanding of Foucault's coverage of the Iranian revolution and their claim that it was part of an Orientalist appropriation and fascination with pre-modern mystical practices that was evident in his work, including his writings on sexuality: Janet Afary and Kevin B. Anderson, *Foucault and the Iranian Revolution: Gender and the Seductions of Islam* (Chicago: University of Chicago Press, 2005), pp. 17–21, 139–44, 155–62. Their work represents Foucault as a cultural relativist who 'lumped together premodern Western societies and modern Oriental ones', exposing his troubled relationship with feminism: Afary and Anderson, *Foucault and the Iranian Revolution*, p. 139. While this volume received many positive reviews, those of a more critical nature pointed to the misreading of Foucault's work that was, in part, based on the 'orientalist' premise adopted by Afary and Anderson. Their analysis pitted modernity against tradition and secularism against Islam, where Islam was portrayed as hegemonic, anti-women, anti-democratic and anti-modern. They also largely ignored Foucault's more subversive and nuanced reading of the Iranian revolution: see Babak Rahimi, 'Rahimi on Afary and Anderson: *Foucault and the Iranian Revolution: Gender and the Seductions of Islamism*', *H-Gender-MidEast*, October 2006, www.h-net.org/reviews/showrev.php?id=12437; Jonathan Rée, 'The Treason of the Clerics', *The Nation*, 28 July 2005, www.thenation.com/article/treason-clerics/; Bonnie Honig, 'What Foucault Saw at the Revolution: On the Use and Abuse of Theology for Politics', *Political Theory* 36, no. 2 (2008): 301–12. See more recently Behrooz Ghamari-Tabrizi, *Foucault in Iran: Islamic Revolution after the Enlightenment* (Minneapolis: University of Minnesota Press, 2016).
17. Michel Foucault, 'What Are the Iranians Dreaming [*Rêvent*] About?' *Le Nouvel Observateur*, 16–22 October 1978 (reproduced in Afary and Anderson, *Foucault and the Iranian Revolution*, pp. 203–9); Michel Foucault, *The Hermeneutics of the Subject: Lectures at the Collège de France, 1981–1982*, ed. Frédéric Gros, trans. Graham Burchell (New York: Palgrave Macmillan, 2005); Michel Foucault, 'Questions of Method', in *The Foucault Effect: Studies in Governmentality*, eds. Graham Burchell, Colin Gordon and Peter Miller (Chicago: University of Chicago Press, 1991), p. 82.
18. Most of these views appear in articles written from 1978 to 1979 for the *Corriere della sera*, a respected Italian newspaper, as well as the French papers *Le Monde* and *Le Nouvel Observateur*. Translated and reprinted in Afary and Anderson, *Foucault and the Iranian Revolution*.
19. Michel Foucault and Baqir Parham, 'Dialogue between Michel Foucault and Baqir Parham', *Nameh-yi Kanun-I Nevisandegan*, no. 1 (Spring 1979): 9–17 (reproduced in Afary and Anderson, *Foucault and the Iranian Revolution*, pp. 183–9). For further detailed consideration of Foucault's writings on the Iranian Revolution, see also Corey McCall,

'Ambivalent Modernities: Foucault's Iranian Writings Reconsidered', *Foucault Studies*, no. 15 (February 2013): 27–51; Ghamari-Tabrizi, *Foucault in Iran.*

20. Foucault and Parham, 'Dialogue', p. 185.
21. Ibid.
22. The Sunnis, in contrast, have held the view that as there was no designated successor, the community could elect a rightful heir from among the Islamic community. They believe that Abu Bakr, Prophet Muhammad's close friend and advisor, was chosen as his successor. The Sunni–Shia schism is partly based on this central disagreement over who was the rightful leader of the believers after the death of the Prophet. This schism became permanent after the Prophet's grandson Hussain was killed in the battle of Karbala in 680 AD. While the Sunni caliphs killed every subsequent Imam, the Twelfth Imam ostensibly escaped such a fate.
23. Ali Shari'ati, 'A Discussion of Shahid', in *Jihād and Shahādat: Struggle and Martyrdom in Islam: Essays and Addresses by Mahmūd Ṭaleqāni, Murtaḍa Muṭahhari, Ali Shari'ati*, eds. Mehdi Abedi and Gary Legenhausen (Houston, TX: Institute for Research and Islamic Studies, 1986), pp. 230–43; Ali Shari'ati, *Where Shall We Begin? Enlightened Thinkers and the Revolutionary Society* (Penang: Citizens International, 2002); Kingshuk Chatterjee, *'Ali Shari'ati and the Shaping of Political Islam in* Iran (New York: Palgrave Macmillan, 2011). For an elaborate discussion on the ideological foundations of the Iranian revolution, see Hamid Dabashi, *Theology of Discontent: The Ideological Foundation of the Islamic Revolution in Iran* (Abingdon: Routledge, 2017).
24. Ghamari-Tabrizi, *Foucault in Iran*, p. 25, see also p. 92; Ali Shari'ati, *What Is to Be Done: The Enlightened Thinkers and an Islamic Renaissance* (BookBaby ebook, 2015). See further Siavash Saffari, *Beyond Shariati: Modernity, Cosmopolitanism, and Islam in Iranian Political Thought* (Cambridge: Cambridge University Press, 2017), on the revolutionary potential of Shari'ati's thought. See also Chatterjee, *Shaping of Political Islam.*
25. Ali Shari'ati, *Marxism and Other Western Fallacies: An Islamic Critique*, trans. R. Campbell (Berkeley, CA: Mizan Press, 1980); Drucilla Cornell and Stephen D. Seely, *The Spirit of Revolution: Beyond the Dead Ends of Man* (Cambridge: Polity, 2016), pp. 66, 67.
26. Cornell and Seely, *The Spirit of Revolution*, p. 65. See also Arash Davari, 'A Return to Which Self? Ali Shari'ati and Frantz Fanon on the Political Ethics of Insurrectionary Violence', *Comparative Studies of South Asia, Africa and the Middle East* 34, no. 1 (2014): 86–105, discussing how the notion of a 'return to the self', found in the writings of Shariati, constituted a call to return not to some lost imagined historical past, but 'to a self that exists immediately in the present but is yet to be realized' (at p. 89).
27. Foucault and Parham, 'Dialogue', p. 185.
28. Cornell and Seely, *The Spirit of Revolution*, p. 65.
29. Ghamari-Tabrizi, *Foucault in Iran*, p. 93.
30. This interest in the Iranian revolution coincided with the period of textual work on *The History of Sexuality*, in which Foucault argued that certain forms of sexual freedom were partly expressions of the worst forms of capitalism – namely, that market forces coerced the subject to think of herself as most liberated at precisely the point when she was most objectified and commodified as a unit of capital, valued only as a substitutable variable in a transactional equation.
31. The ambivalence of Foucault's position on the subject, which has been the source of much debate, stems from the appearance of at least two contradictory understandings of the subject in his work. The first idea present in his early work is that the subject is constituted by power relations – that is, through the technologies of domination; the second is the idea of the self or subject as resistive to domination and capable of critical reflection. While these two different understandings of the subject appear at one level incompatible and contradictory, several scholars have examined how they are indeed consistent and can, in fact, be reconciled: see Golder, *Foucault and the Politics of Rights*; Allen, *Politics of Our Selves: Power, Autonomy, and Gender in Contemporary Critical Theory* (New York: Columbia University Press, 2008); Lois McNay, *Foucault and Feminism: Power, Gender and the Self* (Cambridge: Polity Press, 1992). See generally Cornell and Seely, *The Spirit*

of Revolution, on how to think about revolutionary politics in the aftermath of feminist and queer critiques of the human. See also Kathy Butterworth, 'The Decentred Autonomous Subject', in *Identity and Difference: Contemporary Debates on the Self*, ed. Rafael Winkler (Cham: Palgrave Macmillan, 2016), pp. 155–75.

32. Foucault, *Hermeneutics of the Subject*.
33. Cornell and Seely, *The Spirit of Revolution*, pp. 53–80. See also Michiel Leezenberg, 'Power and Political Spirituality: Michel Foucault on the Islamic Revolution in Iran', in *Cultural History After Foucault*, ed. John Neubauer (New York: Aldine de Gruyter, 1999), pp. 63–80.
34. Cornell and Seely, *The Spirit of Revolution*, pp. 54–5. Cornell and Seely challenge Lee Edelman's identification of queerness with a death drive, which they argue rejects a futurity: Cornell and Seely, *The Spirit of Revolution*, p. 11. Instead, they offer a different understanding of futurity and inheritance, and how to be in the world, by returning queer theory to revolution rather than the logic of annihilation. See Edelman, *No Future*. See also Lee Edelman, 'Ever After', in *After Sex? On Writing Since Queer Theory*, eds. Janet Halley and Andrew Parker (Durham, NC: Duke University Press, 2011), pp. 110–18.
35. Cornell and Seely, *The Spirit of Revolution*, p. 55.
36. Michel Foucault, 'The Ethics of the Concern of the Self as a Practice of Freedom', in *Ethics: Subjectivity and Truth*, ed. Paul Rabinow, trans. Robert Hurley, vol. 1 (New York: The New Press, 1997). For an elaboration of Foucault's work on ethical practice and spiritual self-cultivation, see Edwin Ng, 'The Critique of Mindfulness and the Mindfulness of Critique: Paying Attention to the Politics of Our Selves with Foucault's Analytic of Governmentality', in *Handbook of Mindfulness: Culture, Context, and Social Engagement*, eds. Ronald E. Purser, David Forbes and Adam Burke (Cham: Springer International Publishing, 2016), pp. 135–52.
37. Claire Brière and Pierre Blanchet, 'Iran: The Spirit of a World Without Spirit', in *Iran: La revolution au nom de Dieu* (Paris: Seuill, 1979), pp. 227–41 (reproduced in Afary and Anderson, *Foucault and the Iranian Revolution*, pp. 250–60); Georg Stauth, 'Revolution in Spiritless Times: An Essay on Michel Foucault's Enquiries into the Iranian Revolution', in *Michel Foucault: Critical Assessments*, ed. Barry Smart, vol. 3 (London: Routledge, 1994), pp. 379–401.
38. Foucault, 'Ethics of the Concern of the Self', p. 294.
39. Foucault, *Hermeneutics*, pp. 14–19. See further Ghamari-Tabrizi's discussion of Foucault's understanding of spirituality and the Ethical Subject: Ghamari-Tabrizi, *Foucault in Iran*, pp. 173–80.
40. Foucault, *Hermeneutics*, p. 14.
41. Ibid.
42. Ibid., p. 18.
43. Ibid., p. 16.
44. Ibid., p. 18.
45. Michel Foucault, *The Courage of Truth: The Government of Self and Others II – Lectures at the Collège de France, 1983–1984*, ed. Frédéric Gros, trans. Graham Burchell (Basingstoke: Palgrave Macmillan, 2012), p. 184; Michel Foucault, *The Care of the Self: The History of Sexuality, Volume III*, trans. Robert Hurley (London: Penguin, 1990); Ladelle McWhorter, 'Foucault's Political Spirituality', *Philosophy Today* 47, Suppl. (2003): 39–44.
46. This preoccupation inspired the fourth book in his famed series – a volume on the theme of Christianity, titled *The History of Sexuality: Confessions of the Flesh*, which he worked on in the last years of his life. He died before its completion, and it remains unpublished.
47. Michel Foucault, 'Technologies of the Self', in *Ethics: Subjectivity and Truth*, ed. Paul Rabinow, trans. Robert Hurley, vol. 1 (New York: The New Press, 1997), pp. 223–51; Golder, *Foucault and the Politics of Rights*, pp. 71–3.
48. This aspect of Foucault's work was ignored for many years following his death, but has subsequently been addressed – primarily by scholars of theology, religious studies and philosophy – and has become an important resource for analysing his deployment of

spirituality: see, for example, David Chidester, 'Michel Foucault and the Study of Religion', *Religious Studies Review* 12, no. 1 (1986): 1–39; Christian Jambet, 'The Constitution of the Subject and Spiritual Practice', in *Michel Foucault, Philosopher: Essays Translated from the French and German*, ed. Timothy J. Armstrong (New York: Harvester Wheatsheaf, 1992), pp. 233–47; James W. Bernauer, *Michel Foucault's Force of Flight: Towards an Ethics for Thought* (Atlantic Heights, NJ: Humanities, 1990). See generally Jeremy R. Carrette, ed., *Religion and Culture: Michel Foucault* (New York: Routledge, 1999); Jeremy Carrette, *Foucault and Religion* (London: Routledge, 1999); Jeremy Carrette, 'Rupture and Transformation: Foucault's Concept of Spirituality Reconsidered', *Foucault Studies*, no. 15 (2013): 52–71. On political spirituality, see McWhorter, 'Foucault's Political Spirituality'; James Bernauer and Jeremy Carrette, eds., *Michel Foucault and Theology: The Politics of Religious Experience* (Abingdon: Routledge, 2017).

49. Ghamari-Tabrizi, *Foucault in Iran*, pp. 125–35.
50. Ibid. Ghamari-Tabrizi specifically targets the interventions by Kate Millet and Simone de Beauvoir: pp. 113–58. See also my discussion in Chapter 4.
51. Claudie Broyelle and Jacques Broyelle, 'What Are the Philosophers Dreaming About? Was Michel Foucault Mistaken About the Iranian Revolution', *Le Matin*, 24 March 1979 (reproduced in Afary and Anderson, *Foucault and the Iranian Revolution*, pp. 247–9); Maxime Rodinson, 'Khomeini and the "Primacy of the Spiritual"', *Le Nouvel Observateur*, 19 February 1979 (reproduced in Afary and Anderson, *Foucault and the Iranian Revolution*, pp. 241–5); James Miller, *The Passion of Michael Foucault* (New York: Simon & Schuster, 1993). See more generally Afary and Anderson, *Foucault and the Iranian Revolution*, who adopt the position that Foucault misread events.
52. Michel Foucault, 'What Is Enlightenment?' in *The Foucault Reader*, ed. Paul Rabinow (New York: Pantheon Books, 1984), pp. 32–50; Michel Foucault, 'Open Letter to Prime Minister Mehdi Bazargan', *Le Nouvel Observateur*, 14 April 1979 (reproduced in Afary and Anderson, *Foucault and the Iranian Revolution*, pp. 260–3); Michel Foucault, 'Confronting Governments: Human Rights', in Michel Foucault, *Power*, ed. James D. Faubion, trans. Robert Hurley et al., vol. 3 (London: Penguin Books, 1994), pp. 474–5. For assertions that this work was evidence of his embrace of humanism, see Alain Beaulieu, 'Towards a Liberal Utopia: The Connection between Foucault's Reporting on the Iranian Revolution and the Ethical Turn', *Philosophy & Social Criticism* 36, no. 7 (2010): 801–18; Eric Paras, *Foucault 2.0: Beyond Power and Knowledge* (New York: Other Press, 2006); Richard Wolin, 'From the "Death of Man" to Human Rights: The Paradigm Change in French Intellectual Life, 1968–86', in *The Frankfurt School Revisited: And Other Essays on Politics and Society* (New York: Routledge, 2006), pp. 171–84. In contrast, see Golder, *Foucault and the Politics of Rights*, where he effectively refutes the positions characterizing Foucault's turn to human rights as exemplifying his capitulation to liberal humanism.
53. Golder argues that these responses do not consider how Foucault's later understanding of rights was consistent with his earlier work on juridical discourse. He provides an eloquent and meticulous critical reading of Foucault's later work on rights, which is structured around three related arguments (Golder, *Foucault and the Politics of Rights*): that rights are contingent and not based on conventional normative grounds (at pp. 61–88); that rights are ambivalent as opposed to liberating (at pp. 89–113); and that rights are tactical and strategic political instruments (at pp. 115–47). See Ratna Kapur, 'Review of *Foucault and the Politics of Rights*, by Ben Golder', *UNSW Law Journal* 39, no. 4 (2016): 1472–8. See also Jessica Whyte, 'Is Revolution Desirable? Michel Foucault on Revolution, Neoliberalism and Rights', in *Re-Reading Foucault: On Law, Power and Rights*, ed. Ben Golder (Abingdon: Routledge, 2013), pp. 207–28.
54. Ben Golder, 'Foucault and the Unfinished Human of Rights', *Law, Culture and the Humanities* 6, no. 3 (2010): 354–74; Golder, *Foucault and the Politics of Rights*. See also Amy Allen's incisive analysis of Foucault's later work envisaging new modes of subjectification as consistent with his earlier call rejecting a specific Kantian notion of the

transcendental subject: Allen, *Politics of Our Selves*. See also Sokhi-Bulley, *Governing (Through) Rights*.

55. Foucault, *Birth of Biopolitics*, p. 65.
56. See, for example, Michel Foucault, 'Michel Foucault and Zen: A Stay in a Zen Temple (1978)' in *Religion and Culture: Michel Foucault*, ed. Jeremy R. Carrette (New York: Routledge, 1999), pp. 110–14; Michel Foucault, 'On the Genealogy of Ethics: An Overview of Work in Progress', in *Ethics: Subjectivity and Truth*, ed. Paul Rabinow, trans. Robert Hurley, vol. 1 (New York: The New Press, 1997), pp. 253–80.
57. Foucault, 'A Stay in a Zen Temple', p. 113.
58. Michel Foucault, 'Is It Useless to Revolt?' *Le Monde*, 11–12 May 1979 (reproduced in Afary and Anderson, *Foucault and the Iranian Revolution*, pp. 263–7); Foucault, 'Open Letter'.
59. For a discussion on how 'ethics as politics' is useful for feminist thinking and understandings of freedom, see generally Dianna Taylor and Karen Vintges, eds., *Feminism and the Final Foucault* (Urbana, IL: University of Illinois Press, 2004); in particular, Mariana Valverde, 'Experience and Truth Telling in a Post-Humanist World: A Foucauldian Contribution to Feminist Ethical Reflections', in *Feminism and the Final Foucault*, pp. 91–117.
60. Michel Foucault, 'What Is Critique?' in *What is Enlightenment? Eighteenth-Century Answers and Twentieth-Century Questions*, ed. James Schmidt (Berkeley, CA: University of California Press, 1996), pp. 382–98.
61. Judith Butler, 'Bodies and Power Revisited', in *Feminism and the Final Foucault*, p. 190. Butler develops a more nuanced analysis of this 'I' in her later work, which I discuss in Chapter 7. See Judith Butler, *Senses of the Subject* (New York: Fordham University Press, 2015), pp. 1–16.
62. For a more detailed account of the relationship between Shams-i-Tabrizi and Rumi, as well as the philosophy of dissolution of the self/other in the Sufi doctrine of Rumi, see, for example, William C. Chittick, *The Sufi Doctine of Rumi* (Bloomington, IN: World Wisdom, 2005). See also Shams-i Tabrizi, *Me and Rumi: The Autobiography of Shams-i Tabrizi*, trans. William C. Chittick (Louisville, KY: Fons Vitae, 2004).
63. Jalāl al-Dīn Rūmī, *The Masnavi: Book One*, trans. Jawid Mojaddedi (Oxford: Oxford University Press, 2008); Jalāl al-Dīn Rūmī, *Selected Poems from the Divan-e Shams-e Tabrizi*, trans. and ed. Reynold A. Nicholson (Bethesda, MD: Ibex, 2001).
64. Jalāl al-Dīn Rūmī, *The Essential Rumi*, trans. Coleman Barks (San Francisco, CA: Harper, 1995), p. 104.
65. Ibid., p. 105.
66. The dervish tradition can be traced back at least 5,000 years among the ancient Indo-Iranians. It is a way of life, marked by austerity and asceticism, and finds spiritual expression in the collective form of meditative dance practice of 'whirling'.
67. Mansur Al-Hallaj, *The Tawsin of Mansur Al-Hallaj*, trans. Aisha Abd Ar-Rahman At-Tarjumana (Berkeley, CA: Diwan Press, 1974).
68. For Sufis, this is the experience of annihilation of the self, which was attained by supreme mystics such as Al-Hallaj. For a more general discussion on Sufism and the self/subjectivity, see Paola Abenante and Fabio Vicini, 'Interiority Unbound: Sufi and Modern Articulations of the Self', *Culture and Religion* 18, no. 2 (2017): 57–71.
69. For a more detailed account of the writings and martyrdom of Al-Hallaj, see Louis Massignon, *The Passion of Al-Hallaj: Mystic and Martyr of Islam*, trans. Herbert Mason, 4 vols. (Princeton, CA: Princeton University Press, 1982). At a political level, Sufism was a powerful democratizing political force, and a source of moral and ethical authority that served as a local counter to the British legal system in north India, among other regions. More generally, from the time of its historical emergence to the present day, the Sufi movement has continued to invite considerable opposition, with the orthodox establishment viewing it as subversive and as offering a form of undesirable intoxication.

70. Khanna, 'Touching, Unbelonging, and the Absence of Affect', p. 217. See also Jenna Haring, 'Contemporary Visual Art and Iranian Feminism', *Global Societies Journal* 5 (2017): 70–84.
71. See, for example, 'Buoyancy', in Rūmī, *The Essential Rumi*, pp. 104–5.

7. Freedom from the fishbowl

Will a body such as mine fetter or free me?
—Devdutt Pattnaik, *The Pregnant King*[1]

It takes imagination and courage to picture what would happen to the West … if its temporal fortress were suddenly invaded by the Time of its Other.
—Johannes Fabian, *Time and Its Others*[2]

Who is dragging this corpse here?
—Hsu Yun[3]

EMBODIMENT AND THE 'FAILED SUBJECT'

The Indian film *Chitrangada: The Crowning Wish* (2012), directed by Rituparno Ghosh, is a potent allegory that operates at three different levels.[4] The primary plot is nested within a myth-based frame narrative that forms the film's backdrop. Rudrajit Chatterjee, or Rudra, a choreographer, is directing a performance based on Rabindranath Tagore's 1892 dance drama *Chitrangada*. Tagore's story is itself based on a minor sequence from the well-known Indian epic the *Mahabharata*, involving the king of Manipur, who raises his daughter Chitrangada as a son so that she will be able to inherit his throne. However, once she meets the warrior prince Arjuna (one of the five husbands of Draupadi, the dishonoured queen described in Chapter 5 of this book), Chitrangada becomes infatuated and wants to reoccupy her gender as a woman so that she can marry him.[5]

The second level of the plot focuses on Rudra's intense relationship with Partho Majumdar, the percussionist in the dance troupe. As their relationship develops, Rudra embarks on sex reassignment surgery to acquire female anatomy in the hope that he and Partho can then be accepted as a 'normal' couple and be able to adopt a child. Rudra's options are framed within a freedom-and-happiness script that is primarily structured by a reproductive, heteronormative order, as well as by the idea that subjectivity and identity are essentially anchored, delineated and reinforced through the imperatives of one's personal embodiment. In terms of a wider theme, the criminalization of homosexuality in India –

discussed in Chapter 2 of this book – as well as the state's denial to gay couples of the right to adopt or have children through surrogacy are important, though tangential, subtexts in the narrative.

However, Partho prefers Rudra as a biological man and is repelled by the latter's proposed sex transformation, something he has never requested that his lover undergo. Rudra's pursuit of homonormativity and choice to acquire a gender through the arduous process of reassignment surgery has devastating effects on the relationship. During a tense conversation with Rudra, Partho declares that he would prefer a 'real' woman to a synthetic one, or mimetic 'half-thing'. At the precise moment at which the transformation is to be completed, the third level of the plot emerges, as Rudra is forced to engage and come to terms with several internal and external tensions.

In the context of conventional familial and social expectations, Rudra is quite explicitly, and on several fronts, an exemplar of the 'failed subject'. He acknowledges his parents' disappointment in him: he has refused to become an engineer and instead chooses a career as a choreographer; he is a gay son (although his parents do come to terms with this fact); and finally, he wants to take the irreversible step of sex reassignment in pursuit of personal happiness and social fulfilment. In all of these ways, Rudra is the complete antithesis of the 'successful' queers and aspirational normativity represented in *Dostana*, the Bollywood film discussed in Chapter 2. There is also a deeper internal struggle that occurs, represented in the film as an imaginary dialogue between Rudra and his alter ego, Shubho. During this conversation, Rudra comes to recognize the body as impermanent and accept that it is always subject to change, whether through age or one's own initiative. This realization is brought about in part through Rudra's reflection upon the erotic plot twists of the classical Chitrangada myth. When the young 'prince' Chitrangada meets Arjuna and falls in love, he asks the god of love, Madana, to make him into a beautiful woman for a year. Arjuna falls in love with the divinely refashioned prince, now named Surupa ('beautiful form'). Ultimately, Surupa reverts back to Chitrangada, in 'her' masculine incarnation. Through a deep interrogation of the phenomenon of embodiment and its imperatives, which condition subjectivity and identity, Rudra arrives at the metaphysical insight that *any* modality of attachment to the personal and social script of biological absolutes is illusory/erroneous/false, and a root obstacle to the experience of lasting freedom.

I read Rudra's realization in consonance with the deeper philosophical grain of the film, in which it is recognized that there is an observing 'self' distinct from the body and that, unlike the body, this self is present, continuous and unchanging. This fundamental realization is grounded in the non-liberal tradition of non-dualism, which understands that everything falling within the phenomenal world can be observed and is transient, subject to change and death, and thereby cannot bring about permanent freedom. Rudra's decision to abandon the final stage of sex transformation arises as he experiences a profound epistemic shift, a direct insight (noumenal apperception, unmediated by the senses) that the material body and one's primary epistemic error – the thought 'I am the body'/(mis)identification of the self, or of 'I' with the object that is the body – *both* stand in contrast to the intimate, continuous, unlimited awareness that is self-existence. In symbolic terms, this metaphysical insight transforms Rudra's consciousness just as irreversibly as the sex reassignment would have altered his anatomy. His ultimate decision not to proceed with the surgery is based on the realization that one's true being – the self – is not the inscribed, identified, politicized body; he experiences the insight that freedom *from* identification with the body, as opposed to freedom experienced *through* the body, is what brings about emancipation from suffering. This distinction mirrors, in some ways, Foucault's distinction between the self and the individual subject discussed in Chapter 6 – the former is subject to self-scrutiny leading to transformation and fulfilment, while the latter regards the thinking subject as inherently capable and as the starting point for the pursuit of knowledge, where the subject is not put into play in this pursuit.

The narrative trajectory of *Chitrangada* is thus simultaneously existential and philosophical. At the level of embodiment, Rudra initially assumes that his happiness rests in his relationship with Partho and the materialization of his desire for a family. Recognition of same-sex relationships through rights acquisition might 'solve' his physical and social dilemma, and provide a less troubled journey towards freedom through the complicated mechanics of a 'happy' homonormative life. Self-identified queers who are recognized as equal under law to other humans, and who proceed to assimilate the normative practices supported by a rights regime – which include marriage, adoption, inheritance and other legal and state benefits – do so to become legitimate and successful in contrast to 'failed' subjects, and also to become socially respectable. For the marginalized queer, the choice to actively assimilate in terms of either lifestyle or acquisition of a specific gender may have equivocal outcomes: legitimacy may formally ensure social tolerance and safety, while not necessarily ensuring a deeper social acceptance and the crucial understanding that queers are as equal and worthy, and valuable, as any other subjects. But assimilation may be seen as a better choice than trying to survive the harrowing pressures of marginality and the daily sense of embattlement that dominates queer lives in many parts of the world. For the gender and sexual subaltern, the active move from being a non-subject and/or 'failed subject' living without legibility or affirmation, to consciously seeking normativity – and, through its swathe of protections and privileges, becoming what may be called a 'successful queer' – is often undertaken as the only, and in fact a desirable, option for social and psychological survival. However, as discussed in Chapter 2, the adoption of 'normative' identity practices through assimilation does not automatically bestow freedom upon 'successful' queer subjects. The struggle for gender and sexual legitimacy within a broader neoliberal universe is heavily based upon the production of gender dualisms, as well as a certain type of privileged and desirable queer: the cosmopolitan Western/Westernized 'global gay', an identity thoroughly inscribed within and through human rights and mainstream international market terms.

Rudra's dilemma crystallizes the various philosophical, political and discursive tensions around the constitution of the subject and the pursuit of freedom in relation to gender and alterity – a theme that I have addressed throughout the various chapters in this book. I have situated this discussion within the context of human rights – a centrepiece in the liberal project's conception of autonomy and subjectivity, and integral to the entitled autonomous subject's enjoyment of freedom. The hegemonic discourse of human rights has come to overwhelmingly occupy the space of emancipatory possibilities and to effectively marginalize or negate any potential frameworks for freedom that are based on other epistemes. Ghosh's *Chitrangada* is an example of a creative work that provokes the spectator into thinking about freedom in alternative registers, that is, outside of the liberal fishbowl. It addresses the fraught issue of the recalcitrant who refuses to comply; those (non)subjects who turn away from the normative liberal script and gender dualisms within which both straight and queer lives are framed and deemed liveable and worthy under law, and who seek other modalities of self-affirmation.

The following sections of this chapter explore the idea of freedom outside of the liberal imaginary. I continue to draw upon the idea of the 'failed subject', as well as the implications of the turn away from human rights and its normative prescriptions – an inquiry initiated in Chapter 4 in relation to the veiled female subject, as well as in Chapter 6 via my discussion of Shirin Neshat's video installation *Overruled.* I develop this argument through reference to the distinct tradition of non-dualism found within Indian philosophical thought, to expand the meaning of freedom and to delineate the epistemological field in relation to which this expanded meaning is attached.

DECONSTRUCTING DUALITY

In emphasizing the need to expand the scope of inquiry through a turn towards non-liberal alternatives found in non-Western contexts, it is not my intention to extol the values of non-West as against West, and thus reproduce the very binary critiqued in this book. As I discussed briefly in Chapters 2 and 3, it is evident that 'developed' India and privileged Indians are making a grand entry onto the neoliberal global stage through aggressive wealth accumulation and cosmopolitan consumer lifestyles. India is mimetically navigating precisely that route to modernity implicated in the emerging sense of critical and political impasse, despair and paralysis. So my suggestion that we turn to alternative registers is not about the positing of a crude divide of 'the West and the Rest', but about entering a wider and deeper philosophical script. My concern is partially mirrored in a dialogue between the female philosopher Maitreyi and Yajnavalkya, a great Indian teacher and philosopher from 1800 BCE. Maitreyi asks Yajnavalkya whether she would become 'immortal' – that is, everlastingly free – if she acquired all the wealth in the world. Yajnavalkya replies that she would not and that all she would acquire is the life of a rich person, to which Maitreyi responds rhetorically: 'What should I do with that by which I do not become immortal?'[6] Neither India's nor indeed any society's entry to the global stage of 'progress' results in freedom – what Maitreyi metaphorically invokes as immortality.

At the same time, the sub-continent is home to extraordinary philosophical and intellectual traditions that have infused and influenced everyday life, and continue to do so. And it is precisely for this reason that the core liberal assumptions on which human rights are based can only either co-exist, exist in tension with or be subsumed within, rather than supplant, the ideas of time, subjectivity and freedom that configure entrenched world-views and ways of living in the subcontinent. Unfortunately, epistemologies that are non-liberal, especially in the non-West, have invariably been regarded as exotic, esoteric or rooted in religion and magical thinking. These knowledge traditions are relegated to a space below the ideals and concerns of the liberal secular project, and are regarded as distant and even primitive. Liberal biases fail to recognize the religious tone of some intellectuals in Western (and non-Western) liberal traditions, and also fail to address the religiosity that overtly and/or covertly influences liberal secularism, including within human rights.[7] While the emergence of the liberal subject ostensibly marks the displacement of religious attachment in favour of a rational ideal – an attachment that is disavowed through the norm of secular neutrality – the modern secular state is, somewhat paradoxically, exalted as the heir of a 'Judeo-Christian' past that values justice, liberty and love.[8] It is an essentially Christian understanding of secularism as well as secular neutrality.[9]

Further, the intellectual lineage of many non-Western traditions utilizes a system of logic and dialectics based on inference, deductive analysis and rigorous interrogation of the processes of knowledge. Sub-continental epistemes have a rich genealogy of thinkers who reformulated older knowledge paradigms or founded new schools of thought over millennia of philosophical inquiry, including folk and oral trajectories along with classical schemas. I name just three here, which are relevant to the themes of this book: the Buddha (583–483 BCE), an agnostic; Nāgārjuna, the extraordinary second-century Mahayana philosopher, who further developed the core doctrine of the 'empty' nature of all phenomena including the self, as described in the Chapter 6 discussion of Eve Sedgwick's 'turn' to Buddhism;[10] and Adi Śaṅkara (788–820 CE), the immensely influential scholar who expounded the theory of non-dualism or Advaita, the core aspects of which are presented in this chapter through a reading of his central work, *A Thousand [Verses of] Teachings* (*Upadeśasāhasrī*).[11] Contemporary scholars have mapped the history of sub-continental dialectics, debate and even scepticism; for instance, Amartya Sen, a Nobel laureate in economics, concludes in *The Argumentative Indian* that these knowledge systems are illustrative of everything being open to question. There are also a host of contemporary intellectuals such as Bimal Krishna Matilal, a leading exponent of logic and epistemology in Indian philosophy, who foregrounds the value of inference as a method.[12] Scrupulous examination and critique of the metaphysics of knowledge is an integral and fundamental aspect of sub-continental philosophies; as modes of systematic inquiry, they challenge the dominant assumption that human flourishing can only take place through a liberal framework, and that this framework is superior to all other ways of being in the world.

Moreover, the liberal logic that tends to corral these diverse non-monotheistic epistemologies under the single unifying category of 'religion' is both arbitrary and flawed. As Talal Asad has argued, 'religion' as an historical category emerged in Europe, and subsequently became a trans-historical phenomenon conceived of as a distinct space of human practice and belief, and as having an autonomous essence.[13] European scholars developed the taxonomy of world religions, including 'Hinduism' and 'Buddhism', modelled upon a distinctly Christian epistemology and ontology.[14] Christianity was not only regarded as the highest form of religion, it was also integral to the colonial project. As a category, religion came to be defined as having key components that included a belief system and a central scripture or text, which aligned with the secular idea that political power and religious authority could be segregated into entirely separate domains of influence. The entire construction of the category of 'religion' is thus not only thoroughly modern; it is also limited, exclusive and based on a Christian/Abrahamic genealogical schema. In the modern liberal state, the articulation of religion ensures its containment, not only in terms of space and time, but – as already briefly touched upon – also through the discourse of secularism, which is constituted partly by the way in which religion is politically understood, organized and publicly defined.[15] Within the spectrum of philosophical traditions available in non-liberal contexts which do not comply with the European criteria, there are 'other' belief systems that cannot simply be collapsed, and instantiated, into a more general abstraction – that is, into the category of 'religion'. Rather, being neither 'liberal' nor 'religious' in the terms just discussed, they eloquently insist on the presence – or enable the narration of – alternative registers of being and different paradigms with regard to being free.

In this chapter, I explore some aspects of non-dualism or Advaita ('not two'), a major sub-continental episteme of which Adi Śaṅkara was a central exponent. Three caveats are necessary, prior to any discussion of the principles of this philosophy and their relevance to the themes in his book. First, the critical emphasis on a non-liberal episteme has certain risks – in particular, the possibility that it may be taken up by conservative or right-wing forces and utilized to advance ideological agendas that are regressive and exclusive. It may also be met with charges from those on the left of the political spectrum, including feminists, that any spiritual emphasis in political critique is a betrayal of the cause of secularism. There is no doubt that a discussion of Śaṅkara's philosophical stance could be taken up, within the contemporary context, by the forces of the Hindu Right to advance their project of establishing India as a Hindu state, to actively persecute religious and other minorities and to vilify Christians and Muslims – in particular, as aliens, outsiders and threats to the integrity of the (Hindu) nation state.[16] My position is that the fact that the Hindu Right (as well as right-wing, conservative political agendas elsewhere) has proved very adept at being able to advance its conservative agenda, in and through rights discourses – including the discourse on women's rights, equality, tolerance and secularism – speaks to an urgent need to retrieve and counter these encroachments through focused critique. This strategy requires engagement with the issues of 'religion' as a political force, as well as scrutiny of the productive possibilities for recovering or seizing upon heterodox, esoteric and radical components within different philosophical traditions which have been obscured or marginalized, or where the tradition itself has been co-opted for myopic and destructive ends. There has been a deep reluctance on the part of the Left globally, including critical legal scholars, to engage the terrain of religion – critique invariably and reflexively falls back upon uninterrogated understandings of secularism as a political counter to religious right-wing agendas. Such reluctance cannot countenance new conceptions of freedom that have even the slightest whiff of 'religion'. The fact that the Right has been able to advance their agendas in and through the discourse of secularism and the possibility that secularism may have exacerbated religious tensions make urgent the need to problematize both religion *and* secularism.[17]

Second, it would not be accurate to classify Advaita under either the category of 'culture' or that of 'religion', even though Hindu revivalism in the fourteenth century attempted to claim this tradition within its embrace, and the Hindu Right continues to do so in contemporary times. Despite having an orthodox background, Śaṅkara, perhaps the most famous exponent of Advaita, was actually the nemesis of conservative upper-caste Brahmins, as he explicitly declared that the entrenched and prevalent practices of religious ritualism, deification and institutionalism were unrelated to the philosophical goal of emancipation of the self.[18]

Third, while non-dualism is not the only non-liberal philosophical tradition that makes a persuasive argument for lasting freedom, I have established it as the primary focus of my discussion. I focus on it here partly because of its compelling and radical reinscription of conventional understandings of time, subjectivity and freedom.

The use of 'Eastern' or non-European philosophy is *one* way in which to take forward the project of freedom. The rest of this chapter provides a tentative analysis of three epistemic fundamentals in the tradition of Advaita (non-dualism) as understood and expounded by Adi Śaṅkara: time, the subject and freedom.[19] Although Śaṅkara provided commentaries on numerous texts and scriptures, as well as manuals addressing the central aspects of non-dualism, I focus on the text authored by him entitled *Upadeśasāhasrī* or *A Thousand Teachings*. In this text Śaṅkara sets out the central features of Advaita, which are useful for the arguments about non-liberal understandings of freedom that are the main focus of this chapter.[20] Where necessary, I supplement this text with references from *The Realization of the Absolute: The 'Naiśkarmya Siddhi' of Śrī Sureśvara*, the work of Śaṅkara's student (and direct disciple) Śrī Sureśvara.[21] My endeavour is not to provide a comprehensive or exhaustive account of Advaita – the focus of a vast and complex field of scholarship[22] – but rather to highlight some of its central features, which sharply distinguish it from accounts of freedom and the subject in the liberal human rights tradition, and in the process to highlight the productive value of such inquiries.

Time

A hallmark of the liberal tradition is its unapologetic schematization of unilinear, progressive, teleological and Eurocentric history as the dominant, appropriate and authentic mode of documenting human presence and its imprint on the world. In this knowledge project, the domain of the 'Other' is viewed as Europe's regressive past, while Europe's present is posited as the 'Other's' desirable future. It is an anthropological and socio-political construct in which nations and individuals only attain maturity when they are fully conscious of themselves as subjects within this liberal template, and it is only such individuals who are entitled to freedom. Those outside this narrative have no claims or rights to enfranchisement, and therefore may rightfully continue to be subjugated. They remain 'in the imaginary waiting room of history', cast outside of linear secular time.[23]

Cultural distancing was partly produced through the concept of secularized, naturalized, linear time, which enabled the depiction of the 'Other' as barbarous and distant, and which set up the binary opposition between the advanced West and the backward 'Other'.[24] This temporal device was embedded in a civilizational project and political–moral concerns, and deployed to set up a spatialized relationship with the 'Other' where difference implied distance – a reference to the 'Other' 'out there' 'in the field'.[25] While the idea of distance between the 'West' and the 'Rest' has been largely exposed within anthropology, the very discipline that instituted it, the notion of the primitive as a temporal construct – a notion that has been central to liberal thought – continues to inform the ways in which human rights engage with difference and the 'Other'. While human rights appear expansive and inclusive if viewed within the terms of linear time, as discussed in the early chapters of this book, they have also simultaneously been based upon a hierarchical classification of the human, where distinct cultural traits and traditions are assessed and allocated merit primarily in accordance with the liberal index of material and technical progress, and social sophistication.

The logic of non-dualism posits time very differently. In epistemic terms, it rejects the notion that history consists of linear movement involving the material transition of dark and primitive eras towards more progressive ones. In non-dualism, all dimensions of the subject's relationship with time, space and causality are equivalent, and all require equal attention to be paid through the practice of deep and systematic reflection. Such reflection can produce the space to understand temporal relations, in particular the nature of the relationship between the concept of time and the subject who experiences time, and the nature of what manifests when this constructed experience recedes. Non-dualism locates time in thought, and thought resides in the thinker. Take, for example, memory. When an individual recalls an event or someone from the past, this thought resides in the individual thinker. Similarly, the thought about the future, about someone or something in the future, also resides in the thinker. Both are rooted in the now, in the present. The thought of the past and the future are in the present, and thus both are inseparable from the present. In other words, the three periods of time – the chronology we take for granted – actually do *not* exist in the way that they are universally perceived and engaged with. When we speak about the past and the future, these exist *now*. From the non-dualist perspective there is no past, only memory or the recollection of events that have already occurred, and there is no future, only thoughts or the projection of events that have yet to happen. True being/self is the constant witnessing of experience as it unfolds in the present – not as past or future. 'Past' and 'future' are arbitrary segregations of a single experiential continuum, the 'present', the *now*.[26]

The indivisible 'present' cannot be negated by time, by the logic of past or future. Nor can the present be classified as 'time'. *Now* is not something that comes and goes. We are conditioned to constantly attach to thoughts of either the past or the future; in fact, both constructs arise from the present, our true location, which we rarely inhabit due to the practice of ceaseless engagement with processes of recall and/or future projection. Experience of the 'present' consists of recalling the past and visualizing the future based on that recall. But this experience of the present is illusory. The present 'is', it is 'now' – timeless – autonomous of temporal categorizations. We may superimpose the categories of 'past' and 'future' upon the present, but the present is unchanging: it is experienced when thoughts about the past and the future are absent. *Now* does not refer to a temporal moment. 'To be' cannot be calibrated as a unit of duration; it simply *is*. *Now* is a moment that is without dimension. It is not time. It is not a thought. *To be* is not a thought. By this logic, the past and future are elided with the present, or the truth of *now*. The present is the *now*, devoid of time-based recollections and visualizations; 'now', which is not time, is a word that refers to being, to the unlimited consciousness or awareness that observes the limited components of time but does not exist in time. Time as an imposed category – linear, secular, naturalized, subjective – is thus an epistemic distortion of the experience of being; and *now* is the being undistorted by the subjective experience of time.

Proof of this experience is provided through the universal relationship between the state of wakefulness and the states of sleep/dreaming/deep dreamless sleep.[27] The sleeper may experience dreamless sleep, may dream and not remember what was experienced in the dream state, or may partially or totally recall her dream experience upon waking – but none of these are an experience of time experienced as systematic duration, that is, the linear chronology of the waking state. The fact that the sleeping/dreaming subject experiences no time/altered time is incontrovertible evidence of the existence of the self – the continuous 'who' experiencing the absence of time/altered time in sleep/dream, as well the experience of waking into the conditioned, discontinuous experience of constructed time and instantaneously reoccupying all dimensions of it. This disappearance and appearance of time, as earlier described, establishes that time is not a natural or absolute but an arbitrary modality. The conscious self exists as 'stainless and non-dual';[28] as an unbroken, unlimited continuum, regardless of whether time, space and causality are experienced as discrete or not, in the states of waking, sleep/dreaming or deep dreamless sleep.[29] The attributes of the subject are ephemeral in these different states, manifest and non-manifest, and can 'perish like clothes and wealth'.[30]

Thus, within the logic of non-dualism, the universal markers of time known as 'birth' and 'death' are not distinct causal events experienced as linear, naturalized time and manifested through a somatic process. The apparently distinct and causal events of birth and death, as well as every modification of body and mind during the life that has a physical beginning and end, exist only in relation to the witness/observer of birth and death – the conscious self, which is neither born nor dies, but is continuously present in the instant between one breath and the next; between one thought and the next; between one action and the next. Our universal experience of time as a calibrated progression of discrete, causal, sequential, teleological units arises from our lack of discriminating knowledge – the inability to foreground that which is continuous and present, namely, the changeless, imperishable conscious self, birthless and deathless, where all dualisms are absent and into which all action resolves.[31]

Once time is thus conceptually disaggregated, we arrive at the fundamental conclusion that 'I am'/'I am aware'/'I am aware that I am (this particular) body', and that *this is the now*. The 'now' is neither positive nor negative, and cannot be modified by any concepts of time or replaced by time. It also means that freedom is not an experience of time; that is, of a forward progression, a trajectory, or telos. Rather, freedom is asynchronous, non-categorical and not reliant upon synchronies or categories for validation. Release from the binding concept of linear time – and its understanding of history as events in time – is enabled by correcting the root error of equating the self/'I am' (immutable continuous being, the *now*) with the body. *Now* simply 'is' – the self/subject or consciousness: an awareness that witnesses time, but is not itself embedded in the constructs of time, and which is unaffected by time and all other constructs. This self continually exists and is continually experienced by the subject, whether or not time or any other construct is experienced.

The Subject/Self

The liberal subject is identified with the body, mind, intellect, memory, emotions, material objects, discourses and social labels. This identification with what the text refers to as 'name-and-form'[32] can include titles or words that connote marital status or educational qualifications, as well as professional position and location in the hierarchy of the workplace. Within a liberal universe, this fixed understanding of the subject does not question the relationship of the subject to the modality of action/agency, as a material, biological entity who is a doer/agent with end goals, as well as individually and collectively entitled to the freedom promised by the instruments of rights.

A non-dualist perspective offers a very different way of conceptualizing the subject or the self. It propounds a notion of the self as indivisible – as one, a non-fragmented whole – who, ultimately, is not defined by her labels or identities, or exclusively as a classifiable entity such as 'woman', 'black', 'Muslim' or 'homosexual', for instance. The self is the location where all phenomena and their descriptions are simultaneously produced and available for ontological resolution through the process of their true nature being discerned – in terms of the metaphor used elsewhere in this book, it is the conscious seer/witness correctly discriminating the apparent snake from the actual rope. The subject is emancipated from the state of ignorance/unfreedom when the error is understood through discernment that is directed at what one *is*, rather than what one *knows*. It is a self that is available to be discerned, but the 'I'-thought remains unavailable to engage in this process of self-reflection and error correction. The discerner is not the object of awareness, but the self – that is, awareness – unaffected by time, space and causality. The subject in this tradition is not observed but experienced and cannot be objectified.[33] Using this logic, the equation of the body with the subject also falls within the realm of awareness. What is observed is distinct from that which continuously observes, or is the witness or seer that is not available to be observed. If the seer/subject could be observed, it too would be a discontinuous object. Equation of the seer/subject with the form is the error that needs to be corrected, just as the equation of the rope with the snake needs to be discerned.[34] Time cannot correct these errors; only discernment of the error can correct the misunderstanding.

Everything that can be objectified – that is, everything other than the subject/seer/self – has the same metaphysical value. The same logic applies with regard to the primary attributes of embodiment – the senses and emotions – where the senses and emotions include the subject's identification with them. Without this identification, the objects that are the senses and emotions cannot exist. The self is unaffected by this dynamic of externalization–objectification–identification, because the self is not an object to be observed/identified with, nor is it sustained by identifications.[35]

Non-dualism endeavours to completely delink the equation of the self with all attributes and labels, and foreground the limitless space of consciousness or awareness from which all of these labels and attributes arise and are observed and where errors, if recognized, are available for correction through discernment. This self or 'I' is not the same as the 'I' that is equated with the body, name and form which, in turn, produces a relationship with the world and denotes action.[36] The experiencing 'I' is not a conclusion arrived at through logic. The 'I' is consciousness that continues to exist and be experienced in the states of waking, sleep/dreaming and deep/dreamless sleep.[37] In the states of dreaming and deep sleep, all labels, categories and identities are altered, dispersed or non-existent, attesting to the fact that these attributes are ephemeral and not constitutive of the subject. However, upon waking, the subject instantaneously and wholly equates herself with the form and her prior attributes, without experiencing any compulsion to reflect upon their seamless transmutation from insubstantiality to materiality. Upon waking, she is also immediately, incontrovertibly aware that she has slept and dreamed, even if the dream content is imperfectly or not recalled.[38] The question that arises then is: 'who' recalls the dream or registers that, in deep sleep, the sleeper was absent – that the 'I' was not there? 'Who' is the 'I' recalling that 'I was not there'? It is this seamless, self-established, self-evident consciousness that is the witness of all phenomena – continuously aware, but not an object of its own awareness.[39]

A famous example of the failure to recognize this understanding of the self is illustrated in the literature through the compelling analogy of the 'tenth person'.[40] In this analogy, ten people cross a river; after they have crossed, the tenth person counts the others to make sure that everyone has made it safely across. She counts only nine people, becomes alarmed, and begins to search all over for the 'missing' tenth person. She has, of course, forgotten to count herself. This failure to discern causes the tenth person, the seeker herself, to become obsessed with the other nine and the search for the 'missing' tenth. This very obsession prevents her from discerning the solution to her problem. Similarly, the obsession with the world, others, difference, labels, materiality and corporeality is akin to the tenth person's overlooking of herself and instead becoming fixated on the other nine in order to find the tenth, *herself* – ever present yet, in her distracted state of mind, an illusory absence. The seer of all ten people cannot be observed by any of the other nine, who are the objects of her obsession; nor can she be observed by the obsessive person – herself – as long as she remains obsessed. She signifies a universal human characteristic – distraction – which forecloses the possibility of the introspection or reflection necessary for correct discernment to take place. The misperception that draws her into a circuit of reaction, and distress, over the 'missing' tenth person is corrected through the process of eventually discerning that she herself is the 'missing' tenth person. This process is not an external achievement or discovery, but an internal recognition or uncovering. The antidote to the error is the practice of introspection which can lead to discernment; such 'seeing' is an experience of freedom not contingent upon *doing* and the relationship between doer and deed, or between cause and effect, but upon *being*.[41]

The continuous inherency of the subject as timeless *being* – distinct from everything that she observes and does, even though she may be present in everything she observes and does – needs to be distinguished from affect and its focus on the binding energies of the senses, even though the turn to the granular, experiential and personal can serve as a powerful mode of inquiry with regard to the nature of the conscious self, the claims of the 'I'. Feminist engagements with affect confidently locate subjectivity in the expressive and intimate emotional aspects of the subject. However, there remains a core theoretical tension regarding how the affective subject is formed, and whether she exists as an entity outside of discourse and social norms or is in fact constituted by them.

Butler has engaged this tension throughout the course of her work. Most recently, she discusses how the senses are assumed to mark a moment prior to the *thinking* 'I': 'To say that I am affected prior to ever becoming an 'I' is to deliver the news by using the very pronoun that was not yet put into play, confounding this temporality with that one.'[42] The assumption informing this argument is that there is an affected 'I', which precedes the deliberate and conscious 'I' that is aligned with thought. A second strand of this inquiry is whether the *thinking* 'I', which comes later in the process and is a retrospective position, can describe the prior affective situation at all, as this 'I' is not present for the affective process, and 'I myself, that is the *thinking* "I", seem to be one of its various effects'.[43] If this is true, the non-presence of the thinking 'I' renders any narrative of subject formation impossible. And yet an 'I' is necessary to understand how the subject is initially animated by affect, and how this understanding in turn affects the subsequent processes of her animated life.[44] Who can narrate the process of subject formation when the 'who' only comes into existence subsequent to this formation?

Butler accepts the paradox, and finds partial resolution through reference to the clusters of norms with spatial and temporal dimensions that already exist, are in operation and circulate in the world before touching us and impressing themselves upon us. They open up affective regimes and both act upon and form sensibility, producing feelings that can enter thinking at the moment 'I' – the corporeal being – is born; constructing and being assimilated into the self, these norms continue to operate through the subject's immediate life and are also perpetuated beyond it. They continue to exist and circulate when life ends, and before life begins.[45] What is crucial here is the rejection of causality – the idea that a subject is produced through the action of a single norm – and the suggestion of an essential continuity beyond the immediate. Clusters of norms act upon us before we are born, and impress themselves upon our embodied existence through racial, gendered, religious, socio-political and cultural discourses. In cognitive terms, we cannot be reduced to authors of our own actions; rather, being acted upon and acting are simultaneous – and the 'I' is not thinkable without this formation.[46]

Butler's focus on the senses represents her continuing challenge to the sovereign 'I', a core principle of liberal episteme, which assumes that our individuality renders us inherently capable of acting with complete autonomy. This sovereign individualism disavows the normative coercions of subject formation and the constitutive relationships with the 'Other' against and with which the 'I' calibrates itself. The aggressive liberal disavowal of dependency and interdependency, based on the assumption that disregard for and the arbitrary severing of these constitutive relationships is critical to the process of transitioning from non-being into being – that is, becoming the 'I' – produces a 'brittle' subject.[47] Butler argues against the possibility of a radical break with this normative order, even when the being that emerges is a broken, muted, racialized non-being. While new subject formations can come into being, they cannot overthrow or completely break with the existing normative order. In her discussion of the senses, including the conditions for touching, feeling and sensing the world, the so-called independent 'I' in fact continues to be established through a set of formative relations rather than via a complete break from them. Crucial to Butler's argument is her assertion that the existence of the 'I' requires affirming a world without which the 'I' would not be, since it is constituted through its susceptibility to clusters of already circulating norms with spatial and temporal dimensions.[48] And this process of self-constitution would include affirming whatever happens to me, the subject, without my willing it – everything 'that precipitates my sensing and knowing the world as I do'.[49] We are unable to liberate ourselves from such self-formation, even though the process is neither definitive nor final, but continuous and repetitive. Thus, the subject – unable to transcend the web of relations permeating the world that gives rise to the subject – cannot act 'without first being formed as one with the capacity to act'.[50]

Butler's discussion of the impressionable self is part of her extended effort to address the critique of her influential earlier theorization that the subject was fully constituted by and hemmed in by discourse alone.[51] Her clarifications delineate, in greater detail, the layered nature of the subject and subject formation through the idea of an affective self.[52] But this level of intimate inquiry and reflection results in a description of subjectivity that is profoundly different from subjectivity as narrated in non-dualism, and presents neither a purely analytical 'I' nor a purely affective 'I'. The source of all analysis and affect – the non-dual 'I' – continuously observes the instruments, operations and outcomes of both, without being either.

The axiomatic position of the Cartesian subject – 'I think, therefore I am' – as well as more critical positions, including Butler's view discussed above, equate 'I am' with the notion that 'I am the body' or 'I am the senses' or 'I am the thought'. In fact, in the tradition of non-dualism, the body is no more than matter which becomes sentient due to the identification of the conscious being with the body. This primary association is the genesis of all the logic that constitutes liberal individualism. Butler's analysis extricates itself from the dominant concept of a biological, naturalized 'I' by referring to the process of subject formation through clusters of norms that manifest in the world, and are continuous and repetitive. While this argument comes close to the idea of a continuous, ever-present self, it is, of course, not the same thing.

Non-dualism posits that the self – that is, consciousness – exists even when the material and normative world experienced in the waking state, through the sentient, animated body, ceases to exist for the experiencer; an example is in sleep, a daily physiological event. There is thus a distinction between the conscious being-as-subject (intrinsic, self-evident and self-established); the animated, contingent body, with its labels; and a subject formed within clusters of pre-existent functioning norms.

This articulation of the self within Advaita provides the logic through which to understand that which we are not/recognize that which we are. Such discernment is a simultaneous, not sequential, process. The unlimited conscious self is not the limited mind and its content, the intellect, or thought.[53] Nor is it equated with the norms that constitute the material subject. Consciousness is not a cognitive faculty or mental function, although we experience it as if it is. Thought is matter and the thinker/thought are finite – they begin and end. There can be no thought without this self, although the self can and does exist without thought. The mutable subject – that is, the subject that equates with thought, name and form – cannot exist apart from the immutable conscious self that is its source. Similarly, while norms remain continuous, repetitive and tenacious, and are indifferent to the finitude of the material body, non-dualism draws attention to 'who' observes the norm. The non-dual self is not the Cartesian thinking 'I' nor the *a priori* transcendent 'I', but pure consciousness; the being, *now*, that *is*, ever constant, existent, present. This unchanging, dispassionate self observes the erroneous equation of consciousness with the impermanent body, and all of the relationships that flow from this ever mutable equation. Turning the argument here to the specific terms of critique, there cannot be a denial of the deconstructive postulate that the body is constituted in and through language, or that subject formation is inseparable from clusters of norms that are continuous and repetitive. But the self that observes this inscribed form remains constant, regardless of whether the form has inherent existence outside of discourse, or is indeed wholly constituted by discourse.

The conscious self is like the transparent crystal that looks red because of its proximity to the red flower, but is not qualified by the colour of the flower.[54] The senses may be needed in order for the subject to act, to achieve, to engage with phenomena, but the senses are not required in order to experience one's true existence, *to feel who one is*. While the term 'feel' is used here in relation to the self, it does not signify a finite affective experience. Nor can the experience of self-existence be invoked through logic, imagination or any other mode of willed awareness. The self is choicelessly and intimately felt. It is ever-present *being*; the experience of being utilizes the senses, but is not the senses. Thoughts, the body and senses are not the continuous, cognizing 'I', but resolve in the unlimited conscious self in the same way that sound resolves in silence. Silence and sound are different modalities: silence cannot be objectified, modified or negated into sound; nor can it be transposed or juxtaposed with sound. Silence continues to exist regardless of whether sound is superimposed on it or not, in the experience of the hearer; silence simply *is*.

The tenacious and intractable psycho-physiological habit of identifying consciousness with the material form is what occludes the potential to experience the true self that is ever-available to be experienced. This habit manifests through the belief that '*I* am the performer/doer/agent and *I* am the enjoyer of the actions', and that without continually engaging in action, *I* do not have an identity, *I* am not, *I* do not exist.[55] The pursuit of rights, fully centred on the categories and politics of selfhood as identity, inevitably takes the subject in the direction of 'doing' and away from 'being'. Within both the discursive and the material terrain of human rights, there is regrettably little or no pause for reflection, but rather a continuous focus on how we as individual selves, such as feminists or human rights scholars, can theorize and/or even actualize freedom for others even before we have successfully freed ourselves from our own deep conditioning, unmitigated phobias, discriminatory schemas and powerful sense of privilege and entitlement. A fundamental shift from the philosophical position based on *doing* (good) action, including well-intentioned interventions, to a position of reflection based upon discerning what it means to *be* is central to non-dualism and its understanding of freedom.

Thus, conscious, self-reflective practices should be essential ingredients in human rights advocacy or any project directed towards ensuring freedom. All too often, failure in this respect – in many cases arising from a myopic impulse to misread and mislabel self-reflection as inaction – results in the systematic categorizing and politicizing of particular grievances, prioritizing some as more urgent than others. This inequitable approach shapes interventions and policies that, in the name of rights and emancipation, may in fact reinscribe a legacy of physical and emotional trauma, and may also irretrievably move the marginalized and oppressed – the focus of such advocacy – even further away from the goal of freedom.

Freedom

As discussed in earlier chapters, the concept of freedom in human rights is linked to liberal freedom. However, as evidenced by the violence that marks the contemporary moment, the bestowal of more rights does *not* necessarily result in more freedom or meaningful happiness for disenfranchised, stigmatized and abjected populations. As I argued in Chapter 1, human rights do not simply intervene to ensure 'bare survival' or attend only to address situations of 'human suffering', for example through deployment of humanitarian assistance in response to complex, overlapping and multiple crises. Rather, rights today are active conduits for structures and relations of power, for avid as well as insidious policing and for increased regulation and governance of both the entitled and the disenfranchised.

Taking the context of women's lives globally as an obvious example, it is not at all evident that increased rights have actually produced more freedom and equality for women. Human rights interventions confronting the unrelenting nature of violence, trafficking or rape have not brought about significant emancipation; rather, rights have facilitated and intensified the moral surveillance and regulation of women's lives. The reflexive liberal equation of freedom with more rights also informs a specific strand of feminist legal thought. For example, Martha Nussbaum and Catharine MacKinnon, who articulate very different visions of this quest, are nevertheless similarly committed to the idea of all women enjoying the rights to equality and life to the same degree as their American sisters, either by being free of tradition (and presumably also history),[56] or by wresting power from men and developing a feminist jurisprudence that asserts the view or 'standpoint of all women'.[57] Yet, both scholars not only eschew the agency of these oppressed female 'Others',[58] but also fail to address a major underpinning of the inclusion–exclusion dialectic: the numerous and interdependent ways in which racial, sexual, gendered and cultural 'Others' are produced in and through liberal rights discourses, and then identified as subjects for the preferential bestowal of human rights within the liberal schema. Nussbaum contends that such exclusions are a result of the liberal project becoming ideologically distracted or derailed, while MacKinnon views all exclusions through the homogenizing lens of an adversarial relationship: male dominance and female subordination. Neither theorist considers the argument that these exclusions *themselves* become constitutive of the liberal rights project and its self-arrogated mandates of intervention.

Human rights and the liberal tradition are premised upon the political idea of the individual as the centre of freedom projects, and the perception that freedom lies in the respectful and peaceful coexistence of a multitude composed of such individuals. But this formulation goes no deeper. Freedom through rights – the fulcrum of liberal advocacy – is identified as something external; as an end goal to be reached based upon liberal individualism, which foregrounds the sovereign 'I' and equates the self with material embodiment/identity based upon the particularities of embodiment.

Deconstructing this position becomes the primary focus of critique, as noted in Chapter 1. Yet, as affect theorists have argued, critique privileges the sovereignty of the critic and provides a symptomatic reading which overlooks the way in which everyday life is lived, disregards this existential substrate as an authentic source of knowledge and tends to exclude this from the rights discourse. Feminist engagement with affect seeks to draw attention to that which has been excluded through a focus on the intimate, expressiveness, and the everyday. But while it provides a rich tapestry of how daily life is lived, endured and sustained, dwelling on affective atmospheres does not provide a recipe for freedom and happiness – which is the ultimate aspiration.

Theoretical conclusions that regard life as a modality of 'cruel optimism', that regard life experience as primarily the relentless struggle of survival–endurance–sustenance and that foreground the vulnerable subject's resultant drift into melancholia and despair are not productive options. And affect theorists' prioritization of the senses and emotions is also a limiting perspective when contrasted with non-dualism, which mandates that all concerns of embodiment need to be viewed in relation to the self as the continuum of self-existence – that which animates the body, but is not the body.

A non-dualist position would argue that the pursuit of rights in a desire for freedom is an expression of faith and belief that freedom is an external project which does not involve self-inquiry. The goal of freedom in non-dualism is not confined to material embodiment and everything associated with it, in terms of action and doing, or to the normative realm (resistance, disruption and rearrangement of the social). Rather, it is focused on the deeper journey, where committed practices of self-inquiry and self-reflection have the potential to bring about insights and fundamental shifts in awareness – a crucial reorienting of aspiration towards possibilities of permanent rather than temporary freedom. The desirable practice of continually engaging in rigorous internal and external scrutiny before, during and after undertaking any action is, indeed, far removed from the liberal paradigm of freedom to be acquired through the rights dispensation. An epistemic overhaul is required to fully comprehend this entirely different account of the relationship between the conscious self and the constructed subject, as well as the liberal subject. There is a complete turn away from the focus on how a subject can exist in the world and discover freedom, which implies distance between the subject and her object – freedom – and a turn towards how the subject can uncover freedom, which is her true intimate state, and from which there is never a sense of distance. While this mode of self-inquiry and the resulting self-transformation is reminiscent of Foucault's interest in the 'care of the self' – and essential to the project of freedom discussed in Chapter 6 – non-dualism goes much further. It requires a renunciation of the axiomatic understanding of the subject as a doer and creator, and a shift towards accepting the subject as the observer/witness – the subject as being, as what continually is, rather than what becomes, appears and disappears. Non-dualism rejects action in any form, or accepts it only to the extent that it takes place before acquiring knowledge of the self, which is the ultimate means to freedom.[59]

The understanding of the self as always present, as intimate rather than transcendent, which continues despite the cleavages that seem to abound in the world around us, is indeed a form of emancipation. This freedom is experienced at the site of the correction of the epistemic error; it involves recognition that the self continually infuses the corporeal, material, anatomical subject and also remains present when the corporeal subject decays, is destroyed or is deconstructed. To identify unlimited, indivisible, unchanging self/consciousness with fluctuating, perishable embodiment is the crux of the error. To correct this profound misidentification at its root – in metaphorical terms, to distinguish the apparent snake from the actual rope – is an experience of lasting freedom. And this radical re-experiencing of awareness does not produce an epistemic void or dismiss subjectivity. When the subject is brought within the purview of critique, it does not inevitably have to be accompanied by anxiety, pessimism, hopelessness, despair or negation. Rather, the act of relegating cherished analytical frameworks opens up new conceptual spaces, thus enabling the emergence of other philosophic registers, and other readings and inscriptions of the vital relationship between one's self and one's action in the world.

The turn towards introspection and a non-dualistic perspective, while foundational to the freedom project, should not be equated with indifference or solipsism. As argued throughout this book, efforts towards procuring rights *are* necessary, but they should be delinked from their connection with freedom. The invocation of non-dualism offers a different way to be, and to be free; and it presents a dynamic challenge to the current scheme of rights, which is evidently failing in its promise of freedom.

What does this philosophical exposition on non-dualism – with its assertion that freedom is the experience of freedom from identification with all forms – offer in a world built primarily around the experience of form, where bodies are classified, counted, inscribed with particular identities, differentially valued and treated? How does this understanding of freedom address itself to the intractable human habit of 'othering' – of reflexively accepting/affiliating with bodies that are more or less similar to one's own, and rejecting/abjecting forms that are different from it? In terms of the rope-snake metaphor frequently invoked in this book, one might say that the primary response to 'otherness' is the error of mistaking the rope for a snake, thereby confusing appearance with actuality, and what is not with what is. This profound misperception produces fear or uncertainty that feels palpably true, although the source of the fear is an illusion. The initial response to the rope-perceived-as-snake ranges from the instinct to protect oneself by retreating from it, to finding something to use as a weapon against it, to attempting to ascertain whether it is poisonous or not, to determining whether it can be safely captured without harm to it and to oneself, and whether it can be safely released in a place where it cannot harm other life. However, none of these pragmatic responses will assist in the process of permanently rectifying the root perceptual error – namely, that the phenomenon being observed is in fact a rope and not a snake.[60] This correction can only occur through the subjective practice of discernment, which frees the perceiver from the *real* fear of the *imagined* snake. Even if the perceiver is authoritatively assured that the snake is a rope, this information is inadequate for the resolution of fear. Investigating the phenomenon through empirical analysis, discourse and affect does not sufficiently enable insight into its fundamentals. If the rope was perceived to be a garland or other attractive object, rather than a frightening one, the perceiver would not feel fear but would still be in a state of illusion: her deductions would still be based on error, as she still does not see the rope. Thus the fear can only be resolved through correct knowledge of what the 'snake' actually is. Until then, the phenomenon remains concretely present and problematic for the perceiver, regarded as a dangerous object that can become the focus of obsession and/or become the target of all manner of bigotry, phobias and violence, as posited in the Introduction to this book.

Transposing this logic onto the territory of human rights, responses to the gendered, sexual, religious and cultural 'Other' requiring the bestowal of individual or collective rights are all too often based on the perception and objectification of the 'Other' as dangerous or threatening, and thus needing to be incarcerated, contained, or destroyed; or as an exotic cultural curiosity that can be exhibited and re-narrated at the narrator's desire; or as an abject victim needing to be rescued, rehabilitated, restituted, in accordance with the rescuer's norms and practices. These perceptions and objectifications are manifest in human rights interventions, which have produced failed outcomes that are no longer prompting the more familiar question of how human rights can advance freedom. Instead, they raise an entirely different critical and political question: whose project of freedom is being advanced, for whom, and at what cost?

THE TECTONICS OF INCOMMENSURABILITY

The arguments presented in favour of a non-liberal understanding of freedom bring us back to the two sets of paradoxes that characterize Rudra's struggle, described at the beginning of this chapter – one at the level of embodiment, the other at an epistemic level. At the first level, we recognize how – in social terms – Rudra is a 'failed subject' whose happiness rests in his relationship with Partho and the desire for a family. As stated earlier, recognition of same-sex relationships through rights acquisition might 'solve' Rudra's dilemma and provide a less troubled journey towards a 'happy' homonormative life based on gender dualisms. Yet this desired 'turn away' from queer 'illegitimacy' – and the 'turn towards' rights and becoming a 'successful' queer – might be understood as the manifestation of a struggle and a search for legibility, rather than for freedom. For those who are denied the right to live and to love freely, surrendering alterity and preferring subordinating types of recognition is preferable to invisibility and non-recognition. In contrast, strategies of self-affirmation actively pursued by those who might be termed 'queerly' queer – that is, those who have queered gender and have chosen to 'turn away' from rather than 'turn towards' the offerings of homonormativity, gender dualism, legibility and assimilation – may not be a default choice but a conscious preference, and one that must not be reductively interpreted as merely an effort to find effective ways of surviving the multiple traumas of marginality.

At the epistemic level, Rudra's process of reflection represents another paradox articulated along the suture of different positions thrusting against and abrading each other like tectonic plates – the existential and the metaphysical, the liberal and the non-dual – each testing the massive potential force and resistance of the other. While Rudra's narrative is about the role of human rights in the subaltern's desire for freedom, it is also about the possibility of obtaining meaningful and absolute freedom *beyond* the relative, sceptical and contingent. The material, social and political exclusion of marginalized subjects, their consequent suffering and the very parameters of self-understanding are all relinquished in the tradition of non-dualism. This paradox appears to defy resolution, with the contrast in knowledge claims appearing to be absolute; the methodologies of the encounter appear incompatible, not amenable to prevailing upon one another or to being synthesized into any sort of conclusion, let alone a satisfactory one. Given the embedded template of liberal understandings of freedom, and the very different relationship of self and world delineated in non-dualist conceptions of being, it may be that commensurability is not even desirable. Such reconciliation might, instead, leach away the subversive and transformative potential of alterity, and therefore make it more appropriate to accept that it is illogical and unfeasible to try and align liberal and non-dual conceptions within the framework of a freedom project.

But the effort here is not to seek commensurability – recalling that my argument in part characterizes human rights as a governance project, not a freedom project, and that freedom may be more productively and effectively articulated from alternative registers. However, given that human rights and the lack of rights remains a crucial feature in the lives of abjected ‘Others’, the analysis suggests that it is incumbent upon feminists and human rights advocates to become more self-aware with regard to precisely what they are advancing in and through their human rights advocacy, and also recognize the need for them to develop the practice of double consciousness, which is an integral feature of postcolonial critiques. While the positing of direct commensurability between liberal and non-liberal schemas may be illusive and possibly counterproductive, it nevertheless may be helpful to identify the ways in which these two projects may be able to work *around* one another. A critical approach to human rights reveals how, within the liberal episteme, the subject and freedom are constituted through discourse and social norms, suggesting that there is no sovereign ‘I’ or doer behind the deed. On the other hand, the reparative turn in feminist affect theory, through its focus on the existential, expressive and emotional, begins the process of turning away from the world and the promises on which we have relied, and towards the ‘I’ as affective self, the entity that experiences devastation and betrayal when those promises of freedom are not fulfilled. However, affect-based strategies are not stable; they may provide temporary relief in crisis but cannot offer long-term sustainability. The reparative turn does not correct the erroneous equation of the subject with the body. And given that affect is based on writing the body back into theory, it cannot accommodate what non-dualism asserts is the root error in self-understanding: identifying the subject with the fluctuating, transient body, rather than understanding the subject as self, as the unchanging, imperishable witness to all material fluctuations and transience. This is the starting point for unmasking the limits of existing liberal claims about freedom.

The freedom offered in non-dualism is the personal experience of freedom from name and form, and, as discussed, it frees us from the notion of the 'Other' – that is, a manifestation of name and form different from oneself – as always unequal to oneself, and from the instinct of arrogating to oneself the general right to perceive and treat the 'Other' as a being always less worthy, less valid, less deserving than oneself. Re-invoking the rope-snake metaphor here, the (mis)judgement about the 'Other' ceases once we discern the true nature of the 'snake'. As mentioned earlier, an obsession with the details of the 'snake' – its origins, qualities and propensities – cannot bring about an understanding of the 'snake's' essence; nor can this approach rectify the fundamental misperception of perceiving a 'snake' as what is actually a rope. Freedom from this fixation involves reflection and discernment rather than the logic of reflexive action, as well as taking a vertical and a lateral approach, and engaging in modes of relationship with the 'Other' in order to cease one's unthinking objectification of the 'Other'. Only then will it become possible to detach from the profound illusion that the 'Other' is in any way inferior to oneself. In its most evolved manifestation, this act completely subsumes the notion that the 'Other' is in any way other to oneself.

An emphasis on consciousness provides a very different critical location from which to view the world and its proliferating injustices. If we engage with rights by understanding them in terms of their deployment today – not as tools for the purpose of obtaining freedom, but as being fully implicated in schemas of power and governance – while *also* deeply engaging in the process of self-reflection (the 'turn away' that is synchronous with the 'turn within'), we may be able to arrest the epistemic freefall that occurs subsequent to any thorough dismantling of embedded influential frameworks, and thus seek to recuperate the ideal of lasting freedom. The discussion in this book offers a different epistemology within which to understand and negotiate the concepts of freedom, and also offers a different basis for the fresh imagining of a political position – one that would eschew despair, paranoia and paralysis on the one hand, and consistently refute liberal reformism on the other. It points to the possibility of realizing freedom through a deeper engagement with other influential knowledge paradigms and their metaphysical locations, trajectories and goals. My argument for 'thinking freedom' outside the fishbowl and within non-liberal spaces is intended to push the dialogues within human rights discourses closer to the fundamental issues that continue to trouble feminists and critical legal scholars. We cannot abandon human rights advocacy, but we must recognize its inability to procure freedom. We must therefore not only evolve truly mindful, equitable and inclusive strategies of rights deployment, but also actively direct our attention beyond the fishbowl of familiar liberal hegemonies and seek out alternative registers for their capacity to realize the promise of lasting freedom.

NOTES

1. Devdutt Pattanaik, *The Pregnant King* (New Delhi: Penguin Books, 2008), p. 332.
2. Johannes Fabian, *Time and the Other: How Anthropology Makes Its Object* (New York: Columbia University Press, 2014), p. 35.
3. Lu K'uan-yü (Charles Luk), trans. and ed., *Master Hsu Yun's Discourses and Dharma Words* (Taipei: Corporate Body of the Buddha Educational Foundation, 1996), p. 5 (emphasis added).
4. Rituparno Ghosh was a young lyricist and writer, and one of the most enigmatic and creative filmmakers to emerge on the cultural scene in India. He was unique in putting issues of sexuality – including homosexuality, adultery, divorce and remarriage – into the public domain, and was one of the few openly homosexual persons in the film industry, inserting himself and his sexuality into some of his films. He died unexpectedly, at the age of 49, in 2013, and *Chitrangada: The Crowning Wish* was his final film. For a more detailed commentary on the life and works of Ghosh, see Sangeeta Datta, Kaustav Bakshi and Rohit K. Dasgupta, eds., *Rituparno Ghosh: Cinema, Gender and Art* (New Delhi: Routledge, 2016).
5. Tagore's heroine differs from the figure of Chitrangada in the *Mahabharata*. In the Indian epic, composed around 3000 BCE, Arjuna, the central heroic character, falls in love with Chitrangada, a warrior princess of Manipur. The king, who has no sons, gives Arjuna permission to marry his daughter provided that they remain in Manipur, thereby securing succession through his daughter. Different readings have been offered by scholars of the representations of gender and sexuality in Ghosh's film. See, for example, Daisy Hasan, '"Kissed on One Cheek and Slapped on the Other": Rituparono Ghosh's *Chitrangada* as an Allegory of Oppositional Readings', *South Asian History and Culture* 6, no. 4 (2015): 500–9.
6. Amartya Sen, *The Argumentative Indian: Writings on Indian History, Culture and Identity* (London: Allen Lane, 2005), p. 8.
7. Talal Asad, *Formations of the Secular: Christianity, Islam, Modernity* (Stanford, CA: Stanford University Press, 2003); John Haskell, 'The Religion/Secularism Debate in Human Rights Literature: Constitutive Tensions between Christian, Islamic, and Secular Perspectives', in *International Law and Religion: Historical and Contemporary Perspectives*, eds. Martti Koskenniemi, Mónica García-Salmones Rovira and Paolo Amorosa (Oxford: Oxford University Press, 2017), pp. 135–53.
8. Saba Mahmood, *Religious Difference in a Secular Age: A Minority Report* (Princeton, CA: Princeton University Press, 2016), quoting Jürgen Habermas, pp. 7–8. See also Haskell, 'The Religion/Secularism Debate', discussing how human rights are situated within a Christian legacy, whereas Islam is often cast as being incompatible with democratic traditions and processes (at pp. 137–8).
9. See discussion of *Lautsi v. Italy* in Chapter 4.
10. Nāgārjuna, *The Fundamental Wisdom of the Middle Way: Nāgārjuna's Mūlamadhyamakakārikā*, trans. Jay L. Garfield (New York: Oxford University Press,

1995); K. Venkata Ramanan, *Nāgārjuna's Philosophy* (Rutland, VT: Charles E. Tuttle Company, 1966).

11. Adi Śaṅkara, *A Thousand Teachings: The Upadeśasāhasrī of Śaṅkara*, trans. and ed. Sengaku Mayeda (New York: State University of New York Press, 1992).
12. Bimal Krishna Matilal, *Perception: An Essay on Classical Indian Theories of Knowledge* (Oxford: Clarendon Press, 1986).
13. Talal Asad, *Genealogies of Religion: Discipline and Reasons of Power in Christianity and Islam* (Baltimore, MD: Johns Hopkins University Press, 1993), pp. 27–8.
14. Ibid.; Tomoko Masuzawa, *The Invention of World Religions, Or, How European Universalism was Preserved in the Language of Pluralism* (Chicago: University of Chicago Press, 2005); Peter van der Veer, *Imperial Encounters: Religion and Modernity in India and Britain* (Princeton, CA: Princeton University Press, 2001).
15. Balagangadhara similarly argues that religion is not a cross-cultural universal phenomenon, but has emerged over the past three centuries as a framework based on Christian, Judaic and Islamic theological templates, while every other practice or way of life is viewed and treated as paganistic: S.N. Balagangadhara, *'The Heathen in His Blindness': Asia, the West, and the Dynamic of Religion* (Leiden: E.J. Brill, 1994).
16. Brenda Cossman and Ratna Kapur, *Secularism's Last Sigh? Hindutva and the (Mis)Rule of Law* (Delhi: Oxford University Press, 2001).
17. Cossman and Kapur, *Secularism's Last Sigh?*; Asad, *Formations*; Mahmood, *Minority Report*. See also Timothy Fitzgerald, '"Postcolonial Remains": Critical Religion, Postcolonial Theory, and Deconstructing the Secular–Religious Binary', in *The Postcolonial World*, eds. Jyotsna G. Singh and David D. Kim (Abingdon: Routledge, 2017); Haskell, 'The Religion/Secularism Debate'.
18. Śaṅkara, *A Thousand Teachings*, p. 85. Sureśvarācārya, *The Realization of the Absolute: The 'Naiṣkarmya Siddhi' of Śrī Sureśvara*, trans. A.J. Alston, 2nd ed. (London: Shanti Sadan, 1971), p. 16.
19. Core aspects that are also distinguishing features for some of the other traditions briefly discussed in Chapter 5: Mahayana Buddhism, Sufism and Twelver Shi'ism.
20. Śaṅkara, *A Thousand Teachings*. Mayeda's translation includes an introductory section by him: Śaṅkara, *A Thousand Teachings*, pp. 1–97. The text is divided into two parts. Part I, the metrical part, consists of 19 chapters, is addressed to students and sets out the main questions raised in non-dualist reasoning. Part II, the prose part, consists of three chapters, and is addressed to teachers. Chapter 2 of Part II is largely in the form of a dialogue between a teacher and a student on the nature of the self/subject, and constitutes the central philosophical core of the text.
21. Sureśvarācārya, *Realization of the Absolute*. The text consists of four books. The contents, as well as the structure of the text, are similar to *A Thousand Teachings*. Each book consists of roughly 100 stanzas followed by the author's commentary, and is also supplemented by footnoted commentary from the translator. The text is entirely centred on the shift from action to being, and on how action is incompatible with knowledge of the 'I' and being. The text refutes the claim that freedom can be secured through action alone or action combined with knowledge: Sureśvarācārya, *Realization of the Absolute*, Book I. Its central philosophical argument is that freedom can only be secured through self-knowledge: Sureśvarācārya, *Realization of the Absolute*, Book II.
22. For a brief overview of some of the competing positions and understandings of Advaita, see T.M.P. Mahadevan, 'Contemporary Relevance of the Insights of Advaita', in *Contemporary Indian Philosophy: Series II*, ed. Margaret Chatterjee (Delhi: Motilal Barnarsidass Publishers, 1998), pp. 109–32.
23. Chakrabarty, 'Radical Histories'; Fabian, *Time and the Other*. This linear account of time has been recalibrated in the context of neoliberal temporalities, where market clock-time determines the consumer calendars of travel, shopping, and even the celebration of relationships that has become part of the consumer lifestyle. This recalibration has, in turn, altered the relationship between time and its others.

24. Said, *Orientalism*.
25. Fabian, *Time and the Other*, p. 16.
26. Śaṅkara, *Thousand Teachings*, Pt. I, 14:1, 14:16, 18:129.
27. Ibid., pp. 43–6, 70; Pt. I, 14:2, 14:8, 14:26, 15:24–5, 17:18, 17:24–5.
28. Ibid., pp. 44, 45; Pt. I, 15:25, 18:97; Pt. II, 2:45–111.
29. Ibid., pp. 69–72; Pt. I, 1, 2, 4; Pt. II, 2:110.
30. Ibid., p. 45; Pt. II, 2:86–96.
31. Ibid., pp. 74; Pt. I, 16:6, 16:57; Pt. II, 2:73; Sureśvarācārya, *Realization of the Absolute*, Book II, verse 35.
32. Śaṅkara, *Thousand Teachings*, pp. 20–2; Pt. II, 1:18–22.
33. Ibid., pp. 36–7; Sureśvarācārya, *Realization of the Absolute*, Book II, verses 39–42.
34. Śaṅkara, *Thousand Teachings*, pp. 74–5.
35. Sureśvarācārya, *Realization of the Absolute*, Book II, verses 25–8.
36. Śaṅkara, *Thousand Teachings*, Pt. I, 4:1–5; Pt. II, 2:52, 2:53; Sureśvarācārya, *Realization of the Absolute*, Book II, verses 69–75.
37. Śaṅkara, *Thousand Teachings*; Pt. I, 17:64; Pt. I, 18:97.
38. Ibid., Pt. I, 11:5.
39. Sureśvarācārya, *Realization of the Absolute*, Book II, verses 25–8.
40. Śaṅkara, *Thousand Teachings*, 87; Pt. I, 12:3, 18:170–74, 18:187, 18:190, 18:199; Sureśvarācārya, *Realization of the Absolute*, Book III, verses 68–70.
41. This ultimate recognition in non-dualist philosophy is expressed in the idea 'Thou Art That' (*Tat Tvam Asi*): Śaṅkara, *Thousand Teachings*, pp. 49–50. This statement encapsulates the entire philosophical position of Advaita – to make manifest the central idea that 'I am ever free' – and is the focus of Śaṅkara's work: Śaṅkara, *Thousand Teachings*, Pt. I, 18; Sureśvarācārya, *Realization of the Absolute*, Book III.
42. Butler, *Senses of the Subject*, p. 4.
43. Ibid., p. 2.
44. Ibid., p. 4.
45. Ibid., p. 5.
46. Ibid., p. 6.
47. Ibid., pp. 8–9.
48. Ibid., p. 12.
49. Ibid.
50. Ibid., p. 8.
51. Butler, *Gender Trouble*.
52. See, for example, Butler, *The Psychic Life of Power*. For a critical and valuable engagement with the paradox of the self and how it is implicated in power, yet still allows for autonomy as outlined, for example, in Butler's work, see Allen, *Politics of Our Selves*, pp. 72–95.
53. Śaṅkara, *Thousand Teachings*, 74; Pt. I, 7:1–6; Sureśvarācārya, *Realization of the Absolute*, Book II, verses 113–15. For an elaborate discussion on how neither the intellect nor the mind is the conscious 'I' or self, see Sureśvarācārya, *Realization of the Absolute*, Book II, verses 66–97.
54. Sureśvarācārya, *Realization of the Absolute*, Book II, verse 94.
55. Śaṅkara, *Thousand Teachings*, Pt. I, 1:11, 1:15, 4:3–4.
56. Martha C. Nussbaum, *Sex and Social Justice* (New York: Oxford University Press, 1999), p. 37.
57. Catharine A. MacKinnon, 'Feminism, Marxism, Method, and the State: Toward Feminist Jurisprudence', *Signs* 8, no. 4 (1983): 636–7; Catharine A. MacKinnon, *Feminism Unmodified: Discourses on Life and Law* (Cambridge, MA: Harvard University Press, 1987).
58. Spivak has offered a critique of prescriptive Western feminist theories of agency and freedom, in the context of interventions targeting the practice of *sati*, where a widow burns herself on her dead husband's funeral pyre: Spivak, 'Can the Subaltern Speak?', pp. 28–37.

59. Śaṅkara, *Thousand Teachings*, pp. 87, 92; Pt. I, 1:8–12, 1:15.
60. Śaṅkara, *Thousand Teachings*, p. 77; Pt. II, 2:109–10; Sureśvarācārya, *Realization of the Absolute*, Book II, verses 30, 31.

Epilogue

VALIDATING ALTERNATIVE EPISTEMES OF FREEDOM

This book argues for a fundamental shift in the conceptualization of freedom. As suggested in the preceding chapters, if we continue to think of freedom in terms of the further accumulation of rights, of freedom in terms of a teleological trajectory, of freedom in terms of a political end goal and of freedom through liberal individualism, then we are unlikely to get closer to it. Extending rights discourses, counter-critique and politico-legal commitment beyond the liberal paradigm would enable us to be open to another way of being in the world, where freedom is addressed not as an explicit, imposed process but as a modality of self-transformation that functions as a catalyst for external emancipation. For some disenfranchised populations the struggle to move into a space of recognition and legibility is unending, and even while some existent norms are troubled or defied, new norms emerge that operate along new boundaries of inclusion and exclusion. This constant struggle repeatedly raises questions as to whether such rights-based recognition can offer release from suffering, ensure well-being and, ultimately, provide protection. The formal recognition of precarious subjects – in this sense, securing legibility in and through the discourse of rights – enables those who conform with the terms of legibility to belong, thus providing them with a reliable way in which to become a secure part of the whole. However, this apparent whole is in fact a part, and this part is in fact not freedom but itself a form of containment – that is, freedom in a fishbowl, delineated, calibrated and deployed within the normative parameters that constitute and govern gender and alterity.

The arguments put forward in this book are an effort to move beyond the confines of the fishbowl. While the process of deconstructing human rights, as well as tracing the work they do in the pursuit of rights advocacy, is itself an aspect of re-conceptualizing freedom, I propose that more is required of such a critique, which otherwise leaves us with a result that seems very politically impotent and personally discouraging. I further propose that this *more* is found not simply in expanding the aperture of our epistemological vision, but in seeking out and validating other epistemes rooted in expanded or radical/revisionary understandings of freedom. The discussion in Chapters 6 and 7 indicates that there are other epistemological universes within which to think about freedom when the human rights project has proved incapable of delivering on this promise. It may not be the most obvious shift to make, especially when the templates of alternative epistemologies may not be readily accessible or reassuringly familiar to the liberal mind. But the ever elusive efforts to catalyse the revolutionary aspect of human rights, and the jagged efforts at repair, renewal and reinvestment of the rights schema, are proving to be constrictive rather than emancipatory. Hence, nothing short of a radical epistemic shift is required.

The argument that human rights are a defence against power assumes that power is something to be wrested from the state and placed in the hands of the excluded or precarious subject. It also renders invisible the ways in which this understanding of human rights ratifies the social and economic imperatives within which the aspirations for freedom may be realized. As I have argued throughout this book, rights constitute and regulate the subject of human rights within a specific set of normative arrangements. The demand for human rights by gender or sexual subalterns or precarious subjects does not necessarily challenge the normative terms on which freedom is based. In fact, recognition through rights discourse incorporates the subject into the coercive apparatus of a justice regime. The end result is not freedom but acquiescence to the contemporary context – historical legacies of colonialism, structural adjustments, market reforms and the reduction of life to economic values remain insufficiently interrogated. Existential suffering becomes a question of cultural or racial primitiveness, or lack of access to the market. How human rights contributes to the production of inequalities – by establishing a hierarchy of humans or in producing precariousness – is simply not adequately acknowledged, let alone effectively and honestly addressed.

Accepting that human rights can only ever be an intervention in an already existing structure, rather than a tool for wresting freedom from the tyranny of the state – that rights cannot give us what we want – serves as a space for pursuing alternative trajectories. This understanding compels us to take a step back, to turn away from human rights as a freedom project and explore other lines of inquiry – including epistemological possibilities that exist outside the liberal fishbowl. One such move is the turn to affective and intimate temporalities which aim to address the 'everydayness' of life and investigate how individuals continue to survive despite the seeming hopelessness of their situations. Yet, as I have argued, this turn towards the intimate, while crucial, is not adequate to address the yearning for freedom. It does, however, mark a shift in critique towards validating interiority and emotion as a source of knowledge.

My discussion of alternative registers within which to understand freedom leads to consideration of what a post-liberal human rights future – including the role of human rights in that future – might look like when combined with or considered alongside a non-liberal understanding of freedom and happiness. As mentioned earlier, perhaps the most significant result is that it expands the optic through which we approach the issues of gender and alterity, which have been the central focus of this book. Bringing non-liberal epistemes within our range of critical vision not only brings greater clarity to the issues of gender, sexuality and alterity – where we seek to intervene – but also, simultaneously, produces a more mindful and thoughtful politics in human rights interventions. The result may be a much more considered debate; one that produces responses which are informed and thoughtful. At the same time, we should be open to the possibility that such an expanded vision will bring an awareness of the tectonics and incommensurability of liberal and non-liberal paradigms, and may also invoke the possibility that human rights could be completely displaced in any pursuit of lasting freedom.

BEING AS FREEDOM/FREEDOM TO BE

This section presents an episodic narration of four stories – all of which emerge from the subcontinent – through which I briefly outline the subtleties of how such an expanded aperture might bring other ways of being, and being free, within view. This narration is not a proposal to recover or recuperate that which has been lost. Rather, it is an effort to shift focus, and foreground alternative registers and archives of the experience of freedom – modalities that have been abundant and prolific, and yet often ignored or unexamined or simply dismissed as irrelevant, exotic and/or insignificant vis-à-vis the liberal arena and agenda. In these registers, freedom is not conceptualized in terms of identity-based recognition and empowerment, but invoked as the experience of clearly discerning and understanding the relationship of the self to others and to the world in which one engages others – a relationship based on seeing those others. Hypothetically, a rights strategy that considers non-liberal understandings of freedom would not only constitute an effort at expanding the claustrophobic aperture that currently exists, but would restructure the way in which the subject is understood, and thus reimagine how freedom is experienced through that reconfigured awareness. Each narrative incorporates the broader features of freedom around marginalized, gendered and sexual subjects and alterity that have been addressed in the various chapters of this book. And each narrative is a tentative indication of the capacity to envision and conceptualize freedom in a more complex way, as well as positing how such a reimagining may ultimately depose rights as the imprimatur of freedom.

The Female Renunciate

I begin with the story of Lalla (also known as Lal Ded or Lalleswari), a young female mystic and poet who was born, circa 1320, into an upper-caste family in Kashmir, a divided state in present-day northern India. While Lalla's biography is sketchy at best, one of the few known facts is that she was married at the age of 12 into a family where she was starved and subjected to untold physical abuse and emotional trauma. Yet her poetry only has one oblique reference to this period: she states, '[w]hether they kill a ram or a sheep, Lalla will get a stone to eat'.[1] At the age of 26 she chose to leave her marital home, renouncing marriage and material life. Defying all social conventions, she forged her life as a mystic within the tradition of the Kashmiri Shaivite sect of renouncers.[2] Despite experiencing social sanction and humiliation, she remained committed to her quest as a seeker and shrugged off such abuses, as illustrated by one of her utterances: 'They lash me with insults, serenade me with curses./Their barking means nothing to me./Even if they came with soul-flowers to offer,/I couldn't care less. Untouched, I move on.'[3]

The provocation seen in Lalla's choice (and that of many other women who chose a similar path) was met with distrust as well as ridicule.[4] The hostility towards renunciates, and female renunciates in particular, emanates from the traditional social privileging, validation and valorization of the status attributed to householders. As noted by Madan:

> Apparently they are cynical about those who leave home because most such people never had families of their own … or their relations with their kin have been strained. At a deeper level, however, one might detect a fear of the renouncer, for he [*sic*] poses a threat to the ideology of the householder and plenitude.[5]

The renunciate not only seeks release from 'the web of kinship and other worldly ties but also denigrates these as a trap and an illusion. The renouncer is too powerful an adversary to be contemplated with equanimity.'[6]

As she set off on her own journey, Lalla became an ascetic who wandered about naked, producing a mystic poetry called *vatsun* or *vakh* ('speech' or, more accurately, 'utterance') and reciting proverbs as part of her process of introspection, self-reflection and meditation.[7] Her entire corpus of work was transmitted orally between the fourteenth and twentieth centuries. As Hoskote argues, given that the transmission of Lalla's work occurred over a number of centuries, any effort to establish her origins or to ascertain the 'true' Lalla remains futile and fatuous – rather, 'to the ear that receives her poems, the body of the *vākh* is the only true Lalla there is'.[8] Consistent with her life as a renunciate, Lalla is not the biographical persona constructed from the bricolage of scant data, rumours and fables, but 'breathe[s] within the text' of the poems attributed to her or produced in her name and communicated through a rich oral tradition.[9]

Lalla's life and work embody the syncretic tradition within Kashmir, which draws upon the spiritual vocabularies of Sufism, Buddhism and Kashmir Shaivism and which views the world as a series of traps for the unwary, who remain ignorant of their true nature and of the illusion posed by dualistic thinking. Lalla deplored formal religion and religious practice, especially rituals and external worship, which she felt could never provide the means for what she described as self-realization or freedom. While Lalla's inward journey is neither sexually explicit nor based on sexual identity, her journey at the metaphysical and philosophical level represents an experience outside of binary thought, rather than one reliant upon gender identity and sexual acts, which tend to be the focus of human rights advocacy. Both her life and poetry exemplify her refusal to be bound by social expectations and their accompanying prohibitions and constraints. Lalla was an itinerant wanderer, an 'isolated dissident',[10] who founded no school or movement, and had no disciples or successors. Freedom from fear and vacillation was central to her quest. This fearlessness was manifest in her life and forms a characteristic theme in her *vakh* – deeply philosophical poetic utterances about freedom that are seminal and influential in Kashmir and elsewhere. Lalla's *vakh* is a position that simultaneously produces dissidence while also introducing an alternative and radical understanding of freedom – providing a space outside the established gender and sexual norms, and an alterity that does not exist in opposition to such arrangements, but thrives despite these constraints.

The Widow's Turn Away from Rights

Shenkottai Avudai Akkal (popularly known as 'Akka') was a female sage from Tamil Nadu, a south Indian state, in the eighteenth century. She was a child bride widowed at a very young age.[11] Belonging to an ultraorthodox Brahmin household in south India, she was regarded as inauspicious, relegated to a dark inner room, compelled to do arduous household labour, denied sociality and abjected in numerous ways – as was the customary treatment of widows.[12] When the sage Venkatesh Ayyawal, a highly venerated teacher, passed by her home, the despairing Akka escaped from her confinement and fell at his feet, begging him to rescue her from her traumatic fate.[13] The sage 'initiated' her into *Advaita*, the philosophy of non-dualism discussed in Chapter 7, and thereafter she began to compose songs about this experience of release into freedom. Akka appalled and outraged the orthodox establishment, who flinched at her audacity in seeking freedom and in accessing knowledge, which was traditionally considered the prerogative of high-caste men and forbidden to women, especially widows. Regardless, Akka intervened on her own behalf to escape the personal torment and multiple restrictions imposed by orthodox caste and gender hierarchies. Her songs, composed in the simple colloquial vernacular of her home district, often drew their unforgettable allegories of transcendence from the daily domestic lives of women.

Though preserved by women who sang them while doing household work, and thus transmitted orally for two centuries, Akka's songs remained largely ignored until the early 1940s, when they were eventually collected and compiled for publication. Paradoxically, there is no mention of her, an itinerant, maverick poetic genius, in the official historical or cultural record. Whether deliberate or partly due to her radical mode of self-expression – and her use of erotic metaphors and women-centric tropes referencing, among other things, menstruation and kitchen chores – her effacement from the record initially renders her story as simply that of a suffering child widow – a subject that has been described in some contemporary feminist scholarship as akin to a 'discarded adjunct[]' or 'half dead thing[]'.[14] Framed in this way, when considered from the liberal fishbowl, the implication is that such a non-subject can find freedom as a subject imbued with choice and agency through exposure to the possibilities of liberal individualism. This position reinforces the dominant narrative of the rescue and rehabilitation of the suffering 'Other' by a superior civilizational power – an act that, overtly or covertly, reconditions the subaltern subject into stigmatizing and rejecting her own cultural, historical and political context, and thus brings her into the realm of ostensible freedom. In terms of rights discourses, while reformist colonial laws permitting widows to remarry might counter social ostracism, they continue to prioritize marriage as central to the salvation of the widowed woman: the 'failed' or unworthy subject can be redeemed primarily and/or solely through the mechanism of marriage. This illustrates how rights, rather than being counter-hegemonic or disruptive of the normative gender and sexual order, may in fact instigate the subject's return to and re-confinement within these very categories.

From a human rights perspective, Akka draws attention because of her stigmatized, abjected status as a widow subject to patriarchal injustices. But she was also a metaphysician and poet. And the *only* autobiographical episode invoked in her songs relates to how she encountered her teacher and was initiated by him into the method of self-inquiry. For her, once initiated, all other aspects of her life become irrelevant; and, to use an Advaitic metaphor, when she realizes the self, her ego-bound body consciousness is subsumed like a salt doll immersed in the ocean – 'she', the particularized identity of the suffering widow, cannot be reconstituted. In many songs, she sharply rebukes and challenges orthodox social codes, religious hypocrisy and punitive customs prescribed for widows; her descriptions of freedom are also a challenge to sexual conformity. She uses her poetry to challenge established gender and caste orthodoxies, partly through her prolific use of erotic and sexual descriptions of the process of acquiring knowledge: 'Revealing tender, self-luminous breasts./The gold earrings called 'doubt' fell off/Along with the strap of the gold necklace/Called "I-am-the-doer"/ … Profusely trickling sweat soaked and smeared/The decorative insignia called "wrong knowledge"/ That marked the dancers' foreheads.'[15] However, her songs cannot be read exclusively as songs of resistance. They are just as powerfully about Akka's absolute interior emancipation, the transcending of all dualities. She writes, for example: 'Rambling and wandering/as male and female embodiments, vanished./Unmoving rest in the abode of Knowledge, manifested',[16] or 'As the raging forest fire consumes without discrimination/All the wood – trees, stumps, trunks – in its path,/So the fire of Knowledge completely devoured/The categories of time, space, name and form.'[17] It is this reflective knowledge, rather than the chronological details of the life of the individual seeking the knowledge, that becomes central to her narrative. She refutes the status of an abject widowed subject and avails the space provided through *Advaita* to re-invent herself as a seeker. She seeks her freedom through the process of self-inquiry, non-dualism, and a fearless resistance to dominant gender and sexual norms, all reflected in the philosophical dimensions of her subversive songs and expressions.

The Eunuch and the Theatre of Emancipation

The Supreme Court of India's decision in 2014 recognizing the right to equality of transgender persons – including the rights to health, education and marriage – was considered a landmark ruling. As discussed in Chapter 2, while transgender persons were allocated full selfhood and legal recognition as a 'third gender', such incorporation into a rights framework does not necessarily equate to freedom. And while LoF scholars may argue that the reduction of stigma and suffering is the best that can be hoped for in the pursuit of human rights, as previously discussed, this obscures the broader liberal and neoliberal projects advanced in and through human rights, which are hegemonically cast as the obvious and singular option for those who seek freedom, and its attendant goals of happiness and the good life.

While important, the bestowal of rights neither displaces nor discourages the diverse ways in which the freedom to be, and to do, in alignment with a particular sense of self is navigated by the different groups of sexual subalterns. For example, the *hijras*, or eunuch community, and transgender and cross-dressing persons congregate every year on the full moon in May, in the small village of Koovagam in the south Indian state of Tamil Nadu. They gather before a unique deity – Iravan, patron god of the transgender community, son of the warrior prince Arjuna and Chitrangada, whose story from Indian mythology opens Chapter 7 of this book – to perform the ritual of marriage and claim their status as the brides of Iravan.[18] While they hold beauty pageants, seminars on their social and legal status and discussions on health matters and human rights prior to the full moon event, the ritual marriage is the symbolic and literal fulcrum of the gathering. Temporarily liberated from the legal delineation of their sexuality, subjectivity and agency, the *hijras* express who they are, their very being, through devotional frenzy and ecstatic expression of an altered state of consciousness.[19]

Through rights recognition, this queer subject becomes implicated in the production of governmental power through which she also acquires visibility and presence, ultimately collaborating with the very power she sets out to challenge. Securing traction through rights releases the subject into a space of greater regulation and constraint, rather than freedom. As a resistive subject, she brings an element of disruption to the governing normative order, but these capacities recede through this very traction, and rights increasingly become techniques of assimilation and co-option.

The transgender dance proposes another possible trajectory, removing the subject from the pain and humiliation of daily life and seemingly endless struggle. It is not based on sex acts or sexuality, which are embedded within ancient literature and different philosophical traditions from the subcontinent, but represents the radical direction that freedom can take.[20] Neither gender nor sexual identity lie at the heart of such expressions of freedom.

While visibility and an aggressive strategy in favour of recognition through the pursuit of more rights may be critical in a sexist and homophobic world, as I have argued, it does not move in the direction of more freedom. The ecstatic expressions of freedom reflected in the transgender dance, as well as the philosophical utterances, poetry and songs of Lalla and Akka, all propose other possible trajectories of freedom that are not based on gender binaries or sexual hierarchies. Linking alterity to non-liberal philosophical and alternative registers of freedom can be both productive and liberating.

Fasting unto Freedom

Santhara or *Sullekhna* is a practice of the Jain community which involves a conscious decision on the part of an individual to stop eating and drinking and await release from her body. The vow is undertaken when an individual concludes that the body has served its purposes in life, or that it is unable to perform any other purpose. The process is witnessed by the community, considered a highly spiritual act and regarded with reverence. The choice to fast is a conscious and informed one, grounded in the epistemological view shared by Hindus, Buddhists and Jains that the self/consciousness continues after it is released from the corporeal form. The decision can be reconsidered and the individual is free to resume eating at any time. This is a living practice, integral to a community that understands freedom as freedom *from* identification of the self with the body – as opposed to the notion of freedom as experiencing the self *through* the body – and is a concept central to non-Judeo-Christian traditions. Freedom is understood as an interior and intimate experience, secured through self-reflection.

Some members within the Jain community, as well as some women's rights advocates, have claimed that the practice of *Santhara* is coercive and largely imposed on dependent elderly women considered economically burdensome. It has been considered analogous to the coercive historical practice of *Sati*, the burning of a widow on her husband's funeral pyre. In 2006 a legal challenge was brought to outlaw the practice of *Santhara* and to have it declared equivalent to suicide and thus a punishable act under the Indian Penal Code (IPC), 1860.[21] Lord Macaulay, a British liberal politician who was also a devout Christian, drafted the IPC provisions on suicide under the colonial regime, and the theological basis of the suicide provisions is informed by a Christian view that regards the human body as sacred and suicide as a sin. In August 2015, the court upheld the petitioner's claim that the practice involved nothing less than the intentional self-destruction of the human subject which the state was obliged to protect.[22] In this holding, the individual corporeal subject was regarded as supreme and entitled to her fundamental rights, including the right to life under Article 21 of the Indian Constitution. Confronted with judicial diktat, in their appeal to the Indian Supreme Court the Jain community claimed not only that the right to life must include the right to stop living, but also that the practice was protected by the freedom of religion clauses under Articles 25 and 26 of the Indian Constitution and Article 18 of the Universal Declaration of Human Rights. In a short order, the Indian Supreme Court stayed the lower court's decision. Much like the veil cases discussed in Chapter 4, the human rights framing of the issue entirely eclipsed the broader epistemic challenge to liberal freedom and the limited understanding of the subject on which it is based.

By confining the issue within a rights paradigm, the deeper philosophical aspects implicated in the debate on *Santhara* – which draws a distinction between suicide, that is, giving up on life, and those who choose to fast unto death to purify the self before leaving the world – remained invisible. When presented as a conflict of rights – that is, between the right to freedom of religion and the right to life – *Santhara* is cast as merely a ritual or a religious practice; an action, rather than a way of knowing and being. The rights discourse and its legal manifestation posits *Santhara* as a choice to die, rather than as a fast unto freedom. The practice exemplifies how the subject or self is regarded as continuing after breath leaves the body. The *Santhara* vow, made by both men and women in the Jain community, is made for an evolved spiritual purpose and not for any of the highly problematic reasons provided in the language of familial codes and sacrality to justify violent acts against women. The non-corporeal experience of freedom – one that dissociates from the body – is entirely eclipsed in a rights analysis, and in the process an alternative non-liberal epistemological framing of this experience is entirely excluded from consideration.

DIFFRACTING THE EPISTEMIC HORIZON

Human rights reify the concept of a 'civilized' community and safeguard various populations of 'failed subjects'. The preceding four narratives serve as metaphors for the crowd of 'failures' and outcasts, as well as dissidents, that refute state and social abjection, marginality, disenfranchisement and penalization via commitment to a radical alternative mode of being.[23] This affirmation is not based on gender identity or sexuality, but on an inherent sense of self – one not aligned with the normative script of desirable sociality, and apparently apolitical. While it may be argued that this position represents a capitulation – the clear envisioning, and perhaps the redemptive experience, of freedom based on an alternative epistemology – this self-replenishing modality counters what contemporary history has proved: that more rights ultimately and inevitably goose-step the entitled and disenfranchised down the road of security, governance and regulation, and may be complicit or explicit in furthering a lethal and destructive agenda.

These narratives are not an attempt to either focus exclusively on particular modes of marginality or romanticize socio-cultural systems that, like systems everywhere, are freighted with injustices and inequalities. I present these as examples of freedom lived *outside* of a liberal fishbowl, and here experienced by the subaltern subject. In the case of the transgender devotees of Iravan, while the pursuit of freedom bestowed through law and rights is part of their collective struggle for recognition, emancipation in its complete aspect is experienced and expressed through an entirely self-replenishing, extra-judicial register – that of ecstasy. Freedom for Lalla and Akka is expressed through a turn away from or renouncement of marital and material domesticity, and through their deeply provocative and compelling metaphysical poems and songs, which testify to complete liberation from a marital, reproductive, heteronormative social schema. Self-realization is experienced through an inward journey; the subject/self is something ever present and ever available to be accessed; it is an uncovering rather than a discovering. For the practitioner of *Santhara*, while the legal right to die can enable this personal choice, it is the deeper philosophical trajectory that prevails and overrides judicial logic and rights – that is, the practitioner identifying with the self as a continuous, immutable consciousness, and not with the transient, inscribed, perishable body. A reparative turn towards rights cannot create genuine social space for these failed subjects, or, in the case of the transgender community, truly ensure the dignity and social acceptance that is rarely forthcoming even though this often despised sexual minority now has legal entitlements.

As I have argued throughout this book, engagement with human rights must continue, but not because it will give us what we want. Indeed, the constant struggle and investment in a project that continues to offer hope but is unable to deliver is a form of psychological attrition, ultimately unable to protect the seeker of freedom. On the one hand, the rights regime classifies claimants by interpreting subjectivity as it is expressed through particular bodies, histories and practices, and seems to support these. On the other, when the rights regime reneges on its promises of freedom for particular claimants, the subjectivity of the disenfranchised, disillusioned and embattled subject is worn threadbare. Clinging to these tatters of selfhood might indeed manifest endurance and resistance – but if the rights regime's failure to free the subject is pre-determined, this arduous, tenacious grasping for a social place through a secure, judicially inscribed and allocated identity seems unintelligible. And in many cases, those 'failed subjects' who successfully make the journey into the 'normal', through a legal inscription of identity, may sooner or later find that the process invites incorporation not into the space of freedom, but into the parameters of a regulatory apparatus. The now successful subject acquires a sense of belonging, but such affiliation may co-exist with despair and perhaps even mourning for the aspects of selfhood that she lets die or actively annihilates in the process of securing recognition and social safety. A stark shift in focus, and a re-articulation of the subject in terms of the intimate or conscious self, can counter such despair and the desperation to stitch oneself into a firm identity within the discourse of assimilation.

Human rights are based on the embedded liberal axiom that to live as a rational, entitled, sovereign bearer of rights is the only way to be appropriately human; for the liberal ideologue, this is the unassailable definition of what it means to fully, incontrovertibly, *be*. This very framing of the subject disavows any conception of the self outside the terms of the liberal template. Rights cannot bring about a resolution between the absolutely polarized terms of the 'liberal' and 'non-liberal' (not illiberal) paradigms of subjectivity. The liberal conception of the right to life stands at complete odds, for instance, with the *Santhara* vow and the individual who understands fasting as a form of empowerment and agency, that is, in terms of freedom rather than as a form of criminality and self-inflicted violence. It is a perfect example of the incommensurability of two philosophical matrices, two different world-views. This book is a call to think differently. Rather than present these completely different worldviews as ever incompatible and adversarial, it invokes the need to shift from thinking linearly and in terms of cause and effect, to thinking in terms of removing the errors in perception that are the primary obstacles to actualizing lasting freedom – *to discern the apparent snake from the real rope*. A radical epistemic shift is required if we are not simply to rejuvenate the politics of feminist and queer advocacy, but to understand that the politics *itself* may be core to the problem.

This book provides a starting point for a different kind of conversation on freedom. It takes seriously the quest to address freedom in ways that work through the binary of 'us' and 'them', the liberal subject and her 'Other'. I have not sought tidy outcomes and resolutions, but have focused on scrutinizing the horizon of epistemic possibilities and envisioning the insightful critique that might manifest once the solipsism and self-reflexiveness of the liberal episteme that is evident in human rights is exposed. I have touched on a range of options, consciously selecting some of the more esoteric and heterodox registers within non-liberal spaces. A radical alterity asserted in relation to the complex terrain of gender, sexuality and difference may serve as a heuristic that has the potential to profoundly reconfigure our thinking about rights more generally. The persistence of such alterity may also, perhaps, finally bring some humility to a project whose conceit has implicated it in the very violence and perpetuation of unfreedom that it was originally envisaged to eliminate. And most importantly, it offers the seeker immense hope in the possibility of a lasting and revolutionary freedom beyond the fishbowl.

NOTES

1. A Kashmiri saying attributed to Lalla: Ranjit Hoskote, trans., *I, Lalla: The Poems of Lal Děd* (New Delhi: Penguin Books, 2011), p.xvii.
2. This tradition focuses on transmuting everything that is externally observable into visualizations and experiments in consciousness, and the development of meditative depth.
3. Hoskote, *I, Lalla*, pp.xvii, 94.
4. See also, for example, the female Kashmiri mystic poet, Rupa Bhavani (c.1620–c.1720), and Akka Mahadevi (c.1130–1160), a female poet from the south Indian state of Karnataka.
5. T.N. Madan, *Non-Renunciation: Themes and Interpretations of Hindu Culture* (New Delhi: Oxford University Press, 1988), pp. 41–2, quoted in Hoskote, *I, Lalla*, p. xviii.
6. Ibid.
7. Hoskote, *I, Lalla*. Jaishree Kak, trans., *Mystical Verses of Lallā: A Journey of Self-Realization* (Delhi: Motilal Banarsidass Publishers, 2007).
8. Hoskote, *I, Lalla*, p.xxxvi.
9. Ibid.
10. Ibid., p.xxiii.

11. Kanchana Natarajan, trans., *Transgressing Boundaries: The Advaitic Songs of Shenkottai Avudai Akkal* (New Delhi: Zubaan, 2012), p. 48.
12. Ibid., pp. 48–9.
13. Ibid., p. 52.
14. Nussbaum, *Sex and Social Justice*, p. 67.
15. Natrajan, *Transgressing Boundaries*, p. 204.
16. Ibid., p. 174.
17. Ibid., p. 13.
18. Before Iravan goes into battle in the 18-day war recounted in the Mahabharata, he requests a boon in return for his self-sacrifice – to be married prior to being killed in war. Krishna, Arjuna's charioteer and enunciator of the epic's scriptural core, the Bhagavad Gita, honours this request on the battlefield by manifesting in female form as Mohini (lit. 'she who enchants/seduces/allures'). Iravan marries Mohini, consummates the marriage, goes to war and dies in battle. At their annual festival, the transgender community takes on the role of the brides of Iravan and re-enacts the ceremonial marriage, as well as their widowhood after his sacrifice.
19. See Gayatri Reddy, *With Respect to Sex: Negotiating Hijra Identity in South India* (Chicago: University of Chicago Press, 2006). Reddy discusses how the shifting forms of sexuality including 'third-natured individuals, transposed genders, sexual masquerades, and same-sex procreation' are incorporated into the myths, folklore and literature of wide-ranging communities: Reddy, *With Respect to Sex*, 19. See also Aniruddha Dutta and Raina Roy, 'Decolonizing Transgender in India: Some Reflections', *TSQ: Transgender Studies Quarterly* 1, no. 3 (2014): 320–37.
20. Reddy, *With Respect to Sex*, pp. 18–22. See also Vanja Hamzić, *Sexual and Gender Diversity in the Muslim World: History, Law and Vernacular Knowledge* (London: I.B. Tauris, 2015), especially pp. 171–2, 175–6, 186–7, on the spiritual aspects of the subjectivity of sexually diverse and gender-variant Muslims.
21. Suicide is prosecutable under section 309 of the IPC, 1860.
22. *Nikhil Soni v. Union of India*, No. 7414 of 2006 (High Court of Judicature for Rajasthan, August 10, 2015).
23. See, for example, Gandhi, 'A Case of Radical Kinship' and her discussion of the 'homosexual dissident': p. 92.

Bibliography

TREATIES

Convention for the Protection of Human Rights and Fundamental Freedoms (European Convention on Human Rights, as amended). 4 November 1950. 213 UNTS 221 (ECHR).

Convention for the Suppression of the Traffic in Persons and of the Exploitation of the Prostitution of Others. 21 March 1950. 96 UNTS 271.

Convention on the Elimination of All Forms of Discrimination against Women. 18 December 1979. 1249 UNTS 13.

International Convention for the Suppression of the Traffic in Women and Children. 30 September 1921. 9 LNTS 415.

International Convention for the Suppression of the Traffic in Women of Full Age. 11 October 1933. 150 LNTS 431.

International Convention for the Suppression of White Slave Traffic. 4 May 1910. 211 CTS 45.

International Convention on the Elimination of All Forms of Racial Discrimination. 21 December 1965. 660 UNTS 195.

International Convention on the Protection of the Rights of All Migrant Workers and Members of their Families. 18 December 1990. 2220 UNTS 3.

International Covenant on Civil and Political Rights. 19 December 1966. 999 UNTS 171.

International Covenant on Economic, Social and Cultural Rights. 16 December 1966. 993 UNTS 3.

Optional Protocol to the Convention on the Elimination of All Forms of Discrimination against Women. 10 December 1999. 2131 UNTS 83.

Protocol to Prevent, Suppress and Punish Trafficking in Persons, Especially Women and Children. 16 November 2000. 2237 UNTS 319.

Rome Statute of the International Criminal Court. 17 July 1998. 2187 UNTS 90.

United Nations Convention against Transnational Organized Crime. 15 November 2000. 2225 UNTS 209.

Universal Declaration of Human Rights. 10 December 1948. GA Res 217A (III).

CASES

Belcacemi v. Belgium, App. 37798/13 ECtHR 2017.
Dahlab v. Switzerland, 2001-V ECtHR 447.
Dogru v. France (2009) 49 EHRR 8.
Ebrahimian v. France, App. 64846/11 ECtHR 2015.
Justice K.S. Puttaswamy (Retired) v. Union of India. No. 494 of 2012 (Supreme Court of India, 24 August 2017).
Lautsi v. Italy (2012) 54 EHRR 3.
Leyla Şahin v. Turkey (2005) 41 EHRR 8.
National Legal Services Authority of India v. Union of India (2014) 5 SCC 438.
Naz Foundation v. Government of NCT of Delhi. 160 Delhi Law Times 277 (2009).
Nikhil Soni v. Union of India. No. 7414 of 2006 (High Court of Judicature for Rajasthan, 10 August 2015).
S.A.S. v. France (2015) 60 EHRR 11.
Suresh Kumar Koushal v. Naz Foundation (2014) 1 SCC 1.

LEGISLATION

Circulaire No. 2004-084 of May 18, 2004. *Journal Officiel de la République Française [JO] [Official Gazette of France]*. 22 May 2004.
Criminal Law (Amendment) Act, 2013 (India).
Indian Penal Code, 1860 (IPC).
Loi n° 2004-228 du 15 mars 2004 encadrant, en application du principe de laïcité, le port de signes ou de tenues manifestant une appartenance religieuse dans les écoles, collèges et lycées publics. *Journal Officiel de la République Française [JO] [Official Gazette of France]*. 17 March 2004. 5190.
Loi n° 2010-1192 du 11 octobre 2010 interdisant la dissimulation du visage dans l'espace public. *Journal Officiel de la République Française [JO] [Official Gazette of France]*. 12 October 2010. 18344.
Loi n° 2013-404 du 17 mai 2013 ouvrant le mariage aux couples de personnes de même sexe. *Journal Officiel de la République Française [JO] [Official Gazette of France]*. 18 May 2013. 8253.

UNITED NATIONS/NONGOVERNMENT ORGANIZATIONS

'Anti-Terror Campaign Cloaking Human Rights Abuse.' *Human Rights Watch*. 16 January 2002. www.hrw.org/news/2002/01/16/anti-terror-campaign-cloaking-human-rights-abuse.

Committee on the Elimination of Discrimination against Women. *Statement of the Committee on the Elimination of Discrimination against Women on the 10th Anniversary of Security Council Resolution 1325 on 'Women, Peace and Security'*. 12–30 July 2010. http://www2.ohchr.org/english/bodies/cedaw/docs/statements/Statement_SCR_1325.pdf.

Council of Europe. *Prostitution, Trafficking and Modern Slavery in Europe*. Resolution 1983. 8 April 2014.

International Commission of Jurists. *The Yogyakarta Principles: Principles on the Application of International Human Rights Law in Relation to Sexual Orientation and Gender Identity*. March 2007. icj.wpengine.netdna-cdn.com/wp-content/uploads/2012/08/Yogyakarta-Principles-publication-2007-eng.pdf.

UN Secretary-General. 'Secretary-General Calls for Council Action to Ensure Women are Involved in Peace and Security Decisions.' Press release SG/SM/7598. 24 October 2000.

United Nations. *Report of the Fourth World Conference on Women (Beijing, 4–15 September 1995)*. UN Doc. A/CONF.177/20/Rev.1. 17 October 1995. Annex I ('Beijing Declaration') and Annex II ('Platform for Action').

United Nations. *Report of the Fourth World Conference on Women (Beijing, 4–15 September 1995)*. UN Doc. A/CONF.177/20/Rev.1. 27 October 1995. Annex IV ('Statement by the President of the Conference on the Commonly Understood Meaning of the Term "Gender"').

United Nations, World Conference on Human Rights. *Vienna Declaration and Programme of Action*. UN Doc. A/CONF.157/23. 12 July 1993.

United Nations Commission on Human Rights. *Question of Integrating the Rights of Women into the Human Rights Mechanisms of the United Nations and the Elimination of Violence against Women*. Res. 1994/45. UN Doc. E/CN.4/1994/132. 4 March 1994.

United Nations Commission on the Status of Women. *Report on the Fifty-seventh Session, 4–15 March 2013, Economic and Social Council*. UN Doc. E/2013/27–E/CN.6/2013/11. 2 April 2013.

United Nations General Assembly. *Accelerating Efforts to Eliminate Violence against Women: Preventing and Responding to Violence against Women and Girls, including Indigenous Women and Girls*. UN Doc. A/HRC/RES/32/19. 19 July 2016.

United Nations General Assembly. *Addressing the Impact of Multiple and Intersecting Forms of Discrimination and Violence in the Context of Racism, Racial Discrimination, Xenophobia and Related Intolerance on the Full Enjoyment of All Human Rights by Women and Girls*. UN Doc. A/HRC/RES/32/17. 18 July 2016.

United Nations General Assembly. *Declaration on the Elimination of Violence against Women*. UN Doc. A/RES/48/104. 20 December 1993.

United Nations General Assembly. *Intensification of Efforts to Prevent and Eliminate All Forms of Violence against Women and Girls: Domestic Violence*. UN Doc. A/RES/71/170. 7 February 2017.

United Nations General Assembly. *Report of the Committee on the Elimination of Discrimination against Women*. UN Doc. A/47/38 (1993).

United Nations General Assembly. *Trafficking in Persons, especially Women and Children: Protecting Victims of Trafficking and Persons at Risk of Trafficking, especially Women and Children in Conflict and Post-Conflict Situations*. UN Doc. A/HRC/RES/32/3. 20 July 2016.

United Nations General Assembly. *Violence against Women Migrant Workers*. UN Doc. A/RES/70/130. 8 February 2016.

United Nations High Commissioner for Human Rights. *Discrimination and Violence against Individuals Based on their Sexual Orientation and Gender Identity*. UN Doc. A/HRC/29/23. 4 May 2015.

United Nations High Commissioner for Human Rights. *Discriminatory Laws and Practices and Acts of Violence against Individuals Based on Their Sexual Orientation and Gender Identity*. UN Doc. A/HRC/19/41. 17 November 2011.

United Nations High Commissioner for Refugees. *Sexual and Gender-Based Violence against Refugees, Returnees and Internally Displaced Persons: Guidelines for Prevention and Response*. May 2003. www.unhcr.org/en-au/protection/women/3f696bcc4/sexual-gender-based-violence-against-refugees-returnees-internally-displaced.html.

United Nations Human Rights Council. *Report of the Independent Expert on Protection against Violence and Discrimination Based on Sexual Orientation and Gender Identity*. UN Doc. A/HRC/35/36. 19 April 2017.

United Nations Office of the High Commissioner for Human Rights. *Born Free and Equal: Sexual Orientation and Gender Identity in International Human Rights Law*. UN Doc. HR/PUB/12/06. 2012.

United Nations Office of the High Commissioner for Human Rights. *Living Free and Equal: What States are Doing to Tackle Violence and Discrimination against Lesbian, Gay, Bisexual, Transgender and Intersex People*. UN Doc. HR/PUB/16/3. 2016.

United Nations Population Fund (UNFPA). *Report of the International Conference on Population and Development*. UN Doc. A/CONF.171/13/Rev.1. (1995).

United Nations Security Council. *Resolution 1325 (2000)*. UN Doc. S/RES/1325. 31 October 2000.

United Nations Security Council. *Resolution 1820 (2008)*. UN Doc. S/RES/1820. 19 June 2008.

United Nations Security Council. *Resolution 1888 (2009)*. UN Doc. S/RES/1888. 30 September 2009.

United Nations Security Council. *Resolution 1889 (2009)*. UN Doc. S/RES/1889. 5 October 2009.

United Nations Security Council. *Resolution 2242 (2015)*. UN Doc. S/RES/2242. 13 October 2015.

United Nations Security Council. *Resolution 2282 (2016)*. UN Doc. S/RES/2282. 27 April 2016.

BOOKS/CHAPTERS/ARTICLES/OTHER

'76 Countries Where Homosexuality is Illegal.' *Erasing 76 Crimes*. Last updated 19 May 2017. https://76crimes.com/76-countries-where-homosexuality-is-illegal/.

Abenante, Paola, and Fabio Vicini. 'Interiority Unbound: Sufi and Modern Articulations of the Self.' *Culture and Religion* 18, no. 2 (2017): 57–71.

Adamczyk, Ed. 'New German Law Broadens Definition of Rape.' *UPI*. 7 July 2016. http://www.upi.com/Top_News/World-News/2016/07/07/New-German-law-broadens-definition-of-rape/9361467899775/.

Adichie, Chimamanda Ngozi. *Half of a Yellow Sun*. New York: Anchor Books, 2006.

Aditya, A.K. 'What the Right to Privacy Bench Has Said about Emergency and Section 377.' *Bar and Bench*. 24 August 2017. https://barandbench.com/right-privacy-bench-said-adm-jabalpur-suresh-koushal/.

Adrian, Melanie. *Religious Freedom at Risk: The EU, French Schools, and Why the Veil Was Banned*. Cham: Springer International Publishing, 2016.

Afary, Janet, and Kevin B. Anderson. *Foucault and the Iranian Revolution: Gender and the Seductions of Islam*. Chicago: University of Chicago Press, 2005.

Agamben, Giorgio. *Stanzas Word and Phantasm in Western Culture*. Translated by Ronald L. Martinez. Minneapolis: University of Minnesota Press, 1993.

Agence-France Presse. 'Mayor of Cannes Bans Burkinis on Resort Beaches.' *The Guardian*. 12 August 2016. https://www.theguardian.com/world/2016/aug/11/cannes-mayor-bans-burqinis-beachwear-must-respect-secularism.

Ahmed, Sara. 'Deconstruction and Law's Other: Towards a Feminist Theory of Embodied Legal Rights.' *Social & Legal Studies* 4, no. 1 (1995): 55–73.

Ahmed, Sara. 'Embodying Strangers.' In *Body Matters: Feminism, Textuality, Corporeality*, edited by Avril Horner and Angela Keane, pp. 85–96. Manchester: Manchester University Press, 2000.

Ahmed, Aziza. '"Exploitation Creep" and Development: A Response to Janie Chuang.' *AJIL Unbound* (blog). 11 June 2015. www.asil.org/blogs/%E2%80%9Cexploitation-creep%E2%80%9D-and-development-response-janie-chuang.

Ahmed, Sara. 'Affective Economies.' *Social Text 79* 22, no. 2 (2004): 117–39.

Ahmed, Sara. *The Cultural Politics of Emotions*. Edinburgh: Edinburgh University Press, 2004.

Ahmed, Sara. *The Promise of Happiness*. Durham, NC: Duke University Press, 2010.

Akan, Murat. '*Diversité*: Challenging or Constituting *Laïcité*?' *French Cultural Studies* 28, no. 1 (2017): 123–37.

Akan, Murat. *The Politics of Secularism: Religion, Diversity, and Institutional Change in France and Turkey*. New York: Columbia University Press, 2017.

Aligarh. Film. Directed by Hansal Mehta. India: Eros International/Karma Pictures, 2015.

Allen, Amy. *The Politics of Our Selves: Power, Autonomy, and Gender in Contemporary Critical Theory*. New York: Columbia University Press, 2008.

Al-Hallaj, Mansur. *The Tawsin of Mansur Al-Hallaj*. Translated by Aisha Abd Ar-Rahman At-Tarjumana. Berkeley, CA: Diwan Press, 1974.

Al-Saji, Alia. 'The Racialization of Muslim Veils: A Philosophical Analysis.' *Philosophy and Social Criticism* 36, no. 8 (2010): 875–902.

An-Na'im, Abdullahi A. *Toward an Islamic Reformation: Civil Liberties, Human Rights, and International Law*. Syracuse: Syracuse University Press, 1996.

Anghie, Antony. *Imperialism, Sovereignty, and the Making of International Law*. Cambridge: Cambridge University Press, 2007.

Anghie, Antony. 'International Human Rights Law and a Developing World Perspective.' In *Routledge Handbook of International Human Rights Law*, edited by Scott Sheeran and Nigel Rodley, pp. 109–25. London: Routledge, 2013.

Anker, Elisabeth. 'The Liberalism of Horror.' *Social Research* 81, no. 4 (2014): 795–823.

Arondekar, Anjali R. *For the Record: On Sexuality and the Colonial Archive in India*. Durham, NC: Duke University Press, 2009.

Asad, Talal. *Genealogies of Religion: Discipline and Reasons of Power in Christianity and Islam*. Baltimore: Johns Hopkins University Press, 1993.

Asad, Talal. 'On Torture, or Cruel, Inhuman, and Degrading Treatment.' *Social Research* 63, no. 4 (1996): 1081–1109.

Asad, Talal. 'What Do Human Rights Do? An Anthropological Enquiry.' *Theory & Event* 4, no. 4 (2000): muse.jhu.edu/article/32601.

Asad, Talal. *Formations of the Secular: Christianity, Islam, Modernity*. Stanford, CA: Stanford University Press, 2003.

Asad, Talal. *On Suicide Bombing*. New York: Columbia University Press, 2007.

Asad, Talal. 'Reflections on Violence, Law, and Humanitarianism.' *Critical Inquiry* 41, no. 2 (2015): 390–427.

Bagchi, Subrata Sankar, and Arnab Das, eds. *Human Rights and the Third World: Issues and Discourses*. Lanham, MD: Lexington Books, 2012.

Balagangadhara, S.N. *'The Heathen in His Blindness': Asia, the West, and the Dynamic of Religion*. Leiden: E.J. Brill, 1994.

Balasubramanian, Savina. 'Contextualizing the Closet: *Naz*, Law and Sexuality in Postcolonial India.' In *Perverse Politics? Feminism, Anti-Imperialism, Multiplicity*, edited by Ann Shola Orloff, Raka Ray and Evren Savci, pp. 135–58. Bingley: Emerald, 2016.

Balgamwalla, Sabrina. 'Trafficking in Narratives: Conceptualizing and Recasting Victims, Offenders, and Rescuers in the War on Human Trafficking.' *Denver Law Review* 94, no. 1 (2016): 1–41.

Bardan, Margot. *Feminism in Islam: Secular and Religious Convergences*. Oxford: Oneworld, 2009.

Barreto, José-Manuel. 'Ethics of Emotions as Ethics of Human Rights: A Jurisprudence of Sympathy in Adorno, Horkheimer and Rorty.' *Law and Critique* 17, no. 1 (2006): 73–106.

Barreto, José-Manuel. 'Rorty and Human Rights: Contingency, Emotions and How to Defend Human Rights Telling Stories.' *Utrecht Law Review* 7, no. 2 (2011): 93–112.

Barreto, José-Manuel. *Human Rights from a Third World Perspective: Critique, History and International Law*. Newcastle upon Tyne: Cambridge Scholars Publishing, 2013.

Barreto, José-Manuel. 'Epistemologies of the South and Human Rights: Santos and the Quest for Global and Cognitive Justice.' *Indiana Journal of Global Legal Studies* 21, no. 2 (2014): 395–422.

Barry, Ellen. 'Broadcast of India Gang Rape Documentary is Banned by Court.' *The New York Times*. 4 March 2015. www.nytimes.com/2015/03/05/world/asia/indian-court-bans-broadcast-of-documentary-on-delhi-gang-rape.html.

Baxi, Upendra. 'Voices of Suffering and the Future of Human Rights.' *Transnational Law and Contemporary Problems* 8, no. 2 (1998): 125–69.

Baxi, Upendra. *The Future of Human Rights*. 3rd ed. New Delhi: Oxford University Press, 2008.

Beaulieu, Alain. 'Towards a Liberal Utopia: The Connection between Foucault's Reporting on the Iranian Revolution and the Ethical Turn.' *Philosophy & Social Criticism* 36, no. 7 (2010): 801–18.

Behdad, Ali. 'Inhospitability, European Style: The Failures of Human Rights.' In *The Postcolonial World*, edited by Jyotsna G. Singh and David D. Kim, pp. 291–307. Abingdon: Routledge, 2016.

Bennoune, Karima. 'Secularism and Human Rights: A Contextual Analysis of Headscarves, Religious Expression, and Women's Equality under International Law.' *Columbia Journal of Transnational Law* 45, no. 2 (2007): 367–426.

Bentham, Jeremy. *An Introduction to the Principles of Morals and Legislation*. London: T. Payne, and Son, 1789.

Bentham, Jeremy. *The Book of Fallacies: From Unfinished Papers of Jeremy Bentham*. London: J. and H.L. Hunt, 1824.

Bentham, Jeremy. *A Comment on the Commentaries and A Fragment on Government*. Edited by J.H. Burns and H.L.A. Hart. London: Athlone Press, 1977.

Berlant, Lauren. 'Slow Death (Sovereignty, Obesity, Lateral Agency).' *Critical Inquiry* 33, no. 4 (2007): 754–80.

Berlant, Lauren. 'Starved.' *South Atlantic Quarterly* 106, no. 3 (2007): 434–44.

Berlant, Lauren. *Cruel Optimism*. Durham, NC: Duke University Press, 2011.

Berlin, Isaiah. 'Two Concepts of Liberty.' In *Four Essays on Liberty*, pp. 118–72. Oxford: Oxford University Press, 1969.

Berman, Paul. *Terrorism and Liberalism*. New York: W.W. Norton & Company, 2003.

Bernasconi, Robert. 'Who Invented the Concept of Race? Kant's Role in Enlightenment Construction of Race.' In *Race*, edited by Robert Bernasconi, pp. 11–36. Malden, MA: Blackwell Publishers, 2001.

Bernauer, James W. *Michel Foucault's Force of Flight: Towards an Ethics for Thought*. Atlantic Highlands, NJ: Humanities, 1990.

Bernauer, James, and Jeremy Carrette, eds. *Michel Foucault and Theology: The Politics of Religious Experience*. Abingdon: Routledge, 2017.

Bernstein, Elizabeth. 'Militarized Humanitarianism Meets Carceral Feminism: The Politics of Sex, Rights, and Freedom in Contemporary Anti-trafficking Campaigns.' *Signs* 36, no. 1 (2010): 45–71.

Bernstein, Elizabeth. 'Carceral Politics as Gender Justice? The 'Traffic in Women' and Neoliberal Circuits of Crime, Sex, and Rights.' *Theory & Society* 41, no. 3 (2012): 233–59.

Bogain, Ariane. 'Security in the Name of Human Rights: The Discursive Legitimation Strategies of the War on Terror in France.' *Critical Studies on Terrorism*. 7 April 2017, doi: 10.1080/17539153.2017.1311093: 1–25.

Bonnet, Sebastian. 'Overcoming Eurocentrism in Human Rights: Post-colonial Critiques – Islamic Answers?' *Muslim World Journal of Human Rights* 12, no. 1 (2015): 1–24.

Bottomley, Ciara. 'Unintended Consequences of International Human Rights Advocacy in Uganda.' *SOAS Law Journal* 2, no. 1 (2015): 49–75.

Bracke, Sarah. 'Is the Subaltern Resilient? Notes on Agency and Neoliberal Subjects.' *Cultural Studies* 30, no. 5 (2016): 839–55.

Breakey, Hugh. 'Positive Duties and Human Rights: Challenges, Opportunities and Conceptual Necessities.' *Political Studies* 63, no. 5 (2015): 1198–1215.

Brent, Barbara G. 'Neoliberalism's Market Morality and Heteroflexibility: Protectionist and Free Market Discourses in Debates for Legal Prostitution.' *Sexuality Research and Social Policy* 13, no. 4 (2016): 402–16.

Brière, Claire, and Pierre Blanchet. 'Iran: The Spirit of a World Without Spirit.' In *Iran: La revolution au nom de Dieu*, pp. 227–41. Paris: Seuill, 1979. Reproduced in Janet Afary and Kevin B. Anderson. *Foucault and the Iranian Revolution: Gender and the Seductions of Islam*. Chicago: University of Chicago Press, 2005, pp. 250–60.

Brodie, Kerry. 'In a Historic First, UN Security Council Convenes to Discuss LGBT Rights.' *Human Rights Campaign* (blog). 24 August 2015. www.hrc.org/blog/in-a-historic-first-u.n.-security-council-convenes-to-discuss-lgbt-rights.

Brooks, Thom. 'Bernard Williams, Republicanism, and the Liberalism of Fear: Problems and Prospects.' In *The Moral Philosophy of Bernard Williams*, edited by Alexandra Perry and Chris Herrera, pp. 107–13. Newcastle upon Tyne: Cambridge Scholars Publishing, 2013.

Brown, Kate. 'Introduction: Vulnerability and Social Justice.' *Social Policy and Society* 16, no. 3 (2017): 423–7.

Brown, Wendy. *States of Injury: Power and Freedom in Late Modernity*. Princeton, NJ: Princeton University Press, 1995.

Brown, Wendy. *Politics Out of History*. Princeton, NJ: Princeton University Press, 2001.

Brown, Wendy. 'Suffering the Paradoxes of Rights.' In *Left Legalism/Left Critique*, edited by Wendy Brown and Janet Halley, pp. 420–34. Durham, NC: Duke University Press, 2002.

Brown, Wendy. 'Resisting Left Melancholia.' In *Loss: The Politics of Mourning*, edited by David L. Eng and David Kazanjian, pp. 458–65. Berkeley, CA: University of California Press, 2003.

Brown, Wendy. '"The most we can hope for …": Human Rights and the Politics of Fatalism.' *South Atlantic Quarterly* 103, nos. 2–3 (2004): 451–63.

Brown, Wendy. *Undoing the Demos: Neoliberalism's Stealth Revolution*. New York: Zone Books, 2015.

Brown, Wendy. 'Sacrificial Citizenship: Neoliberalism, Human Capital, and Austerity Politics.' *Constellations* 23, no. 1 (2016): 3–14.

Broyelle, Claudie, and Jacques Broyelle. 'What Are the Philosophers Dreaming About? Was Michel Foucault Mistaken about the Iranian Revolution.' *Le Matin*, 24 March 1979. Reproduced in Janet Afary and Kevin B. Anderson, *Foucault and the Iranian Revolution: Gender and the Seductions of Islam*, pp. 247–9. Chicago: University of Chicago Press, 2005.

Bumiller, Kristin. 'Victims in the Shadow of the Law: A Critique of the Model of Legal Protection.' *Signs* 12, no. 3 (1987): 421–39.

Bumiller, Kristin. *In An Abusive State: How Neoliberalism Appropriated the Feminist Movement against Sexual Violence*. Durham, NC: Duke University Press, 2008.

Buss, Doris, and Ambreena Manji, 'Introduction.' In *International Law: Modern Feminist Approaches*, edited by Doris Buss and Ambreena Manji, pp. 1–16. Oxford: Hart, 2005.

Butler, Judith. *Bodies That Matter: On the Discursive Limits of 'Sex'*. New York: Routledge, 1993.

Butler, Judith. *The Psychic Life of Power: Theories in Subjection*. Stanford, CA: Stanford University Press, 1997.

Butler, Judith. *Gender Trouble: Feminism and the Subversion of Identity*. New York: Routledge, 1999. First published 1990.

Butler, Judith. 'Explanation and Exoneration, Or What We Can Hear.' *Grey Room* 7 (Spring 2002): 56–67.

Butler, Judith. 'Afterword: After Loss, What Then?' In *Loss: The Politics of Mourning*, edited by David L. Eng and David Kazanjian, pp. 467–73. Berkeley, CA: University of California Press, 2003.

Butler, Judith. 'Bodies and Power Revisited.' In *Feminism and the Final Foucault*, edited by Dianna Taylor and Karen Vintges, pp. 183–94. Urbana: University of Illinois Press, 2004.

Butler, Judith. *Precarious Life: The Powers of Mourning and Violence*. London: Verso, 2004.

Butler, Judith. *Frames of War: When Is Life Grievable?* London: Verso, 2009.

Butler, Judith. *Senses of the Subject*. New York: Fordham University Press, 2015.

Butterworth, Kathy. 'The Decentred Autonomous Subject.' In *Identity and Difference: Contemporary Debates on the Self*, edited by Rafael Winkler, pp. 155–75. Cham: Palgrave Macmillan, 2016.

Calvain Endong and Floribert Patrick. 'LGBT Rights Movement in Africa and the Myth of the Whiteman's Superiority.' *Journal of Globalization Studies* 7, no. 1 (2016): 139–51.

Campbell, Letitia M., and Yvonne C. Zimmerman. 'Christian Ethics and Human Trafficking Activism: Progressive Christianity and Social Critique.' *Journal of the Society of Christian Ethics* 34, no. 1 (2014): 145–72.

Carrette, Jeremy. *Foucault and Religion*. London: Routledge, 1999.

Carrette, Jeremy R., ed. *Religion and Culture: Michel Foucault*. New York: Routledge, 1999.

Carrette, Jeremy. 'Rupture and Transformation: Foucault's Concept of Spirituality Reconsidered.' *Foucault Studies*, no. 15 (2013): 52–71.

Castillo, Debra A., and Kavita Panjabi, eds. *Cartographies of Affect: Across Borders in South Asia and the Americas*. Delhi: Worldview, 2011.

Chakrabarty, Dipesh. 'Radical Histories and Question of Enlightenment Rationalism: Some Recent Critiques of *Subaltern Studies*.' *Economic and Political Weekly* 30, no. 14 (1995): 751–59.

Chakrabarty, Dipesh. *Provincializing Europe: Postcolonial Thought and Historical Difference*. Oxford: Princeton University Press, 2000.

Chandler, David, ed. *Rethinking Human Rights: Critical Approaches to International Politics*. Houndmills: Palgrave Macmillan, 2002.

Chang, Stewart. 'The Postcolonial Problem for Global Gay Rights.' *Boston University International Law Journal* 32, no. 2 (2014): 309–54.

Charlesworth, Hilary. 'Cries and Whispers: Responses to Feminist Scholarship in International Law.' *Nordic Journal of International Law* 65, nos. 3–4 (1996): 557–68.

Charlesworth, Hilary. 'Feminist Methods in International Law.' *The American Journal of International Law* 93, no. 2 (1999): 379–94.

Charlesworth, Hilary. 'Talking to Ourselves? Feminist Scholarship in International Law.' In *Feminist Perspectives on Contemporary International Law: Between Resistance and Compliance?*, edited by Sari Kouvo and Zoe Pearson, pp. 17–32. Oxford: Hart Publishing, 2011.

Charlesworth, Hilary, Christine Chinkin and Shelley Wright. 'Feminist Approaches to International Law.' *The American Journal of International Law* 85, no. 4 (1991): 613–45.

'"Charlie Hebdo": Riss imagine le petit Aylan en 'tripoteur de fesses." *Le Point*. 13 January 2016. www.lepoint.fr/societe/charlie-hebdo-riss-imagine-le-petit-aylan-en-tripoteur-de-fesses-13-01-2016-2009640_23.php.

Chatterjee, Kingshuk. *'Ali Shari'ati and the Shaping of Political Islam in Iran*. New York: Palgrave Macmillan, 2011.

Chatterjee, Partha. 'Postcolonialism and the New Imperialism.' In *The Present as History: Critical Perspectives on Contemporary Global Power*, edited by Nermeen Shaikh, pp. 71–93. New York: Columbia University Press, 2007.

Chaudhry, Lakshmi. 'Rape in the "New India".' *The Nation*. 16 January 2013. www.thenation.com/article/rape-new-india/.

Cheah, Pheng. *Inhuman Conditions: On Cosmopolitanism and Human Rights*. Cambridge, MA: Harvard University Press, 2006.

Chidester, David. 'Michel Foucault and the Study of Religion.' *Religious Studies Review* 12, no. 1 (1986): 1–39.

Chimni, B.S. *International Law and World Order: A Critique of Contemporary Approaches*. Cambridge: Cambridge University Press, 2017.

Chitrangada: The Crowning Wish. Film. Directed by Rituparno Ghosh. India: Shree Venkatesh Films, 2012.

Chittick, William C. *The Sufi Doctrine of Rumi*. Bloomington, IN: World Wisdom, 2005.

Cho, Seo-Young. 'Liberal Coercion? Prostitution, Human Trafficking and Policy.' *European Journal of Law and Economics* 41, no. 2 (2016): 321–48.

Choudhary, Shweta. 'Unarmed Mutiny of Draupadi in Mahashweta Devi's Draupadi.' *Language in India* 16, no. 1 (2016): 271–9.

Choudhury, Bibhash. *Reading Postcolonial Theory: Key Texts in Context*. Florence: Taylor & Francis, 2016.

Choudhury, Cyra Akila. 'Governance Feminism's Imperial Misadventure: Progress, International Law, and the Security of Afghan Women.' In *Contesting Feminisms: Gender and Islam in Asia*, edited by Huma Ahmed-Ghosh, pp. 227–50. New York: State University of New York Press, 2015.

Chowdhry, Geeta, and Sheila Nair, eds. *Power, Postcolonialism and International Relations: Reading Race, Gender, and Class*. New York: Routledge, 2002.

Chuang, Janie. 'Redirecting the Debate over Trafficking in Women: Definitions, Paradigms, and Contexts.' *Harvard Human Rights Journal* 11 (1998): 65–107.

Chuang, Janie A. 'Rescuing Trafficking from Ideological Capture: Prostitution Reform and Anti-Trafficking Law and Policy.' *University of Pennsylvania Law Review* 158, no. 6 (2010): 1655–1728.
Chuang, Janie A. 'Exploitation Creep and the Unmaking of Human Trafficking Law.' *American Journal of International Law* 108, no. 4 (2014): 609–49.
Cohen, Nick. *What's Left? How Liberals Lost Their Way*. London: Fourth Estate, 2007.
Commission de Reflexion sur l'application du Principe de Laïcite dans la Republique. *Rapport au President de la Republique*. 11 December 2003. http://lesrapports.ladocumentationfrancaise.fr/BRP/034000725/0000.pdf.
Cornell, Drucilla, and Stephen D. Seely. *The Spirit of Revolution: Beyond the Dead Ends of Man*. Cambridge: Polity, 2016.
Cossman, Brenda. 'Gender Performance, Sexual Subjects and International Law.' *Canadian Journal of Law and Jurisprudence* 15, no. 2 (2002): 281–96.
Cossman, Brenda. *Sexual Citizens: The Legal and Cultural Regulation of Sex and Belonging*. Stanford, CA: Stanford University Press, 2007.
Cossman, Brenda and Ratna Kapur. *Secularism's Last Sigh? Hindutva and the (Mis)Rule of Law*. Delhi: Oxford University Press, 2001.
Coughlan, Sean. 'Tony Blair Warns of "Flabby Liberalism".' *BBC News*. 22 March 2016. www.bbc.com/news/education-35862598.
Craven, Sri. 'Challenging Queer as "Neoliberal": The Radical Politics of South Asian Diasporic Lesbian Representational Culture.' *Journal of International Women's Studies* 18, no. 2 (2017): 45–58.
Cronin, Anne M. 'Consumerism and "Compulsory Individuality": Women, Will and Potential.' In *Transformations: Thinking Through Feminism*, edited by Sara Ahmed, Jane Kilby, Celia Lury, Maureen McNeil and Beverley Skeggs, pp. 273–87. London: Routledge, 2000.
Cvetkovich, Ann. *An Archive of Feelings: Trauma, Sexuality, and Lesbian Public Cultures*. Durham, NC: Duke University Press, 2003.
Cvetkovich, Ann. *Depression: A Public Feeling*. Durham, NC: Duke University Press, 2012.
Dabashi, Hamid. *Islamic Liberation Theology: Resisting the Empire*. New York: Routledge, 2008.
Dabashi, Hamid. *Can Non-Europeans Think?* London: Zed Books, 2015.
Dabashi, Hamid. *Theology of Discontent: The Ideological Foundation of the Islamic Revolution in Iran*. Abingdon: Routledge, 2017.
Da Costa, Dia. 'Cruel Pessimism and Waiting for Belonging: Towards a Global Political Economy of Affect.' *Cultural Studies* 30, no. 1 (2016): 1–23.

Dancy, Geoff, and Christopher J. Fariss. 'Rescuing Human Rights Law from International Legalism and its Critics.' *Human Rights Quarterly* 39, no. 1 (2017): 1–36.

Das, Veena. *Life and Words: Violence and the Descent into the Ordinary*. Berkeley, CA: University of California Press, 2007.

Dasgupta, Rohit K. *Digital Queer Cultures in India: Politics, Intimacies and Belonging*. New Delhi: Routledge, 2017.

Datta, Sangeeta, Kaustav Bakshi and Rohit K. Dasgupta, eds. *Rituparno Ghosh: Cinema, Gender and Art*. New Delhi: Routledge, 2016.

Davari, Arash. 'A Return to Which Self? Ali Shari'ati and Frantz Fanon on the Political Ethics of Insurrectionary Violence.' *Comparative Studies of South Asia, Africa and the Middle East* 34, no. 1 (2014): 86–105.

Davies, Caroline. 'Girl becomes First Briton Convicted of Trying to Join Fight Against Islamic State in Syria.' *The Guardian*. 21 November 2015. www.theguardian.com/uk-news/2015/nov/20/girl-becomes-first-briton-convicted-of-trying-to-join-fight-against-islamic-state-in-syria.

Davies, Margaret. *Delimiting the Law: 'Postmodernism' and the Politics of Law*. London: Pluto Press, 1996.

Davies, Margaret. 'Taking the Inside Out: Sex and Gender in the Legal Subject.' In *Sexing the Subject of Law*, edited by Ngaire Naffine and Rosemary J. Owens, pp. 25–46. North Ryde: LBC Information Services, 1997.

Dedh Ishqiya. Film. Directed by Abhishek Chaubey. India: Shemaroo Entertainment, 2014.

de Jong, Sara. *Complicit Sisters: Gender and Women's Issues across North-South Divides*. New York: Oxford University Press, 2017.

Demirsu, Ipek. *Counter-Terrorism and the Prospects of Human Rights: Securitizing Difference and Dissent*. Cham: Palgrave Macmillan, 2017.

Desai, Manali. 'Gendered Violence and India's Body Politic.' *New Left Review* 99 (May/June 2016): 67–83.

Devi, Mahasweta. 'Draupadi.' In *In Other Worlds: Essays in Cultural Politics*, edited by Gayatri Chakravorty Spivak, pp. 245–69. Abingdon: Routledge, 1998.

Devi, Mahashweta, and Usha Ganguli. *Rudali: From Fiction to Performance*. Translated by Anjum Katyal. Calcutta: Seagull Books, 1997.

Dhawan, Nikita. 'Affirmative Sabotage of the Master's Tools: The Paradox of Postcolonial Enlightenment.' In *Decolonizing Enlightenment: Transitional Justice, Human Rights and Democracy in a Postcolonial World*, edited by Nikita Dhawan, pp. 19–78. Opladen: Barbara Budrich Publishers, 2014.

Dhawan, Nikita. 'Introduction.' In *Decolonizing Enlightenment: Transitional Justice, Human Rights and Democracy in a Postcolonial World*, edited by Nikita Dhawan, pp. 9–16. Opladen: Barbara Budrich Publishers, 2014.

Dhawan, Nikita. 'Can Non-Europeans Philosophize? Transnational Literacy and Planetary Ethics in a Global Age.' *Hypatia* 32, no. 3 (2017): 488–505.

Donnelly, Jack. *Universal Human Rights in Theory and Practice*. 3rd ed. Ithaca, NY: Cornell University Press, 2013.

Douzinas, Costas. *The End of Human Rights: Critical Legal Thought at the Turn of the Century*. Oxford: Hart Publishing, 2000.

Douzinas, Costas. *Human Rights and Empire: The Political Philosophy of Cosmopolitanism*. Abingdon: Routledge-Cavendish, 2007.

Douzinas, Costas. *The Radical Philosophy of Rights*. Abingdon: Routledge, 2018.

Duggan, Lisa. 'The New Homonormativity: The Sexual Politics of Neoliberalism.' In *Materializing Democracy: Toward a Revitalized Cultural Politics*, edited by Russ Castronovo and Dana D. Nelson, pp. 175–94. Durham, NC: Duke University Press, 2002.

Dutta, Aniruddha, and Raina Roy. 'Decolonizing Transgender in India: Some Reflections.' *TSQ: Transgender Studies Quarterly* 1, no. 3 (2014): 320–37.

Dworkin, Andrea. *Pornography: Men Possessing Women*. London: Women's Press, 1981.

Edelman, Lee. *No Future: Queer Theory and the Death Drive*. Durham, NC: Duke University Press, 2004.

Edelman, Lee. 'Ever After.' In *After Sex? On Writing Since Queer Theory*, edited by Janet Halley and Andrew Parker, pp. 110–18. Durham, NC: Duke University Press, 2011.

Edwards, Alice. 'Traffic in Human Beings: At the Intersection of Criminal Justice, Human Rights, Asylum/Migration and Labor.' *Denver Journal of International Law & Policy* 36, no. 1 (2007): 9–53.

Engle, Karen. 'International Human Rights and Feminisms: When Discourses Keep Meeting.' In *International Law: Modern Feminist Approaches*, edited by Doris Buss and Ambreena Manji, pp. 47–66. Oxford: Hart, 2005.

Engle, Karen. 'Anti-Impunity and the Turn to Criminal Law in Human Rights.' *Cornell Law Review* 100, no. 5 (2015): 1069–1127.

Eng, David L., and David Kazanjian, eds. *Loss: The Politics of Mourning*. Berkeley, CA: University of California Press, 2003.

Evans, Carolyn. 'The "Islamic Scarf" in the European Court of Human Rights.' *Melbourne Journal of International Law* 7, no. 1 (2006): 52–73.

Ewald, François. 'A Power without an Exterior.' In *Michel Foucault Philosopher*, edited by Timothy J. Armstrong, pp. 169–75. New York: Harvester Wheatsheaf, 1992.

Eze, Emmanuel Chukwudi. 'The Color of Reason: The Idea of "Race" in Kant's Anthropology.' In *Postcolonial African Philosophy: A Critical Reader*, edited by Emmanuel Chukwudi Eze, pp. 103–40. Cambridge, MA: Blackwell Publishers, 1997.

Fabian, Johannes. *Time and the Other: How Anthropology Makes Its Object*. New York: Columbia University Press, 2014.

Fanon, Franz. *A Dying Colonialism*. Translated by Haakon Chevalier. New York: Grove Press, 1965.

Fanon, Frantz. *The Wretched of the Earth*. Translated by Constance Farrington. New York: Grove Press, 1966.

Fanon, Franz. *Black Skin, White Masks*. Translated by Charles Lam Markmann. New York: Grove Press, 1967.

Fanon, Frantz. 'The Fact of Blackness.' In *The Post-Colonial Studies Reader*, edited by Bill Ashcroft, Gareth Griffiths and Helen Tiffin, pp. 323–6. London: Routledge, 2003. First published 1952.

Farris, Sara R. *In the Name of Women's Rights: The Rise of Femonationalism*. Durham, NC: Duke University Press, 2017.

Fernandes, Sujatha. 'Stories and Statecraft: Afghan Women's Narratives and the Construction of Western Freedoms.' *Signs* 42, no. 3 (2017): 643–67.

Fernando, Mayanthi L. *The Republic Unsettled: Muslim French and the Contradictions of Secularism*. Durham, NC: Duke University Press, 2014.

Fernando, Mayanthi L. 'The Unpredictable Imagination of Muslim French: Citizenship, Public Religiosity, and Political Possibility in France.' In *Muslim Youth and the 9/11 Generation*, edited by Adeline Masquelier and Benjamin F. Soares, pp. 123–50. Santa Fe: School for Advanced Research Press; Albuquerque: University of New Mexico Press, 2016.

Ferrari, Alessandro, and Sabrina Pastorelli, eds. *The Burqa Affair Across Europe: Between Public and Private Space*. Farnham: Ashgate, 2013.

Fineman, Martha. *The Autonomy Myth: A Theory of Dependency*. New York: New Press, 2004.

Fineman, Martha Albertson. 'The Vulnerable Subject: Anchoring Equality in the Human Condition.' *Yale Journal of Law & Feminism* 20, no. 1 (2008): 1–23.

Fineman, Martha Albertson. 'The Vulnerable Subject and the Responsive State.' *Emory Law Journal* 60, no. 2 (2010): 251–75.

Fineman, Martha Albertson, and Anna Grear. *Vulnerability: Reflections on a New Ethical Foundation for Law and Politics*. Farnham: Ashgate Publishing Company, 2013.

Fitzgerald, Timothy. '"Postcolonial Remains": Critical Religion, Postcolonial Theory, and Deconstructing the Secular-Religious Binary.' In *The Postcolonial World*, edited by Jyotsna G. Singh and David D. Kim, pp. 169–83. Abingdon: Routledge, 2017.

Fitzmaurice, Andrew. 'Scepticism of the Civilizing Mission in International Law.' In *International Law and Empire: Historical Explorations*, edited by Martti Koskenniemi, Walter Rech and Manuel Jiménez Fonseca, pp. 359–84. Oxford: Oxford University Press, 2017.

Flikschuh, Katrin. *Freedom: Contemporary Liberal Perspectives*. Cambridge: Polity, 2007.

Foucault, Michel. *The Order of Things: An Archaeology of the Human Sciences*, edited by R.D. Laing. New York: Pantheon Books, 1970.

Foucault, Michel. *The History of Sexuality: Volume I – An Introduction*. Translated by Robert Hurley. New York: Pantheon Books, 1978.

Foucault, Michel. 'What Are the Iranians Dreaming [*Rêvent*] About?' *Le Nouvel Observateur*. 16–22 October 1978. Reproduced in Janet Afary and Kevin B. Anderson. *Foucault and the Iranian Revolution: Gender and the Seductions of Islam*, pp. 203–9. Chicago: University of Chicago Press, 2005.

Foucault, Michel. 'Is It Useless to Revolt?' *Le Monde*. 11–12 May 1979. Reproduced in Janet Afary and Kevin B. Anderson. *Foucault and the Iranian Revolution: Gender and the Seductions of Islam*, pp. 263–7. Chicago: University of Chicago Press, 2005.

Foucault, Michel. 'Open Letter to Prime Minister Mehdi Bazargan.' *Le Nouvel Observateur*. 14 April 1979. Reproduced in Janet Afary and Kevin B. Anderson. *Foucault and the Iranian Revolution: Gender and the Seductions of Islam*, pp. 260–3. Chicago: University of Chicago Press, 2005.

Foucault, Michel. 'What Is Enlightenment?' In *The Foucault Reader*, edited by Paul Rabinow, pp. 32–50. New York: Pantheon Books, 1984.

Foucault, Michel. *The Care of the Self: The History of Sexuality, Volume III*. Translated by Robert Hurley. London: Penguin, 1990.

Foucault, Michel. 'Confronting Governments: Human Rights.' In Michel Foucault, *Power*, edited by James D. Faubion, translated by Robert Hurley et al., pp. 474–5. Vol. 3. London: Penguin Books, 1994.

Foucault, Michel. 'Questions of Method.' In *The Foucault Effect: Studies in Governmentality*, edited by Graham Burchell, Colin Gordon, and Peter Miller, pp. 73–86. Chicago: University of Chicago Press, 1991.

Foucault, Michel. 'The Subject and Power.' In Michel Foucault, *Power*, edited by James D. Faubion, translated by Robert Hurley et al., pp. 326–48. Vol. 3. London: Penguin Books, 1994.

Foucault, Michel. 'The Body of the Condemned.' In Michel Foucault, *Discipline and Punish: The Birth of the Prison*, edited by Alan Sheridan, pp. 3–31. New York: Vintage, 1995.

Foucault, Michel. *Discipline and Punish: The Birth of the Prison*. Edited by Alan Sheridan. New York: Vintage, 1995.

Foucault, Michel. 'What is Critique?' In *What is Enlightenment? Eighteenth-Century Answers and Twentieth-Century Questions*, edited by James Schmidt, pp. 382–98. Berkeley, CA: University of California Press, 1996.

Foucault, Michel. 'The Ethics of the Concern of the Self as a Practice of Freedom.' In *Ethics: Subjectivity and Truth*, edited by Paul Rabinow, translated by Robert Hurley, pp. 281–301. Vol. 1. New York: The New Press, 1997.

Foucault, Michel. 'On the Genealogy of Ethics: An Overview of Work in Progress.' In *Ethics: Subjectivity and Truth*, edited by Paul Rabinow, translated by Robert Hurley, pp. 253–80. Vol. 1. New York: The New Press, 1997.

Foucault, Michel. 'Technologies of the Self.' In *Ethics: Subjectivity and Truth*, edited by Paul Rabinow, translated by Robert Hurley, pp. 223–51. Vol. 1. New York: The New Press, 1997.

Foucault, Michel. 'Michel Foucault and Zen: A Stay in a Zen Temple (1978).' In *Religion and Culture: Michel Foucault*, edited by Jeremy R. Carrette, pp. 110–14. New York: Routledge, 1999.

Foucault, Michel. *'Society Must Be Defended': Lectures at the Collège de France, 1975–76*. Edited by Mauro Bertani and Alessandro Fontana, translated by David Macey. London: Allen Lane, 2003.

Foucault, Michel. *The Hermeneutics of the Subject: Lectures at the Collège de France, 1981–1982*. Edited by Frédéric Gros, translated by Graham Burchell. New York: Palgrave Macmillan, 2005.

Foucault, Michel. *The Birth of Biopolitics: Lectures at the Collège de France, 1978–79*. Edited by Michel Senellart, translated by Graham Burchell. Basingstoke: Palgrave Macmillan, 2008.

Foucault, Michel. *The Courage of Truth: The Government of Self and Others II – Lectures at the Collège de France, 1983–1984*. Edited by Frédéric Gros, translated by Graham Burchell. Basingstoke: Palgrave Macmillan, 2012.

Foucault, Michel, and Baqir Parham. 'Dialogue between Michel Foucault and Baqir Parham.' *Nameh-yi Kanun-I Nevisandegan*, no. 1 (Spring 1979): 9–17. Reproduced in Janet Afary and Kevin B. Anderson.

Foucault and the Iranian Revolution: Gender and the Seductions of Islam, pp. 183–9. Chicago: University of Chicago Press, 2005.

'France: LOI° n 2013-404 du 17 mai 2013 ouvrant le mariage aux couples de personnes de même sexe.' *Fabregat Perulles Sales Abogados* (blog). 29 May 2013. www.fabregat-perulles-sales.com/blog/france-loi-n-2013-404-du-17-mai-2013-ouvrant-le-mariage-aux-couples-de-personnes-de-meme-sexe/.

Frankenberg, Günter. 'The Innocence of Method – Unveiled: Comparison as an Ethical and Political Act.' *Journal of Comparative Law* 9, no. 2 (2014): 222–58.

Frankenberg, Günter. 'Human Rights and the Belief in a Just World.' *International Journal of Constitutional Law* 12, no. 1 (2014): 35–60.

Frankenberg, Günter. *Political Technology and the Erosion of the Rule of Law: Normalizing the State of Exception*. Cheltenham: Edward Elgar Publishing, 2014.

Fredman, Sandra. *Human Rights Transformed: Positive Rights and Positive Duties*. Oxford: Oxford University Press, 2008.

Freeman, Elizabeth. *Time Binds: Queer Temporalities, Queer Histories*. Durham, NC: Duke University Press, 2010.

Gallagher, Anne T., and Joy Ngozi Ezeilo. 'The UN Special Rapporteur on Trafficking: A Turbulent Decade in Review.' *Human Rights Quarterly* 37, no. 4 (2015): 913–40.

Gandhi, Leela. 'A Case of Radical Kinship: Edward Carpenter and the Politics of Anti-Colonial Sexual Dissidence.' In *The Phobic and the Erotic: The Politics of Sexualities in Contemporary India*, edited by Brinda Bose and Subhabrata Bhattacharyya, pp. 91–116. London: Seagull Books, 2007.

Gearty, Conor. *Can Human Rights Survive?* Cambridge: Cambridge University Press, 2006.

Gemie, Sharif. 'In Search of the Good Muslim: French Muslims, the French State, and the Politics of Identity.' In *The State of Social Progress of Islamic Societies: Social, Economic, Political, and Ideological Challenges*, edited by Habib Tiliouine and Richard J. Estes, pp. 321–35. Cham: Springer International Publishing, 2016.

George, Aaron Rohan. 'Bollywood's Queer Dostana: Articulating a Transnational Queer Indian Identity and Family in 2008's *Dostana*.' *Asia Colloqiua Papers: 2014 Critical Approaches to South Asian Studies Workshop* 5, no. 2 (2015): 1–14.

Gerber, Paula, and Joel Gory. 'The UN Human Rights Committee and LGBT Rights: What Is It Doing? What Could It Be Doing?' *Human Rights Law Review* 14, no. 3 (2014): 403–39.

Ghamari-Tabrizi, Behrooz. *Foucault in Iran: Islamic Revolution after the Enlightenment*. Minneapolis: University of Minnesota Press, 2016.

Ghosh, Apoorva. 'LGBTQ Activist Organizations as "Respectably Queer" in India: Contesting a Western View.' *Gender, Work and Organization* 22, no. 1 (2015): 51–66.

Ghosh, Palash. 'Delhi Gang-Rape: Right-Wing Leader Claims Sex Crimes Caused by Western Influences, Urban Living.' *International Business Times*, 1 August 2013, www.ibtimes.com/delhi-gang-rape-right-wing-leader-claims-sex-crimes-caused-western-influences-urban-living-999992

Gibran, Kahlil. 'On Freedom.' In Kahlil Gibran, *The Prophet*, edited by Suheil Bushrui, pp. 47–9. London: Oneworld Publications, 2012.

Gilligan, Carol. *In a Different Voice: Psychological Theory and Women's Development*. Cambridge, MA: Harvard University Press, 2003.

Gilroy, Paul. *Postcolonial Melancholia*. New York: Columbia University Press, 2005.

Global Alliance Against Traffic in Women (GAATW). *Collateral Damage: The Impact of Anti-Trafficking Measures on Human Rights around the World*. 2007.

Golder, Ben. 'Foucault and the Unfinished Human of Rights.' *Law, Culture and the Humanities* 6, no. 3 (2010): 354–74.

Golder, Ben. 'Foucault, Rights, and Freedom.' *International Journal for the Semiotics of Law* 26, no. 1 (2013): 5–21.

Golder, Ben. 'Beyond Redemption? Problematising the Critique of Human Rights in Contemporary International Legal Thought.' *London Review of International Law* 2, no. 1 (2014): 77–114.

Golder, Ben. *Foucault and the Politics of Rights*. Stanford, CA: Stanford University Press, 2015.

Golder, Ben, and Peter Fitzpatrick. *Foucault's Law*. Hoboken, NJ: Taylor & Francis, 2009.

Gopinath, Gayatri. 'On *Fire*.' *GLQ: A Journal of Lesbian and Gay Studies* 4, no. 4 (1998): 631–6.

Gordon, Daniel. '"Civilization" and the Self-Critical Tradition.' *Society* 54, no. 2 (2017): 106–23.

Grewal, Inderpal. *Transnational America: Feminisms, Diasporas, Neoliberalisms*. Durham, NC: Duke University Press, 2005.

Groll, Elias. 'A Record Year in Misery: The World Has Never Seen a Refugee Crisis this Bad.' *Foreign Policy*. 18 June 2015. http://foreignpolicy.com/2015/06/18/a-record-year-in-misery-the-world-has-never-seen-a-refugee-crisis-this-bad/.

Gross, Aeyal M. 'Sex, Love, and Marriage: Questioning Gender and Sexuality Rights in International Law.' *Leiden Journal of International Law* 21, no. 1 (2008): 235–53.

Guha, Ranajit. 'On Some Aspects of the Historiography of Colonial India.' In *Subaltern Studies: Writings on South Asian History and*

Society, edited by Ranajit Guha, pp. 1–8. Delhi: Oxford University Press, 1982.

Guha, Ranajit, and Partha Chatterjee. *The Small Voice of History: Collected Essays*. Ranikhet: Permanent Black, 2010.

Gunkel, Henriette. 'Some Reflections on Postcolonial Homophobia, Local Interventions, and LGBTI Solidarity Online: The Politics of Global Petitions.' *African Studies Review* 56, no. 2 (2013): 67–81.

Gwong, Gerrit W. *The Standard of 'Civilization' in International Society*. Oxford: Clarendon Press, 1984.

Hagen, Jamie J. 'Queering Women, Peace and Security.' *International Affairs* 92, no. 2 (2016): 313–32.

Halberstam, Judith. *The Queer Art of Failure*. Durham, NC: Duke University Press, 2011.

Halley, Janet. *Split Decisions: How and Why to Take a Break from Feminism*. Princeton, NJ: Princeton University Press, 2006.

Halley, Janet. 'Rape at Rome: Feminist Interventions in the Criminalization of Sex-Related Violence in Positive International Criminal Law.' *Michigan Journal of International Law* 30, no. 1 (2008): 1–123.

Halley, Janet. 'Rape in Berlin: Reconsidering the Criminalisation of Rape in the International Law of Armed Conflict.' *Melbourne Journal of International Law* 9, no. 1 (2008): 78–124.

Halley, Janet. 'Introduction to Governance Feminism.' In *Governance Feminism: An Introduction*, edited by Janet Halley, Prabha Kotiswaran, Rachel Rebouché, and Hila Shamir, pp. ix-xxii. Minneapolis: University of Minneapolis Press, 2018.

Halley, Janet, Prabha Kotiswaran, Hila Shamir and Chantal Thomas. 'From the International to the Local in Feminist Legal Responses to Rape, Prostitution/Sex Work, and Sex Trafficking: Four Studies in Contemporary Governance Feminism.' *Harvard Journal of Law & Gender* 29, no. 2 (2006): 335–423.

Halperin, David M. *One Hundred Years of Homosexuality: And Other Essays on Greek Love*. New York: Routledge, 1990.

Hamzić, Vanja. *Sexual and Gender Diversity in the Muslim World: History, Law and Vernacular Knowledge*. London: I.B. Tauris, 2015.

Harcourt, Bernard E. *The Illusion of Free Markets: Punishment and the Myth of Natural Order*. Cambridge, MA: Harvard University Press, 2011.

Haring, Jenna. 'Contemporary Visual Art and Iranian Feminism.' *Global Societies Journal* 5 (2017): 70–84.

Hasan, Daisy. '"Kissed on One Cheek and Slapped on the Other": Rituparono Ghosh's *Chitrangada* as an Allegory of Oppositional Readings.' *South Asian History and Culture* 6, no. 4 (2015): 500–9.

Haskell, John. 'The Religion/Secularism Debate in Human Rights Literature: Constitutive Tensions between Christian, Islamic, and Secular Perspectives.' In *International Law and Religion: Historical and Contemporary Perspectives*, edited by Martti Koskenniemi, Mónica García-Salmones Rovira and Paolo Amorosa, pp. 135–53. Oxford: Oxford University Press, 2017.

Hassan, Oz, and Andrew Hammond. 'The Rise and Fall of American's Freedom Agenda in Afghanistan: Counter-Terrorism, Nation-Building and Democracy.' *International Journal of Human Rights* 15, no. 4 (2011): 532–51.

Hasson, Kevin J. 'Religious Liberty and Human Dignity: A Tale of Two Declarations.' *Harvard Journal of Law & Public Policy* 27, no. 1 (2003): 81–92.

Hawley, John C., ed. *Postcolonial, Queer: Theoretical Intersections*. Albany, NY: State University of New York Press, 2001.

Hemmings, Clare. 'Affective Solidarity: Feminist Reflexivity and Political Transformation.' *Feminist Theory* 13, no. 2 (2012): 147–61.

Hemmings, Clare. 'Invoking Affect: Cultural Theory and the Ontological Turn.' *Cultural Studies* 19, no. 5 (2005): 548–67.

Hess, Andreas. *The Political Theory of Judith N. Shklar*. Basingstoke: Palgrave Macmillan, 2014.

Hinchy, Jessica. 'The Eunuch Archive: Colonial Records of Non-Normative Gender and Sexuality in India.' *Culture, Theory and Critique* 58, no. 2 (2017): 127–46.

Hirschkind, Charles, and Saba Mahmood. 'Feminism, the Taliban, and Politics of Counter-Insurgency.' *Anthropological Quarterly* 75, no. 2 (2002): 339–54.

Honig, Bonnie. 'What Foucault Saw at the Revolution: On the Use and Abuse of Theology for Politics.' *Political Theory* 36, no. 2 (2008): 301–12.

Hoover, Joe. *Reconstructing Human Rights: A Pragmatist and Pluralist Inquiry into Global Ethics*. Oxford: Oxford University Press, 2016.

Hopegood, Stephen. *The Endtimes of Human Rights*. Ithaca, NY: Cornell University Press, 2013.

Hoskote, Ranjit, trans. *I, Lalla: The Poems of Lal Děd*. New Delhi: Penguin Books, 2011.

Huckerby, Jayne. 'Same, but Different: Assessing the Interaction of the Migrant Workers' Rights and Anti-Trafficking Regimes Under International Law.' *New York University Journal of International Law and Politics* 47, no. 3 (2015): 593–645.

Hudson, Natalie Florea. *Gender, Human Security and the United Nations: Security Language as a Political Framework for Women*. Hoboken: Taylor & Francis, 2009.

Hunt, Lynn. *Inventing Human Rights: A History*. New York: W.W. Norton, 2007.

Hunter, Rosemary. 'Deconstructing the Subjects of Feminism: The Essentialism Debate in Feminist Theory and Practice.' *The Australian Feminist Law Journal* 6 (1996): 135–62.

Ibhawoh, Bonny. *Imperialism and Human Rights: Colonial Discourses of Rights and Liberties in African History*. New York: State University of New York, 2007.

Ibrahim, Amrita. '*India's Daughter* and How Not to Talk About Rape.' *Dissent* (blog). 19 March 2015. www.dissentmagazine.org/blog/indias-daughter-and-how-not-to-talk-about-rape.

Ignatieff, Michael. 'The Seductiveness of Moral Disgust.' *Social Research* 62, no. 1 (1995): 77–97.

Ignatieff, Michael. 'I. Human Rights as Politics; II. Human Rights as Idolatry.' Lecture, Princeton University, April 4–7, 2000.

Ignatieff, Michael. 'The American Empire: The Burden.' *The New York Times Magazine*. 5 January 2003. www.nytimes.com/2003/01/05/magazine/the-american-empire-the-burden.html.

Ignatieff, Michael. *Empire Lite: Nation Building in Bosnia, Kosovo and Afghanistan*. London: Vintage, 2003.

Ignatieff, Michael. *Human Rights as Politics and Idolatry*. Princeton, NJ: Princeton University Press, 2011.

Ignatieff, Michael. 'Human Rights, Global Ethics, and the Ordinary Virtues.' *Ethics & International Affairs* 31, no. 1 (2017): 3–16.

India's Daughters. Film. Directed by Leslee Udwin. United Kingdom: Berta Film, 2015.

Ingram, James D. *Radical Cosmopolitics: The Ethics and Politics of Democratic Universalism*. New York: Columbia University Press, 2013.

Invernizzi-Accetti, Carlo. 'Is the European Union Secular? Christian Democracy in the European Treaties and Jurisprudence.' *Comparative European Politics*. 24 March 2017. doi: 10.1057/s41295-017-0091-0: 1–26.

Iyer, Shruti. 'Taking a Break from the State: Indian Feminists in the Legal Reform Process.' *Journal of International Women's Studies* 17, no. 2 (2016): 18–29.

Jacobsen, Christine M., Mayanthi Fernando, and Janet Jakobsen. 'Gender, Sex and Religious Freedom in the Context of Secular Law.' *Feminist Review*, no. 113 (2016): 93–102.

Jamal, Amina. 'Piety, Transgression, and the Feminist Debate on Muslim Women: Resituating the Victim-Subject of Honor-Related Violence from a Transnational Lens.' *Signs* 41, no. 1 (2015): 55–79.

Jambet, Christian. 'The Constitution of the Subject and Spiritual Practice.' In *Michel Foucault, Philosopher: Essays Translated from the French and German*, edited by Timothy J. Armstrong, pp. 233–47. New York: Harvester Wheatsheaf, 1992.

Jansson, Maria, and Maud Eduards. 'The Politics of Gender in the UN Security Council Resolutions on Women, Peace and Security.' *International Feminist Journal of Politics* 18, no. 4 (2016): 590–604.

Jawad, Huda. 'The Burkhini Ban is Misogynistic – and Western Feminists Are Turning a Blind Eye.' *Independent*. 13 August 2016. www.independent.co.uk/voices/burkini-cannes-islamophobia-banning-the-burkini-is-misogynistic-and-western-feminists-are-turning-a-a7188806.html.

Jones, Spence. 'Towards a Universal Construction of Transgender Rights: Harmonizing Doctrinal and Dialogic Strategies in Indian Jurisprudence.' *The Indonesian Journal of International & Comparative Law* 4, no. 1 (2017): 91–121.

Joshi, Yuvraj. 'Respectable Queerness.' *Columbia Human Rights Law Review* 43, no. 2 (2012): 415–67.

Joshi, Yuvraj. 'The Trouble with Inclusion.' *Virginia Journal of Social Policy & the Law* 21, no. 2 (2014): 207–65.

Kak, Jaishree, trans. *Mystical Verses of Lallā: A Journey of Self-Realization*. Delhi: Motilal Banarsidass Publishers, 2007.

Kant, Immanuel. *Groundwork for the Metaphysics of Morals*. Translated and edited by Allen W. Wood. New Haven, CT: Yale University Press, 2002.

Kapoor, Ilan. *The Postcolonial Politics of Development*. London: Routledge, 2008.

Kapur, Ratna. 'The Tragedy of Victimization Rhetoric: Resurrecting the "Native" Subject in International/Post-Colonial Feminist Legal Politics.' *Harvard Human Rights Journal* 15 (Spring 2002): 1–37.

Kapur, Ratna. *Erotic Justice: Law and the New Politics of Postcolonialism*. London: Glass House Press, 2005.

Kapur, Ratna. 'Unruly Desires, Gay Governance and the Makeover of Sexuality in Postcolonial India.' In *Global Justice and Desire: Queering Economy*, edited by Nikita Dhawan, Antke Engel, Christoph F. E. Holzhey, and Volker Woltersdorff, pp. 115–31. Abingdon: Routledge, 2015.

Kapur, Ratna. Review of *Foucault and the Politics of Rights*, by Ben Golder. *UNSW Law Journal* 39, no. 4 (2016): 1472–8.

Keller, Catherine, Michael Nausner and Mayra Rivera, eds. *Postcolonial Theologies: Divinity and Empire*. St Louis, MO: Chalice Press, 2004.

Kennedy, David. 'The International Human Rights Movement: Part of the Problem?' *Harvard Human Rights Journal* 15 (Spring 2002): 101–25.

Kennedy, David. *The Dark Sides of Virtue: Reassessing International Humanitarianism*. Princeton, NJ: Princeton University Press, 2004.

Kennedy, David. 'Reassessing International Humanitarianism: The Dark Sides.' In *International Law and Its Others*, edited by Anne Orford, 131–55. Cambridge: Cambridge University Press, 2006.

Kennedy, David. 'The International Human Rights Regime: Still Part of the Problem?' In *Examining Critical Perspectives on Human Rights*, edited by Rob Dickinson, Elena Katselli, Colin Murray and Ole W. Pederson, pp. 19–34. Cambridge: Cambridge University Press, 2012.

Khanna, Ranjana. 'Touching, Unbelonging, and the Absence of Affect.' *Feminist Theory* 13, no. 2 (2012): 231–2.

Khoja-Moolji, Shenila S. 'The Making of Humans and Their Others in and through Transnational Human Rights Advocacy: Exploring the Cases of Mukhtar Mai and Malala Yousafzai.' *Signs* 42, no. 2 (2017): 377–402.

Kingsolver, Barbara. *The Poisonwood Bible*. New York: HarperFlamingo, 1998.

Kirchner, Stephanie, and Rick Noack. 'New Stricter Sexual-Assault Laws in Germany are Making Refugee Activists Uneasy.' *The Washington Post*. 7 July 2016. www.washingtonpost.com/news/worldviews/wp/2016/07/07/why-stricter-sexual-assault-laws-in-germany-make-refugee-activists-uneasy/?utm_term=.62a764bc34c9.

Klein, Naomi. *The Shock Doctrine: The Rise of Disaster Capitalism*. London: Allen Lane, 2007.

Klose, Fabian. 'Human Rights For and Against Empire: Legal and Public Discourses in the Age of Decolonisation.' *Journal of the History of International Law* 18, nos. 2–3 (2016): 317–38.

Kohn, Sally. 'Hillary, "The Family" and Uganda's Anti-Gay Christian Mafia.' *The Daily Beast*. 25 February 2014. www.thedailybeast.com/hillary-the-family-and-ugandas-anti-gay-christian-mafia.

Korycki, Katarzyna. 'Desire Recast: The Production of Gay Identity in Iran.' *Journal of Gender Studies* 25, no. 1 (2016): 50–65.

Kotiswaran, Prabha. *Dangerous Sex, Invisible Labor: Sex Work and the Law in India*. Princeton, NJ: Princeton University Press, 2011.

Kouvo, Sari. 'Taking Women Seriously? Conflict, State-Building and Gender in Afghanistan.' In *Feminist Perspectives on Contemporary International Law: Between Resistance and Compliance?*, edited by Sari Kouvo and Zoe Pearson, pp. 159–76. Oxford: Hart Publishing, 2011.

Kouvo, Sari, and Zoe Pearson, eds. *Feminist Perspectives on Contemporary International Law*. Oxford: Hart, 2011.

Krieg, Andreas. *Commercializing Cosmopolitan Security: Safeguarding the Responsibility to Protect*. New York: Palgrave Macmillan, 2016.

Kymlicka, Will. *Liberalism, Community and Culture*. Oxford: Clarendon Press, 1989.
Lacayo, Richard. 'Lifting the Veil.' *Time*. 3 December 2001.
Lægaard, Sune. 'Burqa Ban, Freedom of Religion and "Living Together".' *Human Rights Review* 16, no. 3 (2015): 203–19.
Larking, Emma. 'Human Rights Rituals: Masking Neoliberalism and Inequality, and Marginalizing Alternative World Views.' *Canadian Journal of Law and Society/Revue Canadienne Droit et Société* 32, no. 1 (2017): 1–18.
Lavers, Michael K. 'Islamic State Focus of UN Security Council's First LGBT Meeting.' *Washington Blade*. 25 August 2015. www.washingtonblade.com/2015/08/24/islamic-state-focus-of-u-n-security-councils-first-lgbt-meeting/.
Lazaro, Elaine M. 'Thinking with Irigaray: On Asian Women as Objects of Conquest and Exchange.' *Kritike* 11, no. 1 (2017): 94–107.
Leezenberg, Michiel. 'Power and Political Spirituality: Michel Foucault on the Islamic Revolution in Iran.' In *Cultural History after Foucault*, edited by John Neubauer, pp. 63–80. New York: Aldine de Gruyter, 1999.
'Le magazine Elle lance un appel contre le voile.' *Elle*. 5 December 2003.
Locke, John. *Two Treatises of Government*. Vol. 5. London: Thomas Tegg, 1823. Prepared by Rob Hay for McMaster University Archive of the History of Economic Thought, 2000.
Love, Heather. *Feeling Backward: Loss and the Politics of Queer History*. Cambridge, MA: Harvard University Press, 2007.
Lu K'uan-yü (Charles Luk), trans. and ed. *Master Hsu Yun's Discourses and Dharma Words*. Taipei: Corporate Body of the Buddha Educational Foundation, 1996.
MacKinnon, Catharine A. 'Feminism, Marxism, Method, and the State: Toward Feminist Jurisprudence.' *Signs* 8, no. 4 (1983): 635–58.
MacKinnon, Catharine A. *Feminism Unmodified: Discourses on Life and Law*. Cambridge, MA: Harvard University Press, 1987.
MacKinnon, Catharine A. *Toward a Feminist Theory of the State*. Cambridge, MA: Harvard University Press, 1989.
Mahadevan, T.M.P. 'Contemporary Relevance of the Insights of Advaita.' In *Contemporary Indian Philosophy: Series II*, edited by Margaret Chatterjee, pp. 109–32. Delhi: Motilal Barnarsidass Publishers, 1998.
Mahmood, Saba. *Politics of Piety: The Islamic Revival and the Feminist Subject*. Princeton, NJ: Princeton University Press, 2005.
Mahmood, Saba. *Religious Difference in a Secular Age: A Minority Report*. Princeton, NJ: Princeton University Press, 2016.
Majeed, Javed. *Ungoverned Imaginings: James Mill's The History of British India and Orientialism*. Oxford: Oxford University Press, 1992.

Mamdani, Mahmood. 'Good Muslim, Bad Muslim: A Political Perspective on Culture and Terrorism.' *American Anthropologist* 104, no. 3 (2002): 766–75.

Mamdani, Mahmood. 'Beware Human Rights Fundamentalism!' *Mail & Guardian*. 20 March 2009. https://mg.co.za/article/2009-03-20-beware-human-rights-fundamentalism.

Mamdani, Mahmood. *Saviors and Survivors: Darfur, Politics, and the War on Terror*. London: Verso, 2009.

Mancini, Susanna. 'The Power of Symbols and Symbols as Power: Secularism and Religion as Guarantors of Cultural Convergence.' *Cardozo Law Review* 30, no. 6 (2009): 2629–68.

Mancini, Susanna. 'The Tempting of Europe, the Political Seduction of the Cross: A Schmittian Reading of Christianity and Islam in European Constitutionalism.' In *Constitutional Secularism in an Age of Religious Revival*, edited by Susanna Mancini and Michel Rosenfeld, 111–35. Oxford: Oxford University Press, 2014.

Mantena, Karuna. *Alibis of Empire: Henry Maine and the Ends of Liberal Imperialism*. Princeton, NJ: Princeton University Press, 2010.

Mari, Ruti. *The Ethics of Opting Out: Queer Theory's Defiant Subjects*. New York: Columbia University Press, 2017.

Marks, Susan. 'Exploitation as an International Legal Concept.' In *International Law on the Left: Re-Examining Marxist Legacies*, edited by Susan Marks, pp. 281–307. Cambridge: Cambridge University Press, 2008.

Marks, Susan. 'Four Human Rights Myths.' London School of Economics and Political Science, LSE Law, Society and Economy Working Papers 10/2012, 2012. www.lse.ac.uk/collections/law/wps/WPS2012-10_Marks.pdf.

Martinez, Jenny S. *The Slave Trade and the Origins of International Human Rights Law*. Oxford: Oxford University Press, 2012.

Massad, Joseph. 'Re-Orienting Desire: The Gay International and the Arab World.' *Public Culture* 14, no. 2 (2002): 361–85.

Massad, Joseph A. *Desiring Arabs*. Chicago: University of Chicago Press, 2007.

Massignon, Louis. *The Passion of Al-Hallaj: Mystic and Martyr of Islam*, translated by Herbert Mason. 4 vols. Princeton, NJ: Princeton University Press, 1982.

Massumi, Brian. 'The Autonomy of Affect.' In *Deleuze: A Critical Reader*, edited by Paul Patton, pp. 217–39. Oxford: Blackwell, 1996.

Masuzawa, Tomoko. *The Invention of World Religions, Or, How European Universalism Was Preserved in the Language of Pluralism*. Chicago: University of Chicago Press, 2005.

Matilal, Bimal Krishna. *Perception: An Essay on Classical Indian Theories of Knowledge*. Oxford: Clarendon Press, 1986.
Mbembe, Achille. 'Necropolitics.' Translated by Libby Meintjes. *Public Culture* 15, no. 1 (2003): 11–40.
McCall, Corey. 'Ambivalent Modernities: Foucault's Iranian Writings Reconsidered.' *Foucault Studies*, no. 15 (February 2013): 27–51.
McCrudden, Christopher. 'Human Rights Histories.' *Oxford Journal of Legal Studies* 35, no. 1 (2015): 179–212.
McGoldrick, Dominic. *Human Rights and Religion: The Islamic Headscarf Debate in Europe*. Oxford: Hart Publishing, 2006.
McNay, Lois. *Foucault and Feminism: Power, Gender and the Self*. Cambridge: Polity Press, 1992.
McNeilly, Kathryn. 'After the Critique of Rights: For a Radical Democratic Theory and Practice of Human Rights.' *Law and Critique* 27, no. 3 (2016): 269–88.
McWhorter, Ladelle. 'Foucault's Political Spirituality.' *Philosophy Today* 47, Suppl. (2003): 39–44.
Mehta, Uday Singh. *The Anxiety of Freedom: Imagination and Individuality in Locke's Political Thought*. Ithaca, NY: Cornell University Press, 1992.
Mehta, Uday Singh. *Liberalism and Empire: A Study in Nineteenth-Century British Liberal Thought*. Chicago: University of Chicago Press, 1999.
Memmi, Albert. *The Colonizer and the Colonized*. New York: Orion Press, 1963.
Meyers, Diana Tietjens. 'Recovering the Human in Human Rights.' *Law, Culture and the Humanities* 12, no. 3 (2016): 474–84.
Mignolo, Walter D. *The Darker Side of the Renaissance: Literacy, Territoriality, and Colonization*. 2nd ed. Ann Arbor, MI: University of Michigan Press, 2003.
Milivojevic, Sanja, and Marie Segrave. 'Responses to Sex Trafficking: Gender, Borders and "Home".' In *Trafficking and Human Rights: European and Asia-Pacific Perspectives*, edited by Leslie Holmes, pp. 37–55. Cheltenham: Edward Elgar Publishing, 2010.
Mill, John Stuart. *Essays on Equality, Law, and Education*. Vol. 21 of *Collected Works of John Stuart Mill*, edited by John M. Robson. Toronto: University of Toronto Press, 1984.
Mill, John Stuart. *Utilitarianism*. London: Parker, Son and Bourn, 1863.
Mill, John Stuart. *Utilitarianism*. 2nd ed. London: Longman, Green, 1864.
Millan, Anna, and Ali Can Yildirim. 'Decolonizing Theories of Global Justice.' In *Decolonizing Enlightenment: Transnational Justice, Human*

Rights and Democracy in a Postcolonial World, edited by Nikita Dhawan, pp. 195–208. Opladen: Barbara Budrich Publishers, 2014.

Miller, James. *The Passion of Michael Foucault*. New York: Simon & Schuster, 1993.

Moaveni, Azadeh. 'ISIS Women and Enforcers in Syria Recount Collaboration, Anguish and Escape.' *The New York Times*. 21 November 2015. www.nytimes.com/2015/11/22/world/middleeast/isis-wives-and-enforcers-in-syria-recount-collaboration-anguish-and-escape.html?_r=0.

Morefield, Jeanne. *Empires Without Imperialism: Anglo-American Decline and the Politics of Deflection*. New York: Oxford University Press, 2014.

Motha, Stewart. 'Liberal Cults, Suicide Bombers, and Other Theological Dilemmas.' *Law, Culture and the Humanities* 5, no. 2 (2009): 228–46.

Moyn, Samuel. *The Last Utopia: Human Rights in History*. Cambridge, MA: Harvard University Press, 2010.

Moyn, Samuel. 'Judith Shklar versus the International Criminal Court'. *Humanity* 4, no. 3 (2013): 473–500.

Moyn, Samuel. *Human Rights and the Uses of History*. London: Verso, 2014.

Munro, Vanessa E. 'Navigating Feminisms: At the Margins, in the Mainstreams or Elsewhere? Reflections on Charlesworth, Otomo and Pearson.' In *Feminist Perspectives on Contemporary International Law: Between Resistance and Compliance?*, edited by Sari Kouvo and Zoe Pearson, pp. 13–16. Oxford: Hart Publishing, 2011.

Munt, Sally. *Queer Attachments: The Cultural Politics of Shame*. Aldershot: Ashgate, 2008.

Muthu, Sankar. *Enlightenment against Empire*. Princeton, NJ: Princeton University Press, 2003.

Mutua, Makau. 'What is TWAIL?' *ASIL Proceedings* [2000]: 31–8.

Mutua, Makau. 'Savages, Victims, and Saviors: The Metaphor of Human Rights.' *Harvard International Law Journal* 42, no. 1 (2001): 201–45.

Mutua, Makau. *Human Rights Standards: Hegemony, Law, and Politics*. Albany: State University of New York Press, 2016.

My Brother … Nikhil. Film. Directed by Onir. India: Yash Raj Films, 2005.

Nāgārjuna, *The Fundamental Wisdom of the Middle Way: Nāgārjuna's Mūlamadhyamakakārikā*, translated by Jay L. Garfield. New York: Oxford University Press, 1995.

Naik, Yeshwant. *Homosexuality in the Jurisprudence of the Supreme Court of India*. Cham: Springer International Publishing, 2017.

Nandy, Ashis. *The Intimate Enemy: Loss and Recovery of Self under Colonialism*. Delhi: Oxford University Press, 1983.

Naravane, Vaiju. 'The Burqa Debate Splits France.' *The Hindu*. 14 July 2009. www.thehindu.com/todays-paper/tp-international/The-burqa-debate-splits-France/article16555357.ece.
Natarajan, Kanchana, trans. *Transgressing Boundaries: The Advaitic Songs of Shenkottai Avudai Akkal*. New Delhi: Zubaan, 2012.
Nedelsky, Jennifer. *Law's Relations: A Relational Theory of Self, Autonomy, and Law*. New York: Oxford University Press, 2011.
Nesiah, Vasuki. 'Feminism as Counter-Terrorism: The Seduction of Power.' In *Gender, National Security and Counter-Terrorism: Human Rights Perspectives*, edited by Margaret L. Satterthwaite and Jayne C. Huckerby, pp. 127–51. Abingdon: Routledge, 2013.
Nesiah, Vasuki. 'The Specter of Violence that Haunts the UDHR: The Turn to Ethics and Expertise.' *Maryland Journal of International Law* 24, no. 1 (2009): 135–54.
Ng, Edwin. 'The Critique of Mindfulness and the Mindfulness of Critique: Paying Attention to the Politics of Our Selves With Foucault's Analytic of Governmentality.' In *Handbook of Mindfulness: Culture, Context, and Social Engagement*, edited by Ronald E. Purser, David Forbes and Adam Burke, pp. 135–52. Cham: Springer International Publishing, 2016.
Nguyen, Mimi Thi. 'The Biopower of Beauty: Humanitarian Imperialisms and Global Feminisms in an Age of Terror.' *Signs* 36, no. 2 (2011): 359–83.
Nilsen, Alf Gunvald, and Srila Roy. 'Introduction.' In *New Subaltern Politics: Reconceptualizing Hegemony and Resistance in Contemporary India*, edited by AlfGunvald Nilsen and Srila Roy, pp. 1–26. New Delhi: Oxford University Press, 2015.
Ní Mhaoileoin, Niamh. 'The Ironic Gay Spectator: The Impacts of Centring Western Subjects in International LGBT Rights Campaigns.' *Sexualities*. 5 June 2017, doi: 10.1177/1363460717699778: 1–17.
Nouwen, Sarah M.H. 'Justifying Justice.' In *The Cambridge Companion to International Law*, edited by James Crawford and Martti Koskenniemi, pp. 327–51. Cambridge: Cambridge University Press, 2012.
Nozick, Robert. *Anarchy, State, and Utopia*. New York: Basic Books, 1974.
Nussbaum, Martha C. 'Human Capabilities, Female Human Beings.' In *Women, Culture, and Development: A Study of Human Capabilities*, edited by Martha C. Nussbaum and Jonathan Glover, pp. 61–104. Oxford: Clarendon Press, 1995.
Nussbaum, Martha C. *Sex and Social Justice*. New York: Oxford University Press, 1999.
Nussbaum, Martha C. 'Capabilities and Human Rights.' *Fordham Law Review* 66, no. 2 (1997): 273–300.

Nussbaum, Martha. *Creating Capabilities: The Human Development Approach*. Cambridge, MA: Harvard University Press, 2011.

O'Grady, Helen. 'An Ethics of the Self.' In *Feminism and the Final Foucault*, edited by Dianna Taylor and Karen Vintges, pp. 91–117. Urbana, IL: University of Illinois Press, 2004.

Olsson, Louise. *Gender, Peace and Security: Implementing UN Security Council Resolution 1325*. Hoboken, NJ: Taylor & Francis, 2015.

Orford, Anne. 'Feminism, Imperialism and the Mission of International Law.' *Nordic Journal of International Law* 71, no. 2 (2002): 275–96.

Orford, Anne. *Reading Humanitarian Intervention: Human Rights and the Use of Force in International Law*. Cambridge: Cambridge University Press, 2003.

Otto, Dianne. 'Rethinking the "Universality" of Human Rights Law.' *Columbia Human Rights Law Review* 29, no. 1 (1997): 1–46.

Otto, Dianne. 'A Sign of "Weakness"? Disrupting Gender Certainties in the Implementation of Security Council Resolution 1325.' *Michigan Journal of Gender & Law* 13, no. 1 (2006): 113–75.

Otto, Dianne. 'The Exile of Inclusion: Reflections on Gender Issues in International Law Over the Last Decade.' *Melbourne Journal of International Law* 10, no. 1 (2009): 11–26.

Otto, Dianne. 'The Security Council's Alliance of Gender Legitimacy: The Symbolic Capital of Resolution 1325.' In *Fault Lines of International Legitimacy*, edited by Hilary Charlesworth and Jean-Marc Coicaud, pp. 239–75. Cambridge: Cambridge University Press, 2009.

Otto, Dianne, ed. *Gender Issues and Human Rights*. 3 vols. Cheltenham: Edward Elgar Publishing, 2013.

Otto, Dianne. 'International Human Rights Law: Towards Rethinking Sex/Gender Dualism.' In *The Ashgate Research Companion to Feminist Legal Theory*, edited by Margaret Davies and Vanessa E. Munro, pp. 197–215. Farnham: Ashgate, 2013.

Otto, Dianne. 'Queering Gender [Identity] in International Law.' *Nordic Journal of Human Rights* 33, no. 4 (2015): 299–318.

Otto, Dianne, ed. *Queering International Law: Possibilities, Alliances, Complicities, Risks*. Abingdon: Routledge, 2018.

Otto, Dianne, and Gina Heathcote. 'Rethinking Peacekeeping, Gender Equality and Collective Security: An Introduction.' In *Rethinking Peacekeeping, Gender Equality and Collective Security*, edited by Gina Heathcote and Dianne Otto, pp. 1–20. Basingstoke: Palgrave Macmillan, 2014.

Pahuja, Sundhya. 'This Is the World: Have Faith' (Review: Shelley Wright, *International Human Rights, Decolonisation and Globalisation: Becoming Human*. London and New York: Routledge, 2001). *European Journal of International Law* 15, no. 2 (2004): 381–94.

Paras, Eric. *Foucault 2.0: Beyond Power and Knowledge*. New York: Other Press, 2006.

Pattanaik, Devdutt. *The Pregnant King*. New Delhi: Penguin Books, 2008.

Pedwell, Carolyn, and Anne Whitehead, 'Affecting Feminism: Questions of Feeling in Feminist Theory.' *Feminist Theory* 13, no. 2 (2012): 115–29.

Perreau, Bruno. *Queer Theory: The French Response*. Stanford: Stanford University Press, 2016.

Perugini, Nicola, and Neve Gordon. *The Human Right to Dominate*. New York: Oxford University Press, 2015.

Peters, Anne. 'Humanity as the A and Ω of Sovereignty'. *European Journal of International Law* 20, no. 3 (2009): 513–44.

Pettit, Philip. *A Theory of Freedom: From the Psychology to the Politics of Agency*. New York: Oxford University Press, 2001.

Phir Milenge. Film. Directed by Revathi. India: Percept Picture Company, 2004.

Pitts, Jennifer. *A Turn to Empire: The Rise of Imperial Liberalism in Britain and France*. Princeton, NJ: Princeton University Press, 2005.

'PM's Speech at Munich Security Conference.' *GOV.UK*. February 2011. www.gov.uk/government/speeches/pms-speech-at-munich-security-conference.

Posner, Eric A. *The Twilight of Human Rights Law*. New York: Oxford University Press, 2014.

Power, Samantha. 'The Enforcer: A Christian Lawyer's Global Crusade.' *The New Yorker*. 19 January 2009. www.newyorker.com/magazine/2009/01/19/the-enforcer.

Probyn, Elspeth. *Blush: Faces of Shame*. Minneapolis: University of Minnesota Press, 2005.

Puar, Jasbir K. *Terrorist Assemblages: Homonationalism in Queer Times*. Durham, NC: Duke University Press, 2007.

Puri, Jyoti. *Sexual States*. Durham, NC: Duke University Press, 2016.

Quinn, Ben. 'French Police Make Woman Remove Clothing on Nice Beach Following Burkini Ban.' *The Guardian*. 24 August 2016. www.theguardian.com/world/2016/aug/24/french-police-make-woman-remove-burkini-on-nice-beach.

Rahimi, Babak. 'Rahimi on Afary and Anderson: *Foucault and the Iranian Revolution: Gender and the Seductions of Islamism*.' *H-Gender-MidEast*. October 2006. www.h-net.org/reviews/showrev.php?id=12437.

Rahman, Momin. *Homosexualities, Muslim Cultures and Modernity*. Basingstoke: Palgrave Macmillan, 2014.

Rajagopal, Balakrishnan. *International Law from Below: Development, Social Movements and Third World Resistance*. Cambridge: Cambridge University Press, 2003.

Ramanan, K. Venkata. *Nāgārjuna's Philosophy*. Rutland, VT: Charles E. Tuttle Company, 1966.

Rao, Rahul. *Third World Protest: Between Home and the World*. Oxford: Oxford University Press, 2010.

Rawls, John. *Lectures on the History of Moral Philosophy*. Edited by Barbara Herman. Cambridge, MA: Harvard University Press, 2000.

Raz, Joseph. *The Morality of Freedom*. Oxford: Clarendon, 1986.

Reddy, Gayatri. *With Respect to Sex: Negotiating Hijra Identity in South India*. Chicago: University of Chicago Press, 2006.

Rée, Jonathan. 'The Treason of the Clerics.' *The Nation*. 28 July 2005. https://www.thenation.com/article/treason-clerics/.

Richardson, Diane. 'Desiring Sameness? The Rise of a Neoliberal Politics of Normalisation.' *Antipode* 37, no. 3 (2005): 515–35.

Richardson, Diane. 'Rethinking Sexual Citizenship.' *Sociology* 51, no. 2 (2017): 208–24.

Rittich, Kerry. 'The Future of Law and Development: Second-Generation Reforms and the Incorporation of the Social.' In *The New Law and Economic Development*, edited by David M. Trubek and Alvaro Santos, pp. 203–52. Cambridge: Cambridge University Press, 2006.

Roberts, William Clare. 'The Idea of Emancipation after Postcolonial Theory.' *Interventions: International Journal of Postcolonial Studies* 19, no. 6 (2017): 747–63.

Robin, Corey. *Fear: The History of a Political Idea*. Oxford: Oxford University Press, 2004.

Rodinson, Maxime. 'Khomeini and the "Primacy of the Spiritual".' *Le Nouvel Observateur*. February 19, 1979. Reproduced in Janet Afary and Kevin B. Anderson. *Foucault and the Iranian Revolution: Gender and the Seductions of Islam*, pp. 241–5. Chicago: The University of Chicago Press, 2005.

Root, Amanda. *Market Citizenship: Experiments in Democracy and Globalization*. Los Angeles: SAGE, 2007.

Rorty, Richard. *Contingency, Irony, and Solidarity*. Cambridge: Cambridge University Press, 1989.

Rorty, Richard. 'Human Rights, Rationality, and Sentimentality.' In Richard Rorty, *Truth and Progress: Philosophical Papers*, pp. 167–85. Vol. 3. Cambridge: Cambridge University Press, 1998.

Rorty, Richard. 'Hope and the Future.' *Peace Review* 14, no. 2 (2002): 149–55.

Rosenblum, Darren. 'Unsex CEDAW, Or What's Wrong with Women's Rights.' *Columbia Journal of Gender and Law* 20, no. 2 (2011): 98–194.

Roth, Brad R. 'Marxian Insights for the Human Rights Project.' In *International Law on the Left: Re-Examining Marxist Legacies*, edited by Susan Marks, pp. 220–51. Cambridge: Cambridge University Press, 2006.

Rothschild, Cynthia, edited by Scott Long and Susana T. Fried. *Written Out: How Sexuality Is Used to Attack Women's Organizing*. New York: International Gay and Lesbian Human Rights Commission; Center for Women's Global Leadership, 2005.

Roychowdhury, Poulami. '"The Delhi Gang Rape": The Making of International Causes.' *Feminist Studies* 39, no. 1 (2013): 282–92.

Rudaali. Film. Directed by Kalpana Lajmi. India: Doordarshan/National Film Development Corporation of India, 1993.

Rūmī, Jalāl al-Dīn. *The Essential Rumi*, translated by Coleman Barks. San Francisco, CA: Harper, 1995.

Rūmī, Jalāl al-Dīn. *Selected Poems from the Divan-e Shams-e Tabrizi*. Translated and edited by Reynold A. Nicholson. Bethesda, MD: Ibex, 2001.

Rūmī, Jalāl al-Dīn. *The Masnavi: Book One*, translated by Jawid Mojaddedi. Oxford: Oxford University Press, 2008.

Ruti, Mari. *The Ethics of Opting Out: Queer Theory's Defiant Subjects*. New York: Columbia University Press, 2017.

Saeed, Tania. *Islamophobia and Securitization: Religion, Ethnicity and the Female Voice*. Basel: Springer/Palgrave Macmillan, 2016.

Saffari, Siavash. *Beyond Shariati: Modernity, Cosmopolitanism, and Islam in Iranian Political Thought*. Cambridge: Cambridge University Press, 2017.

Said, Edward. *Orientalism*. London: Penguin Books, 1978.

Śaṅkara, Adi. *A Thousand Teachings: The Upadeśasāhasrī of Śaṅkara*, translated and edited by Sengaku Mayeda. New York: State University of New York Press, 1992.

Śaṅkarācārya. *Śaṅkara on the Absolute*. Translated by A.J. Alston. London: Shanti Sadan, 2004.

Santos, Boaventura de Sousa. *Epistemologies of the South: Justice against Epistemicide*. Boulder, CO: Paradigm Publishers, 2014.

Santos, Boaventura de Sousa. *If God Were a Human Rights Activist*. Stanford, CA: Stanford University Press, 2015.

Santos, Boaventura de Sousa and César A. Rodríquez-Garavito. 'Law, Politics, and the Subaltern in Counter-Hegemonic Globalization.' In *Law and Globalization from Below: Towards a Cosmopolitan Legacy*, edited by Boaventura de Sousa Santos and César A. Rodríquez-Garavito, pp. 1–26. Cambridge: Cambridge University Press, 2005.

Sarasvati, Pundita Ramabai. *The High Caste Hindu Woman*. Philadelphia: Jas. B. Rodgers Printing Co., 1888.

Scheinin, Martin, and Mathias Vermeulen. 'Unilateral Exceptions to International Law: Systematic Legal Analysis and Critique of Doctrines that Seek to Deny or Reduce the Applicability of Human Rights Norms in the Fight Against Terrorism.' In *Terrorism and Human Rights*, edited by Martin Scheinin, pp. 3–56. Cheltenham: Edward Elgar Publishing, 2013.

Scott, Joan Wallach. *The Politics of the Veil*. Princeton, NJ: Princeton University Press, 2007.

Sedgwick, Eve Kosofsky. *Epistemology of the Closet*. Berkeley: University of California Press, 1990.

Sedgwick, Eve Kosofsky. 'Introduction: Queerer than Fiction.' *Studies in the Novel* 28, no. 3 (1996): 277–80.

Sedgwick, Eve Kosofsky. 'Introduction.' In *Touching Feeling: Affect, Pedagogy, Performativity*, pp. 1–25. Durham, NC: Duke University Press, 2003.

Sedgwick, Eve Kosofsky. 'Making Things, Practicing Emptiness.' In *The Weather in Proust*, edited by Jonathan Goldberg, pp. 69–122. Durham, NC: Duke University Press, 2011.

Sedgwick, Eve Kosofsky. 'Paranoid Reading and Reparative Reading, Or, You're So Paranoid, You Probably Think This Essay Is About You.' In *Touching Feeling: Affect, Pedagogy, Performativity*, pp. 123–51. Durham, NC: Duke University Press, 2003.

Sedgwick, Eve Kosofsky. 'Pedagogy of Buddhism.' In *Touching Feeling: Affect, Pedagogy, Performativity*, pp. 153–81. Durham, NC: Duke University Press, 2003.

Sedgwick, Eve Kosofsky. 'Reality and Realization.' In *The Weather in Proust*, edited by Jonathan Goldberg, pp. 206–15. Durham, NC: Duke University Press, 2011.

Sedgwick, Eve Kosofsky. *Between Men: English Literature and Male Homosocial Desire*. New York: Columbia University Press, 2016. First published 1985.

Sedgwick, Eve Kosofsky, and Michael D. Snediker. 'Queer Little Gods: A Conversation.' *The Massachusetts Review* 49, nos 1/2 (2008): 194–218.

Selmeczi, Anna. 'Who Is the Subject of Neoliberal Rights? Governmentality, Subjectification and the Letter of the Law.' *Third World Quarterly* 36, no. 6 (2015): 1076–91.

Sen, Amartya. *Commodities and Capabilities*. Amsterdam: Elsevier Science Publishing Company, 1985.

Sen, Amartya. *Development as Freedom*. Oxford: Oxford University Press, 1999.

Sen, Amartya. *The Argumentative Indian: Writings on Indian History, Culture and Identity*. London: Allen Lane, 2005.

Shah, Svati Pragna. *Street Corner Secrets: Sex, Work, and Migration in the City of Mumbai*. Durham, NC: Duke University Press, 2014.

Shaikh, Nermeen. 'Saba Mahmood.' In *The Present as History: Critical Perspectives on Contemporary Global Power*, pp. 148–71. New York: Columbia University Press, 2007.

Sharapov, Kiril. '"Traffickers and Their Victims": Anti-Trafficking Policy in the United Kingdom.' *Critical Sociology* 43, no. 1 (2017): 91–111.

Shari'ati, Ali. *Marxism and Other Western Fallacies: An Islamic Critique*. Translated by R. Campbell. Berkeley, CA: Mizan Press, 1980.

Shari'ati, Ali. 'A Discussion of Shahid.' In *Jihād and Shahādat: Struggle and Martyrdom in Islam: Essays and Addresses by Mahmūd Ṭaleqāni, Murtaḍa Muṭahhari, Ali Shari'ati*, edited by Mehdi Abedi and Gary Legenhausen, pp. 230–43. Houston, TX: Institute for Research and Islamic Studies, 1986.

Shari'ati, Ali. *Where Shall We Begin? Enlightened Thinkers and the Revolutionary Society*. Penang: Citizens International, 2002.

Shari'ati, Ali. *What Is to Be Done: The Enlightened Thinkers and an Islamic Renaissance*. BookBaby ebook, 2015.

Sherwood, Harriet. 'Polish Magazine's "Islamic Rape of Europe" Cover Sparks Outrage.' *The Guardian*. 18 February 2016. www.theguardian.com/world/2016/feb/18/polish-magazines-islamic-of-europe-cover-sparks-outrage.

Shklar, Judith N. *Legalism*. Cambridge, MA: Harvard University Press, 1964.

Shklar, Judith N. 'Putting Cruelty First.' *Daedalus* 111, no. 3 (1982): 17–27.

Shklar, Judith. *Ordinary Vices*. Cambridge, MA: Harvard University Press, 1984.

Shklar, Judith N. 'The Liberalism of Fear.' In *Liberalism and the Moral Life*, edited by Nancy L. Rosenblum, pp. 21–38. Cambridge, MA: Harvard University Press, 1989.

Shklar, Judith N. *The Faces of Injustice*. New Haven: Yale University Press, 1990.

Shnayderman, Ronen. 'On "Being Forced to Be Free" Between Republican and Liberal Freedom.' *Ethical Perspectives: Journal of the European Ethics Network* 22, no. 2 (2015): 247–70.

Singh, Pawan. 'Staging Sexuality through the Familial, the Performative and the Activist: Bollywood's Queer Repertoire in the Twenty-First Century.' *South Asian Popular Culture* 13, no. 2 (2015): 125–39.

Sinha, Mrinalini. *Colonial Masculinity: The 'Manly Englishman' and the 'Effeminate Bengali' in the Late Nineteenth Century*. Manchester: Manchester University Press, 1995.

Smart, Carol. 'The Women of Legal Discourse.' *Social & Legal Studies* 1, no. 1 (1992): 29–44.

Snediker, Michael D. *Queer Optimism: Lyric Personhood and Other Felicitous Persuasions*. Minneapolis: University of Minnesota Press, 2009.

Sokhi-Bulley, Bal. 'Government(ality) by Experts: Human Rights as Governance.' *Law and Critique* 22, no. 3 (2011): 251–71.

Sokhi-Bulley, Bal. *Governing (through) Rights*. Oxford: Hart Publishing, 2016.

Spivak, Gayatri Chakravorty. *Outside in the Teaching Machine*. New York: Routledge, 1993.

Spivak, Gayatri Chakravorty. 'Can the Subaltern Speak?' In *The Post-Colonial Studies Reader*, edited by Bill Ashcroft, Gareth Griffiths and Helen Tiffin, pp. 24–8. London: Routledge, 1995.

Spivak, Gayatri Chakravorty. *A Critique of Postcolonial Reason: Toward a History of the Vanishing Present*. Cambridge, MA: Harvard University Press, 1999.

Spivak, Gayatri Chakravorty. 'Can the Subaltern Speak?' In *The Post-Colonial Studies Reader*, edited by Bill Ashcroft, Gareth Griffiths and Helen Tiffin, pp. 28–37. 2nd ed. London: Routledge, 2006.

Stauth, Georg. 'Revolution in Spiritless Times: An Essay on Michel Foucault's Enquiries into the Iranian Revolution.' In *Michel Foucault: Critical Assessments*, edited by Barry Smart, pp. 379–401. Vol. 3. London: Routledge, 1994.

Stephens, George M. *Locke, Jefferson, and the Justices: Foundations and Failures of the US Government*. New York: Algora Publishing, 2002.

Stevenson, Nick. *Human Rights and the Reinvention of Freedom*. Abingdon: Routledge, 2017.

Stoler, Ann Laura. *Duress: Imperial Durabilities in Our Times*. Durham, NC: Duke University Press, 2016.

Stychin, Carl F. *Law's Desire: Sexuality and the Limits of Justice*. London: Routledge, 1995.

Sung, Jung Mo. *The Subject, Capitalism, and Religion: Horizons of Hope in Complex Societies*. New York: Palgrave Macmillan, 2011.

Sureśvarācārya. *The Realization of the Absolute: The 'Naiśkarmya Siddhi' of Śrī Sureśvara*, translated by A.J. Alston. 2nd ed. London: Shanti Sadan, 1971.

Svendsen, Lars. *A Philosophy of Freedom*. London: Reaktion Books, 2014.

Tabrizi, Shams-i. *Me and Rumi: The Autobiography of Shams-i Tabrizi*, translated by William C. Chittick. Louisville, KY: Fons Vitae, 2004.

Talisse, Robert. 'On the Liberalism of Fear: A Reply to Brooks.' In *The Moral Philosophy of Bernard Williams*, edited by Alexandra Perry and Chris Herrera, pp. 114–18. Newcastle upon Tyne: Cambridge Scholars Publishing, 2013.

Tamale, Sylvia. 'A Human Rights Impact Assessment of the Ugandan Anti-Homosexuality Bill 2009.' *The Equal Rights Review* 4 (2009): 49–57.

Taylor, Dianna, and Karen Vintges, eds. *Feminism and the Final Foucault*. Urbana, IL: University of Illinois Press, 2004.

The Wire Staff. 'Right to Privacy Judgement Sets Stage to Decriminalise Gay Sex For All Time.' *The Wire*. 24 August 2017. https://thewire.in/170565/section-377-right-to-privacy-supreme-court/.

Thornton, Margaret. 'Neoliberal Governmentality and the Retreat from Gender Equality.' In *Feminisms of Discontent: Global Contestations*, edited by Ashleigh Barnes, pp. 71–96. New Delhi: Oxford University Press, 2015.

Thrupkaew, Noy. 'The Crusade against Sex Trafficking.' *The Nation*. 16 September 2009. www.thenation.com/article/crusade-against-sex-trafficking/.

Tomkins, Silvan S. *Affect, Imagery, Consciousness*. 4 vols. New York: Springer, 1963.

Tomuschat, Christian. *Human Rights: Between Idealism and Realism*. Oxford: Oxford University Press, 2014.

Transgressing Boundaries: The Advaitic Songs of Shenkottai Avudai Akkal. Translated by Kanchana Natarajan. New Delhi: Zubaan, 2012.

Trispiotis, Ilias. 'Two Interpretations of 'Living Together' in European Human Rights Law.' *The Cambridge Law Journal* 75, no. 3 (2016): 580–607.

United Nations Secretary-General's Campaign to End Violence against Women (UniTE). www.un.org/en/women/endviolence/.

US Department of State. 'UN Security Council Holds Inaugural Meeting on LGBT Issues.' News release. 24 August 2015. https://2009-2017.state.gov/r/pa/prs/ps/2015/08/246296.htm.

Valdez, Inés. 'Nondomination or Practices of Freedom? French Muslim Women, Foucault, and the Full Veil Ban.' *American Political Science Review* 110, no. 1 (2016): 18–30.

Valverde, Mariana. 'Experience and Truth Telling in a Post-humanist World: A Foucauldian Contribution to Feminist Ethical Reflections.' In *Feminism and the Final Foucault*, edited by Dianna Taylor and Karen Vintges, pp. 67–90. Urbana, IL: University of Illinois Press, 2004.

Van der Veer, Peter. *Imperial Encounters: Religion and Modernity in India and Britain*. Princeton, NJ: Princeton University Press, 2001.

Van Leuven, Dallin, Dyan Mazurana and Rachel Gordon. 'Analysing the Recruitment and Use of Foreign Men and Women in ISIL through a Gender Perspective.' In *Foreign Fighters under International Law and Beyond*, edited by Andrea de Guttry, Francesca Capone, and Christophe Paulussen, pp. 97–120. The Hague: T.M.C. Asser Press, 2016.

Vasilaki, Rosa. 'The Politics of Postsecular Feminism.' *Theory, Culture & Society* 33, no. 2 (2016): 103–23.

Veitch, Scott. *Law and Irresponsibility: On the Legitimation of Human Suffering*. Abingdon: Routledge-Cavendish, 2007.

Verma, J.S., Leila Seth, and Gopal Subramanium. *Report of the Committee on Amendments to Criminal Law*. New Delhi: Centre for Social Research, 2013.

Volpp, Leti. 'Feminist, Sexual, and Queer Citizenship.' In *The Oxford Handbook of Citizenship*, edited by Ayelet Shachar, Rainer Bauböck, Irene Bloemraad and Maarten Vink, pp. 153–77. Oxford: Oxford University Press, 2017.

Wadud, Amina. *Inside the Gender Jihad: Women's Reform in Islam*. Oxford: Oneworld, 2006.

Waldron, Jeremy. 'Theoretical Foundations of Liberalism.' *The Philosophical Quarterly* 37, no. 147 (1987): 127–50.

Walker, Kristen L. 'Capitalism, Gay Identity and International Human Rights Law.' *Australasian Gay and Lesbian Law Journal* 9 (2000): 58–73.

Walzer, Michael. 'The Politics of Rescue.' *Social Research* 62, no. 1 (1995): 53–66.

Walzer, Michael. 'On Negative Politics.' In *Liberalism without Illusions: Essays on Liberal Theory and the Political Vision of Judith N. Shklar*, edited by Bernard Yack, 17–24. Chicago: University of Chicago Press, 1996.

Walzer, Michael. 'The European Crisis.' *Dissent* (blog). 11 September 2015. www.dissentmagazine.org/blog/michael-walzer-european-refugee-crisis.

Ward, Ellis, and Gillian Wylie, eds. *Feminism, Prostitution and the State: The Politics of Neo-Abolitionism*. London: Routledge, 2017.

Ward, Kevin. 'The Role of the Anglican and Catholic Churches in Uganda in Public Discourse on Homosexuality and Ethics.' *Journal of Eastern African Studies* 9, no. 1 (2015): 127–44.

Weber, Cynthia. *Queer International Relations: Sovereignty, Sexuality and the Will to Knowledge*. New York: Oxford University Press, 2016.

Weed, Elizabeth. 'Gender and the Lure of Postcritical.' *Differences* 27, no. 2 (2016): 153–77.

West, Robin. *Caring for Justice*. New York: New York University Press, 1997.

Whyte, Jessica. 'Is Revolution Desirable? Michel Foucault on Revolution, Neoliberalism and Rights.' In *Re-Reading Foucault: On Law, Power and Rights*, edited by Ben Golder, pp. 207–28. Abingdon: Routledge, 2013.

Wiegman, Robyn. 'The Times We're In: Queer Feminist Criticism and the Reparative 'Turn'.' *Feminist Theory* 15, no. 1 (2014): 4–25.

Wiegman, Robyn, and Elizabeth A. Wilson. 'Introduction: Antinormativity's Queer Conventions.' *Differences: A Journal of Feminist Cultural Studies* 26, no. 1 (2015): 1–25.

Wilder, Gary. *The French Imperial Nation-State: Negritude & Colonial Humanism Between the Two World Wars*. Chicago: University of Chicago Press, 2005.

Williams, Bernard. 'The Liberalism of Fear.' In *In the Beginning Was the Deed: Realism and Moralism in Political Argument*, edited by Geoffrey Hawthorn, pp. 52–61. Princeton, NJ: Princeton University Press, 2005.

Wintemute, Robert. 'From "Sex Rights" to "Love Rights": Partnership Rights as Human Rights.' In *Sex Rights: The Oxford Amnesty Lectures 2002*, edited by Nicholas Bamforth, pp. 186–224. Oxford: Oxford University Press, 2005.

Wolin, Richard. 'From the "Death of Man" to Human Rights: The Paradigm Change in French Intellectual Life, 1968–86.' In *The Frankfurt School Revisited: And Other Essays on Politics and Society*, pp. 171–84. New York: Routledge, 2006.

Yack, Bernard. 'Political Liberalism: Political, not Philosophical.' *Perspectives on Politics* 15, no. 1 (2017): 116–21.

Zakaria, Rafia. 'Women and Islamic Militancy.' *Dissent* 62, no. 1 (2015): 118–25.

Zembylas, Michalinos. 'Emotions, Critical Pedagogy, and Human Rights Education.' In *Human Rights Education: Theory, Research, Praxis*, edited by Monisha Bajaj, pp. 47–68. Philadelphia, PA: University of Pennsylvania Press, 2017.

Zimmerman, Yvonne C. 'Christianity and Human Trafficking.' *Religion Compass* 5, no. 10 (2011): 567–78.

Index